T0310671

Social, Legal, and Ethical Implications of IoT, Cloud, and Edge Computing Technologies

Gianluca Cornetta
Universidad CEU San Pablo, Spain

Abdellah Touhafi
Vrije Universiteit Brussel, Belgium

Gabriel-Miro Muntean
Dublin City University, Ireland

A volume in the Advances in Information Security,
Privacy, and Ethics (AISPE) Book Series

Published in the United States of America by
IGI Global
Information Science Reference (an imprint of IGI Global)
701 E. Chocolate Avenue
Hershey PA, USA 17033
Tel: 717-533-8845
Fax: 717-533-8661
E-mail: cust@igi-global.com
Web site: http://www.igi-global.com

Copyright © 2020 by IGI Global. All rights reserved. No part of this publication may be reproduced, stored or distributed in any form or by any means, electronic or mechanical, including photocopying, without written permission from the publisher. Product or company names used in this set are for identification purposes only. Inclusion of the names of the products or companies does not indicate a claim of ownership by IGI Global of the trademark or registered trademark.

Library of Congress Cataloging-in-Publication Data

Library of Congress Cataloging-in-Publication Data

Names: Cornetta, Gianluca, 1969- editor. | Touhafi, Abdellah, 1970- editor.
  | Muntean, Gabriel-Miro, 1972- editor.
Title: Social, legal, and ethical implications of IoT, cloud, and edge
  computing technologies / Gianluca Cornetta, Abdellah Touhafi, and
  Gabriel-Miro Muntean, editors.
Description: Hershey, PA : Information Science Reference, an imprint of IGI
  Global, [2020] | Includes bibliographical references and index. |
  Summary: "This book provides vital research on the non-technical
  repercussions of IoT technology adoption. While highlighting topics such
  as smart cities, environmental monitoring, and data privacy, this
  publication explores the regulatory and ethical risks that stem from
  computing technologies"-- Provided by publisher.
Identifiers: LCCN 2019060056 (print) | LCCN 2019060057 (ebook) | ISBN
  9781799838173 (hardcover) | ISBN 9781799852117 (paperback) | ISBN
  9781799838180 (ebook)
Subjects: LCSH: Internet of things--Social aspects. | Cloud
  computing--Social aspects | Internet of things--Industrial applications.
  | Cloud computing--Industrial applications. | Smart cities.
Classification: LCC TK5105.8857 .S63 2020 (print) | LCC TK5105.8857
  (ebook) | DDC 303.48/34--dc23
LC record available at https://lccn.loc.gov/2019060056
LC ebook record available at https://lccn.loc.gov/2019060057

This book is published in the IGI Global book series Advances in Information Security, Privacy, and Ethics (AISPE) (ISSN: 1948-9730; eISSN: 1948-9749)

British Cataloguing in Publication Data
A Cataloguing in Publication record for this book is available from the British Library.

All work contributed to this book is new, previously-unpublished material. The views expressed in this book are those of the authors, but not necessarily of the publisher.

For electronic access to this publication, please contact: eresources@igi-global.com.

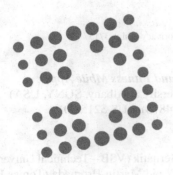

Advances in Information Security, Privacy, and Ethics (AISPE) Book Series

Manish Gupta
State University of New York, USA

ISSN:1948-9730
EISSN:1948-9749

MISSION

As digital technologies become more pervasive in everyday life and the Internet is utilized in ever increasing ways by both private and public entities, concern over digital threats becomes more prevalent.

The **Advances in Information Security, Privacy, & Ethics (AISPE) Book Series** provides cutting-edge research on the protection and misuse of information and technology across various industries and settings. Comprised of scholarly research on topics such as identity management, cryptography, system security, authentication, and data protection, this book series is ideal for reference by IT professionals, academicians, and upper-level students.

COVERAGE

- Information Security Standards
- Telecommunications Regulations
- Data Storage of Minors
- Electronic Mail Security
- Security Information Management
- Cyberethics
- Security Classifications
- Privacy Issues of Social Networking
- Risk Management
- Internet Governance

IGI Global is currently accepting manuscripts for publication within this series. To submit a proposal for a volume in this series, please contact our Acquisition Editors at Acquisitions@igi-global.com or visit: http://www.igi-global.com/publish/.

The Advances in Information Security, Privacy, and Ethics (AISPE) Book Series (ISSN 1948-9730) is published by IGI Global, 701 E. Chocolate Avenue, Hershey, PA 17033-1240, USA, www.igi-global.com. This series is composed of titles available for purchase individually; each title is edited to be contextually exclusive from any other title within the series. For pricing and ordering information please visit http://www.igi-global.com/book-series/advances-information-security-privacy-ethics/37157. Postmaster: Send all address changes to above address. Copyright © 2020 IGI Global. All rights, including translation in other languages reserved by the publisher. No part of this series may be reproduced or used in any form or by any means – graphics, electronic, or mechanical, including photocopying, recording, taping, or information and retrieval systems – without written permission from the publisher, except for non commercial, educational use, including classroom teaching purposes. The views expressed in this series are those of the authors, but not necessarily of IGI Global.

Titles in this Series

For a list of additional titles in this series, please visit:
http://www.igi-global.com/book-series/advances-information-security-privacy-ethics/37157

Privacy Concerns Surrounding Personal Information Sharing on Health and Fitness Mbile Apps
Devjani Sen (Independent Researcher, Canada) and Rukhsana Ahmed (University at Albany, SUNY, USA)
Information Science Reference • © 2020 • 300pp • H/C (ISBN: 9781799834878) • US $215.00

Safety and Security Issues in Technical Infrastructures
David Rehak (VSB – Technical University of Ostrava, Czech Republic) Ales Bernatik (VSB – Technical University of Ostrava, Czech Republic) Zdenek Dvorak (University of Zilina, Slovakia) and Martin Hromada (Tomas Bata University in Zlin, Czech Republic)
Information Science Reference • © 2020 • 499pp • H/C (ISBN: 9781799830597) • US $195.00

Cybersecurity Incident Planning and Preparation for Organizations
Akashdeep Bhardwaj (University of Petroleum and Energy Studies, Dehradun, India) and Varun Sapra (University of Petroleum and Energy Studies, India)
Information Science Reference • © 2020 • 300pp • H/C (ISBN: 9781799834915) • US $215.00

Blockchain Applications in IoT Security
Harshita Patel (KLEF, Vaddeswaram, Guntur, Andhra Pradesh, India) and Ghanshyam Singh Thakur (MANIT, Bhopal, Madhya Pradesh, India)
Information Science Reference • © 2020 • 300pp • H/C (ISBN: 9781799824145) • US $215.00

Modern Theories and Practices for Cyber Ethics and Security Compliance
Winfred Yaokumah (University of Ghana, Ghana) Muttukrishnan Rajarajan (City University of London, UK) Jamal-Deen Abdulai (University of Ghana, Ghana) Isaac Wiafe (University of Ghana, Ghana) and Ferdinand Apietu Katsriku (University of Ghana, Ghana)
Information Science Reference • © 2020 • 302pp • H/C (ISBN: 9781799831495) • US $200.00

Handbook of Research on Multimedia Cyber Security
Brij B. Gupta (National Institute of Technology, Kurukshetra, India) and Deepak Gupta (LoginRadius Inc., Canada)
Information Science Reference • © 2020 • 372pp • H/C (ISBN: 9781799827016) • US $265.00

Security and Privacy Applications for Smart City Development
Sharvari C. Tamane (MGM's Jawaharlal Nehru Engineering College, India)
Information Science Reference • © 2020 • 300pp • H/C (ISBN: 9781799824985) • US $215.00

701 East Chocolate Avenue, Hershey, PA 17033, USA
Tel: 717-533-8845 x100 • Fax: 717-533-8661
E-Mail: cust@igi-global.com • www.igi-global.com

Editorial Advisory Board

Diana Bogusevschi, *Dublin City University, Ireland*
Guadalupe Cantarero García, *Universidad CEU San Pablo, Spain*
Jan Helsen, *Vrije Universiteit Brussels, Belgium*
Cristina Muntean, *National College of Ireland, Ireland*
Nieves Navarro Cano, *Universidad Politécnica de Madrid, Spain*
José Luís Piñar Mañas, *Universidad CEU San Pablo, Spain*
Kris Steenhaut, *Vrije Universiteit Brussels, Belgium*
Magdalena Suárez, *Universidad Complutense Madrid, Spain*
Abderrahim Tahiri, *Abdelmalek Essaädi University, Morocco*
Zhenhui Yuan, *Hangzhou Dianzi University, China*

Table of Contents

Section 1
Enabling Technologies and Applications

Detailed Table of Contents

Section 1
Enabling Technologies and Applications

Chapter 1
Software-Defined Networking: An Architectural Enabler for the IoT 1
Víctor M. López Millán, Universidad CEU San Pablo, Spain

The connection of billions of devices to the internet poses numerous challenges to the networking infrastructure. The traditional networking paradigm is anticipated to be unable to cope with a scenario of myriad heterogenous devices connected through both wireless and wired links. The mobility and instability of a significant portion of the devices of the IoT demand a flexible and agile response of the network to adapt and keep the appropriate policies in effect. Software-defined networking (SDN) moves the intelligence of the network to a central controller with a global vision of the network capable of issuing timely instructions to the network nodes to accommodate the constant changes. This chapter presents the SDN paradigm, covering its architecture, functional blocks, interfaces, and protocols. The focus is put on the application of SDN to IoT environments supporting different applications, each with its specific difficulties, exploring current trends to tackle the identified challenges.

Chapter 2
Wireless Sensor Networks in IPM 28
Mina Petrić, Ghent University, Belgium & University of Novi Sad, Serbia & Avia-GIS NV, Belgium
Cedric Marsboom, Avia-GIS NV, Belgium
Jurgen Vandendriessche, Vrije Universiteit Brussel, Belgium

An emerging field for environmental wireless sensor networks (WSN) is entomological vector surveillance. Sensor technology can be used to shoulder ecologically friendly practices within the integrated pest management (IPM) approach. Proper surveillance and subsequent modelling of the impact that pest and disease have on human health and crop agriculture is a pressing issue in numerous segments. Complex numerical models are being developed to generate information regarding the population dynamics of vector species and the expected circulation of vector-borne disease (VBD). These models require detailed micrometeorological forcing representative of the vector habitat to generate accurate simulations. Near real-time data offload in remote areas with flexible channels of communication for complex and heterogeneous topographies is an important component in this type of application. In this chapter, the authors provide an overview of the scope and best-practice approaches in applying WSN technology to drive IPM models.

Chapter 3

Abdellah Touhafi, Vrije Universiteit Brussel, Belgium
Gianluca Cornetta, Universidad CEU San Pablo, Spain

Engineering education requires a rather difficult learning process, which aims at building the student's capacities in theoretical insights in science, project-oriented thinking and co-operation, experimental verification of basic concepts in specific labs, deductive and creative thinking, and multi-disciplinary engineering. Many education techniques to help in that learning process have been proposed in literature and have found their way into the daily learning process. Two very prominent active learning techniques used in engineering education are on one hand the virtual and remote laboratories and on the other hand the fab labs. The upcoming internet of things paradigm is now adding new possibilities to further enhance those two techniques to support engineering education. In this chapter, the authors introduce some of those possibilities, describe use cases, and draw some conclusions on the current state of research.

Chapter 4

Kimaya Arun Ambekar, K. J. Somaiya Institute of Management Studies and Research, India
Kamatchi R., ISME School of Management and Entrepreneurship, India

Cloud computing is based on years of research on various computing paradigms. It provides elasticity, which is useful in the situations of uneven ICT resources demands. As the world is moving towards digitalization, the education sector is expected to meet the pace. Acquiring and maintaining the ICT resources also necessitates a huge amount of cost. Education sector as a community can use cloud services on various levels. Though the cloud is very successfully running technology, it also shows some flaws in the area of security, privacy and trust. The research demonstrates a model in which major security areas are covered like authorization, authentication, identity management, access control, privacy, data encryption, and network security. The total idea revolves around the community cloud as university at the center and other associated colleges accessing the resources. This study uses OpenStack environment to create a complete cloud environment. The validation of the model is performed using some cases and some tools.

Chapter 5

Gianluca Cornetta, Universidad CEU San Pablo, Spain
Abdellah Touhafi, Vrije Universiteit Brussel, Belgium
Gabriel-Miro Muntean, Dublin City University, Ireland

Cloud and IoT technologies have the potential to enable a plethora of new applications that are not strictly limited to remote sensing, data collection, and data analysis. In such a context, the IoT paradigm can be seen as an empowering technology rather than a disruptive one since it has the capability to improve the standard business processes by fostering more efficient and sustainable implementations and by reducing the running costs. Cloud and IoT technologies can be applied in a broad range of contexts including entertainment, industry, and education, among others. This chapter presents part of the outputs of the NEWTON H2020 European project on technology-enhanced learning; more specifically, it introduces the concept of fabrication as a service in the context of educational digital fabrication laboratories. Fab Labs can leverage cloud and IoT technologies to enable resource sharing and provide remote access to distributed expensive fabrication resources over the internet. Both platform architecture and impact on learning experience of STEM subjects are presented in detail.

Section 2
Technologies in a Smart City Context

Eduardo J. López-Fernández, Universidad CEU San Pablo, Spain
Francisco Alonso-Peralta, Technical University of Madrid, Spain
Gastón Sanglier-Contreras, Universidad CEU San Pablo, Spain
Roberto A. González-Lezcano, Universidad CEU San Pablo, Spain

This chapter analyses the urban water cycle in the smarts cities, describes the current situation, which constitutes a valid but outdated knowledge, adopting the perspective of improving and extending the measures that lead to greater efficiency of the water collection, treatment, supply, sewage, purification, and reuse systems at all stages of the water cycle: the sites, construction, operation, and maintenance of the networks and systems that enable the cycle to be completed effectively. The process of converting a city into smart city includes resources, processes, and services, and all stages of the water cycle are a set of processes, with water as a fundamental resource, which condition the different services to citizens, and therefore, it is necessary to try to establish efficiency improvements in all of them.

Elizabeth Frank, Universidad CEU San Pablo, Spain
Gloria Aznar Fernández-Montesinos, Universidad CEU San Pablo, Spain

With a rapidly growing world population, urban populations are estimated to increase significantly over the next decades. This trend is reason for concern since the planet's resources are limited, and climate change is inherent. This chapter focusses on the question about whether new technologies employed in smart cities can be the answer to current and future needs of a city population. Cutting-edge technological advances are reshaping our ecosystem; transforming society, living, and work environments; transport systems; energy grids; healthcare; communications; businesses; and education. How can cities respond to the multitude of challenges by employing technology and at the same time ensure the public well-being, improve the quality of life of city inhabitants, and make sure that the human is still at the center of decisions?

Implementation of the smart city concept in architectural school programs is neither evident nor simple. The starting point is a historical heritage of established patterns shaped to different schools of thought that have independently worked on territories at different scales: urban planning and building construction. The Spanish scenario understands the smart city as the ICTs (information and communication technologies) applied to security, data processing, logistics, energy management, among others, but we must not forget the Spanish urban plans born from the architecture discipline and how buildings are positioned within a site. The aim of this study is to highlight some reflections on the need to unite multiple and artificial intelligences so that the latter does not monopolize or gain exclusivity within the smart city design guidelines and listens to the city's demands.

Chapter 9

Smart destinations provide value for the tourist experience. Platforms where dialogue arises are important to develop an adequate integration of smart technology as a resource for the cooperative creation of valuable tourist experiences. The incorporation of digital technologies in historical disciplines as a part of humanistic knowledge design is a new paradigm that encourages the creation of innovative content. Taking as a reference the Spanish routes that the war journalists visited during the First Carlista War, it is possible to transform the villages that were protagonists of these historical landmarks as smart tourist destinations. Digital content based on geolocation, GIS developments, apps, audiovisual pieces with videomapping, and augmented reality techniques are the key to bring the traveler the experience in an interactive, personalized, integrative, and participatory environment while the data provided by the different sensors allows measuring their economic and social impact.

Section 3
Data Privacy and eGovernment

Chapter 10

Big data and analytics have not only changed how businesses interact with consumers, but also how consumers interact with the larger world. Smart cities, IoT, cloud, and edge computing technologies are all enabled by data and can provide significant societal benefits via efficiencies and reduction of waste. However, data breaches have also caused serious harm to customers by exposing personal information. Consumers often are unable to make informed decisions about their digital privacy because they are in a position of asymmetric information. There are an increasing number of privacy regulations to give consumers more control over their data. This chapter provides an overview of data privacy regulations, including GDPR. In today's globalized economy, the patchwork of international privacy regulations is difficult to navigate, and, in many instances, fails to provide adequate business certainty or consumer protection. This chapter also discusses current research and implications for costs, data-driven innovation, and consumer trust.

Chapter 11

Cloud computing, internet of things (IoT), edge computing, and fog computing are gaining attention as emerging research topics and computing approaches in recent years. These computing approaches are rather conceptual and contextual strategies rather than being computing technologies themselves, and in practice, they often overlap. For example, an IoT architecture may incorporate cloud computing and fog computing. Cloud computing is a significant concept in contemporary computing and being adopted in almost every means of computing. All computing architectures incorporating cloud computing are termed as cloud-based computing (CbC) in general. However, cloud computing itself is the basis of CbC because it significantly depends on resources that are remote, and the remote resources are often under third-party ownership where the privacy of sensitive data is a big concern. This chapter investigates various privacy issues associated with CbC. The data privacy issues and possible solutions within the context of cloud computing, IoT, edge computing, and fog computing are also explored.

Chapter 12

Recently, digital health solutions are taking advantage of recent advances in information and communication technologies. In this context, patients' health data are shared with other stakeholders. Moreover, it's now easier to collect massive health data due to the rising use of connected sensors in the health sector. However, the sensitivity of this shared healthcare data related to patients may increase the risks of privacy violation. Therefore, healthcare-related data need robust security measurements to prevent its disclosure and preserve patients' privacy. However, in order to make well-informed decisions, it is often necessary to allow more permissive security policies for healthcare organizations even without the consent of patients or against their preferences. The authors of this chapter concentrate on highlighting these challenging issues related to patient privacy and presenting some of the most significant privacy preserving approaches in the context of digital health.

The smart city is a concept that began to take shape at the end of the last century, emerging as a consequence of the real evolution of urban requirements. Whilst in bygone eras the need arose to equip cities with elements such as security, public health services, and public adornment, which were primordial for development of said cities, nowadays the—increasingly demanding—citizenry calls for a type of services related to the introduction of information and communications technology (ICT), aside from the cities' own evolution, as well as growth of the social and environmental capital. A smart city could be defined as a city which uses information and communications technology to ensure that both its critical infrastructure and the public services and components it offers are more interactive and efficient and that citizens can become more aware of them.

Preface

Cloud computing and Internet of Things (IoT) are technologies that have become an integral part of our everyday life. However, while Cloud computing is now an established technology, IoT is still in its early stages. The concept of "Cloud" refers to the ability to access remote hardware and software resources through a network or the Internet. This computing paradigm originated in the late 60s with the implementation of mainframe computers accessible through thin clients. The technology has evolved in the past five decades into the modern elastic Cloud computing systems that rely on hardware virtualization technologies to outsource network and computing resources and that have the capability to scale the available resources either horizontally or vertically. Cloud computing system are characterized by different deployment and service models. A deployment model defines the location of the cloud infrastructure: public (open infrastructure on the cloud service provider premises), private (infrastructure located on the organization premises), hybrid (a mixture of public and private clouds), and community (infrastructure whose access is restricted to a group of organizations). A service model defines the way in which either a hardware or a software cloud resource is delivered to the end user. There are three basic cloud service models: Infrastructure as a Service (IaaS, which provides access to basic computing resources such as remote machines, virtual machines, remote storage), Platform as a Service (PaaS, which provides access to runtime and deployment environments), and Software as a Service (SaaS, which provides remote software service on a subscription basis).

IoT can be considered as the natural evolution of embedded computing. The term "Internet of Things" was first used in 1999 by the British technology pioneer Kevin Ashton to describe a system where the physical world is connected to the Internet through sensors. Today, IoT is associated with a scenario in which the capabilities of objects of everyday life, sensors, actuators and other "smart" devices are enhanced with computing capabilities and Internet connectivity. IoT technological paradigm embraces several areas related to device design, communication, integration, as well as storage, management and analysis of the data generated by the network of smart objects.

IoT is a disruptive technology; however, its impact on the enterprise business models is not the same as the one that the Internet had in mid 90s. The introduction of the Internet implied a complete rethink and redesign of the enterprise business processes; conversely, IoT can be considered as an empowering technology that can seamlessly integrate with the available infrastructure and business processes without the need to redesign all of them from scratch. In such a context, IoT can be considered as a disruptive technology for its capability to penetrate into all the aspects of the society, for its potential to impact in our lives and to generate new business opportunities and models that leverage the data produced by the network of smart objects to generate new value. The interaction between Cloud and IoT technologies has the potential to enable many new applications and added value services in practically all the markets, from energy and transportation, logistic and supply chain management, environmental monitoring and farming and livestock management, to health, public administration, education, domotic and ambient assisted living. IoTis driving profound changes in the way we live, work and interact with the environment and with each other, and is inspiring a new way to perceive our cities that are becoming a symbiotic mix between technology and architecture. In the "smart" cities of the future, the network of smart objects will be seamlessly and pervasively integrated in the urban fabric.

The social implications of the digital revolution prompted by the new Cloud and IoT technological paradigm are evident and cannot be overlooked. The way to ethically exploit the new technologies must be fully understood by all the stakeholders involved in the digitalization process so that the technological progress could really contribute to the social welfare and people benefit.

To fully exploit the potential of the IoT technological paradigm many technical and non-technical challenges must be properly addressed. These include system scalability, standardization and device interoperability, service discovery, power and energy management, just to mention a few of them. However, the main concerns with IoT are privacy and ethical issues related to the sensing, storage and processing of the data generated by the network of smart objects. This is where this book comes into play.

The main purpose of this book is to provide the reader with an overview of the potential applications of Cloud and IoT technologies and their potential to create new value and business opportunities. The book also aims to explore and analyze the privacy and ethical issues that could arise when using those technologies.

The book content is presented in a coordinated manner and is divided into three sections:

1. Enabling Technologies and Applications
2. Technologies in the Smart City Context
3. Data Privacy and eGovernment

The Introduction introduces the book aims and scope, also emphasizing the potential impact on society of the new Cloud and IoT technological paradigm. Section 1 (Chapters 1 to 5) explores Cloud and IoT enabling technologies and applications with particular emphasis to education. Section 2 (Chapters 6 to 9) deals with IoT and Cloud technologies in the Smart City context, Finally, Section 3 (Chapters 10 to 13) addresses data privacy and regulations with a special focus to the context of Cloud computing and digital health.

The editors hope you will enjoy your reading!

June 2020

Gianluca Cornetta
Universidad CEU San Pablo, Spain

Abdellah Touhafi
Vrije Universiteit Brussel, Belgium

Gabriel-Miro Muntean
Dublin City University, Ireland

Acknowledgment

We are grateful to IGI Global for permitting us to edit this volume. In particular, we want to thank Carlee Nilphai and Morgan Brajkovich of IGI staff that assisted us throughout the whole editorial process.

A very special thanks goes to Mrs. Guadalupe Cantarero of the Book Editorial Advisory Board, for her valuable support, suggestions and encouragement offered during the review process.

Also, we are thankful to all the authors for their insightful contributions and to the reviewers for their constructive suggestions and their effort for improving the quality of the submitted chapters.

Dr. Muntean would like to acknowledge the support of Science Foundation Ireland for the Enable (16/SP/3804) and Insight (12/RC/2289\P2) research centres.

Introduction:
Internet of Things and Cloud Technologies – The Roadmap Towards a Networked World and Its Implications for the 21st Century Global Society

Internet of Things (IoT) is a novel networking concept in which objects of everyday life (e.g. household appliances, cars, medical equipment, etc.) can be integrated with sensors and provided with the capability to implement simple processing tasks and communicate with other smart devices through the Internet. IoT device networks are usually short-range and with limited size; however, the integration with Cloud technology can empower the IoT infrastructure by providing deployed devices with ubiquitous access and by enabling many new networked applications (Botta et al, 2015).

The Internet, the network of networks, is constantly evolving. During the last two decades we have seen it evolve from a static network of documents in hypertext format (HTML) to its present form, that is also known as WEB 2.0.

The WEB 2.0 involves technologies and services which most of us are very familiar with, such as social networks, blogs and wikis that enable participation, collaboration and interaction among people. However, the work of the researchers is never stopping, and the technological basis has already been set for the forthcoming WEB 3.0 or semantic web.

Semantic web targets development of a markup language that can be easily understood by machine and search engines and that can enable integration of "intelligence" in the present and future applications. The standardization of the contents' markup will allow the machines to process, share and generate data autonomously, without any need for human supervision or intervention.

The last decade has also seen development of technologies and protocols aimed at the deployment, remote monitoring and connectivity of sensor networks supported by simple and inexpensive devices. These technologies include Near Field Communication (NFC), RFID sensors and tags, and machine-to-machine communication protocols such as MQTT that implement a publish/subscribe paradigm on top of the TCP/IP communication layer. Recently, new connectivity standards have also gained certain level of attention. These include standards such as Li-Fi (Light Fidelity), that allows wireless communication through high-frequency modulated light, and LoRAWAN (Long Range Wide Area Network), a protocol suite for wide area networks of "things".

Internet of Things (IoT), a network of autonomous and self-configurable objects that can publish and analyze information through the conventional WEB, arises from the convergence of these new technologies with the already consolidated and familiar WEB.

Many of the core technologies of the IoT, such as for example RFID and sensor networks, have been used during years in industrial environments for real-time warehouse management, asset tracking and logistics in general. Also, the idea of machine-to-machine protocols is not new since it already provides the core technological support for communications between clients, servers and routers in conventional networks. However, IoT represents an evolution of these technologies in a completely new context: a network of billions of heterogeneous devices with different requirements in terms of power consumption, connectivity, functionality and transmission rate. In other words, the IoT paradigm aims at providing every kind of device (e.g. household appliances, smoke detectors, LED lights, audio and video transceivers, etc.) with the same functionality and connectivity of a server or a desktop computer and making them visible over the Internet. The great promise of the IoT paradigm is the possibility to provide the environment in which we live, work and move with intelligence, so that not only the people could interact with the environment, but also the environment with the people in a simple and straightforward way, making decisions and adapting to their needs.

A world full of smart and "invisible" objects will have, potentially, a great impact on the way in which we will live, work and interact in a future not very far away. However, this transformation will not only be limited to the social sphere, but it will also encompass all the aspects of the modern society, including the business processes which will be radically affected by the new IoT paradigm and will lead to an unprecedented breakup with the traditional enterprise models. This unavoidable change, that we are already experiencing with the creation and consolidation of the first cloud-based business and services, will soon extend to all the aspects of the society including education, medicine, architecture and urbanism.

HARDWARE, SOFTWARE, AND ARCHITECTURES

The deployment of the network of smart objects has already started and is a reality; the supporting technologies are in continuous development and are reaching their maturity at an incredible pace; nonetheless, there are still a lot of technological and ethical challenges that need to be solved. Like a conventional system, the IoT paradigm will rely on a combination of hardware, software and architectures. However; while the hardware layer is formed, in large part, by known technologies, the software layer needs an extensive redesign in order to support scenarios in which many heterogeneous devices shall operate jointly, and data must be searched and collected asynchronously.

Managing such a scenario is extremely complex and requires a device virtualization layer (middleware) to decouple the application from the underlying hardware. In other words, the middleware layer abstracts the hardware characteristics and data of the device network providing to the application a set of services that allow seamless access to the network resources without needing to write a specific code for each type of device and/or supported data type.

It will also be necessary to adapt the characteristics of the browsers and search engines to the new scenarios enabled by IoT. Actual browsers and search engines are designed to index a relatively stable data set; nonetheless, the objects that form the network of things are mobile, extremely dynamic and generate with high frequency huge and heterogeneous data amounts. This scenario requires a web browser with the capability to identify smart objects, discover the available services in the network of things and interact in real time with all of them. Moreover, the search engine of the future shall be able to find in real time the information in the network, as soon as it is generated by the smart objects.

The architecture of an information system in general, and of the network of things in particular, represents the set of structural and design patterns aimed at finding a configuration to maximize the effectiveness and the efficiency of the whole system.

The heterogeneous and distributed nature of the network of things requires the application of these design principles at different abstraction levels, by defining a hardware and network architecture, a software architecture and a process architecture capable to provide efficient support to the services of the network of things and to all the workflows built on top of those services.

The software architecture must clearly define the functionalities to allow device access and to share the services offered by the network of things. In such context, software models already used in WEB programming such as Service Oriented Architecture (SOA) and Representational State Transfer (REST) are really appealing due to their flexibility and their service-oriented nature. On the other hand, business processes leveraging the network of things shall lean on architectures capable to efficiently manage the workflows and to support pervasive and ubiquitous computing.

APPLICATION FIELDS

The possible applications of the network of things are only limited by the designer's creativity. Nevertheless, all the applications available to date can be grouped into four subdomains: intelligent infrastructure, health, logistics and supply chain, and social applications.

Integrating smart objects into a physical infrastructure can improve its flexibility, reliability and efficiency leading to a drastic reduction of the personnel's costs and to a security improvement. For example, smart grids are used to carry out remote meter reading and to collect data on energetic and hydric consumption (Al-Turjman & Abujubbeh, 2019). Measured data can be automatically embedded in the bills to provide to the end user a global perspective on the consumption patterns and recommendations on how reducing them.

Houses, buildings and office spaces can be equipped with sensors and actuators that implement real-time monitoring of the energetic consumption and configure the heating or air conditioning system automatically in order to either reduce or optimize them (Pan et al, 2016). At a larger scale, IoT technologies can be used to build more efficient and sustainable "smart" cities (Rajab & Cinkerl, 2018). The smart cities goal is leveraging the network of smart objects to provide the citizens with a more comfortable, efficient and healthier environment by improving traffic control, monitoring parking spaces, measuring pollution level or air quality, and even sending to users notifications when waste containers are full.

The main application of the network of things in the health field is in assisted living scenarios. Vital constants sensors with network connectivity can collect and transfer information to relatives or physicians in real time through the internet in order to improve the treatment or the response time in case of critical situations (Wan et al, 2017). Moreover, smart sensors and devices can be used to control a pharmacological treatment and assess the risk related to the introduction of new medicines in the treatment (e.g. allergic reactions or adverse interactions).

The ubiquity of IoT technologies can significantly improve all the logistic processes by extending the monitoring and control at a wider scale through all the supply chain (Tu, Lim & Yang, 2018). IoT technologies can be also used to promote social interactions through social networking by providing user geographic or activity information. An application can automate data collection, analysis and integration and inform the users if there is an event of interest in the proximity.

In a recent study published by Strategy Analytics the number of devices connected to internet reached 22 billion at the end of 2018 and it is expected that by 2025 there will be more than 37 billion connected devices (including PCs, smartphones and tablets). Large part of this device growth will affect business lines related to zero-emission buildings, smart cities, automotive industry, household appliances, logistics and warehouse management, physical activity and vital constants monitoring. However, IoT technologies will also have a remarkable impact to education, affecting process optimization as well as the way of teaching and of interacting with students (Cornetta et al, 2020).

A SUSTAINABLE BUSINESS MODEL

Every new technological advance requires a change in the business models aimed at generating new value and at capturing the attention of potential clients. For example, the technologies of the WEB 2.0 have boosted new models such as platforms that provide the users to access to cloud hardware (this model is known as Infrastructure as a Service - IaaS) or software (this model is known as Software as a Service - SaaS) resources by paying a subscription fee. On the other hand, IoT will foster the development of business models based on ubiquity and data analysis.

IoT, in its essence, is a business model that speeds up business processes, reduces operating costs and promises value creation with limited resources. "More for less" is the key principle of sustainability. However, sustainability is a wider concept that is not only related to the capability to manage a business more efficiently using less resources, but also with the capability to adapt, understand and anticipate social and economic changes, anticipate and resist the impact of disruptive technologies.

The introduction of the Internet in the past century radically changed the business processes and the way to generate value; nonetheless, the impact of IoT in today's business processes and models will be completely different from the first Internet revolution. IoT technologies will be an empowering element rather than a disruptive force. The most important idea underneath the IoT is that it is not a simple technology, but rather a facilitator element that provides the users access to resources and services, adding new value to the traditional business processes we are used with.

"The value of the Internet of Things has very little to do with either the Internet or the things. Rather, the real value lies in harvesting and analyzing the data that all these objects generate, and in turning those insights into meaningful action[1]."

Ubiquitous connectivity among people and processes will enable the network deployment of several adaptive services with consciousness of the operating context. Such services can be automatically delivered to the end user without human mediation and whenever and where they are needed.

The network of things, namely the technological paradigm with the capacity to enable a transparent and seamless connection among people, smart objects and processes, will lead to a series of benefits at short, medium and long term and will positively impact on all the economy sectors from the automotive, till the services sector, logistics and supply chain, health and education. This, in turn, will improve the quality of life of several billion people in the new global digital world without socio-economic barriers that we see being born.

The impact of this new connected world on the way we live and work will be fundamental, and the spreading of the network of things will translate into great social and environmental benefits, such as better medical care, improved security and efficiency in transportation and logistics, better education and smarter and more efficient use of energy.

The ability to capture information in real-time and to remotely control without or with minimum human intervention several kinds of processes, as well as the capability to embed mobile connectivity into objects of every day's life, will enable a more efficient operation of both machine and vehicles, significantly reducing wastes generation and improving productivity.

The new services enabled by IoT technologies will significantly contribute to the economic growth by creating new business opportunities for the mobile carriers, hardware manufacturers as well as other actors that operate in the mobile communication ecosystem and in related industrial fields. All these new emerging business lines will be a positive stimulus for the demand that will prompt the funding and the global deployment of a new and improved infrastructure capable to provide broadband access and IoT connectivity to billion users.

The interconnected device market will generate new cash flows, foster the development of new business models and will significantly improve the efficiency and the way in which several services are delivered in different business and industrial sectors.

The global impact of the network of the network of things in business can be divided into two categories: (i) new income opportunities, and (ii) running costs reduction and service improvement. It is estimated that, by 2020 the incomes due to the sales of IoT device and services as well as derived services such as "pay-as-you-drive" car insurances, will reach 2.5 trillion dollars, 1.2 of which will be gained by the mobile carriers and the remaining by enterprises of the IoT ecosystem[2].

On the other hand, running costs reduction and service improvement are related with the less direct but equally tangible benefits enabled by the implementation of efficient and sustainable business and management processes leveraging the network of things. It is estimated that, by 2020, the benefits in terms of costs reduction due to the adoption of IoT technologies will reach 2 trillion dollars. One trillion will be derived from the deployment of technologies such as smart meters (which will avoid the need for a manual readout by specialized personnel) and one will be generated by service improvements such as telemedicine and remote monitoring of patients with chronic diseases[2].

To speed-up the market entry of these new services, the mobile carriers have established partnerships and alliances with technological ICT enterprises to foster the creation of new standards to allow the short-term integration of the network of objects in the current infrastructure and to create new consumer-oriented IoT services.

In this new context, new commercial models that break with the traditional schemes we are used to are becoming increasingly relevant. One of such new models is the so-called Business to Business to Consumer (B2B2C) in which is the partner company of the mobile carrier which has direct contact with the client and that markets the end product or service. For example, a mobile carrier could partner with a power supply company offering the deployment of a network of smart meters; nonetheless is the power company that offer this service and hires the meters to its clients.

Besides this rethinking of the traditional business models, there also exists a substantial difference in the way value is created and, consequently, in the way the clients are charged for the new services. While for the traditional telecommunication services the client is billed for the use of the infrastructure and, frequently, also for the data consumed; the new services relying on IoT technologies will be related with the intrinsic value of the service itself (of which network connectivity will be an intangible and indistinguishable value).

For example, the users of networked vehicles can be billed monthly for the service jointly with discretionary fees for added value services such as entertainment. In many cases, the mobile carrier that provides the IoT services is not visible to the end client, since its relationship is exclusively with the partner company that markets the final product or service.

Additionally, the mobile carriers can also choose to interact with Small and Medium Enterprises (SME) that may want to develop mobile application and services for the network of things in an economically sustainable way. In such scenario, the next technological challenge to cope with is the cloud integration of the network of things as well as the development of programmatic interfaces (APIs) to expose the resources of the network of things to third-party applications. Such interfaces will allow to develop and monetize the relationships with many heterogeneous industrial partners in related technological sectors.

HAZARDS AND CHALLENGES

IoT goes well beyond the technological challenges related to the deployment, communication and remote monitoring of billions of networked devices. The real issue is understanding how the states and institutions will manage the network of things and how they will use the generated information. What shall we do when we start collecting data about users? Shall the behavioral patterns be considered as personal data and technology and service provider be liable of tracing a personal profile entailing legal issues?

The major hazards that can slow down the diffusion of the IoT paradigm are related to social and ethical issues such as, for example, the lack of a specific legislation and of a feasible diffusion and management plan of the network of things. Security and data privacy in the network of things are the factors with major impact in all the target markets.

The diffusion of embedded devices will allow rapid deployment of complex networks of people and smart object both in the private and public sectors. These devices will enable a new type of relationship and interplay among people and machines. In such new context, the right balance must be found between the benefits brought by the new technologies, and the consciousness of the intrinsic risks related to privacy and security. The only way to achieve this is through a literacy process that must involve all the stakeholders.

Personal and public data shall be treated differently, and the privacy and intimacy of each individual shall be respected and guaranteed. In addition, IoT must guarantee data integrity, authenticity and timely updating. This is the real technological challenge of the new network that, due to the extremely dynamic nature of both data and devices, requires continuous updating and reconfiguration.

CONCLUSION

The new technological revolution prompted by cloud and IoT technologies is driving profound changes that embrace the whole society. Pervasive and ubiquitous computing enabled by the interaction of the network of smart objects with the cloud infrastructure is resulting in the development of new applications and enterprise business and process models based on sustainability and on a more efficient exploitation of the available resources. Cloud and IoT are empowering technologies that can be successfully applied to almost any kind of business such as farming and agri-food industry, healthcare, education, environmental monitoring, supply chain management and logistic, just to mention a few examples. They have the potential to make the place where we work and live smarter, more efficient and comfortable and they are becoming the core technologies behind the smart cities of the future. However, the real value of IoT technology is not in the technology itself, but in the data generated and processed by the deployed infrastructure. The new data-centric paradigm entails both technological and ethical issues that must be comprehensively addressed and understood in order to foster its acceptance by all its potential stakeholders. The dynamic nature of the network of things requires a fast, secure and resilient cloud infrastructure for data storage and processing which could be a hard technological challenge due to the huge amount of data that must be processed in real-time. However, while enterprises and public administrations are more concerned with infrastructure efficiency, security and data integrity and authenticity, policy makers and individuals are more concerned on the ethical use of the information gathered and to ensure that the right to privacy of all the citizens is guaranteed. The social progress and welfare are not just a matter of economic growth and technological advances and cannot be achieved by undermining the legitimate personal rights or interests of part of the society. The lack of legislation and standardization are, so far, the main barriers to the diffusion of IoT technologies. IoT applications embrace several market sectors and leverage many connectivity technologies, this in turn makes very difficult to develop a new regulatory framework since conflicts may arise either with existing legislation or duties of regulatory bodies. There is a need for a cross-sectoral and technology-neutral regulatory approach (Reiter & Gastaut, 2019); however, prior to reach a widespread consensus, all the stakeholders of the new technological paradigm must be involved in the process and must understand what the technology can do, what are the potential benefits for the whole society, but also which are the potential risks related to a misuse or abuse of technology.

Gianluca Cornetta
Universidad CEU San Pablo, Spain

Abdellah Touhafi
Vrije Universiteit Brussel, Belgium

Gabriel-Miro Muntean
Dublin City University, Ireland

REFERENCES

Al-Turjman, F., & Abujubbeh, M. (2019). IoT-enabled smart grid via SM: An overview. *Future Generation Computer Systems*, *95*, 694–712. doi:10.1016/j.future.2019.02.012

Botta, A., Donato, W., Persico, V., & Pescapè, A. (2016). Integration of Cloud Computing and Internet of Things: A Survey. *Future Generation Computer Systems*, *56*, 684–700. doi:10.1016/j.future.2015.09.021

Cornetta, G., Togou, M. A., Touhafi, A., & Muntean, G.-M. (2020). Fabrication-as-a-Service: A Web-Based Solution for STEM Education Using Internet of Things. *IEEE Internet of Things Journal*, *7*(2), 1519–1530. doi:10.1109/JIOT.2019.2956401

Pan, J., Jain, R., Paul, S., Vu, T., Saifullah, A., & Sha, M. (2015). An Internet of Things Framework for Smart Energy in Buildings: Designs, Prototype, and Experiments. *IEEE Internet of Things Journal*, *2*(6), 527–537. doi:10.1109/JIOT.2015.2413397

Rajab, H., & Cinkerl, T. (2018, June). *IoT based Smart Cities*. Paper presented at the IEEE International Symposium on Networks, Computers and Communications (ISNCC). doi: 10.1109/ISNCC.2018.8530997

Reiter, J., & Gastaut, S. (2019). *A new IoT regulatory framework for Europe*. Retrieved from https://www.vodafone.com/content/dam/vodcom/files/public-policy/iot-whitepaper/IoT_whitep aper_.pdf

Tu, M., Lim, M., & Yang, M. (2018). IoT-based production logistics and supply chain system – Part 1: Modeling IoT-based manufacturing supply chain. *Industrial Management & Data Systems*, *118*(1), 65–95. doi:10.1108/IMDS-11-2016-0503

Wan, J., Gu, X., Chen, L., & Wang, J. (2017, October). *Internet of Things for Ambient Assisted Living: Challenges and Future Opportunities*. Paper presented at the IEEE International Conference on Cyber-Enabled Distributed Computing and Knowledge Discovery (CyberC). 10.1109/CyberC.2017.83

ENDNOTES

[1]   Per Simonsen, CEO of Telenor Connexion.
[2]   Source GSM Association (GSMA) www.gsma.com

Section 1
Enabling Technologies and Applications

Chapter 1
Software–Defined Networking:
An Architectural Enabler for the IoT

Víctor M. López Millán
Universidad CEU San Pablo, Spain

ABSTRACT

The connection of billions of devices to the internet poses numerous challenges to the networking infrastructure. The traditional networking paradigm is anticipated to be unable to cope with a scenario of myriad heterogenous devices connected through both wireless and wired links. The mobility and instability of a significant portion of the devices of the IoT demand a flexible and agile response of the network to adapt and keep the appropriate policies in effect. Software-defined networking (SDN) moves the intelligence of the network to a central controller with a global vision of the network capable of issuing timely instructions to the network nodes to accommodate the constant changes. This chapter presents the SDN paradigm, covering its architecture, functional blocks, interfaces, and protocols. The focus is put on the application of SDN to IoT environments supporting different applications, each with its specific difficulties, exploring current trends to tackle the identified challenges.

INTRODUCTION

The pervasive presence of Internet is taking connectivity between users and services to a higher level. In its original meaning, Internet is understood as a large and heterogenous network connecting servers providing computation and data storage capacity on the one hand, and people accessing those services using their Internet Service Provider on the other hand. Current core and access networks provide bandwidth enough to expand the Internet connectivity to elements different from the user terminal (i.e., smartphones, computers, tablets). The goal is to collect data from the "things" surrounding us, process that data in the cloud and use it to make people's lives easier in a very many ways, like guiding our vehicle to a free parking spot, having our fridge order what is needed for the week, monitoring vital signals of patients to anticipate health problems, etc. Not so long ago, navigation systems capable of showing us the fastest route to a destination for the current traffic conditions was something restricted to the science

DOI: 10.4018/978-1-7998-3817-3.ch001

Copyright © 2020, IGI Global. Copying or distributing in print or electronic forms without written permission of IGI Global is prohibited.

fiction realm. The Internet of Thigs (IoT) will geometrically increment the number of devices connected and will make possible applications we cannot imagine yet.

However, the networking infrastructure needs to evolve to become more flexible, agile and easier to control and manage. Software Defined Networking (SDN) is a new networking paradigm that can help to achieve the necessary improvements. This chapter presents the SDN networking paradigm, describing its architecture, functional modules and protocols, focusing on the advantages it can offer to an IoT. Then, the domains of application of the IoT concept are explored, with a view on explaining how SDN can be used in each situation. For each application domain, the benefits from the SDN application and the challenges still to be solved are identified.

BACKGROUND

In the previous decades, Internet connectivity has rocketed from being available to a few government and research institutions, to companies, to homes, and finally to virtually everybody in the planet. The ultimate democratization of Internet access among residential users has been made possible by the advent of several successive access network technologies. First, CATV providers included Internet access in their catalog service with DOCSIS. Along the way, telcos found the way to claim their market share using the ubiquitous telephone line with ADSL and related technologies (xDSL). In these days, providers are pushing the rollout of their FTTH access networks struggling to outperform competitors in getting their optic fibers to the homes. In the meanwhile, digital cellular telephony has evolved through several generations (GSM, CDMA, UMTS, LTE) with ever-increasing bandwidth in the radio interface. Currently, most mobile telcos have deployed their 4G (Advanced LTE) radio access network, providing speed enough to watch multimedia contents on-line on smartphones and other portable devices. In addition, public and private wireless networks are being implemented in companies, hospitals, airports, stores, restaurants, public spots, etc. As a consequence, user traffic keeps soaring as these continuous upgrades of both fixed and wireless access networks are introduced, and this forces network owners to increase their core network capacity accordingly.

The next step in deepening the Internet access ubiquity is the 5th generation (5G) of mobile communications. Many telcos and network equipment providers have been deploying pilot projects for testing and demonstration in the last years (e.g., in the Winter Olympic Games in South Korea in February 2018). A few telcos around the world are already offering commercial service as of the last quarter of 2019. 5G improvements over the previous generation include not only the required increase of bandwidth, which determines the hop to a new generation. Very important aspects are the reduction of latency, essential to real-time conversational applications, and the increment of the number of connected devices, with an impressive 10^6 per square kilometer. The driver for this capability is obviously not the need to connect one million people in such a reduced area. The aim is to be able to connect one million *things* to the Internet with wireless links, opening the door to another conception: the Internet of Things (IoT) (Ejaz, Imran, Jo, Muhammad, Qaisar & Wang 2016). Cisco Systems defines the Internet of Everything to be an expanded IoT connecting virtual entities as well as "physical" things (Evans, 2012). Devices can be connected to the IoT by fixed line access, but it is the availability of a wireless access that will lead to the birth of a new generation of the Internet. The 5G radio access network will play a central role by facilitating the connection and mobility of a massive number of devices.

In the IoT, the user-service paradigm is superseded by a more general machine-to-machine (M2M) interaction model in which, in some cases, a human user will be using one of the end devices to access services. Devices connected to the IoT will range between the simplest sensor to the most sophisticated computer, with home appliances, personal devices, vehicles, traffic lights, cameras, etc. in the range. Improvements in batteries and low-power electronics and protocols make possible to have myriads of small and inexpensive devices that are autonomous over long periods of time and that are connected through the IoT (Dahlqvist, Patel, Rajko & Shulman 2019).

The heterogeneity of these devices, and also of the services and applications they support, and the fact that many of them are mobile, put an enormous challenge on the network infrastructure and its management. End devices can be connected and disconnected to the network dynamically in time and space, and the infrastructure has to cope with this changing demand and react to maintain the desired quality of service and security policies for every application. Traditional network management, based on monitoring and controlling network elements from centralized Network Operation Centers (NOC), is unable to scale to a scenario with billions of heterogeneous fixed and mobile end devices. Network equipment, like routers, switches, firewalls, etc., run operating systems that are operated by means of a command line interface (CLI) and through management protocols (e.g., SNMP). Even though these network elements autonomously cooperate with each other to react to changes in the network (e.g., dynamic routing protocols), and even though they can be controlled remotely through the network by centralized management applications in NOCs, these capabilities are neither fine-grained nor fast enough to correctly enforce network policies in a rapidly changing scenario like the IoT supporting a large number of heterogeneous applications.

A new network paradigm allows to fulfill the demands of the IoT on the network infrastructure. Software Defined Networking (SDN) (The Open Networking Foundation 2013) breaks a network device into the forwarding capabilities, or *data plane*, and the intelligence of the device (routing, quality of service, security, etc.) or *control plane*. An SDN-enabled switch or network element offers an API to control its forwarding capabilities remotely from a centralized control plane (the SDN *controller*) that has a view of all the network elements under its responsibility. The management applications in the controller receive from the network elements information about new traffic flows, and then install new appropriate rules in the network elements to control those flows. Possible actions specified in the rules include the blocking of the packet, the forwarding of the unaltered packet and the modification of the packet before being forwarded.

Three facts give the SDN networking model the ability to react rapidly enough to the changing demands of end devices in the IoT. Firstly, the global view of the network allows to design a more appropriate and coordinated solution for the network current situation. Secondly, the APIs of the network elements offer a fine-grain control over individual traffic flows. Finally, the open nature of the controller allows for the addition of new management applications than can be programmed for the specific needs at hand. This application layer gives a control over the network that is much more flexible than the traditional one based on CLIs and network management protocols.

SDN is still a young technology in the process of consolidation and standardization, with architectures and protocols already widely accepted and used to explore new developments and applications. The Open Networking Foundation (ONF) is an operator-led consortium that promotes SDN standards and the OpenFlow protocol within an open software model. On the research side, a number of projects have been launched in the last years aimed at using the SDN paradigm to meet the challenges posed by the IoT on the network infrastructure. They differ in aspects like the network application domain, the level of the network where they apply SDN, and the approach used.

SOFTWARE DEFINED NETWORKING

This section presents the concept of SDN, explaining its advantages over the traditional network paradigm. In a nutshell, the SDN paradigm allows for the centralized control of the behavior of the network from applications that can be programmed for specific purposes. In contrast, the traditional networking paradigm mostly relies on the autonomous behavior of cooperative network nodes or elements. The traditional network control is decentralized, resembling the distributed nature of the network itself. Crucial network functions like routing are performed by the network elements working cooperatively. Some of these functions, like security, require configuring each element with different instructions to achieve a global goal. Each manufacturer of networking equipment provides different capability sets and configuration language interfaces, which the network administrator must master to instruct the network to do what it is supposed to do and to react in the expected fashion to changes in the topology or in the user traffic demands. Routing decisions, for example, are decided autonomously by the dynamic routing algorithms running in the network (e.g., OSPF, EIGRP). Since this task is distributed, the convergence time can be significant in large networks. In addition, each routing protocol functions according to its own particular features. Specific needs that deviate from the standard behavior can often be accommodated, but only at a general level and still requiring careful and error-prone configuration by the network administrator. Of course, there are centralized spots, the Network Operation Centers (NOCs), which monitor the nodes and offer network administrators a global view of the network, allowing coordinated actions on multiple nodes. Still, the network is not flexible enough to respond to rapidly changing demands.

In SDN, only the forwarding hardware is left in the network elements. The algorithms (the intelligence that decides what to do with each packet) are relocated at a centralized controller that tells each element what to do with new traffic flows. Indeed, this introduces a dependency of the network elements on the controller, but it can be afforded because of the high reliability and reduced latency of current networks. Standard APIs are meant to be used in the interaction between controller and network elements, simplifying the multi-vendor scenario. SDN controllers include standard routines to instruct nodes about new traffic flows according to routing algorithms, standard networking functions (e.g., NAT, Access Control Lists). But what really makes SDN a powerful architecture is that the controller in turn offers APIs to applications. These applications can be programmed to tell the controller the network policies they need for the services to work at the moment, and the controller will enforce these fine-grain networking decisions in real time installing the right forwarding rules in the right network elements. In a sense, the paradigm is shifting towards a general-purpose networking platform controlled by software applications that provide specific services, as it happened with computers decades ago. This will allow the new network to fulfill the requirements changing traffic patterns of billions of devices connected to the IoT.

This new networking paradigm has been driven by several networking trends other than IoT. Nowadays, users require to access data, both corporate and personal, from any kind of device, anywhere, and any time. Public and private cloud computing services play a central role in this, and the network is under pressure to make possible and to control all different types of accesses. In addition, companies are now familiar with the advantages of clouds to instantiate, manage and leave computing and storage resources based on their current needs. SDN makes possible for the network to respond in the same way. Finally, the processing of the huge datasets in big-data analytics demands unprecedented network flexibility to handle the communications among servers in data centers and between data centers.

The notion of separating the traffic plane and the control plane was first conceived for the Public Switched Telephone Networks (PSTN) and dates back to the early 90's. The so-called Intelligent Network was meant to facilitate the introduction of new services in telephone networks. Later, the Internet Engineering Task Force (IETF) created a work group to transpose the idea to packet switched networks. More recently, the Ethane project at Stanford University can be marked as the origin of a what is nowadays understood as SDN, leading to the definition of the OpenFlow protocol. White papers on SDN can be found, for instance, in the Open Networking Foundation (2013) as well as in networking equipment manufacturers (Cisco, 2013) (Juniper, 2016).

SDN Advantages for the IoT

The SDN paradigm introduced above offers the following specific advantages that are directly applicable to the IoT:

- **Centralized control:** Having the network to do what it is supposed to do is made easier from a centralized point than in the current distributed fashion, which requires the separate configuration of individual devices from different manufacturers. This advantage is especially important in a rapidly changing environment with a large number of connected devices generating numerous traffic flows, as is the IoT scenario.
- **Abstraction of physical networking devices:** The view of the network offered to the SDN is based on capability sets rather than on physical networking devices. This eases the programming of the controller and the applications in terms of networking needs, rather than in terms of the specific features of a device.
- **Vendor-independent network control interface:** The added requirement of mastering the proprietary configuration languages of every equipment vendor is removed, since the devices offer standard APIs to the SDN controller. This makes the software development faster and more cost efficient, encouraging the introduction of new IoT applications.
- **Fine grain automation:** The APIs provide control over the forwarding hardware, allowing to tailor its operation to the specific needs of every service and traffic flow. Applications are able to automatically program the network for many different situations.
- **Higher flexibility:** Network control is performed by software running in computers: the controller, and ultimately, the applications telling the controller what network behavior they need at any given time. Only in this way, the network reconfiguration (reprogramming) can be done matching the speed of changes in an IoT scenario.
- **Improved security:** Remote access to the networking devices for configuration is not needed in SDN, so unauthorized accesses can be avoided. Devices are controlled via APIs only available to authorized SDN controllers, with appropriate authentication functions.

All these advantages are achieved by the SDN paradigm. Over the past years, an SDN architecture has stabilized and is now widely accepted. It is described in the next section.

SDN Architecture

According to the Open Networking Foundation (2013), the SDN architecture defines three *planes,* the Data Plane, the Control Plane, and the Application Plane, as shown in Figure 1. These planes and their elements are defined below.

Figure 1. SDN architecture

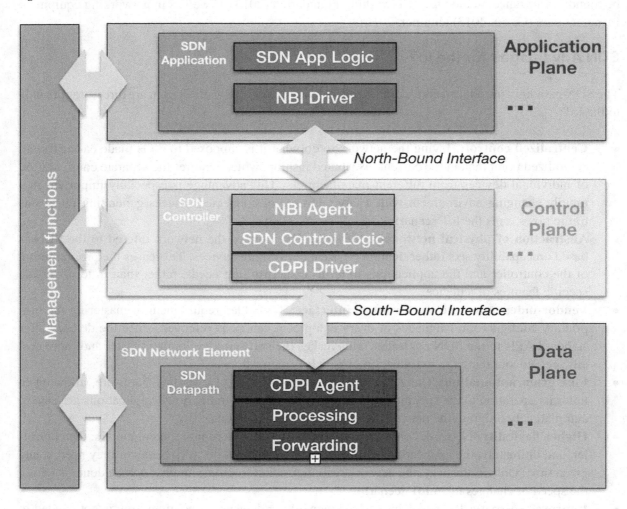

The Data Plane

The Data Plane consists of the SDN Network Elements, i.e., the nodes that actually forward incoming packets to other nodes using the links between them. A network element contains one or more *SDN data-paths*. An SDN datapath is a *logical* network element that provides a representation of part or all of the underlying resources of the node and that offers a logical view of those to the control plane. This concept achieves the separation of the physical network equipment and the logical view of it that is provided to the control plane. An SDN datapath comprises one or more *forwarding engines* and *processing functions* to modify the packets (i.e., their headers) being forwarded, and a Control-to-Data Plane Interface (CDPI) Agent to interact with the control plane. This architecture allows for network elements to contain more than one datapath, and for datapaths to be defined across several physical network elements.

The CDPI is the key element to attain the separation of the data and control planes. It includes the following functions:

- Advertising of the capabilities of the datapath to the SDN controller.
- APIs to control the forwarding of packets.
- Notification of events.
- Reporting of statistics.

These functions should be offered in a vendor-independent fashion, allowing for the interoperation of pieces of equipment from different manufacturers.

The Control Plane

The Control Plane contains the SDN Controller, defined as a centralized element that controls the SDN datapaths of a (sub)network. The controller is responsible for offering an abstract representation of the entire network to the Application Plane so that applications can decide the network policies they need.

The controller is also responsible for interpreting application policies and translating them into specific instructions for each datapath to implement them. These functions are performed by the SDN Control Logic module.

Interfaces with the application plane are called the *North-Bound Interfaces* (NBI) and are managed by the NBI Agent module of the controller. The CDPI Driver function interacts with the CDPI agents of the network elements through the Controller-to-Data plane Interface, also known as the *South-Bound Interface*. Both north-bound and south-bound interfaces are meant to be vendor-independent to allow interoperation of equipment and software from different manufacturers.

The SDN Controller is defined as a logical function, compatible with any organization of the physical servers performing the function. Several alternative control plane designs are described in the next section.

The Application Plane

The Application Plane consists of SDN Applications, programs that interact with the SDN Controller to convey their network behavior requirements for the logical network they see. They consist of the SDN Application Logic and one or more NBI Drivers to interact with the SDN Controller(s). As stated above, the NBIs offer a high-level, easy-to-use means for the applications to interact with the network.

The functions in the three planes are complemented by global management functions for configuration, coordination and monitoring purposes. Figure 2 illustrates where the elements of the SDN architecture are placed in the IoT network. A central SDN controller takes the network policies from several IoT applications and translate them into instructions for the relevant NEs, which are distributed throughout the network core and the network edge, from where the devices are connected to the network via wired and wireless links.

Figure 2. SDN architecture components in the IoT

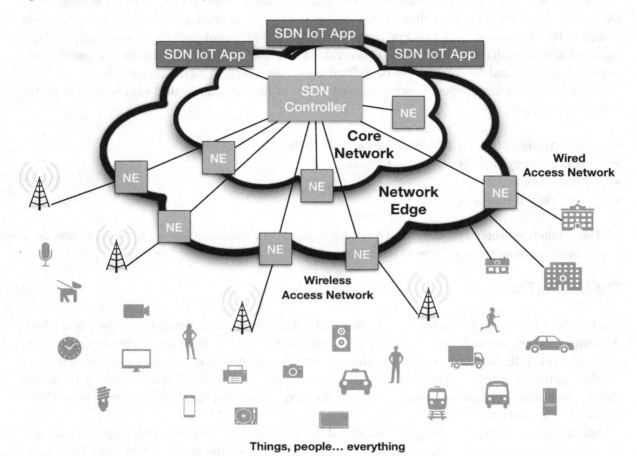

Implementations of Architectural Elements and Systems

Implementations of several elements of the architecture introduced above have been developed in a number of projects in the Open Networking Foundation. These, in turn, have been used as modules in various network systems. A few of those relevant for IoT are mentioned next.

An *OpenFlow Switch* (The Open Networking Foundation, 2015) is a network element that provides a standard CDPI (the south-bound interface) to an SDN controller. The interface is materialized in the *OpenFlow* protocol. OpenFlow is currently becoming widely used, with several network equipment vendors offering OpenFlow support in their devices. In the control plane, the Open Network Operating System (ONOS) is an SDN controller (The Open Networking Foundation, 2014), aimed at providing carrier-grade features like high availability, high performance and scalability. The Open Mobile Evolved Core (OMEC) is an implementation of an Evolved Packet Core (EPC) for LTE mobile networks, designed to be able to handle the large number of devices that will connect to the IoT through the 5G network. OMEC is used in Converged Multiaccess and Core (COMAC), a platform that integrates the management of both fixed and mobile subscribers in their connections to the core network.

Control Plane Design

The central idea in the SDN paradigm is the centralization of the network control function. This leads to the initial notion that the whole network is supposed to be controlled by a single controller, which has a view of the entire network. While this approach may be operational in small networks, it is clearly naïve in a large scenario like the IoT. Important scalability and reliability concerns need to be addressed for SDN to be suitable for real scenarios.

It is therefore acknowledged that the control plane must contain several instances of the SDN controller, with a view to meet reliability and scalability requirements. The SDN architecture accommodates any physical and logical organization of these controllers. On one end is the single controller approach mentioned above. On the other end, a controller would be collocated with each single network element leading, in fact, to the traditional network paradigm (network devices have both a data plane and a control plane). An intermediate solution is sought, with multiple SDN controllers sharing or partitioning the control of a large number of network elements. This opens the door to several architectures of the control plane, illustrated in Figure 3:

Figure 3. Centralized vs. distributed SDN control plane

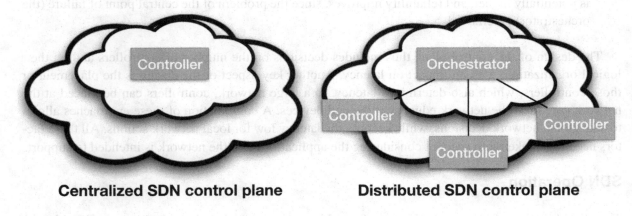

Centralized SDN control plane   **Distributed SDN control plane**

- **Centralized control plane:** This category encompasses not only the single controller solution but any situation in which a cluster of controllers share the task of controlling the whole network for reliability purposes. Existing high-availability solutions and protocols between the servers can be used to implement this approach.
- **Distributed control plane:** This category comprises the solutions where each controller is responsible for a part of the network, with only a local view of that portion of the network. In this case, controllers are autonomous if the desired behavior involves network elements under their control. For global requirements, i.e., involving network elements across the network, the controllers of those elements are required to cooperate. While the distributed approach attains network scalability, it makes programming more difficult, since the reception of notifications from the elements and the decisions on the actions to perform on them has to be done in several communicating controllers. In addition, this creates a synchronization traffic in the control plane. This traffic

flows through the data plane together with its regular user traffic, since the most common situation is that communications in the control and data planes use the same network hardware (the physical network elements and the links among them).

In a distributed control plane, the logical relation among controllers can be designed in several ways:

- **Hierarchical control plane:** The SDN controllers that control a certain network region are under the responsibility of a higher-level controller. In turn, a set of such controllers is under the responsibility of a controller in the next level upwards. This higher-level controller, which has a global view of the network or subnetwork and coordinates the controllers below it, is often called an *orchestrator*. This hierarchical structure seeks to facilitate the adoption of network decisions. If the desired network behavior involves a set of network elements controlled by more than one controller, the decision is taken by a controller in the hierarchy responsible for all the network elements. This approach recovers the centralization in the decision making and the corresponding ease of programming but adds latency to the reaction of the control plane.
- **Fully distributed control plane:** The SDN controllers are peers at the same logical level. They exchange messages to share their respective local views and take decisions cooperatively. Programming of controllers is more difficult because of its distributed nature, although efficiency is potentially higher, and reliability improves, since the problem of the central point of failure (the orchestrator) is removed.

The design of the control plane thus includes decisions on the number of controllers and on their logical organization, with an impact on latency. Another key aspect of the design is the placement of those controllers, which also determines latency. In a large network, controllers can be placed at the network core or at the network edge, near the end devices. A combination of these approaches allows to take global network decisions, while keeping the latency low for local network actions. All these factors need to be taken into account considering the applications that the network is intended to support.

SDN Operation

The main function of a network element of any kind is to forward packets (or frames). For this, the device receives a packet through an incoming interface, stores it and analyzes the header corresponding to the layer of the device in the protocol architecture. Based on this analysis, the device takes a decision of forwarding or dropping the packet. If it is decided to forward the packet, a further decision is made as for the output interface. A multilayer switch is capable of processing the packet according to several headers corresponding to different layers (e.g., L1 to L4).

Interactions between the Controller and Network Elements

Compared to the operation of a generic network element described in the previous lines, an SDN network element in the data plane lacks the logic required to take decisions by itself. It still receives, stores and analyzes the packet headers and is still able to forward or drop the packet. But the decision is taken by a remote, centralized SDN controller. Of course, it would be extremely inefficient to ask the controller what to do with every single packet entering the device. Therefore, an SDN switch has a table (or typically a set of tables) where *rules* are stored. A rule establishes a *traffic flow* and an *action*. The switch takes that action for all packets matching that traffic flow. A traffic flow is defined as a sequence of packets passing through the switch with the same characteristics, i.e., given values in (a subset of) the headers fields. Thus, a traffic flow may identify packets originated from some network and destined to some other network and carrying information related to some service (L4 port), for example.

The SDN controller, interacting through the CDPI of the SDN switch (the southbound interface), populates its table with the appropriate rules. When a packet enters the switch, the corresponding flow (headers fields) is looked up in the table. If found, the switch applies the action set for that flow to the packet. (This is similar to the forwarding process in today switches.) If not found, the switch sends that packet to the controller asking for instructions. In response, the controller will install a new rule in the switch table. Subsequent packets of the same flow will be autonomously processed by the switch with no interaction with the controller.

While packets of known flows can be forwarded at line rates, the interaction of the switch with the controller for the first packet of an unknown flow obviously introduces a delay or latency in the processing of the whole flow. While the switch is asking the controller for instructions and waiting for its response, more packets of the same flow will in general arrive to the switch and will need to be stored in a queue until a rule is installed by the controller. This requires the switch to have enough buffering space, which needs to be carefully dimensioned according to the interface's speeds, the frequency of arrival of new flows, and the expected delay in the controller response. The latter factor depends in turn on the design of the control plane, as noted in the previous section.

The Rule Tables

The matching of an incoming packet to a rule in the table is usually performed using a Contents Addressable Memory (CAM). The bits of the packet headers are presented to the CAM and the matching rule (if there is one in the CAM) is written in an output register in the next clock cycle. In Ternary CAMs (TCAM), the bits in the index field (the headers) of the rules are able to store a '0', a '1' and an 'x' meaning "either '0' or '1'". This introduces the possibility that many different packets (e.g., coming from the same subnetwork but differing in the host portion of the source address) match the same rule. This leads to a beneficial reduction in the number of rules that need to be stored in the table. In addition, this feature allows a single packet to match more than one rule. In that case, several actions would be applied to the packet.

Packet processing in an SDN switch can be organized in a sequence of tables or table *pipeline*. In this case, the packet may go through a sequence of tables, from an ingress table to an egress table. A match of the packet in a table prescribes an action on the packet, and perhaps the forwarding of the packet to another table. If the packet matches an entry on that table, another action is prescribed and the packet may be forwarded to the next table. The process repeats until the packet is ready to be output. At this point, the actions prescribed by all the tables are executed in the order they were added and the packet is transmitted through a switch output interface. Figure 4 illustrates this table pipeline organization of the an SDN datapath in the network element, and shows the processing of a packet from ingress to egress into/from the network element.

Figure 4. Flow table pipeline in an SDN network element

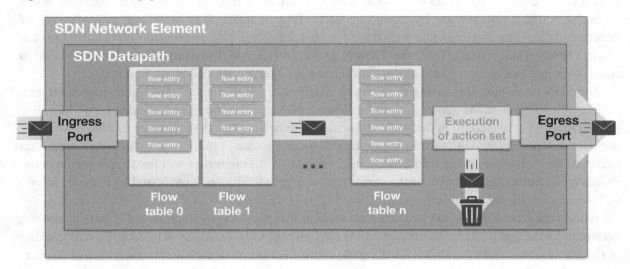

Actions on Packets

As it has already been mentioned, the action prescribed by an entry in a traffic flow table can be *output* or *drop*. However, there are many other actions to be performed on the packet before it is forwarded to another switch. Examples of such actions follow:

- **Output:** The packet starts forwarding process through the indicated output port.
- **Drop:** The packet is discarded.
- **Select queue:** The packet is set to be processed by a particular queue on the selected output interface, which allows for the implementation of Quality of Service policies.
- **Label:** A label is added (or removed) to (from) the packet. This can be used for VLAN tagging in Ethernet, or for LSP tagging in MPLS.
- **Write:** A value is written in the specified header field.
- **Copy:** The value in the specified field is copied. The copied value can be written to a flow entry field, written to another header field, etc.
- **Modify:** An operation is performed on a header field value, and the result is written to that field. An example use of this is the decrement of TTL-like header fields.
- **Measure:** The packet is sent to the specified statistics collector, which can drop the packet if a configurable threshold is reached, depending on the type of the measure being performed.
- **Group:** The packet is sent to a special group table in order to be forwarded through more than one output port.

Any action performed by a traditional network element on a packet can be recreated using the actions types presented above. Therefore, an SDN switch is also able to perform those actions. The difference between the traditional and the SDN switch is that, in the latter, such actions are governed by a set of rules in the flow tables, and those entries are installed by the remote SDN controller.

Flow Table Entries Installation

As stated above, the SDN controller is responsible for the installation of the appropriate rules in the SDN switch tables to handle each traffic flow. Several strategies are possible for this:

- **Reactive mode:** The SDN controller does nothing until the first packet of a new flow is received from an SDN switch. After the packet is processed, the controller sends the rules to be installed to the switch. This behavior introduces a latency in the forwarding of the flow.
- **Proactive mode:** The SDN controller installs rules for all flows in the SDN switch in advance. The switch will not need to send the controller any packet, since all flows are known. This behavior removes the latency of the reactive mode, but requires taking care of all possible flows a priori and lacks flexibility.
- **Hybrid mode:** Some flows can be preconfigured by the controller, following the proactive mode. The rest of the flows can be dynamically configured, using the reactive mode. The hybrid mode thus combines the flexibility and low latency of the other modes. This is comparable to the routing tables of the traditional routers, which can be populated by dynamic routing algorithms and by the network administrator configuring static rules.

Software Defined Storage

Adding to the successful paradigms of cloud computing and software defined networking is the Software Defined Storage (SDS) concept (Raj & Raman 2017). The notion of Software Defined Data Centers (SDDC) is based on these three concepts. Storage in traditional data centers were designed for specific applications, and typically used heterogeneous and multivendor products, leading to storage solutions that were difficult to manage and scale. Expensive Storage Area Networks are an example of these. Along the line of SDN, the key idea behind SDS is to separate the control of the storage equipment and centralize it in a remote controller. This makes possible to use inexpensive commodity storage resources that are managed by the controller. The controller can then implement the storage policies (caching, striping, replication, back-ups, etc.) required by each application. In other words, SDS virtualizes storage making it flexible, scalable, fault-tolerant, dynamic and manageable. In addition, SDS makes it possible to distribute the data in the right place to improve application performance. One additional aspect of SDS hardware is that it offers APIs that give applications control over the storage functions to further improve performance. The joint capabilities of SDS, SDN and cloud computing give the IoT the flexibility and dynamics required for real applications.

SDN in IoT Networks

The Internet of Things is not a unique reality. The concept of having a very large number of connected devices may be applied in networks for different applications and services, in both public and private environments. All of them benefit from the application of the SDN paradigm, in ways that depend on the architecture and purpose of the network. IoT application areas expected to take advantage of SDN include:

- Sensor networks
- Healthcare systems
- Vehicular networks
- Education
- Smart cities and smart grids
- Telecommunications
- Industrial systems

This section describes these areas and explain how SDN can give an answer to some of the challenges posed by each of them.

Sensor Networks

Some systems need to receive measures of diverse types to achieve their goals. Those measures are performed by sensors connected to some central server. Those connections can be wired or, more often nowadays, wireless, making for Wireless Sensor Networks (WSN). Many IoT applications make use of sensor networks, including environmental control systems, home automation, factory lines, biomedical health monitoring systems, etc. Figure 5 illustrates an IoT based on sensor networks, both wired and wireless.

Sensors are typically small inexpensive devices powered by batteries, and their autonomy is critical to keep the system economically feasible. Sometimes, besides the measuring functions, these devices assume forwarding functions to build ad-hoc wireless networks, capable of working with no access point infrastructure. Routing in an ad-hoc network is a challenge because of their particular characteristics like the instability of the radio links and the power restrictions. Some routing protocols have been designed specifically for this type of networks. SDN can streamline the routing in the ad-hoc network since the controller gets a vision of the whole network. In addition, to maximize the batteries lifespan, the SDN controller can organize routing to optimize the use of the wireless bandwidth minimizing power consumption. It can even try to avoid routing messages through devices with low remaining battery capacity. The use of SDN in sensor networks can be seen in Figure 5.

However, taking advantage of SDN in sensor networks implies facing considerable challenges. For example, communications between the SDN controller and the sensor is likely to be unstable because of the unreliability of wireless links. Also, this communication imposes an overhead on the wireless bandwidth, since SDN traffic competes with the regular sensor traffic. It is necessary to reduce the interactions through the CDPI to minimize this traffic, creating a lightweight SDN protocol architecture, like the one proposed in (Baddeley, Nejabaty, Oikonomou, Sooriyabandara, & Simeonidou, 2018).

Wireless sensor networks can host several applications, each requiring different levels of QoS. This can be handled creating virtual networks in the data plane on the same hardware. Network slicing is a technique that assigns the required resources to each *slice* of the network, generally isolating slices to guarantee the QoS demanded by each slice. A network slice is therefore an abstraction that encompasses a portion of the resources of the network behaving as a dedicated network in itself. While this is relatively straightforward in wired networks, it is harder to implement in wireless networks, where radio links may cause interference between slices. In this case, SDN can help in orchestrating the routing in a way that minimizes the interference in high priority slices at the expense of best effort slices (An, Kim, Park, Kwon, & Lim 2019). The multipurpose sensor network has been also called Virtual Sensor Network (VSN).

Figure 5. An IoT based on sensor networks

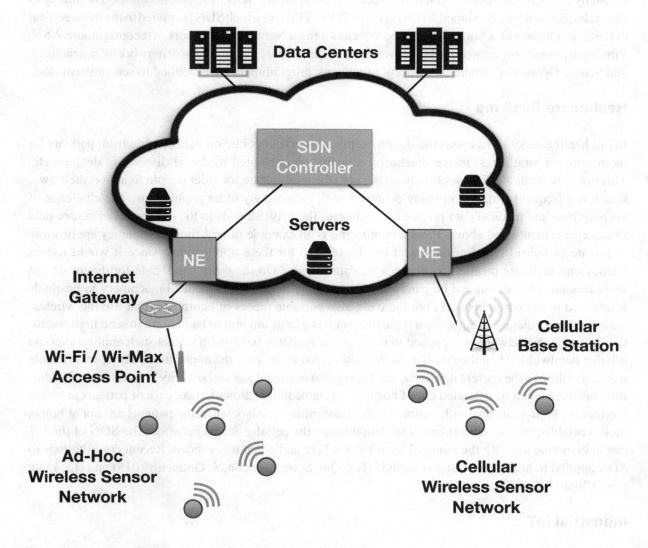

Data gathered by sensors is routed through the network towards the application servers. The latency introduced by the network can be significant and some services are delay-sensitive. To reduce this latency, the path from the sensor to the servers can be shortened moving servers closer to the sensors. This can be done replicating and placing servers and storage resources at the network edge. This approach, known as *fog computing*, essentially introduces an intermediate layer between the sensors and the cloud application servers, in a hierarchical architecture. The flexible routing made possible by SDN is useful here to direct data from sensors to the appropriate servers, that is, the closest servers in the network edge that fulfill the application requirements (Okay, & Ozdemir 2018). The concept of fog computing can be extended if SDN switches themselves are furnished with enough processing capacity to host software to process sensor data, thus minimizing latency. Then, the aggregated or preprocessed data can be sent to other servers in the cloud or at any other network location for further processing.

Many projects have been developed in recent years applying SDN to sensor networks. The survey in (Tayyaba, Shah, Khan, & Ahmed 2017) includes SDN-WISE (in which SDN is applied to the management of the sensor network), a Software Defined Wireless Sensor Network Framework, a reconfigurable WSN, a multipurpose sensor network (where several applications share the same sensor network infrastructure), and Sensor OpenFlow (where the concept of network programmability is applied to sensor networks).

Healthcare Systems

IoT in healthcare systems opens the door to applications that operate on data coming from patients for monitoring of vital signs, image diagnosis, wearable or implanted medicine dispensing devices, etc. This not only includes illnesses treatment but also the remote care for elder people living on their own, which is a frequent situation in many countries with increasingly older populations. The challenge of keeping personal medical data private as it traverses the network adds to the challenges of sensor data management mentioned above. Patient monitoring is an example of real-time low-latency application. A private or hybrid cloud arrangement can be of help for these applications, since it would reduce latency and facilitate meeting regulations on data privacy. On the other hand, data for diagnosis can be processed off-line, but can be bandwidth demanding. Some of the medical machinery in hospitals is attached to the wired network, but there are also portable pieces of equipment that use the wireless network. Image diagnosis equipment typically requires a large amount of bandwidth to send high resolution images. The network is supposed to manage the available bandwidth so that such applications can use that bandwidth when they need it. SDN makes possible to route the applications traffic in a flexible way, according to the current demands, and taking into account QoS and security requirements. In addition, healthcare can be extended out of hospitals. Telemedicine allows to take care of patients at home, monitoring their signs and with remote medical consultancy. Also, when the patients are not at home, their wearable medical sensors can send data through the cellular access network. The SDN of the IoT can help in guaranteeing the required bandwidth where and when it is needed. Recent contributions to SDN applied to healthcare systems include (Hu, Qiu, Song, Hossain, & Ghoneim 2015) and (Li, Liao, Cho, Chien, Lai, & Chao 2017).

Industrial IoT

When the concept of IoT is applied to factories and other industrial processes, collecting data from scores of sensors in the production chains and connecting industrial robots to control software through the network, the Industrial IoT (IIoT) arises. This concept is often presented as part of the Industry 4.0, or fourth industrial revolution, together with artificial intelligence, cloud computing and big data analysis. The intelligent factories of the Industry 4.0, massively connected through the IIoT, will bring gains in operational efficiency and savings in cost reductions. These benefits come from improving manufacturing processes or other industry-related processes by means of data gathering through sensors networks, and the subsequent processing of the data in the cloud (Mourtzis, Vlachou, & Milas 2016). Figure 6 illustrates the Industrial IoT.

The aviation industry, for example, involves both the manufacturing of planes and engines on the one hand, and the operation of airlines on the other hand. Both sides can benefit from the IIoT (Gilchrist 2016). In particular, the monitoring and maintenance of jet engines is a crucial process with very high expenses. With an IIoT, thousands of sensors continuously produce large amounts of data that can be

Figure 6. An industrial IoT

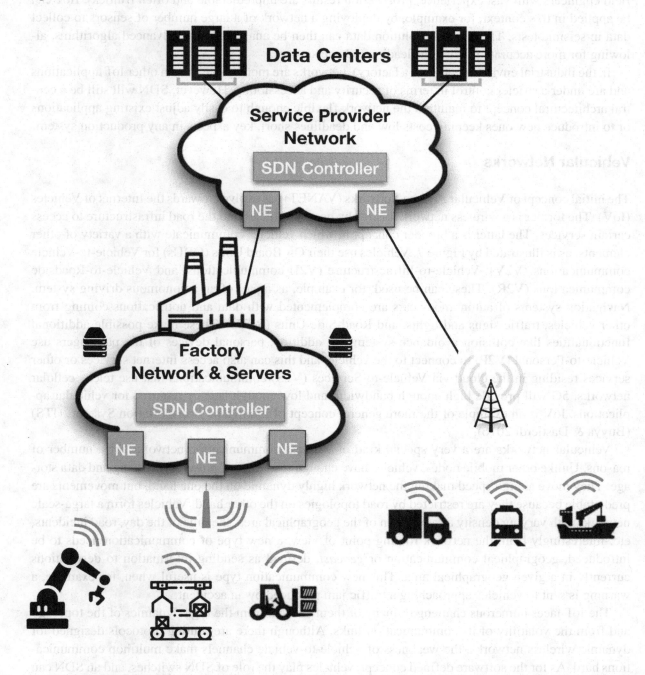

analyzed to discover patterns that anticipate failures. Based on that data, a model of an engine can be constructed and used as a parallel version of its physical engine counterpart. This "digital twin" can be used to detect parts of the engine that need to be serviced avoiding maintenance of parts of the engine that would turn out to be fine.

Processes with very high costs can also be found in the oil and gas industry. Drilling for discovery of new reservoirs takes a huge amount of time and resources. Albeit traditionally led by the expertise of field engineers with vast experience, prospection results are unpredictable and often fruitless. IIoT can be applied in this context, for example, by deploying a network of a large number of sensors to collect data in seismic tests. These high-resolution data can then be analyzed using advanced algorithms, allowing for more accurate predictions leading to huge savings.

In the industrial environment (e.g., a factory), networks are more stable than in other IoT applications and are under a stricter control in terms of security and accessibility. However, SDN will still be a central architectural concept to maintain the network flexible enough to easily adjust existing applications or to introduce new ones keeping costs low and deadlines short, key aspects in any production system.

Vehicular Networks

The initial concept of Vehicular Ad-hoc Networks (VANET) has evolved towards the Internet of Vehicles (IoV). The former is a wireless network formed by nearby vehicles and the road infrastructure to access certain services. The latter is a broader concept in which vehicles communicate with a variety of other elements, as is illustrated by Figure 7. Vehicles use their On-Board Units (OBUs) for Vehicle-to-Vehicle communications (V2V), Vehicle-to-Infraestructure (V2I) communications, and Vehicle-to-Roadside communications (V2R). These can be used, for example, as a part of an autonomous driving system. Navigation systems of autonomous cars are complemented with data and notifications coming from other vehicles, traffic signs and lights, and Road-Side Units (RSUs). These make possible additional functionalities like collision avoidance systems. In addition, personal devices of the passengers use Vehicle-to-Personal (V2P) to connect to the vehicle, and this can also access Internet services or other services residing in the cloud via Vehicle-to-Services (V2S) communications that use telcos cellular networks. 5G will provide high enough bandwidth and low enough latency required for vehicular applications. IoV is an example of the more general concept of Intelligent Transportation Systems (ITS) (Buyya & Dastjerdi 2016).

Vehicular networks are a very special kind of wireless communication networks for a number of reasons. Unlike other mobile nodes, vehicles have enough resources of power, processing and data storage. They move at high speed making the network highly dynamic on the one hand, but movements are predictable because they are restricted by road topologies on the other hand. Vehicles form a large-scale network, with varying density as a function of the geographical area, the time of the day, road incidents, etc. Interestingly from the network routing point of view, a new type of communication needs to be introduced, geographical communication or *geocast*, defined as sending information to destinations currently in a given geographical area. This new communication type is useful when, for example, a warning is sent to vehicles approaching a traffic jam produced by an accident.

The IoT faces numerous challenges, many of them derived from the high dynamics of the topology and from the volatility of its communication links. Although there are routing protocols designed for dynamic wireless networks, the weakness of vehicle-to-vehicle channels make multihop communications hard. As for the software defined concept, vehicles play the role of SDN switches, and an SDN can help in finding the best routes through vehicles. But the speed of changes in the topology of the network demand a very low latency and a high processing power in the SDN controller to keep pace with the network situation. Security is another essential concern in IoVs, where not only the privacy and integrity of information must be preserved, but vehicles must be protected from attacks to their navigation and autonomous driving systems (Chen, Xiang, Liu, & Wang 2019).

Figure 7. Vehicle communications in an IoV

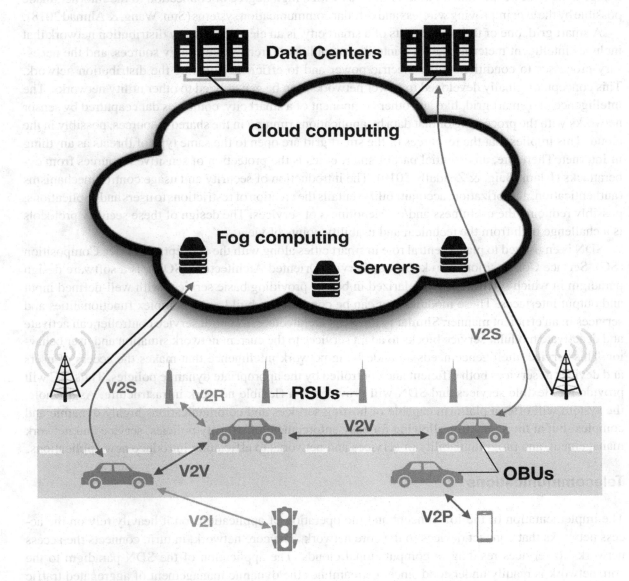

Smart Cities and Smart Grids

One of the most ambitious applications of IoT is the Smarts City concept, which encompasses services to make people's life easier in their daily activities while contributing to solve the crucial challenges that the large concentrations of population are facing today. These challenges include problems as important as global warming, energy shortage, economic and social restructuring, population ageing, migration flows, etc. Smart cities go beyond the technical issues posed by IoT, targeting problems with a strong social component that involves healthcare, environmental issues, energy/utility networks, transportation/delivery networks, people mobility, communications, security, housing, architecture, education, entertainment, etc. In a sense, smart cities are the concentration of all IoT applications in an urban area with a large density of people and all kind of devices with a high degree of connection to the Internet, made possible by the ever improving wireless and cellular communication systems (Sun, Wang, & Ahmad 2018).

A smart grid, one of the components of a smart city, is an electrical energy distribution network that includes intelligent metering devices, intelligent appliances, renewable energy sources, and the necessary processes to conditionate the electric power and to efficiently operate the distribution network. This concept, originally developed in power networks, can be generalized to other utility networks. The intelligence of a smart grid, like any other component of a smart city, combines data captured by sensor networks with the processing of that data by applications running in the shared resources, possibly in the cloud. This implies that the resources of the smart grid are open to the same type of threats as anything in Internet. Therefore, an essential part of smart cities is the protection of sensitive resources from cyberattacks (Islam, Baig, & Zeadally 2019). The introduction of security and usage control mechanisms (authentication, authorization, accountability) entails the creation of restrictions to users and applications, possibly reducing the usefulness and/or friendliness of services. The design of these security protocols is a challenge both from the technical and usability points of view.

SDN is envisaged to play a central role in smart cities along with the concept of Service Composition (SC). Service Composition, also known as Service Oriented Architecture (SOA), is a software design paradigm in which software is modularized in blocks providing basic services with well-defined input and output interfaces. These modules that can be combined to build more complex functionalities and services in an efficient manner. Similar to the SDN architecture, a central service controller can activate and deactivate modular service blocks to adapt services to the current network situation and user behavior. This service intelligence needs an underlying network intelligence that makes the access of users and devices to services both efficient and controlled by the appropriate dynamic policies. Thus, SC will provide for flexible services and SDN will provide for a flexible network infrastructure. As a whole, the system will offer a platform capable of hosting services and communications highly dynamic and complex, but at the same time allowing for easy enforcement of security policies, service and network management, and programmability of services and networks to efficiently introduce new applications.

Telecommunications

The implementation of the IoT concept and the operation of applications on it heavily rely on the access networks that connect devices to the core network. The core network, in turn, connects the access networks to services residing in computational clouds. The application of the SDN paradigm to the core network is readily understood since it streamlines the dynamic management of aggregated traffic flows to adapt the network to the current demands. However, it is in access networks where SDN faces more challenging issues and exhibits greater potential. It is in access networks where the traffic flows must be granted or denied access on a per-user basis. An access network must also be able to handle the mobility of users, with handover and roaming capabilities, and at the same time, reconfigure network nodes to apply the right policies to the new traffic flows resulting from moving users. It is desired that handovers can take place between heterogeneous networks (e.g., between wi-fi and cellular networks, between home and public networks, etc.), allowing for a seamless integration that makes the network transparent to users. This highly dynamic nature of the access network calls for a completely new network paradigm, where the desired reactions of networks can be programmed (Tayyaba, Shah, Khan, & Ahmed 2017) (Akyildiz, Wang, & Lin 2015). The use of SDN in telecommunication networks, which in turn support IoT applications, is illustrated by Figure 8.

Figure 8. SDN in a telecommunication network supporting IoT applications

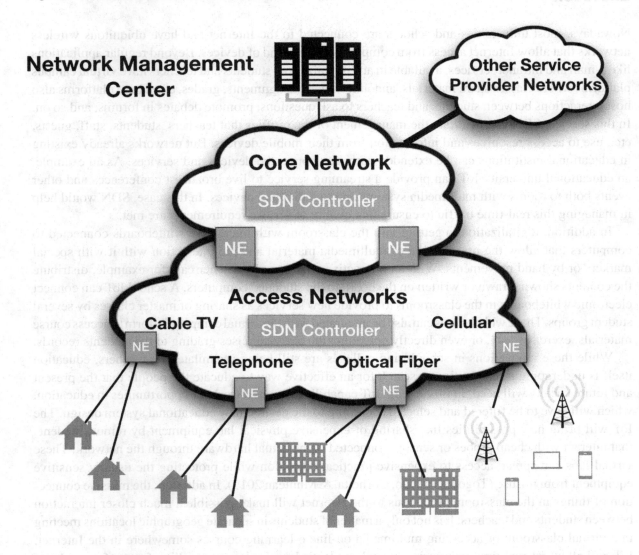

Wireless networks interfaces have their own software defined paradigm. In Software Defined Radio (SDR), many radio signal processing functions that have traditionally been performed by hardware devices (filters, modems, detectors, mixers, etc.) are implemented in software in combination with analog-to-digital and digital-to-analog converters and a radiofrequency stage. This allows for unprecedented flexibility in the air interface, since changing from a physical layer protocol to another in a device (e.g., switching between GSM, UMTS and LTE in a cell phone) is a matter of running different software over the same general purpose processing and radiofrequency hardware. SDR also provides a much more agile means to dynamically allocate resources (frequencies, timeslots, channels, etc.) to users according to their bandwidth needs of the moment, since we have software control over the signal through the antenna. The flexibility provided by SDR in the physical layer complements the flexibility provided by SDN in higher layers of the protocol stack (Namal, Ahmad, Saud, Jokinen, & Gurtov 2015).

Education

Nowadays, most universities and schools are connected to the Internet and have ubiquitous wireless networks that allow Internet access from computers and all kind of devices. Beyond regular applications like e-mail and intranet services, available in any organization, students and teachers have virtual campus platforms where classes share materials, announcements, assignments, grades, etc. These platforms also host interactions between students and teachers to ask questions, promote debates in forums, and so on. In this service, SDN can facilitate the management of the profiles that teachers, students, staff, guests, etc., use to access resources and information from their mobile devices. But networks already existing in educational institutions can be extended with new connected devices and services. As an example, an educational university IoT can provide a streaming service to live broadcast conferences and other events both to rooms with multimedia systems and to individual devices. In this case, SDN would help in managing this real-time traffic to ensure that quality of service requirements are met.

In addition, digitalization is getting into the classroom with interactive whiteboards connected to computers that allow the presentation of multimedia material and the interaction with it with special markers or by hand movements. With an interactive whiteboard a teacher can, for example, distribute the contents shown, drawn or written on the board to the students' computers. A school IoT can connect electronic whiteboards in the classrooms to provide new services as sharing of master classes by several student groups. These whiteboards can also be integrated with the virtual campus platform to access course materials, exercises, etc., or even directly uploading the class exercises grading to the students records.

While these innovations in schools and colleges are still being assimilated by teachers, education itself is undergoing a redefinition in search for an effective way to educate the people that the present and future society will need. In this setting, IoT capabilities opens a world of opportunities in education, which will have to be filtered and selected according to the desired new educational system design. The IoT will bring new possibilities like sharing of expensive physical lab equipment by remote students that interact with cheap probes or sensors connected to the actual hardware through the network. These virtual labs can spread access to expensive practical education while protecting the usually sensitive equipment from misuse (Togou, Lorenzo, Cornetta, & Muntean 2019). In addition, the massive connection of things in the classroom or campus to the Internet will make possible a much closer interaction between students and teachers. It is not only a matter of students in separate geographic locations meeting in a virtual classroom or accessing multimedia on-line e-learning courses somewhere in the Internet. IoT will allow for real-time monitoring of each student's learning process, calling for reinforcement of improvement areas in a personalized educational experience that will speed up the learning process. For instance, the student's tablet computer can send his or her exercise results to the virtual campus, and feedback and new exercises can be sent back according to the needs of that particular student. IoT in Education is also envisaged to relieve teachers' administrative tasks, with automatic class attendance control, periodic progress assessment of students, etc. (Al-Emran, Malik, Al-Kabi 2020).

Finally, the numerous possibilities brought about by IoT can be expanded by combining it with Virtual Reality (VR) and Augmented Reality (AR) to improve the learning experience. Students can have a virtual animal dissection lab session on their tablet computers, with relevant information being displayed when appropriate. They can also be placed in a virtual environment to learn about geography, history, science, etc. This virtual environment can be controlled by the student reactions, which are captured by wearable sensors, resulting in interactive scenarios that can be applied in the design of sophisticated learning experiences. All this will result in a dynamic mix of traffic flows with different requirement that SDN can help to manage and control in a much more easy and flexible way than the traditional networking paradigm.

FUTURE RESEARCH DIRECTIONS

SDN is a promising architectural element for the IoT, although some open issues still need to be addressed in depth. Some research initiatives so far have provided theoretical frameworks or models, but many implementation aspects require further details to be able to move on to an experimental phase to validate the proposals and to prove the suitability of SDN for IoT scenarios. First, the centralization of the control plane needs to be combined with a degree of distribution to avoid reliability and scalability problems. The design of the control plane and the interactions between the SDN controllers need to strike the right balance to achieve low latency, high availability and easy management.

A similar balance is sought in the computation of application software. Centralized cloud computation is easier than distributed fog computation, but the latter achieves lower latency. SDN can also help in balancing the load between servers or data centers. Dynamic adaptation would assure that available network and computation resources are used efficiently to meet application requirements. In fact, the software definition feature of the network should be integrated with its counterparts in application, storage and even in the radio interface for wireless access networks. An effective combination of these elements could really leverage the potential of software definition. As an example, consider an Internet service subject to ample variations in its demand, like the streaming over the Internet of the new season of a popular TV series. The networks of the service providers could detect the rising traffic demand as the season is released, and could adapt the routing of that traffic securing the necessary bandwidth for it using SDN. The network could even react creating mirror streaming servers closer to the areas with higher demand to reduce traffic in the core network. This would be dynamically and efficiently achieved by the combined use of other software definition techniques, like server virtualization and software defined storage.

Security also remains a challenge, due to the enormous number of devices connected to the IoT. All of them need to be properly authenticated to avoid attacks and to guarantee information integrity and confidentiality. Consider for an instance mobile users with different security profiles as they roam through several cellular networks. Each network needs to identify and classify those users to be able to apply the appropriate policies to each of them via SDN. In addition, this scenario requires the interaction of the involved service provider networks to provide the relevant native user information.

On the other hand, interactions among SDN elements themselves (controllers, network elements and applications) must be secured, in a degree equivalent to the current networking protocols. For example, an SDN controller is required to authenticate itself to the network elements it will be controlling, to avoid malicious controllers to gain control of the network resources and traffic.

Finally, SDN must be able to handle the difficulties inherent to the characteristics of many IoT devices, i.e., limited power, limited processing and storage capabilities, and unstable wireless links. These, together with the issues mentioned above, need to be dealt with by an SDN network. For example, consider a small wireless access point in a sensor network. SDN capabilities could be added to such a device only at a significant increase in its price, unless a lightweight protocol is defined and implemented. At the same time, the management and control of that SDN network must be kept simple, which is another challenge in itself.

CONCLUSION

This chapter has presented SDN as a key element to the IoT. SDN provides a new networking paradigm, more flexible and agile than the traditional model, that achieves a better fit to the IoT requirements.

The SDN architecture has been described and its main functional elements and interfaces have been explained. This has allowed to list and understand the advantages that SDN offers to the IoT. These benefits have been related to the specific scenarios of IoTs supporting a variety of applications and services, including vehicular networks, sensor networks, healthcare systems, telecommunications, industrial IoTs, smart cities and grids, and IoTs for education. The prospect is highly promising, albeit open issues have been reviewed that need to be further studied and experimentally tested with actual implementations of the SDN concepts. Once these challenges are met, this networking paradigm will likely be a central element of future IoT services, as it is envisaged for other application areas as cloud computing and big data analysis.

REFERENCES

Akyildiz, I., Wang, P., & Lin, S. (2015). SoftAir: A software defined networking architecture for 5G wireless systems. *Computer Networks*, *85*, 1–18. doi:10.1016/j.comnet.2015.05.007

Al-Emran, M., Malik, S. I., & Al-Kabi, M. N. (2020). A Survey of Internet of Things (IoT) in Education: Opportunities and Challenges. In Toward Social Internet of Things (SIoT): Enabling Technologies, Architectures and Applications (pp. 197-209). Springer.

An, N., Kim, Y., Park, J., Kwon, D.-H., & Lim, H. (2019). Slice Management for Quality of Service Differentiation in Wireless Network Slicing. *Sensors (Basel)*, *19*(12), 2745. doi:10.339019122745 PMID:31248088

Baddeley, M., Nejabaty, R., Oikonomou, G., Sooriyabandara, M., & Simeonidou, D. (2018). Evolving SDN for Low-Power IoT Networks. In *Proceedings of the 4th IEEE Conference on Network Softwarization and Workshops (NetSoft)* (pp. 71-79). Montreal, Canada: IEEE. 10.1109/NETSOFT.2018.8460125

Buyya, R., & Dastjerdi, A. V. (2016). *Internet of Things. Principles and paradigms*. Cambridge, MA: Elsevier.

Chen, C., Xiang, B., Liu, Y., & Wang, K. (2019). A Secure Authentication Protocol for Internet of Vehicles. *IEEE Access : Practical Innovations, Open Solutions*, *7*, 12047–12057. doi:10.1109/ACCESS.2019.2891105

Cisco Systems. (2013). *Software-Defined Networking: Why we like it and how we are building on it.* Cisco White Paper. Retrieved from https://www.cisco.com/c/dam/en_us/solutions/industries/docs/gov/cis13090_sdn_sled_white_paper.pdf

Dahlqvist, F., Patel, M., Rajko, A., & Shulman, J. (2019). *Growing Opportunities in the Internet of Things*. McKinsey & Company. Retrieved from https://www.mckinsey.com/industries/private-equity-and-principal-investors/our-insights/growing-opportunities-in-the-internet-of-things# in January 2020.

Ejaz, W., Imran, M., Jo, M., Muhammad, N., Qaisar, S., & Wang, W. (2016). Internet of Things (IoT) in 5G Wireless Communications. *IEEE Access : Practical Innovations, Open Solutions, 4*, 10310–10314. doi:10.1109/ACCESS.2016.2646120

Evans, D. (2012). *The Internet of Everything. How More Relevant and Valuable Connections Will Change the World*. Cisco Internet Business Solutions Group.

Gilchrist, A. (2016). *Industry 4.0: The industrial Internet of Things*. Bangken, Thailand: Apress. doi:10.1007/978-1-4842-2047-4

Hu, L., Qiu, M., Song, J., Hossain, M. S., & Ghoneim, A. (2015). Software defined healthcare networks. *IEEE Wireless Communications, 22*(6), 67–75. doi:10.1109/MWC.2015.7368826

Islam, S., Baig, Z., & Zeadally, S. (2019). Physical Layer Security for the Smart Grid: Vulnerabilities, Threats and Countermeasures. *IEEE Transactions on Industrial Informatics, 15*(12), 6522–6530. doi:10.1109/TII.2019.2931436

Juniper Networks. (2016). *SDN and NFV: Transforming the service provider organization*. Juniper White Paper. Retrieved from https://www.juniper.net/assets/us/en/local/pdf/whitepapers/2000579-en.pdf

Li, T., Liao, C., Cho, H., Chien, W., Lai, C. F., & Chao, H. (2017). An e-healthcare sensor network load-balancing scheme using SDN-SFC. *Proceedings of the IEEE 19th International Conference on e-Health Networking, Applications and Services (Healthcom)*, 1-4. 10.1109/HealthCom.2017.8210833

Mourtzis, D., Vlachou, E., & Milas, N. (2016). Industrial Big Data as a Result of IoT Adoption in Manufacturing. *Procedia CIRP, 55*, 290–295. doi:10.1016/j.procir.2016.07.038

Namal, S., Ahmad, I., Saud, S., Jokinen, M., & Gurtov, A. (2015). Implementation of OpenFlow based cognitive radio network architecture: SDN&R. *Wireless Networks, 22*(2), 663–677. doi:10.100711276-015-0973-5

Okay, F. Y., & Ozdemir, S. (2018). Routing in Fog-Enabled IoT Platforms: A Survey and an SDN-Based Solution. *IEEE Internet of Things Journal, 5*(6), 4871–4889. doi:10.1109/JIOT.2018.2882781

Raj, P., & Raman, A. C. (2017). *The Internet of Things: Enabling Technologies, Platforms, and Use Cases*. Boca Raton, FL: CRC Press.

Sun, H., Wang, C., & Ahmad, B. I. (2018). *From Internet of Things to Smart Cities. Enabling technologies*. Boca Raton, FL: CRC Press.

Tayyaba, S. K., Shah, M. A., Khan, O. A., & Ahmed, A. W. (2017). Software Defined Network (SDN) Based Internet of Things (IoT): A Road Ahead. In *Proceedings of the International Conference on Future Networks and Distributed Systems* (pp. 15:1-15:8). New York, NY: ACM 10.1145/3102304.3102319

The Open Networking Foundation. (2013). *Software-Defined Networking: the new norm for networks*. ONF White Paper. Retrieved from https://www.opennetworking.org/images/stories/downloads/sdn-resources/white-papers/wp-sdn-newnorm.pdf

The Open Networking Foundation. (2014). *Introducing ONOS – a SDN network operating system for Service Providers*. ONF White Paper. Retrieved from onosproject.org/wp-content/uploads/2014/11/Whitepaper-ONOS-final.pdf

The Open Networking Foundation. (2015). *OpenFlow Switch specification version 1.5.1*. TS-025. Retrieved from https://www.opennetworking.org/software-defined-standards/specifications/

Togou, M. A., Lorenzo, C., Cornetta, G., & Muntean, G. M. (2019). NEWTON Fab Lab Initiative: A Small-Scale Pilot for STEM Education. In Proceedings of EdMedia + Innovate Learning 2019, (pp. 8-17). Waynesville, NC: Association for the Advancement of Computing in Education (AACE).

KEY TERMS AND DEFINITIONS

Application Plane: Part of the SDN architecture consisting of applications implementing services provided to users/devices through the network. Applications interact with the SDN controller through APIs (the northbound interface) to get an abstract global vision of the network they are using and to communicate the network behavior they need at the moment.

Control Plane: Part of the networking function that determines the treatment given to each traffic flow, and lastly to each packet, including switching, routing, quality of service, security, and fault tolerance aspects. It is placed in each network element in the traditional networking paradigm, whereas it is centralized in SDN, allowing for network programmability.

Core Network: Part of the network consisting of network elements connected by high-speeds communication lines (optic fibers and/or point-to-point radio links), typically covering a wide geographical region. It does not include the network infrastructure to connect user devices.

Data Plane: Part of the networking function that handles packets in network elements, including the buffering of the packet, the decision on dropping or forwarding it, the output interface, the queuing policy, and the modification of its headers/contents. The way each of these functions process packets is decided by the control plane. Network elements typically perform these functions at line rate (the speed at which packets enter the element through the input interfaces) in specialized hardware.

Flow Table: List of rules in an SDN network element matching specific traffic flows. For a given flow, actions are specified as to how to treat a packet belonging to that flow. An SDN network element can organize packet processing as a sequence or pipeline of flow tables through which a packet flows from the ingress interface to the egress interface.

Network Edge: Part of the network consisting of access nodes and the wired lines or wireless links to connect user devices. These access nodes are network elements specialized in handling numerous user links, aggregating their traffic flows, and sending them to the core network through high-speed communication lines.

Orchestrator: An SDN controller that has a view of the entire network and coordinates other local SDN controllers covering portions of the network to implement global network policies.

SDN Controller: Central part of the SDN control plane. Through the southbound interfaces, it interacts with SDN network elements through APIs to get notifications about new traffic flows and network changes, and to install forwarding rules in the switches. Through the northbound interfaces, it receives the network behavior needed by applications, translating it to instructions to network elements.

SDN Network Element: A piece of networking equipment consisting of several input/output interfaces and the data plane functions. An SDN Network Element, or SDN switch, also provides APIs to interact with the SDN controller (the southbound interface) to receive instructions to install flow table entries to handle new traffic flows.

Software-Defined Networking (SDN): A networking paradigm in which the control plane is removed from the network elements and placed in a central SDN controller. The controller installs appropriate forwarding rules in the relevant network elements for each new traffic flow, according to the network policies requested by applications.

Chapter 2
Wireless Sensor Networks in IPM

Mina Petrić
Ghent University, Belgium & University of Novi Sad, Serbia & Avia-GIS NV, Belgium

Cedric Marsboom
Avia-GIS NV, Belgium

Jurgen Vandendriessche
Vrije Universiteit Brussel, Belgium

ABSTRACT

An emerging field for environmental wireless sensor networks (WSN) is entomological vector surveillance. Sensor technology can be used to shoulder ecologically friendly practices within the integrated pest management (IPM) approach. Proper surveillance and subsequent modelling of the impact that pest and disease have on human health and crop agriculture is a pressing issue in numerous segments. Complex numerical models are being developed to generate information regarding the population dynamics of vector species and the expected circulation of vector-borne disease (VBD). These models require detailed micrometeorological forcing representative of the vector habitat to generate accurate simulations. Near real-time data offload in remote areas with flexible channels of communication for complex and heterogeneous topographies is an important component in this type of application. In this chapter, the authors provide an overview of the scope and best-practice approaches in applying WSN technology to drive IPM models.

INTRODUCTION

The global burden imposed by pests is manifold. Invading plant pests and pathogens present a constantly increasing risk for agriculture brought on by current environmental shifts (Savary et al., 2019; Spence et al., 2020). Furthermore, disease carrying pest species, i.e. vectors, represent one of the biggest global health issues today, as well as historically, and are only exasperated by the introduction of invasive vector species to new areas through different mechanisms of climate change (Campbell-Lendrum et al., 2015). Vector borne disease (VBD) include diseases such as zika, dengue, malaria, yellow fever, chikungunya, leishmaniasis and trypanosomiasis (National Academies of Sciences & Medicine, 2016).

DOI: 10.4018/978-1-7998-3817-3.ch002

Copyright © 2020, IGI Global. Copying or distributing in print or electronic forms without written permission of IGI Global is prohibited.

These VBDs have accounted for more human death through the last two centuries than all other causes combined (Gubler, 1998; National Academies of Sciences & Medicine, 2016). Over 500 million people are infected by Vector Borne Disease (VBD) every year. WHO estimates that, annually, over 3 billion people are at risk of contracting a VBD, of which a large proportion is diseases transmitted by mosquito vectors. More than 2.5 billion people are at risk of contracting Dengue alone, and Malaria causes over 500,000 deaths every year.

The implementation of pest-control strategies in the mid-20th century to reduce mosquitoes populations succeeded in the localized reduction of these VBDs (National Academies of Sciences & Medicine, 2016). Due to the ethical implication and environmental damage caused by most of the firs-used techniques, a shift in pest control towards more environmentally sound practices is soon observed. This movement and the collection of practices it entails is labelled as Integrated Pest Management (IPM).

Ever since the inception of integrated management in 1959 by Stern et al. (Stern et al., 1959), Integrated Pest Management (IPM) has undergone quite a change and evolved into a large concept covering different fields (Peterson et al., 2018). This evolution also brought in several ethical concerns regarding the direction the concept was going. In his Integrated Control Concept, Stern (Stern et al., 1959) speaks about using chemical and biological control to supplement each other and not look at them as alternatives. Although this core concept hasn't changed, the implementation and technologies have changed quite a bit. Resistance against pesticides was one of the main driving factors behind the conceptualization of integrated management which is still a driving factor today. There are limitations to IPM both in the practical and the ethical sense (Peterson et al., 2018). When it comes to medical pest, completely killing the pest is usually still the preferred way when it comes to public opinion and tolerance. There are several constraints to developing tolerant crops and other hosts. These include identifying tolerance, characterizing tolerance mechanisms, and understanding the genetics underlying tolerance (Delaney & Macedo, 2000; Velusamy & Heinrichs, 1986). Tolerance can be interpreted both as a type of resistance or as the factor for economic injury levels (Pedigo & Rice, 2014; Peterson et al., 2018). The topics of sampling and economic thresholds are closely allied to the focus on management, host stress, and the proper use of tactics (Kogan, 1988, 1998).

Wireless Sensor Network technology is already widely used in a plethora of scientific and commercial applications, and this number will only increase with the expected rise of the IoT market. An emerging field for environmental WSN systems is autonomous vector surveillance. Sensor technology can be used to shoulder ecologically friendly practices within the Integrated Pest Management (IPM) approach. Proper surveillance and subsequent modelling of the impact that pest and disease have on human health and crop agriculture is a pressing issue in numerous segments. In-situ, environmental WSN data support these practices by defining areas and periods of increased risk for the pest as well as providing valuable input to pest distribution and pest population dynamics models. IoT networks can be combined with earth observation (EO) data and expert knowledge to generate information regarding the pest activity levels, current environmental suitability, risk and expected dynamics.

Numerical models are being developed to generate information regarding the population dynamics of vector species and the expected circulation of Vector Borne Disease (VBD). These models require detailed micrometeorological forcing representative of the vector habitat to generate accurate simulations. These applications translate expert knowledge of pest biology and ecology into a tailored control strategy to reduce local vector populations to the lowest level possible. Earth Observation (EO) data can be coupled to the WSN system and used to compliment the collected sensor data. It can be used to determine micro-climatic zones in a region, by providing additional data which the WSN cannot collect such as information on a regional or continental scale and long-term historic data.

Many IPM applications in the form of internet information delivery system already exist (Bajwa et al., 2003). Two main groups can be identified: (i) static data repositories; (ii) more complex models integrated in a spatial decision support system (SDSS). The models range from growing degree day (GDD) models (*MyPest Page*; *Research Models: Insects, Mites, Diseases, Plants, and Beneficials*) more sophisticated phenology and pest population dynamics models (*California PestCast*), to sampling cost calculators for pest monitoring (*IPM Cost Calculator*). Recent studies indicate that SDSS surveillance and management systems could rapidly become an absolute requirement for local, regional as well as international IPM within the One Health concept (Bajwa et al., 2003; Beard et al., 2018; Damos, 2015).

Antonivić et al. (Antonovic et al., 2018) point out the micrometeorological measurements are required to shoulder the risk assessment of invasive species. While the climatological mean measured at standard meteorological stations from national networks which are usually positioned in rural and semirural environment might indicate an unsuitable environment for the mosquito vector, the urban environment which is usually warmed due to the urban island effect, could provide a suitable habitat for the mosquito to overwinter and become established.

Plant disease is often localized and requires targeted and precise treatment to reduce cost and damage to the environment (Abbasi et al., 2014). Sensor information regarding the micrometeorological conditions of crop patches together with the spatial distribution of the crop biomass can be used to shoulder these practices. Thus, the correct positioning of sensors to capture the pest micro-habitat is an important consideration for WSN applications in IPM.

Performing Quality Control (QC) checks and issuing appropriate flags for the raw and processed data in near real time (NRT) is vital for reducing data loss and providing accurate input fields for the numerical models. QC can be considered in the following categories: (i) QC of raw data, performed directly on the gateway; (ii) QC of processed data, performed on a remote server; (iii) Extended QC which deals with the empirical relationship of the observed data. This is an essential step for creating consistent background fields for running pest population dynamics models.

The role of WSN network and IPM health applications is expected to become increasingly more important with the development of automated pest count and identification sensors. Smart IoT ground sensors, deployed in field conditions, integrated with standard commercial pest traps, which can remotely and automatically acquire ground data on pest counts, sex, species, age and local micro-environmental parameters. This data is invaluable as input to vector-borne epidemic models that currently receive their input data from manual counting of dispersed traps. This information can be used by public and private organizations to plan optimal intervention strategies with limited resources.

One of the challenges that one may face when working with autonomous WSN's is energy. A WSN that runs on batteries that only last for one week or one month is not ecological and has a high maintenance cost. On the other hand, powering a WSN from a central power grid can require a lot of cables and nullifies the whole purpose of making the sensor network wireless. One can tackle this problem from two sides: reducing energy consumption or increasing the amount of available energy. To solve the problem of available energy, one can use a technique called energy harvesting or energy scavenging. Energy harvesting means that the natural energy that is present in the environment like wind, thermal, solar,... is converted to useful electrical energy to power the wireless network. When each node in the network has its own energy harvester, the network becomes truly autonomous.

As a final point the issue of data privacy needs to be addressed. Data collected by the WSN can be highly sensitive. Upload to remote servers might be essential to aggregate the different sources of incoming data and convert it to more pragmatic information and knowledge. Especially low-cost devices are vulnerable to this as they have little security features and are often based on similar architecture.

In this chapter we will provide an overview of the scope and best-practice approaches in applying WSN technology to drive IPM models with a focus on the mosquito pest.

ENVIRONMENTAL MONITORING

Ambient temperature, relative humidity and precipitation have been identified as the most significant abiotic parameters driving insect populations, however factors such a soil moisture, wind speed and direction and level of urbanization can also influence the dynamics (Savopoulou-Soultani et al., 2012; Wallner, 1987).

Antonović et al. (Antonovic et al., 2018) use a WSN system which records air humidity, pressure, light intensity, wall temperature and water temperature to assess the meteorological suitability for *Aedes albopictus* in Switzerland. Hur et al. (Hur & Eisenstadt, 2015) demonstrate the application of an environmental WSN using humidity, temperature and wind sensors for mosquito and pathogen research. Similarly, Evans et al. (M. V. Evans et al., 2019) studied the effects of the microclimate on the *Aedes albopictus* mosquito population across an urban gradient and found that urban temperature can have an important effect on emergence and mortality rates of the vector. Several authors (Meyer et al., 1990; Paaijmans et al., 2010; Paaijmans & Thomas, 2011) used sensor technologies to examine the effect of different resting temperatures and found that they have a significant effect on the extrinsic incubation rate of arboviruses in mosquitoes. Both the diurnal temperature range and the difference in temperature between microhabitats can have an important effect on the development and cumulative abundance of the vector population, thus an approach with deploying a WSN in a mesh configuration to capture and quantify these differences across different patches of the study area is suggested (Murdock, n.d.).

Cator et al. (Cator et al., 2013) examined the temperature variations in urban microclimates to define the thermal ecology for the local transmission of Malaria by *Anopheles* mosquitoes in India. They found that the mean daily temperatures within the urban environment was significantly warmer that the ones obtained from the meteorological stations from the national grid and suggest microenvironmental WSN monitoring for more accurate risk assessments of vector borne disease (Cator et al., 2013).

To be of scientific value for IPM monitoring, the data collection and WSN design should be driven by the following requirements: (i) measurement fidelity; i.e. reliable data offload ensuring minimal data loss; (ii) high sampling frequency; (iii) sensor accuracy and precision; the sensor accuracy should not be less than: $<\pm$ 0.5 °C for air temperature; $<\pm$ 5% for relative humidity and $<\pm$ 4% for precipitation. The operation range for the temperature sensor should be - 20 to +70 °C; (iv) power autonomy. The low power aspect of WSNs can allow for exploring energy-efficient options. Such techniques are known as power scavenging or energy harvesting technologies; (v) operability in harsh environments; to ensure reliable data collection over longer periods, both the node hardware and sensors must perform well under harsh conditions.

ENTOMOLOGICAL SENSORS

The current practice in IPM is manual collection and identification of mosquito using traps to lure and capture the mosquito during their active periods. In recent years, the first prototypes for remote monitoring of insect species have been developed (Gustavo E. Batista et al., 2011; Gustavo EAPA Batista et al., 2011; Chen, 2006; Hur & Eisenstadt, 2018). They entail automating the trapping, count, identification process and data transfer. This type of integrated sensor technologies is fairly young but has great potential in IPM applications, allowing for remote monitoring of the pest and effective intervention at the optimal time during the evolution of the pest population. Interestingly enough, first efforts to study insect wing motion date back to studies from 1827 in which a stroboscope was used to determine the resonance frequency of wing-beats of flying insects. The idea to classify mosquito sounds for control purpose has been first suggested already in 1945 by Khan et al. (Kahn et al., 1945). In order to suggest an alternative to spraying with the D.D.T. insecticide, which is very harmful to the ecosystem, they proposed a specific solution that would target only mosquitos:

We have observed that the largest variety of sounds made by this species as well as the others refereed to are outside the energy range of normal hearing. Despite the great variety of sounds, each genus and species have tonal emanations which are so distinctive in character that an experienced observer cannot only readily distinguish one genus from another, but with no difficulty at all can also distinguish the males of a species from the females of the same species. Even such closely related species as Aedes aegypti and Aedes albopictus can be distinguished by sounds alone. (Kahn et al., 1945)

This hypothesis was not tested; however, their research did provide valuable insight into the separate frequency ranges employed by different species and even male and female mosquitoes of the same species:

We have observed that the largest variety of sounds made by this species as well as the others refereed to are outside the energy range of normal hearing. Despite the great variety of sounds, each genus and species have tonal emanations which are so distinctive in character that an experienced observer cannot only readily distinguish one genus from another, but with no difficulty at all can also distinguish the males of a species from the females of the same species. Even such closely related species as Aedes aegypti and Aedes albopictus can be distinguished by sounds alone. (Kahn et al., 1945)

They found that most fundamental tones fell in the 250 Hz – 1500 Hz range. All recorded male frequencies were of a significantly higher pitch than the frequencies of female mosquitoes (Kahn et al., 1945). This was later confirmed to be true for other species as well (Jankauski, 2019).

When looking at this type of sensors application it is important we can distinguish different technologies based on the actual sensor which can be acoustic (Belton & Costello, 1979; Cobb et al., 2016; Mankin et al., 2006; Raman et al., 2007; Reed et al., 1942) or optical (Gustavo E. Batista et al., 2011; Gustavo EAPA Batista et al., 2011; Chen et al., 2014; Evangelista, 2018; Ouyang et al., 2015; Potamitis & Rigakis, 2015).

Most of the existing work that focuses on remote and independent monitoring of insect populations uses a classification method for wing beat frequency for different species and genera. However, the sensing method and the specific classification algorithms can be very different from paper to paper. Batista et al. (Gustavo E. Batista et al., 2011) argue that the integration of low-cost sensors in insect monitoring instruments is opening up a new area of research, i.e. computational entomology. They describe it as a specific branch of data mining since it builds on existing data mining techniques such as clustering, classification, scalability, transfer learning and the processing of distributed and uncertain data.

In the solution proposed by Evangelista (Evangelista, 2018); they use an optical infrared (IR) sensor to detect the frequency. The IR diode serves as an emitter and a photodiode array is used as the receiver screen. The variation caused by the insects body and wings blocking the IR beam towards the receiver, causes voltage variations which is then FFT (Fast Fourier Transform) processed to get the wingbeat frequency (Evangelista, 2018). The wingbeat frequency is calculated as the fundamental FFT frequency. They use Bayesian classification for the prediction of the species.

A schematic representation of the insect sensor with two light sources and the fundamental frequencies of different insect species is shown in Figure 1.

Figure 1. (a) The schematic description of the insect sensor design; and (b) fundamental frequency of different insect species

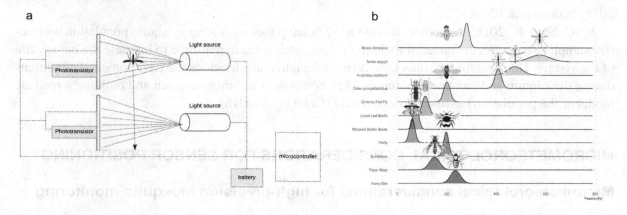

In the design from Batista et al. (Gustavo E. Batista et al., 2011) a laser light source is used with a phototransistor serving as the background of the reflected laser beam; the mechanism for wing beat detection stays the same and is captured in the obstruction of the laser signal by a passing insect, and later processed by FFT and a Bayesian classifier. In a later paper they explain how the system can be adapted in a simple way to measure speed and direction of the incoming insect (Gustavo EAPA Batista et al., 2011). This is achieved by positioning a second parallel beam and measuring the time between the time that it takes for the insect to travel this distance. The circadian rhythm of the specific species is used in estimating the per-species likelihood for the classification algorithm in case of overlapping frequencies (Gustavo EAPA Batista et al., 2011).

Ouyang et al. (Ouyang et al., 2015) similarly use an IR sensor to capture the wingbeat wave which is then converted using an inverse Fourier transform of the log of the absolute value of the Fourier transform of the unprocessed signal. The sequence is then divided into 12 bins on which a Gaussian mixture model estimation using the EM-GMM (Reynolds & Riley, 2002) maximization algorithm is applied. Potamitis et al. (Potamitis & Rigakis, 2015) examined sensor identification of wing-beat frequencies of the olive fruit fly pest Bactrocera oleae, a malaria mosquito *Anopheles* gambiae and the western honey Apis mellifera using an optical sensor based on photodiodes and a microphone. They demonstrated that the accuracy of the optical sensors matches that of the microphone with the advantage of a higher signal-to-noise ratio and higher robustness in field operations (Potamitis & Rigakis, 2015). The photodiodes operated in higher frequencies and could successfully resolve the fundamental frequency as well as the overtones of the wing-beat signal.

Chen et al. (Chen et al., 2014) build on the work by (Gustavo E. Batista et al., 2011; Gustavo EAPA Batista et al., 2011) and improve the Bayesian classifier by augmenting the probability using additional features within the wingbeat signal (Chen et al., 2014), thus reducing the Bayesian error rate. The authors argue that the lack of progress in the complete commercial development and deployment of remote count and identification traps can be attributed to three factors: (i) The use of acoustic instead of optical sensors; (ii) Limited data; (iii) Overfitting with complicated ML classification models (Chen et al., 2014). The authors state the because of the fast attenuation of the acoustic signal and very noisy data for increased microphone sensitivity leads to difficulties in data collection in studies that used acoustic sensors (Belton & Costello, 1979; Cobb et al., 2016; Mankin et al., 2006; Raman et al., 2007; Reed et al., 1942) and a solution with an optical sensor used together with Bayesian clustering is suggested (Gustavo E. Batista et al., 2011; Gustavo EAPA Batista et al., 2011; Chen et al., 2014; Evangelista, 2018; Ouyang et al., 2015; Potamitis & Rigakis, 2015).

In (Cobb et al., 2016) the authors discuss a WSN setup for monitoring mosquito population with active sampling based on the uncertainty in the model predictions in real-time to increase the battery life of the system. However, in the study they do not take into considerations the environmental conditions during the capture and mention that this is a key component in future research and building a realistic model of the population based on observed data (Cobb et al., 2016).

MICROMETEOROLOGICAL CONSIDERATIONS FOR SENSOR POSITIONING

Micrometeorological considerations for high-precision mosquito monitoring

In this chapter we will examine the recommended setup and considerations in environmental monitoring for mosquito vectors. As poikilothermic organisms their body is very sensitive to the current state and rate of change of environmental temperature. The aquatic stages (egg, larva and pupa) are mostly influenced by water temperature of their breeding site, while the adult reacts to the variability of air temperature of the planetary boundary layer (PBL) which constitutes the very dynamics layer of the atmosphere adjacent to the surface (approx. < 1km). The mosquito has different resting and blood-seeking sites with different temperatures (Figure 2). In order to answer the question of optimal sensor positioning to capture the micrometeorology relevant for the mosquito vector we will consider how the vertical and temporal profile change in the PBL within the daily cycle.

Depending on where it spends most of its time the mosquito will be exposed to different temperatures (Figure 2). This can have an effect on the: (i) Duration of the gestating period; (ii) Level of blood-seeking activity; (iii) Oviposition; (iv) In case the mosquito is infected, temperature has an effect on the intrinsic incubation rate of the virus within the resting mosquito.

The physical mechanisms that govern air heating and cooling adjacent to the Earth's surface are: (i) Radiation; (ii) Conduction, convection and advection; (iii) Turbulent mixing; (iv) Evaporation and condensation. The absorption of incoming short-wave ($0.2\mu m \leq \lambda \leq 3.0\mu m$ and long-wave radiation ($\lambda \geq 3$ μm leads to an increase in the temperature of the active surface. Conduction pertains to the molecular

Figure 2. Scheme depicting (1) resting (2) biting and (3) aquatic sites relevant to different stages in the mosquito development cycle

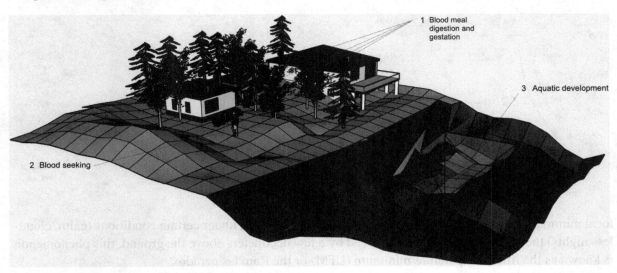

exchange of energy by the two adjacent layers of air and soil, i.e. the very thin surface layer of air. Convection and Advection are governed by the first order moment of moving air, with convection related to vertical motion and advection pertaining to horizontal transfer. Evaporation and condensation in turn generate or require energy in the form of latent heat which is needed for the phase transition of water from vapor to liquid and vice versa. Finally, turbulent eddies, cause mixing between different atmospheric layers and generate a more thermodynamically homogenous state. The extent of turbulence is defined by the turbulent kinetic energy (tke). The rate of change of tke is chiefly influenced by: (i) mean vertical shear; and (ii) the buoyancy force per unit volume (dissipation, transport and pressure work). Vegetation can locally increase the production of tke by creating a strong shear layer just above the top of the canopy, however it would usually lead to area of smaller tke just after the vegetation in the direction of the mean flow (De Maerschalck et al., 2010).

On Figure 3, the evolution of the PBL is shown for a 24 h window. During the day, due to turbulent mixing and the direct heating of the Earth's surface by solar radiation a convective mixed layer (CML) is formed. During the night, less turbulence in the residual layer, with no thermal eddies powered by convection, causes a shear to develop between the surface layer and the rest of the PBL. Again, after the sunrise, the surface energy balance is reversed, the warmer air particles begin to rise up forming a new convective mixed layer.

The areas in which *Culex* and *Aedes* mosquitoes are known to be active are outlined in red. Most species in the *Culex* genera exhibit a biphasic activity profile with increased activity at during dusk, i.e. just before sunrise and just after sunset (Christophers, 1960; Šebesta et al., 2011). *Aedes* species have a slightly shifted diel activity window, with the highest bloodseeking activity for *Ae. aegypti* reported for the 06–08 and 16–18 h (Chadee & Martinez, 2000; Delatte et al., 2010).

On Figure 3a we can see the typical night-time and day-time vertical profile for the PBL. During the day (a) the surface absorbs solar radiation, becomes warmer and heats up the adjacent atmosphere. During the night the air rapidly emits in the IR band which causes an inversion layer to occur with the

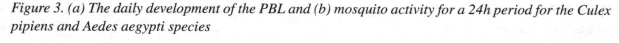

Figure 3. (a) The daily development of the PBL and (b) mosquito activity for a 24h period for the Culex pipiens and Aedes aegypti species

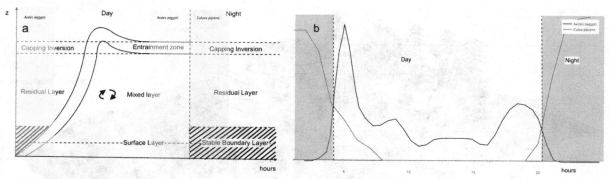

local minimum usually occurring on the surface itself. However, under certain conditions (calm, cloudless nights) the minimum might me displaced by a few decimeters above the ground, this phenomenon is known as the lifted temperature minimum (LTM) or the Ramdas paradox.

Another variability that should be taken into consideration is the diurnal temperature curve which can act as a stressor to mosquito populations. In Figure 4 an example for three study sites in Bahariya (Egypt), Guadeloupe (Lesser Antilles), and Petrovaradin (Serbia). The most pronounced diurnal curve is observed for Bahariya (desert location) while almost no daily observation is observed for the subtropical site in Guadeloupe.

Figure 4. (a) The observed diurnal temperature curve for three locations in Petrovaradin (green), Bahariya (purple) and Guadeloupe (blue); and (b) Position of the observation locations

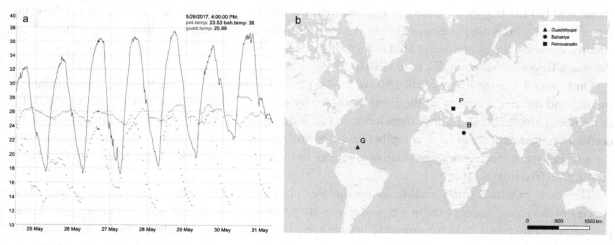

Vegetation can have a significant impact on the vertical temperature profile mainly through its effect on the energy budget. It serves as a buffer or intermediary layer absorbing most of the direct radiation before it reaches the ground. Through its root system vegetation also has an effect on the thermal and hydraulic characteristics of the soil (Lalić et al., 2018). The energy balance components that are most affected are the soil heat flux (G); and the upward radiation, which is a function of the albedo, that now has a pronounced seasonal character following the phenological development of the canopy. The heating from radiation causes higher temperatures to occur within in the canopy, with a minimum occurring on the surface. This can have important implication for the mosquito population with exophilic resting habits. I.e. warmer resting temperatures, which the mosquito can find inside the canopy layer, will have an effect on the development times (shorter), and extrinsic incubation rate (higher), in case the mosquito is infected.

Mosquitoes are known to rest within the vegetation canopy or in natural resting shelters such as hollow wood trunks close to the ground, or sometimes in understory vegetation. During the day they will always choose a shaded area, never resting in full sunlight.

Sensor Positioning

We propose the following sensor setup in order to capture the micrometeorological conditions specific to the different modes of activity for the mosquito vector: (1) standard positioning; (2) inside vegetation; (3) indoor resting; (4) aquatic breeding sites (Figure 5).

1. **Standard Positioning:** One node in the mesh should be positioned to reflect the WMO standard for weather observation. This node serves as a reference when running a comparison with weather reanalysis data or numerical weather prediction outputs. Moreover, it also provides a baseline for the increase/decrease in temperature observed in the indoor and vegetation resting sites. This temperature is used in vector population dynamics models as the temperature that governs the mortality and development parameters of air-borne mosquitoes, actively searching for a blood meal.

    The international standard height for the measurements of air temperature and dew point temperature is at 2 m above the surface ("Locating outside sensors for optimum accuracy," n.d.). The sensors should be placed inside a radiation shield to protect from direct solar radiation. Moreover, the sensors should be positioned at a reasonable distance from any local sources of heat such as building walls and higher vegetation, in a location where free air circulation can develop. The sensors should be placed over a low-grass natural surface, while an urban surface such as concrete can cause substantial errors ("Locating outside sensors for optimum accuracy," n.d.). Humidity reading should be taken together with the temperature observations, and the sensor should be mounted alongside the temperature sensor. Wind speed and direction are greatly influenced by the turbulent air circulation in the PBL. The official sensor height for wind speed is 2 m above surface level and this corresponds to the mosquito flight height (Cribellier et al., n.d.). Similarly to the requirements for temperature, the wind-speed sensors should be placed in an open area where no turbulent eddies generated from local buildings or vegetation can cause turbulent interference. The precipitation sensor should also be located in an open are because rain particles are often carried to a lesser or greater extent by wind field ("Locating outside sensors for optimum accuracy," n.d.).

2. **Inside Vegetation:** Within vegetation mosquitoes will choose to rest in near surface areas, 10 cm above the ground, especially if there is a more permanent shadow cast by the plant or a denser vegetation body (Meyer et al., 1990). The temperature profile within canopy usually has a neutral

Figure 5. Sensor positioning for capturing the micrometeorology affecting the mosquito in different parts of it's activity cycle: (a) Standard positioning, (b) vegetation, (c) indoor, (d) aquatic breeding sites

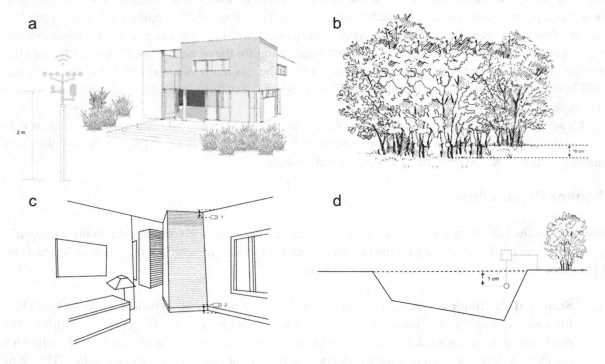

gradient with a slight increase toward the top of the crown (Stoutjesdijk & Barkman, 2014). The temperature maximum is usually achieved just above the canopy, while inside the canopy vertical differences are small (Stoutjesdijk & Barkman, 2014).

3. **Indoor Resting:** In a study by Quinones et al. (Quiñones & Suarez, 1990) most endophilic malaria mosquitoes were found to prefer indoor resting on heights bellow 0.5 m and less predominantly on height between 2 – 2.5 m, independent of feeding condition. The preferred resting height was specific to the vector species, and different species were found to display different preferences for indoor resting (Damar et al., 1981; Pampana, 1966). Placing a sensor at maximum height and one at minimum height allows for the capture of the vertical temperature gradient in the room. This will allow for flexible mosquito resting site temperature assessment. However, there is usually a temperature inversion at the very top adjacent to the wall, because of conductive head transfer adjacent to the colder walls (Overby & Steen-Thøde, 1990; Sikula, n.d.). So the maximum height for the sensor should be calculated with a 0.2 m buffer (Overby & Steen-Thøde, 1990; Sikula, n.d.). Porras-Amores et al. (Porras-Amores et al., 2014) have found that despite seasonal and local variations in the gradient existing caused by different indoor heating and a reaction to different outdoor temperatures the slope of the curve could be approximated quite well with a simple linear regression (Porras-Amores et al., 2014).

4. **Breeding Sites:** For monitoring the breeding site temperatures, a water temperature sensor should be placed 1 cm below the water surface (Asare et al., 2016). This temperature impacts the mortality and development rates of the egg and immature stages (Larva and Pupa) of the mosquito vector.

For best results it is recommended to minimize signal attenuation by restricting the transmission distance and line-of-sight obstacles as far as possible while still retaining the recommended sitting. Transmissions above these distances and attenuation limits is, however quality of reception will begin to suffer or additional effort will need to be taken to improve the secondary factors that affect the node-to-node communication.

INTEGRATED SOLUTION: INTEGRATING SENSOR MEASUREMENTS IN A SPATIAL DECISION SUPPORT SYSTEM

The entomological and meteorological WSN data collected by the sensors is processed and passed on to a remote application or SDSS which translates it to information relevant for IPM applications. The SDSS consist of several models which can generate risk regarding the pest. There are two main classes of models that can be distinguished: (i) Stochastic vector distribution models; (ii) Deterministic pest population dynamics models. The quality of both is dependent on the quality of input data. This means: (i) Accurate sensor data; (ii) Continuous data with minimal loss. In order to build a comprehensive system for IPM monitoring; the WSN network should be supplied with an energy scavenging source and flexible data-offload solution to support remote deployment. The data should be preprocessed, run through an automated cleaning and aggregation algorithm and forwarded to the backend SDSS application which will process the data in order to generate IPM information.

Petrić et al. (Petrić et al., 2019) proposed a comprehensive solution utilizing space assets to ensure reliable data offload in remote areas Figure 6.

Figure 6. Integrated IPM monitoring solution

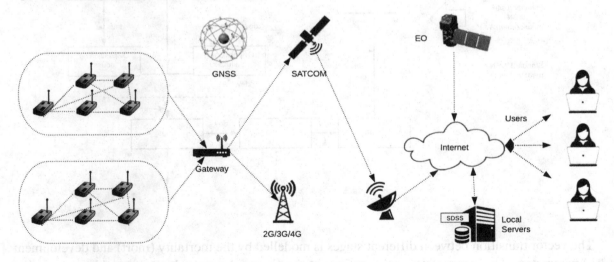

The solution can be divided into three different parts: (a) the sensing and communication part on the left, (b) the remote servers in the middle right and (c) the end-users at the far right. This can be seen in Figure 6 which provides a general overview of the envisioned architectural setup.

The system integrates three space components: global positioning (GNSS), satellite communication (SatCom) and earth observation products (EO). The solution proposed by Petrić et. al (Petrić et al., 2019) combines RF-based sensor networks with terrestrial communication, satellite communication and GNSS localization techniques. To realize this solution, they considered the integration abilities of multiple Single Board Satellite Transceiver Modules which can be embedded into OEM equipment and operate with a dual uplink using both terrestrial and satellite communication to ensure continuous data offload.

At the SDSS the data is passed on to a mosquito population dynamics model. To illustrate how environmental forcing is coupled with vector population dynamics models an ordinary differential equation (ODE) modelling framework following the work by (Cailly et al., 2012; Erickson et al., 2010; Petric, 2020) is presented below (Figure 7). The model is a dynamic 10-dimension nonlinear ODE system in which each equation corresponds to a stage in the mosquito development cycle: (i) egg, (ii) larva; (iii) pupa; (iv) emerging adults; (v) nulliparous bloodseeking adults; (vi) nulliparous gestating adults; (vii) nulliparous ovipositioning adults; (viii) parous bloodseeking adults; (ix) parous gestating adults; (x) parous ovipositioning adults.

Figure 7. Mosquito vector population dynamics model scheme

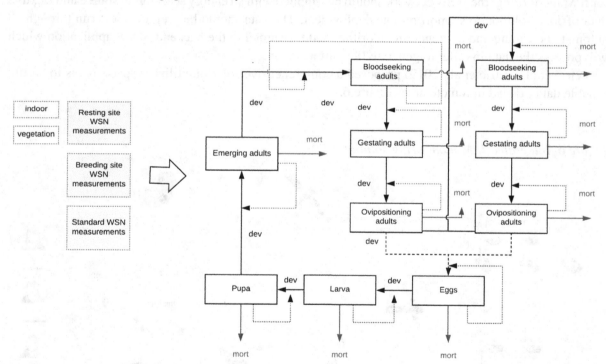

The vector transition between different stages is modelled by the mortality (mort) and development (dev) parameters. These parameters are functions of the observed meteorological variables, i.e. resting micrometeorological conditions, active, bloodseeking, micrometeorological conditions and micrometeorological conditions of the water body for aquatic development. Firstly, the resting meteorology is used to define the parameters for gestating adults. Secondly, the standard 2 m meteorology is used to define the parameters for: (i) emerging adults; (ii) gestating adults; and (iii) ovipositioning adults. Finally, the breeding site water temperature measurements are used to define the parameters for: (i) egg; (ii) larva; and (iii) pupa.

DATA PROCESSING AND QUALITY CONTROL (QC)

After the recordings have been collected; in a first step, the data should be checked for missing readings, error detection and possible error correction in order to achieve a continuous flow of data maintaining the desired level of accuracy. This can be done on the gateway microcontroller and later on the remote server which hosts the WSN database. Quality control (QC) procedures are recommended for all WSNs to control the quality and consistency of the data before it reaches the SDSS models. Three levels of this type of real-time QC can be distinguished: (i) QC of raw data; (ii) QC of processed data (iii) Extended QC (D. Evans et al., 2003; Zahumenskỳ, 2004). QC of raw data is performed in real-time, directly on the gateway and should deal with measurement errors and errors caused by the malfunction of technical components of the system. QC of processed data is also known as the extended QC procedure, is performed on the remote server which hosts the database that stores all the WSN data. It deals with more elaborate check of long-term biases and internal inconsistencies. Extended QC can be performed in the case of a modular system when we have two or more pairs of complementary variables being measured that retain a certain relationship.

Standard meteorological measurements and basic flagging procedure is examined in the next section.

Quality Control of Raw Data

1. **Gross Error Check:** This check is used to evaluate whether the measured values are within the plausible value range for the specific variable. This is done by comparing the numerical reading with the measurement range of the sensor.
2. **Basic Time Checks:** This check is used to verify that the successive measurements have a plausible rate of change, i.e. that there are no unrealistic jumps between measurements. This check performs best for time-series with high serial correlation i.e. measurements taken with a high sampling rate. Each measurement is checked against the previous one. The suggested limits for the sampling frequency of 10 s are: $2°$ for air temperature, dew point temperature, ground and soil temperature; 5% for relative humidity; 20 m/s for wind speed; and 800 W/m2 for solar radiation (D. Evans et al., 2003; Zahumenskỳ, 2004).

The raw data is used to generate aggregated values for larger intervals, e.g. 1 min aggregated reading or 15 min aggregated readings. If there are less than 66% of the sub-sample readings the aggregated value should be flagged as missing.

Quality Control of Processed Data

1. **Plausible Value Check:** This check is performed on the aggregated data and works in the same way as the gross error check on the limits adapted to the aggregated frequency. These limits are defined based on the local climatology of the WSN and on the season. The broader limits for the

most common meteorological variables are: [- 80 °C, 60 °C] for air temperature; [- 80 °C, 60 °C] for dew point temperature; [- 80 °C, 80 °C] for ground temperature; [- 50 °C, 50 °C] for soil temperature; [0%, 100%] for relative humidity; [500 hPa, 1100 hPa] for atmospheric pressure; [0 °, 360 °] for wind direction; [0 m/s, 75 m/s] for wind speed; [0 W/m2, 1600 W/m2] for solar radiation; [0 mm/min, 40 mm/min] for precipitation rate (D. Evans et al., 2003; Zahumenskỳ, 2004).

2. **Time Consistency Check:** This is analogous to the Basic time check for the raw data. The aggregated value should meet the minimum and maximum plausible variability within the sub-sample which is used to create the aggregated value. The recommended maximum and minimum values for the following meteorological variables are shown in the table below. Another metric that can be used for non-standard variables is computing the maximum range as $4 \bullet \sigma_v$ (Zahumenskỳ, 2004) with σ_v being the standard deviation for the aggregated parameter calculated from a period of ≥ 10min (Table 1).

Table 1. Minimum and maximum suggested variability for the time consistency check of processed data

	Air temperature	Dew point temperature	Ground temperature	Soil temperature	Relative humidity	Atmospheric pressure	Wind speed
Minimum variability	0.1°C (Δt=60m)	0.1°C (Δt=60m)	0.1°C (Δt=60m)	0.1°C (Δt=120m)	1% (Δt=60m)	0.1h Pa (Δt=60m)	0.5m/s (Δt=60m)
Maximum variability	3°C	2°C	5°C	1°C	10%	0.5hPa	20m/s

3. **Internal Consistency Check:** The internal consistency check is based on the comparison of two meteorological values whose relationship is quantifiable or at least parametrizable. We will outline the following; The condition that the dew point temperature is lower than the actual temperature should always be satisfied. When the wind speed is 0, the wind direction should display 0. When the wind speed is $\neq$ 0, the wind direction should $\neq$ 9. Both variables should be examined if cloud cover = 0 does not match to amount precipitation = 0. Both variables if total clod cover is 8 or bigger and sun duration is > 0. Both elements should be examined if solar radiation is > 500 W/m^2 and the sunshine duration is = 0 (Zahumenskỳ, 2004).

4. **Extended QC Procedure:** The extended QC procedure can be performed at centres which have analysis field and extended annual measurements for the specific variables in which the QC can be performed for the desired period based on long-term averages.

The outlined QC procedure needs to be tailored to the species of interested based on the model accuracy requirements. And categorical flags need to be assigned to different quality classes according to the user requirements. If the measurements fail any of the QC tests it is rejected and flagged with a missing value identifier. These gaps can later be filled with an appropriate gap-filling algorithm. One method that was tested for in-situ sensor reading for locations in tropical and midlatitude landscapes was a Gap-Filling algorithm using debiased ERA5 reanalysis data (Lompar et al., 2019).

The flagging procedure depends on the threshold sets, some of them can be fixed for the specific variable while most will change as a function of location and season.

ENERGY HARVESTING

There are many types of energy harvesters, and not all of them can be used in the same environment. A sensor network used in the polar regions, where there is no direct sunlight for several months every year. The most known one is photo voltaic, where sunlight is converted into electricity. This is commonly used in small calculators that don't use batteries. Also other forms of energy can be used for energy harvesters. Thermoelectric and pyroelectric energy harvesters use thermal energy to generate electricity. The former is based on the Seebeck effect, where a difference in temperature between a hot and a cold surface in a semiconductor or metal causes a voltage to build up. Harvesters that use this are called thermoelectric generator (TEG). On the other hand, pyroelectric energy harvesters (PEG) produce an output voltage based on changes of the temperature of the complete harvester. To keep generating energy a PEG must continuously cycle between heating and cooling, resulting in an AC voltage. While a TEG doesn't require a direct change in temperature, the cold surface needs to be cooled to keep the temperature difference between the two sides. Also mechanical energy can be converted into electrical energy by energy harvesters. Piezoelectric energy harvesters use crystal materials that generate electricity when stress is applied. This allows to convert vibrations or shocks into electrical energy. Mechanical energy can also be converted into electrical energy by using the triboelectric effect, where friction creates a positive charge in a material, like a plastic comb through hair. There are many more types of energy harvesters like betavoltaic (radiation), bioharvesters (chemical), micro wind turbines, … (KHENG, 2010; Verbelen, 2018).

Because WSNs only have a limited amount of energy available, their power consumption must be limited. Modern microcontrollers reduce energy consumption by only working for a small amount of time, while staying in a sleep mode when no work has to be done. In this mode, the microcontroller only consumes a few μW or even nW of energy. On the other hand, the sensors data has to be transmitted through the sensor network. Communication protocols like Wi-Fi or 4G aim at high throughput which requires a high energy cost, making these protocols not suitable for long term battery operated applications (Mekki et al., 2019; Phung et al., 2018). For this reason, WSNs use other communication technologies that focus on low power consumption at the cost of a lower data rate. A few examples of these technologies are Zigbee, Z-wave, LoRa and SigFox. Zigbee and Z-Wave nodes only send data over a short range (10 to 100 meters) and require a mesh network, where a message is send from node to node, to send a message to the gateway (Raza et al., 2017; *Zigbee FAQ; Z-Wave FAQ*).

These types of low power communication technologies have proven to be useful in both indoor and outdoor battery-operated sensor network applications. Although each sensor node has only a limited communication range, the combination of message-hopping, duty-cycling and self-recovery in the mesh-protocol stack allows sensor data to be transported over several hundreds of meters.

Radically different communication approaches which have been specifically designed for battery operated internet coupled sensing devices are used. Two well-known examples are LoRa, which uses a spread spectrum technique, and SigFox that uses an ultra-narrow band modulation technology (Mekki et al., 2019; Phung et al., 2018; Queralta et al., 2019; Raza et al., 2017). Both have the possibility to communicate over distances in the order of several kilometres, with a power consumption which is in the range of 10 mW. The drawback of these protocols is the very limited throughput which is typically only a few bytes per day. However, these protocols have proven to be very interesting in applications where only a limited amount of data is to be sent per day, e.g. a smart water meter sending its current reading ones a month or a moister sensor in a greenhouse checking if a plant needs more water every day.

DATA PRIVACY

With the internet of things era comes a lot more devices connected to the internet (Perera et al., 2013). This plethora of devices capture a lot of information and although some solutions can and will store this data locally, for many applications this data is sent to an off-site server for processing (Perera et al., 2015). Especially in the big data area, this upload might even be essential to connect the different data sources and turn the data into information and knowledge (Perera et al., 2015).

With the increase of these connected devices and data streams, there also comes an increase in privacy concerns (Mayer, 2009). These IoT devices collect data from the environment, including location data, and possibly personal information (Perera et al., 2015). This data can be (highly) sensitive and are an easy target for hackers. At the time of writing, there were already several incidents involving mismanagement and hacking of IoT devices and its data. Especially low-cost devices are vulnerable to this as they have little security features and are of based on similar architectures and therefore are all vulnerable if one is vulnerable.

The distributed nature and simplicity of LPLC WSN networks consisting of a set of resource constrained nodes, makes them especially vulnerable to a variety of security attacks such as eavesdropping and injecting (Ukil et al., 2010). The attack threats can be considered in the following groups: (i) Network Layer attacks including wormhole attacks (Hu et al., 2003), the Sybil attack (Douceur et al., 2002), the Byzantine attack (Awerbuch et al., 2004) and other attacks directed towards WSN routing (Karlof and Wagner, 2003); (ii) Link layer attacks such as the denial-of-sleep (Raymnod 2006; Akyildiz et al., 2002; Wood 2002); (iii) Transport Layer attacks such as flooding and de-synchronization attacks (Ukil et al., 2010); (iv) Physical layer attacks (Shi et al., 2004; Wang et al., 2005; Wang et al., 2004; Ukil et al., 2010); and (v) (i) Multilayer Denial of service attacks (DoS) which can be executed across any or in a combination of layers (Wood et al., 2002; Ukil et al., 2010).

Off course there is also the threat of an outside third party who can intercept the data streams from the devices to the service severs (Ukil et al., 2014). Therefore, it is important to encrypt all the data to mitigate this risk. A WSN is considered secure if it adheres to the following security properties, i.e. it supports authenticity, confidentiality, integrity and availability (Ukil et al., 2010). Several attributes that can strengthen the security of a particular WSN are: (i) random key pre-distribution cryptography schemes; (ii) Self-organizing networks (Chan et al., 2003; Liu et al., 2005; Ukil et al., 2010). If the network is not self-organizing, one of the most hazardous attacks can be DoS attacks which can: cut off a certain section of the network by malicious node collaboration; jam the communication channel and limiting message transmission; power depletion by repeated requests packets from the nodes leading to exhaustion or death (Ukil et al.,2010). There are a lot of different ways to encrypt data and protect the WSN from outside attacks, listing and comparing them all is beyond the scope of this work. This is a highly specialised area of the IT world which increased significantly in complexity, importance and size over the past few years.

Regulating bodies such as the European Union and national governments are putting legislation into place to prevent such problems, although they seem to be largely aimed at the biggest companies in the industry (Wachter, 2018). The problem is that a lot of users do not know and or care about the privacy risks as long as the product makes their lives easier and that the stakeholder chain can be quite complicated (Article 29, 2014; Miorandi et al., 2012). So, until these regulations, it was a bit a wild west out there of companies basically doing what they liked as the legislation had not caught up yet (Weber, 2009). Current consent requests have proven to be insufficient, inadequate and misleading. With legislation now being put in place, the industry will have to change and will most likely move to a 2 tier system where there is a free tier in which people explicitly consent to their data being collected and used (within the legal framework) and a second tier where people pay for the using the system with guarantees that their data and privacy is protected (Perera et al., 2015).

CONCLUSION AND FUTURE RESEARCH DIRECTIONS

In this chapter the role of WSN networks deployed to monitor the heterogeneous microhabitat of mosquito pests and how this can shoulder ethical IPM practices was examined. An integrated autonomous LPLC solution coupled with space assets such as EO and SatCom that feeds into an IPM SDSS was investigated. This configuration is modular and suitable for small-scale as well as larger-scale studies. The spatial extent of the deployed system needs to be tailored to the pest species and type of real-world application.

The newest generation of climate change projections indicate that most of the northern hemisphere will experience a significant increase in temperature which will enable the establishment of invasive vector species in a much broader region than observed in the previous century. This only enforces the need for a comprehensive and precise IPM monitoring system. The development of IPM should be coupled with the expansions of IoT enabling global coverage and risk assessment in an economically feasible framework.

In future steps, the total network yield for specific IPM applications needs to be explored together with the impact on data loss, delivery and end-to-end delay. Moreover, the authors believe that the development observed in autonomous entomological sensors, which can transmit pest counts and allow for remote monitoring of target vector species, will pave the way for new data assimilation techniques which are instrumental for building more realistic models for forecasting vector population dynamics.

Data privacy and security concerns will need to be factored into these future steps. Data breaches are becoming more and more frequent. Legislation was slow to catch up but is getting put into place now and can enforce large fines on service providers who don't take appropriate measures to mitigate possible breaches and misuse of data. WSN's applications base will grow further in the future and combined with cloud services and space technology, WSN monitoring has the potential to significantly influence the way pest control is conducted worldwide.

Vector-Borne Diseases (VBD) transmitted by insect vectors such as mosquitoes are gaining importance. Examples of diseases transmitted by mosquitoes include malaria, dengue, chikungunya and more recently Zika fever. Early detection and prevention of outbreaks is a key pillar in preventive control. An early warning system can help identify solutions, which allow for the identification of high-risk areas and timely and effective responses to the health issue. The model input data needs to be prepared in a consistent manner by a standardized QC procedure which ensures data consistency and the correct flagging of null and void parts and tuples.

REFERENCES

Abbasi, A. Z., Islam, N., & Shaikh, Z. A. (2014). A review of wireless sensors and networks' applications in agriculture. *Computer Standards & Interfaces*, *36*(2), 263–270. doi:10.1016/j.csi.2011.03.004

Akyildiz, I. F., Su, W., Sakarasubramaniam, Y., & Cayirci, E. (2002). A survey on sensor networks. *IEEE Communications Magazine*, *40*(8), 102–114. doi:10.1109/MCOM.2002.1024422

Antonovic, M. P., Cannata, M., Danani, A., Engeler, L., Flacio, E., Mangili, F., Ravasi, D., Strigaro, D., & Tonolla, M. (2018). ALBIS: Integrated system for risk-based surveillance of invasive mosquito Aedes albopictus. *PeerJ PrePrints*, *6*, e27251v1.

Article 29. (2014). *Opinion 8/2014 on the recent developments on the Internet of Things*. Data Protection Working Party.

Asare, E. O., Tompkins, A. M., Amekudzi, L. K., Ermert, V., & Redl, R. (2016). *Mosquito breeding site water temperature observations and simulations towards improved vector-borne disease models for Africa*. Academic Press.

Awerbuch, B., Curtmola, R., Holmer, D., Nita-Rotaru, C., & Rubens, H. (2004). Mitigating byzantine attacks in ad hoc wireless networks. Department of Computer Science, Johns Hopkins University. *Tech. Rep. Version*, *1*, 16.

Bajwa, W. I., Coop, L., & Kogan, M. (2003). Integrated pest management (IPM) and Internet-based information delivery systems. *Neotropical Entomology*, *32*(3), 373–383. doi:10.1590/S1519-566X2003000300001

Batista, G. E., Keogh, E. J., Mafra-Neto, A., & Rowton, E. (2011). SIGKDD demo: Sensors and software to allow computational entomology, an emerging application of data mining. *Proceedings of the 17th ACM SIGKDD International Conference on Knowledge Discovery and Data Mining*, 761–764. 10.1145/2020408.2020530

Batista, G., Hao, Y., Keogh, E., & Mafra-Neto, A. (2011). Towards automatic classification on flying insects using inexpensive sensors. *2011 10th International Conference on Machine Learning and Applications and Workshops, 1*, 364–369.

Beard, R., Wentz, E., & Scotch, M. (2018). A systematic review of spatial decision support systems in public health informatics supporting the identification of high risk areas for zoonotic disease outbreaks. *International Journal of Health Geographics*, *17*(1), 38. doi:10.118612942-018-0157-5 PMID:30376842

Belton, P., & Costello, R. A. (1979). Flight sounds of the females of some mosquitoes of Western Canada. *Entomologia Experimentalis et Applicata*, *26*(1), 105–114. doi:10.1111/j.1570-7458.1979.tb02904.x

Cailly, P., Tran, A., Balenghien, T., L'Ambert, G., Toty, C., & Ezanno, P. (2012). A climate-driven abundance model to assess mosquito control strategies. *Ecological Modelling*, *227*, 7–17. doi:10.1016/j.ecolmodel.2011.10.027

California PestCast: Disease Model Database—UC IPM. (n.d.). Retrieved January 31, 2020, from http://ipm.ucanr.edu/DISEASE/DATABASE/diseasemodeldatabase.html

Campbell-Lendrum, D., Manga, L., Bagayoko, M., & Sommerfeld, J. (2015). Climate change and vector-borne diseases: What are the implications for public health research and policy? *Philosophical Transactions of the Royal Society B: Biological Sciences, 370*(1665). doi:10.1098/rstb.2013.0552

Cator, L. J., Thomas, S., Paaijmans, K. P., Ravishankaran, S., Justin, J. A., Mathai, M. T., ... Eapen, A. (2013). Characterizing microclimate in urban malaria transmission settings: A case study from Chennai, India. *Malaria Journal, 12*(1), 84. doi:10.1186/1475-2875-12-84 PMID:23452620

Chadee, D. D., & Martinez, R. (2000). Landing periodicity of Aedes aegypti with implications for dengue transmission in Trinidad, West Indies. *Journal of Vector Ecology, 25*, 158–163. PMID:11217215

Chan, H., Perrig, A., & Song, D. (2003). Random key predistribution schemes for sensor networks. *2003 Symposium on Security and Privacy*, 197–213. 10.1109/SECPRI.2003.1199337

Chen, Y., Why, A., Batista, G., Mafra-Neto, A., & Keogh, E. (2014). Flying insect classification with inexpensive sensors. *Journal of Insect Behavior, 27*(5), 657–677. doi:10.100710905-014-9454-4 PMID:25350921

Christophers, S. R. (1960). *Aedes aegypti: The yellow fever mosquito*. CUP Archive.

Cobb, A., Roberts, S., & Zilli, D. (2016). Active sampling to increase the battery life of mosquito-detecting sensor networks. *AIMS CDT Mini Project, 10*.

Cribellier, A., van Erp, J. A., Hiscox, A., Lankheet, M. J., van Leeuwen, J. L., Spitzen, J., & Muijres, F. T. (2018, August). Flight behaviour of malaria mosquitoes around odour-baited traps: Capture and escape dynamics. *Royal Society Open Science, 5*(8), 180246. doi:10.1098/rsos.180246 PMID:30225014

Damar, T., Fleming, G. A., Gandahusada, S., & Bang, Y. H. (1981). Nocturnal indoor resting heights of the malaria vector Anopheles aconitus and other anophelines (Diptera: Culicidae) in Central Java, Indonesia. *Journal of Medical Entomology, 18*(5), 362–365. doi:10.1093/jmedent/18.5.362 PMID:7299790

Damos, P. (2015). Modular structure of web-based decision support systems for integrated pest management. A review. *Agronomy for Sustainable Development, 35*(4), 1347–1372. doi:10.100713593-015-0319-9

De Maerschalck, B., Maiheu, B., Janssen, S., & Vankerkom, J. (2010). CFD-modelling of complex plant-atmosphere interactions: Direct and indirect effects on local turbulence. *Proceedings of the CLIMAQS Workshop 'Local Air Quality and Its Interactions with Vegetation'*, 21–22.

Delaney, K. J., & Macedo, T. B. (2000). The impact of herbivory on plants: Yield, fitness, and population dynamics. In *Biotic stress and yield loss* (pp. 149–174). CRC Press. doi:10.1201/9781420040753.ch9

Delatte, H., Desvars, A., Bouétard, A., Bord, S., Gimonneau, G., Vourc'h, G., & Fontenille, D. (2010). Blood-feeding behavior of Aedes albopictus, a vector of Chikungunya on La Réunion. *Vector Borne and Zoonotic Diseases (Larchmont, N.Y.), 10*(3), 249–258. doi:10.1089/vbz.2009.0026 PMID:19589060

Erickson, R. A., Presley, S. M., Allen, L. J. S., Long, K. R., & Cox, S. B. (2010). A stage-structured, Aedes albopictus population model. *Ecological Modelling, 221*(9), 1273–1282. doi:10.1016/j.ecolmodel.2010.01.018

Evangelista, I. R. S. (2018). Bayesian Wingbeat Frequency Classification and Monitoring of Flying Insects Using Wireless Sensor Networks. *TENCON 2018-2018 IEEE Region 10 Conference*, 2403–2407.

Evans, D., Conrad, C. L., & Paul, F. M. (2003). Handbook of automated data quality control checks and procedures of the National Data Buoy Center. NOAA National Data Buoy Center Tech. Document, 03–02.

Evans, M. V., Hintz, C. W., Jones, L., Shiau, J., Solano, N., Drake, J. M., & Murdock, C. C. (2019). Microclimate and larval habitat density predict adult Aedes albopictus abundance in urban areas. *The American Journal of Tropical Medicine and Hygiene*, *101*(2), tpmd190220. doi:10.4269/ajtmh.19-0220 PMID:31190685

Gubler, D. J. (1998). Resurgent vector-borne diseases as a global health problem. *Emerging Infectious Diseases*, *4*(3), 442–450. doi:10.3201/eid0403.980326 PMID:9716967

Hu, Y.-C., Perrig, A., & Johnson, D. B. (2003). Rushing attacks and defense in wireless ad hoc network routing protocols. *Proceedings of the 2nd ACM Workshop on Wireless Security*, 30–40. 10.1145/941311.941317

Hur, B., & Eisenstadt, W. R. (2015). Low-power wireless climate monitoring system with rfid security access feature for mosquito and pathogen research. *2015 First Conference on Mobile and Secure Services (MOBISECSERV)*, 1–5. 10.1109/MOBISECSERV.2015.7072871

IPM Cost Calculator. (n.d.). Retrieved January 31, 2020, from http://www.ipmcalculator.com/

Jankauski, M. (2019). Flapping at Resonance: Measuring the Frequency Response of the Hymenoptera Thorax. *bioRxiv*.

Kahn, M. C., Celestin, W., & Offenhauser, W. (1945). Recording of Sounds produced by certain Disease-carrying Mosquitoes. *Science*, *101*(2622), 335–336. doi:10.1126cience.101.2622.335 PMID:17789049

Karlof, C., & Wagner, D. (2003). Secure routing in wireless sensor networks: Attacks and countermeasures. *Ad Hoc Networks*, *1*(2–3), 293–315. doi:10.1016/S1570-8705(03)00008-8

Kheng, T. Y. (2010). *Analysis, Design and implementation of Energy Harvesting Systems for Wireless Sensor Nodes* (PhD Thesis).

Kogan, M. (1988). Integrated pest management theory and practice. *Entomologia Experimentalis et Applicata*, *49*(1–2), 59–70. doi:10.1111/j.1570-7458.1988.tb02477.x

Kogan, M. (1998). Integrated pest management: Historical perspectives and contemporary developments. *Annual Review of Entomology*, *43*(1), 243–270. doi:10.1146/annurev.ento.43.1.243 PMID:9444752

Lalic, B., Eitzinger, J., Dalla Marta, A., Orlandini, S., Sremac, A. F., & Pacher, B. (2018). *Agricultural Meteorology and Climatology* (Vol. 8). Firenze University Press. doi:10.36253/978-88-6453-795-5

Liu, D., Ning, P., & Li, R. (2005). Establishing pairwise keys in distributed sensor networks. *ACM Transactions on Information and System Security*, *8*(1), 41–77. doi:10.1145/1053283.1053287

Locating outside sensors for optimum accuracy. (n.d.). *Prodata Weather Systems*. Retrieved January 30, 2020, from https://www.weatherstations.co.uk/gooddata.htm

Lompar, M., Lalić, B., Dekić, L., & Petrić, M. (2019). Filling gaps in hourly air temperature data using debiased ERA5 data. *Atmosphere*, *10*(1), 13. doi:10.3390/atmos10010013

Mankin, R. W., Machan, R., & Jones, R. (2006). Field testing of a prototype acoustic device for detection of Mediterranean fruit flies flying into a trap. *Proc. 7th Int. Symp. Fruit Flies of Economic Importance*, 10–15.

Mayer, C. P. (2009). Security and privacy challenges in the internet of things. *Electronic Communications of the EASST*, 17.

Mekki, K., Bajic, E., Chaxel, F., & Meyer, F. (2019). A comparative study of LPWAN technologies for large-scale IoT deployment. *ICT Express*, *5*(1), 1–7. doi:10.1016/j.icte.2017.12.005

Meyer, R. P., Hardy, J. L., & Reisen, W. K. (1990). Diel changes in adult mosquito microhabitat temperatures and their relationship to the extrinsic incubation of arboviruses in mosquitoes in Kern County, California. *Journal of Medical Entomology*, *27*(4), 607–614. doi:10.1093/jmedent/27.4.607 PMID:2167374

Miorandi, D., Sicari, S., De Pellegrini, F., & Chlamtac, I. (2012). Internet of things: Vision, applications and research challenges. *Ad Hoc Networks*, *10*(7), 1497–1516. doi:10.1016/j.adhoc.2012.02.016

Murdock, C. (n.d.). *Variation in mosquito microclimate and implications for vector-borne disease transmission*. Academic Press.

MyPest Page—IPM Pest and Plant Disease Models and Forecasting. (n.d.). Retrieved January 31, 2020, from http://pnwpest.org/wea/

National Academies of Sciences and Medicine. (2016). *Global health impacts of vector-borne diseases: Workshop summary*. National Academies Press.

Ouyang, T.-H., Yang, E.-C., Jiang, J.-A., & Lin, T.-T. (2015). Mosquito vector monitoring system based on optical wingbeat classification. *Computers and Electronics in Agriculture*, *118*, 47–55. doi:10.1016/j.compag.2015.08.021

Overby, H., & Steen-Thøde, M. (1990). *Calculation of vertical temperature gradients in heated rooms*. Academic Press.

Paaijmans, K. P., Imbahale, S. S., Thomas, M. B., & Takken, W. (2010). Relevant microclimate for determining the development rate of malaria mosquitoes and possible implications of climate change. *Malaria Journal*, *9*(1), 196. doi:10.1186/1475-2875-9-196 PMID:20618930

Paaijmans, K. P., & Thomas, M. B. (2011). The influence of mosquito resting behaviour and associated microclimate for malaria risk. *Malaria Journal*, *10*(1), 183. doi:10.1186/1475-2875-10-183 PMID:21736735

Pampana, E. (1966). *Erradicación de la malaria*. Editorial Limusa-Wiley México.

Pedigo, L. P., & Rice, M. E. (2014). *Entomology and pest management*. Waveland Press.

Perera, C., Ranjan, R., Wang, L., Khan, S. U., & Zomaya, A. Y. (2015). Big data privacy in the internet of things era. *IT Professional*, *17*(3), 32–39. doi:10.1109/MITP.2015.34

Perera, C., Zaslavsky, A., Christen, P., & Georgakopoulos, D. (2013). Context aware computing for the internet of things: A survey. *IEEE Communications Surveys and Tutorials, 16*(1), 414–454. doi:10.1109/SURV.2013.042313.00197

Peterson, R. K., Higley, L. G., & Pedigo, L. P. (2018). Whatever happened to IPM? *American Entomologist (Lanham, Md.), 64*(3), 146–150. doi:10.1093/ae/tmy049

Petric, M. (2020). *Modelling the influence of meteorological conditions on mosquito vector population dynamics (Diptera, Culicidae)*. Ghent University.

Petrić, M., Vandendriessche, J., Marsboom, C., Matheussen, T., Ducheyne, E., & Touhafi, A. (2019). Autonomous Wireless Sensor Networks in an IPM Spatial Decision Support System. *Computers, 8*(2), 43. doi:10.3390/computers8020043

Phung, K.-H., Tran, H., Nguyen, Q., Huong, T. T., & Nguyen, T.-L. (2018). Analysis and assessment of LoRaWAN. *2018 2nd International Conference on Recent Advances in Signal Processing, Telecommunications & Computing (SigTelCom)*, 241–246.

Porras-Amores, C., Mazarrón, F. R., & Cañas, I. (2014). Study of the vertical distribution of air temperature in warehouses. *Energies, 7*(3), 1193–1206. doi:10.3390/en7031193

Potamitis, I., & Rigakis, I. (2015). Novel noise-robust optoacoustic sensors to identify insects through wingbeats. *IEEE Sensors Journal, 15*(8), 4621–4631. doi:10.1109/JSEN.2015.2424924

Queralta, J. P., Gia, T. N., Zou, Z., Tenhunen, H., & Westerlund, T. (2019). Comparative study of LPWAN technologies on unlicensed bands for M2M communication in the IoT: Beyond LoRa and LoRaWAN. *Procedia Computer Science, 155*, 343–350. doi:10.1016/j.procs.2019.08.049

Quiñones, M. L., & Suarez, M. F. (1990). Indoor resting heights of some anophelines in Colombia. *Journal of the American Mosquito Control Association, 6*(4), 602–604. PMID:2098466

Raman, D. R., Gerhardt, R. R., & Wilkerson, J. B. (2007). Detecting insect flight sounds in the field: Implications for acoustical counting of mosquitoes. *Transactions of the ASABE, 50*(4), 1481–1485. doi:10.13031/2013.23606

Raymond, D. R., Marchany, R. C., Brownfield, M. I., & Midkiff, S. F. (2008). Effects of denial-of-sleep attacks on wireless sensor network MAC protocols. *IEEE Transactions on Vehicular Technology, 58*(1), 367–380. doi:10.1109/TVT.2008.921621

Raza, U., Kulkarni, P., & Sooriyabandara, M. (2017). Low power wide area networks: An overview. *IEEE Communications Surveys and Tutorials, 19*(2), 855–873. doi:10.1109/COMST.2017.2652320

Reed, S. C., Williams, C. M., & Chadwick, L. E. (1942). Frequency of wing-beat as a character for separating species races and geographic varieties of Drosophila. *Genetics, 27*(3), 349. PMID:17247046

Research Models: Insects, Mites, Diseases, Plants, and Beneficials—From UC IPM. (n.d.). Retrieved January 31, 2020, from http://ipm.ucanr.edu/MODELS/index.html

Reynolds, D. R., & Riley, J. R. (2002). Remote-sensing, telemetric and computer-based technologies for investigating insect movement: A survey of existing and potential techniques. *Computers and Electronics in Agriculture, 35*(2–3), 271–307. doi:10.1016/S0168-1699(02)00023-6

Savary, S., Willocquet, L., Pethybridge, S. J., Esker, P., McRoberts, N., & Nelson, A. (2019). The global burden of pathogens and pests on major food crops. *Nature Ecology & Evolution, 3*(3), 430–439. doi:10.103841559-018-0793-y PMID:30718852

Savopoulou-Soultani, M., Papadopoulos, N. T., Milonas, P., & Moyal, P. (2012). Abiotic Factors and Insect Abundance [Editorial]. *Psyche, 2012*, 1–2. doi:10.1155/2012/167420

Šebesta, O., Gelbič, I., & Peško, J. (2011). Daily and seasonal variation in the activity of potential vector mosquitoes. *Open Life Sciences, 6*(3), 422–430. doi:10.247811535-011-0019-7

Shi, E., & Perrig, A. (2004). Designing secure sensor networks. *IEEE Wireless Communications, 11*(6), 38–43. doi:10.1109/MWC.2004.1368895

Sikula, O. (n.d.). Vertical Distribution of Air Temperatures in Heated Dwelling Rooms. *Proceedings of Clima 2007 WellBeing Indoors: Rehva World Congress.*

Spence, N., Hill, L., & Morris, J. (2020). How the global threat of pests and diseases impacts plants, people, and the planet. Plants, People. *Planet, 2*(1), 5–13.

Stern, V., Smith, R., Van den Bosch, R., & Hagen, K. (1959). The integration of chemical and biological control of the spotted alfalfa aphid: The integrated control concept. *Hilgardia, 29*(2), 81–101. doi:10.3733/hilg.v29n02p081

Stoutjesdijk, P. H., & Barkman, J. J. (2014). *Microclimate, vegetation & fauna*. Brill. doi:10.1163/9789004297807

Ukil, A. (2010). *Security and privacy in wireless sensor networks*. INTECH Open Access Publisher. doi:10.5772/14272

Ukil, A., Bandyopadhyay, S., & Pal, A. (2014). IoT-privacy: To be private or not to be private. *2014 IEEE Conference on Computer Communications Workshops (INFOCOM WKSHPS)*, 123–124.

Velusamy, R., & Heinrichs, E. A. (1986). Tolerance in crop plants to insect pests. *International Journal of Tropical Insect Science, 7*(6), 689–696. doi:10.1017/S1742758400011747

Verbelen, Y. (2018). *Characterization of Self-Powered Autonomous Embedded Systems for Complementary Balanced Energy Harvesting*. doi:10.13140/RG.2.2.29768.42242

Wachter, S. (2018). Normative challenges of identification in the Internet of Things: Privacy, profiling, discrimination, and the GDPR. *Computer Law & Security Review, 34*(3), 436–449. doi:10.1016/j.clsr.2018.02.002

Wallner, W. E. (1987). Factors Affecting Insect Population Dynamics: Differences Between Outbreak and Non-Outbreak Species. *Annual Review of Entomology, 32*(1), 317–340. doi:10.1146/annurev.en.32.010187.001533

Wang, X., Chellappan, S., Gu, W., Yu, W., & Xuan, D. (2005). Search-based physical attacks in sensor networks. *Proceedings 14th International Conference on Computer Communications and Networks, 2005. ICCCN 2005*, 489–496.

Wang, X., Gu, W., Schosek, K., Chellappan, S., & Xuan, D. (2004). Sensor Network Configuration under Physical Attacks. Department of Computer Science and Engineering, Ohio State University. Technical Report: OSU-CISRC-7/04-TR45.

Weber, R. H. (2009). Internet of things–Need for a new legal environment? *Computer Law & Security Review, 25*(6), 522–527. doi:10.1016/j.clsr.2009.09.002

Wood, A. D., & Stankovic, J. A. (2002). Denial of service in sensor networks. *Computer, 35*(10), 54–62. doi:10.1109/MC.2002.1039518

Z-Wave | Z-Wave Smart Home Products FAQ. (n.d.). Retrieved January 30, 2020, from https://www.z-wave.com/faq

Zahumenský, I. (2004). *Guidelines on quality control procedures for data from automatic weather stations*. World Meteorological Organization.

Zigbee FAQ - Zigbee Alliance. (n.d.). Retrieved January 30, 2020, from https://zigbeealliance.org/zigbee-faq/

Chapter 3
IoT to Support Active Learning in Engineering Education: Test Cases and Lessons Learned

Abdellah Touhafi
Vrije Universiteit Brussel, Belgium

Gianluca Cornetta
https://orcid.org/0000-0001-8614-079X
Universidad San Pablo-CEU, Spain

ABSTRACT

Engineering education requires a rather difficult learning process, which aims at building the student's capacities in theoretical insights in science, project-oriented thinking and co-operation, experimental verification of basic concepts in specific labs, deductive and creative thinking, and multi-disciplinary engineering. Many education techniques to help in that learning process have been proposed in literature and have found their way into the daily learning process. Two very prominent active learning techniques used in engineering education are on one hand the virtual and remote laboratories and on the other hand the fab labs. The upcoming internet of things paradigm is now adding new possibilities to further enhance those two techniques to support engineering education. In this chapter, the authors introduce some of those possibilities, describe use cases, and draw some conclusions on the current state of research.

INTRODUCTION

Academic education programs in engineering are very challenging due to the need to strive at the same time to a sufficiently deep knowledge in theoretical principles of science, technology and mathematics, while the practical concepts and applications should be harnessed up to the level of physical implementations. This requires the educational program to go beyond classic lab-experiments and classic oral sessions in which basic theoretical principles are demonstrated and analytically explained.

DOI: 10.4018/978-1-7998-3817-3.ch003

Copyright © 2020, IGI Global. Copying or distributing in print or electronic forms without written permission of IGI Global is prohibited.

As such a lot of research has been done during the last decades in order to implement educational concepts that help to build the student's capacities in scientific thinking, deductive and creative thinking, project oriented handling, co-operation in group tasks, multi-disciplinary engineering, makers-attitude and a business-oriented attitude.

One of the methods developed to improve educational performance which is broadly applicable to many educational domains is *active learning*. Active learning is a method that impacts the learning process on the level of knowledge, skills and attitudes. By actively involving the students in the learning process it is possible to increase students' abilities on the level of knowledge registration, knowledge absorption and knowledge creation. It also has the potential to increase their capacity to develop practical and methodological skills and to enhance students (lifelong) learning, entrepreneurial, social and professional attitude. The method was first introduced to enhance the effects and experience of classic oral classes at university level. An overview of multiple active learning techniques and their assessment can be found in the work of Benjamin et al. (2017). In the following table a summary of those techniques is given as an informative overview for the reader to get acquainted with those techniques.

All the proposed techniques mentioned in the previous table, are mainly focusing on activating students to acquire knowledge, mainly trying to overcome the problems related to knowledge transfer during passive oral classes. Although some of those techniques are used for active learning in engineering, additional methods to build professional engineering attitude competences and practical engineering skill competences are required.

Within an engineering education program, the creation of competences related to skills and attitudes are at least as important as knowledge related competences. Typically, separate exercise sessions, practicals and group projects are included in the curriculum to invoke skill and attitude creation.

However, the fact that passive teaching and active teaching methods are defined as separate courses that are barely interweaved, leads in our opinion to lower student performance during the practicals and exercise sessions or to a higher study-time requirement to reach a fixed and predefined goal. This is mainly a consequence of the fact that there is no direct cognitive link laid down during the passive oral classes and the practicals or exercises. The authors believe that this has to be changed and a multi-competences oriented active learning approach is required. In this chapter technology supported active learning methods are proposed which try to have a better impact on the three basic competence groups (Engineering Knowledge, Engineering Skills, Engineering Attitude).

In the proposed solution, the authors envision to make the active learning method only loosely coupled to time and location. And next to that, to create a better cognitive linking between the oral learning moments, the practicals, the projects and the exercises.

We believe that IoT technologies, in combination with smart devices and a cloud infrastructure are the technological enablers to implement such a vision. The ubiquitous availability of cloud-based computing power, wired and wireless interconnection, web technologies, mobile computing devices, and low-cost electronic actuators and sensors have been extensively used in that research to implement those new learning concepts. This has led to new types of lab-environments for active learning with multi-disciplinary educational goals.

A first concept that has been implemented by the research community are the virtual laboratories. These laboratories are based on computer-based simulators or emulators that help students to interactively improve their theoretical insights in physics, chemistry, thermo-dynamics, electricity and electronics among others. Students are no longer limited to knowledge gathering by reading textbooks or watching static presentations but get the possibility to discover basic principles by making their own experiments

Table 1. Basic active learning methods

Method	Description of technique
class discussion (McKeachie, 2006) (Weimer, 2015)	During a class discussion, students actively discuss their interpretation of the taught material. It is a very good method to increase critical thinking. This method requires that students have already mastered the knowledge up to a minimal level. Unprepared students will benefit only a little from this method and as such will probably not participate.
think-pair-share (*Robertson, 2006*)	This technique uses a three steps process, where students first think about the learned content, then they discuss it with their peers and at the end they share their final thoughts with the class. This method, just like the previous requires that students are already mastering the subject up to a certain level. The advantage of this method is that the teacher gets valuable feedback, about potential misconceptions that exist among the students.
learning cell (Goldschmid, 1971)	A learning cell is a randomly chosen pair of students, who have to study and learn together. The students alternately ask questions and give answers to each other about the material that must be studied. The teacher is then going from group to group to give feedback. This method works very well if the group is homogenous and the students have a competitive character.
short written exercise	In this method the students are requested to write a one-minute-short paper. It is comparable to an elevator pitch in which the student should explain in one minute the main elements of a business idea. With this method misconceptions can be identified.
collaborative learning group (McKinney, 2010)	In this method, a group of 3 up to 6 students collaborate in a learning group for multiple learning courses and subjects. They are given an exercise or task on which they have to work in group. The multidisciplinary approach in this method makes it remarkable. The group of students are required to have reached a certain level in their knowledge before they can participate in this method. A flexible classroom where small groups can be formed is required.
student debate	This method allows students to train their verbal skills and to take position in a certain matter.
reaction to a video	In this method the students are preferably given some questions prior to watching a movie on the subject they are studying. After the movie, they are divided into groups where they discuss the movie and debate about it.
small group discussion	Students are activated by dividing them in small groups where they can discuss a certain topic. This is more appealing to students, because it is easier to discuss in a small group rather than an open discussion during the lecture, where the number of participating students gets limited.
Just-in-time teaching	In this technique, a common ground is created among students and teachers by providing a set of open problems or open questions prior to the start of the class-period. Students tend to actively retrieve the answer to the questions or problem statement during the class.
class game (McKinney, 2010)	Gamification of the course by trying to achieve certain goals within a subject related game-context, helps the students to prepare themselves better for an examination of the subject.
Learning by teaching	In this set-up, the students first prepare their course and teach it to their peers. In several cases it turns out that the student is able to transmit a certain concept better to his peers, due to his better understanding of the missing knowledge components to grasp the concept.

in the virtual lab environment. It has been proven in many studies that the use of virtual laboratories with well-designed graphical user interfaces is helping students to get in a flow-state which typically leads to spending more time in learning. The fact that contemporary mobile devices like smart phones, tablets and laptops provide high quality screens, computing power and interconnectivity, new learning methods which combine virtual laboratories with those devices has been investigated and a complete community which works on what is called mobile learning arose.

A second concept which is investigated thoroughly are the remote laboratories. Well known problems of lab equipment for engineering education are their cost, and inefficient use. In many cases lab-equipment is used only for a very short time during an academic year. Remote labs tend to solve those problems by providing a digital twin of the lab-equipment which allows students to perform the lab-tasks remotely. The advantage of this approach is that the limitations related to the accessibility of the labs are solved and as such the efficiency of usage is increased. Students can perform the physical lab-experiments during timeslots divided over a full day. Another advantage is that lab-experiments can be exchanged among universities worldwide thanks to the fact that they have a digital twin that allows for full remote controllability and monitoring. Research to bring this method to a level that it can be used very broadly is still ongoing. Advances are made in the automated creation of the digital interfaces for the lab-experiments, the generation of multi-media oriented graphical user interfaces and the automated recording of the lab-states.

A third concept that has gained a big momentum is the use of fabrication labs also called fab labs. Fab labs are laboratories which aim at developing the digital fabrication skills of students. The concept allows for starting with simple and low-cost fabrication devices like 3D-printers and basic tools for electronic system fabrication. However, in the most cases we can remark that fab labs related to academic institutes are often well equipped and tend to focus on fabrication of innovative prototypes related to an engineering project or to prove a new concept. It is also remarkable that the educational concept within a fab lab environment differs among institutes. Some fab labs focus mainly on creative thinking and proof of principle creation, while other fab labs tend to strive to engineer and produce products which are fully functional. Fab labs at academic level come with an important cost related to the management of the fab lab and the maintenance of the equipment. Research to improve the management and the collaboration among fab labs is ongoing and first results have been published the last years. Creating digital twins of the machines and coupling them to a management and remote access platform are some of the advances made in the domain.

The objective of this chapter is to describe experiences on how IoT can impact a learning environment. This is based on use cases which have been developed by the authors during the last years. The authors will also share the learned lessons accumulated during their exploration. The first use case describes the application of IoT to create remote experiments. The second use case describes the inclusion of IoT in a class room to deal with absenteeism and drop-out for oral classes. The third use case describes the integration of IoT devices to enhance accessibility to machines and infrastructure of a fab lab and real-time tracking of learning achievements in the fab lab.

BACKGROUND

Several research groups have integrated IoT in one or another way in the academic learning environment or in the education method. In the works of Suduc et al. (2018) and Veeramanickam et al. (2016) IoT has been used to define the concept of a smart campus and smart school. In Marquez et al. (2016) IoT principles have been used to create learning communities. In Elyamany et al. (2015) IoT was used for teaching infrastructure and to teach basic concepts in computer science. In Gul et al. (2017) a new course named "My Digital Life" for undergraduate students was introduced. In that course IoT was used to give students a better understanding of the world and their role in it. In Wang et al. (2010) IoT devices have been used to improve language learning skills by using voice and visual sensors to correct utterance for English language. In Touhafi et al. (2018) IoT was used as a method to create interconnected virtual and remote laboratories. In Gianluca et al. (2019) IoT is used as a method to create interconnected fab labs between remote campuses. Cheng H-C et al. (2012) reported the influence of integrating IoT, cloud computing and data mining in education. Castellani et al. (2018) presented how IoT was used to evolve from a digital campus to an Intelligent Campus.

In (Bagheri,2016) (Burd,2017) (Chen,2013) (Farahani B,2018) (Magrabi,2018) (Mershad,2018) (Shyr W-J,2018) (Tan,2018) many other applications of IoT in an educational context have been presented.

When put in a broader context we might summarize the impact of IoT on a campus level as inclusion of IoT to create smart learning concepts within smart spaces with smart facilities. This is depicted in figure 1.

Figure 1. IoT in a smart campus

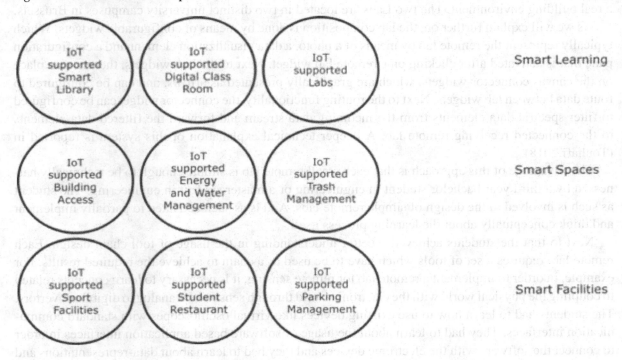

From this overview it becomes clear that IoT has a big impact on the complete campus operation and hence the learning experience of students. However, specific research on IoT to enhance active learning techniques has up to our knowledge not been done before and we consider the provided use cases in the next parts of this chapter as first experimental and empiric contributions to that research.

CASE STUDIES AND LESSONS LEARNED

Case Study 1: IoT for Interconnected Remote Labs

The basic concepts of remote labs that mainly focus on delivering remote access to lab equipment and visualization methods to display the results are well known (Xuemin 2010). In this part of the chapter a method is described to compose new remote labs based on existing labs. Such a lab composer allows for the creation of new lab-experiments by combining the results of physically separated remote laboratories. This creates a flexible way to extend the realm of laboratories and to develop laboratories that are more complex without having to dedicate all the hardware to a single experiment or remote lab setup. This work has been extensively reported by us in (Touhafi, 2018) and is reported here to describe the set of IoT inspired actions that have been developed to improve education at our university.

The basic concept behind the lab composer is shown in Figure 2. The figure demonstrates the lab composer canvas, in which a new Lab is implemented, based on two existing Labs. On the left side of the canvas, a live data-source is used which sends monitored environmental parameters to the second lab which is a Raspberry-Pi computing module and has the ability to be reprogrammed remotely. In this exercise, the students have the ability to implement sensor fusion techniques and to detect anomalies in a real building environment. The two Labs are located in two distinct university campuses in Brussels.

As we will explain further on, the lab composition is done by means of configurable widgets. Which typically represent the remote lab by means of a photo, a data visualization element and a configuration pane that is activated after clicking on a remote lab widget. Next to the Lab widgets, the user can place on the canvas connector-widgets, which are graphically presented as arrows, and can be configured to route data between lab widgets. Next to the routing functionality, the connector widget can be configured to filter specific data elements from the incoming data stream and forward the filtered data-elements to the connected receiving remote lab. A deeper technical explanation of this system is reported in (Touhafi, 2018).

The advantage of this approach is that each small remote lab is simple enough to be technically harnessed by a third year bachelor student in engineering or a master student in engineering. The student as such is involved in the design of simple remote labs. And is as such activated to partially implement and think conceptually about the learning process itself.

Next to that the students achieved a better understanding in the usage of tool chain design. Each remote lab, requires a set of tools which have to be used as a chain to achieve the required results. For example, in order to implement a remote lab for remote sensing, it is necessary to learn concepts related to coupling the physical world with the electronic world through sensors and analog to digital convertors. The students had to learn how to use existing devices like virtual oscilloscopes with standard communication interfaces. They had to learn about the usage of software based application interfaces in order to connect the software with the electronic devices and they had to learn about data-representations and the use of web based communication components to transfer the data to the lab-composer.

The proposed system has proven to be implementable but difficult to maintain. Guaranteeing that the data is formatted in the correct way, such that the different remote labs can exchange their data, seamlessly was one of the major blocking points for the widespread use of this tool. This has learned us that there is need for a toolset which automatically or at least semi-automatically generates a wrapper around an existing remote lab, such that it can be integrated into the lab-composer. Further research on that aspect is required.

Case Study 2: IoT to Reduce Absenteeism and Drop-Out in Oral Class

In this use case we will describe the use of smart phones and web applications to increase interactivity during oral classes and reduce the drop-out.

In our engineering curriculum several projects which are implemented in a fab lab environment have been introduced during the last decade. This has led to a remarkable increase in the technologi-

Figure 2. Remote lab composer

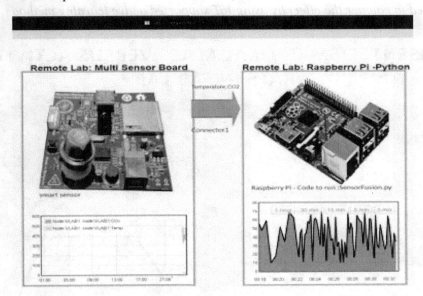

cal, machine handling and digital design skills of our students in the electronics and electromechanics domain. Another remarkable change was the increased students' engagement to work on the project and their competitive attitude towards other students. The size of the workload, however, requires that the students also create a working attitude in which they distribute their project related workload more evenly within the project period. Monitoring the student activity level in the fab lab during a semester is showing however that the typical student's activity is more related to the imposed intermediate and final deadlines and is far from an evenly distributed activity level. This typical behavior seems to cause absenteeism in oral classes and as such creates a new problem. In this use case we have investigated the cause and tried to implement a remedy supported by IoT technological concepts.

In figure 3 we show the measured students' activity during one semester of 12 weeks. The peeks of activity at week 4, week 8 and week 12 are related to the intermediate and final deadlines for the practical project in the fab lab.

The shown data is related to two courses that are organized in the second year bachelor's degree in industrial engineering. The data in black rhombic dotted lines is related to a 5 ECTS credits theoretical course on electronic design principles which is initially organized in a modern multi-media classroom with a smart board, projector and internet connection. During the semester we have recorded the number of absent students. The data in the gray squares dotted line is related to a 6 ECTS credits project-course in which the students have to design and build a small windmill for wind-energy creation. An activity rate of the students for their project work is estimated based on the hours as foreseen in the curriculum and the hours they spend on their project during a week.

Activity= #hours spent per week / #hours per week foreseen in curriculum

These two courses are both organized two days per week and are planned on the same day. During the morning sessions, the electronics-design course is given while in the afternoon the students can

Figure 3. Drop-out in oral class due to deadlines imposed in fab lab related practical works. The last weeks where used to counter the effect by using IoT supported active learning method

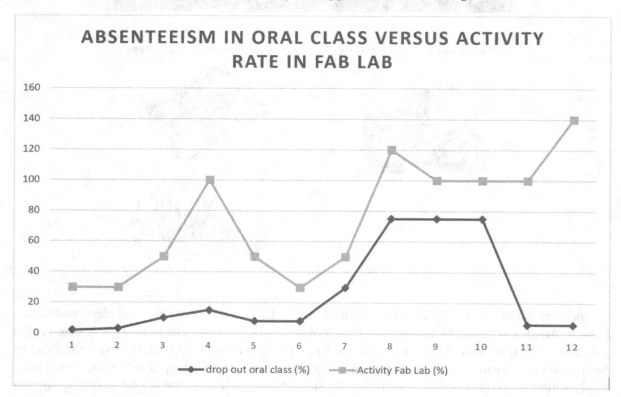

work on their project-course. The fab lab has an open-door policy and the students can work on their project whenever they have free hours in their course schedule. Three deadlines during the semester are foreseen to evaluate the student's progress. The evaluation counts partially for their final mark on the project. The hours foreseen to reach the project goals are the programmed contact hours in the fab lab, during which the students can get support from their coaches from the education team and 2 times the contact hours which are programmed as individual working hours without support from their coaches.

The drop-out which has been remarked as a side effect of the intermediate project deadlines alarmed us, and in order to find the cause, a focus discussion with a small group of students has been elaborated. The discussion showed us, that the drop-out problem was mainly related to the high demands from the practical course, and the fact that skipping the oral course is not perceived as having a negative impact on the long term for their exam results, while otherwise it has a positive impact on the score they receive for the intermediate evaluation of the practices-course.

Another element that can be learned from the drop-out graph, is that after each deadline the number of students that drop-out and don't attend the oral class will fall back after the deadline, but the new steady state of drop-outs is much higher than the previous steady state of the drop-outs.

The focus-discussion of the students shows that this is due to their subjective feeling that they will not be able to catch up the lost parts of the oral course and attending the course has no added value for them anymore.

Based on those elements a strategy to reverse the subjective feelings of the student regarding the value of attending the oral course has been developed. In first instance, sessions have been transformed from classic oral sessions to interactive sessions in which IoT devices and web applications were used for the first time. We introduced the use of an electronic circuit simulator (Touhafi,2018) which can be used on a mobile phone, a tablet or directly run as a web application on a laptop computer.

Secondly, we have introduced a hedonic approach to increase the perceived value of attending the interactive oral session. As such, the sessions were implemented in three parts. First a fast overview of the course concepts that would be handled during that session were repeated. Secondly a guided exercise is worked out which was made interactive by having the students making predictions on the simulator output by logic reasoning instead of analytical calculation. Then the students received exercises which they could solve by using the electronic circuit simulator on their smart phones or their computer. The given exercises were also to be considered examples of exam questions which they finally should be able to solve analytically using pen and paper.

And thirdly, we changed the course environment from a classic classroom to the electronics lab in order to allow for a group work approach. Where students had the ability to co-operate during the time that they were solving the exercises.

This multifaceted approach has led to an immediate dropdown of the number of students that were skipping the oral course and lowered the drop-out to a minimum level of 6% while we had drop-outs in the order of 70% before.

Next to that, the students perceived the courses as valuable, in the sense that they learned new skills which helped them to become less depending on reading material and classic analytical computational methods. Instead they felt that they were trained to explore themselves the solution space by the simulator and to learn by experiencing nearly real time the consequences of their design choices. The simulator supports real time changes of component values and shows the impact in a graphical way immediately.

As a conclusion we can state that practical project-oriented courses with intermediate evaluation moments and deadlines are perceived by students to have a higher hedonic value. As such we have experimented by using a hedonic approach to increase the perceived value of attending oral classes such that their perceived value becomes more equal to the pre mentioned practical project-oriented courses. After applying this approach an immediate and high effect was measured on the drop-out for the courses. The use of mobile computing devices and mobile simulation applications or web applications for creating interaction during the oral course increases the perceived value on the long term and becomes seen as an investment for a better score at examination. A short-term payback is created by giving the students the possibility to make a report on their individual exercises and receive a score which is counting for 10% of the final score for the course.

Use Case 3: Fab Lab and IoT

As explained in the introduction, fab labs have been adopted in higher and secondary education as a new concept to improve the digital creation skills of students. The management of a fab lab is however a limiting factor in terms of manpower and financial cost. The costs related to the management personal and maintenance are rather high and as such require an important yearly operating budget which might exceed the costs related to the educational support personal and as such if not taken care of leads to a non-managed fab lab or a lack of educational support. In this use-case we will tackle this issue by transforming a classic fab lab which is to be seen as a set of individual fabrication machines into an interconnected fab lab with the ability to manage the machines and the users of the machines.

Machine Access Control and Student Monitoring

In the first implementation of the IoT interconnected fab lab, the focus was put on implementing an advanced access control system. Which allows us to implement a student's competence-based access to the machines.

Figure 4. IoT supported system architecture for fab lab management

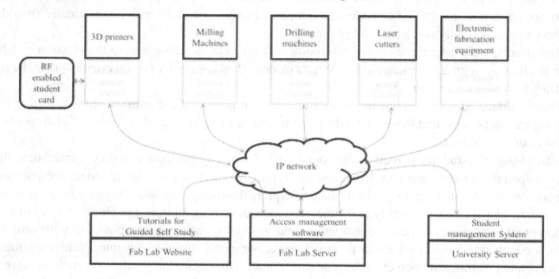

As depicted in figure 4, the system architecture is based on a fab lab server which contains a machine access control software. The fab lab equipment is extended with an IP-enabled access management system which allows the machine to be activated by an RF-ID tag or an RF-ID enabled student card. Further the system contains a fab lab website which gives access to digital tutorials for guided self-study.

Students cannot access the machines in the fab lab until they achieve learning credits by following the guided self-study courses. The self-study courses explain how a student has to operate a machine. Within the course-trajectory multiple stop-points are introduced on which the student will have reached a certain level of understanding which is required to operate the machine under guidance. The student shall then contact the fab lab manager or a fab lab tutor who will guide him to perform the learned machine-operations on the machine. After completing the guided self-study tutorial, the student will be registered in the access management system as a person who has full access to the machines for which the tutorials were completed. Once registered in the system, the student gets access to the machines by his RF-ID enabled student card.

Each time a student makes use of a machine it is registered in the access management software. The more often a student is using a machine, the higher his credits score for that particular machine. Once a certain level of experience and hence credits is reached, the student becomes automatically registered in the system as a fab lab tutor for that specific machine and receives the ability to grant other students' access to that type of machines. This co-tutoring aspect has helped us to maintain a high level of inter-activity and safety in the fab lab without increasing the number of hired fab lab managers.

In figure 5, a photo of the 3D printers in our fab lab that have been extended with the access management pod is shown.

Figure 5. Simplified architecture of the IoT based access management pod and photo of 3D-printer extended with the IoT based access management pod at the authors institution

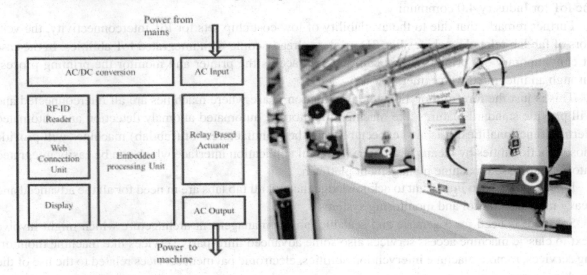

It is worth mentioning that the machine access automation and the logging of machine-activity has impacted the accessibility of the fab lab in a positive way. The fab lab opening hours could be extended until 22h00 in the evening thanks to the intervention of volunteering students who have reached the fab lab tutor level and students that helped to manage the fab lab based on a part time student-job contract.

The logging of the student activity in the fab lab by the access management software has also proven to be a good indicator for the advancement of students in their project work and could be used to define a more precise follow up trajectory of the students.

Service Oriented Fab Lab Management System

While the previously described IoT based access automation approach has been fully implemented and has been operational more than 12 months at the moment of writing, a new architecture has been defined for a more generic fab lab management system which opens possibilities to create a more scalable fab lab management system. Concerning the scalability, we mainly aim for an open system which allows the system to scale in its fab lab support abilities. The need for such an open fab lab management system approach becomes clear once a comparison is made between our current system and the advances in the Industry 4.0 research.

In (Gianluca, 2019) the ability to implement interconnected multi-site fab labs is presented in which students can collaborate and exchange their designs and experiences. As shown in that paper implementing advanced Industry 4.0 principles to support the automated operation of a multi-site fab lab requires an advanced software layer which also includes concepts like security and multi-tenancy control. A first tested implementation of that approach has been reported in (Gianluca, 2019). The paper also discussed and demonstrated innovative collaboration methods in which students share machines remotely or distribute their fabrication tasks over multiple fab lab sites.

Another aspect is the potential to support heterogeneous machine control and monitoring systems in order to avoid vendor lock-in and to have the ability to easily upgrade and surf on the advances made in the IoT for Industry 4.0 community.

Further remark, that due to the availability of low-cost chip sets for IoT interconnectivity, the vendors of fab lab related machines like 3D printers already come with integrated IoT abilities. In the case of contemporary 3D printers, users can remotely access the printer and monitor the printing process through an integrated web camera.

This is just the forefront of a new transformation phase where machines are all interconnected and will provide standard features like machine monitoring, automated anomaly detection and automated alerting functionalities. It is also expectable that the manufacturers of (fab lab) machines will provide those functionalities by means of an open RESTful application interface which can be easily integrated into a cloud-based machine management platform.

It is, however, also important to acknowledge that not all fab labs are in need for all the advanced and heavy machine control and monitoring systems.

So, there is need for a generic and scalable fab lab management architecture which might involve next to classic machine access services also some advanced third-party services like machine monitoring services, remote machine intervention abilities, electronic payment services related to the use of the machines and so on.

Figure 6. Scalable service oriented architecture

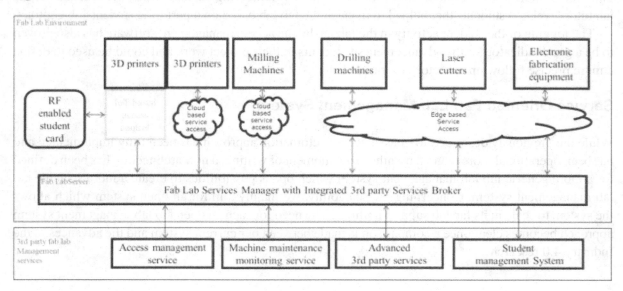

It is also necessary to create an architecture which supports the different interconnectivity models that exist today. As such, the interconnectivity architecture towards the machines should be heterogeneous and should support the straightforward methods like direct IP-based interconnection as in our first implementation but it should also support access through a vendor specific cloud service or via a local edge-computing solution.

As shown in figure 6, the heart of this architecture is built around a service oriented fab lab management server. The Service Oriented fab lab manager is a basic services-handler which supports MQTT communication and RESTful communication with different services. The server also acts as a message router and protocol translator among the different machines and services. The strength of the approach is that the message routing and translation core has also the ability to communicate with the machines through vendor specific cloud-based services, rather than having a direct communication channel with the machine. This allows us to keep the fab lab management server rather light weight.

FUTURE RESEARCH DIRECTIONS

The authors emphasize that specific research on the impact of IoT on active learning is still in a starting phase. Many research directions could evolve.

On the one hand newly IoT inspired active learning techniques might be developed and researched in practical settings. On the other hand the impact of IoT on existing active learning techniques can be researched and improved versions can be developed.

The usage of IoT for evaluation purposes of active learning is also still not investigated yet. Our experience with active learning has learned us the hard way that active learning comes with an important time-cost regarding the evaluation of the students. The authors believe that IoT based tools might help in automating the evaluation process for active learning.

Another promising research track is to start the research in the opposite way and focus on the development of new IoT technologies to support active learning. As an engineering department, we have chosen to follow the latter research path. As such, our research focus is related to the development of IoT tools to further loosen the strong coupling of active learning methods with the physical labs and the time frames in which those active learning techniques are accessible to the students. A first ongoing experiment is the use of Smart Building and Smart City infrastructure in combination with mobile applications to create off-campus learning experiences. The concept and the related tools are built with the aim to be accessible and usable anywhere and anytime. New IoT devices to explore those concepts are being developed. A second ongoing project which also defines our further research path is the setup of an 'IoT Creation Lab' which has as major goal to make IoT more accessible to multiple disciplines in education. The authors believe, that IoT might have its use for the active learning methods in multiple faculties.

CONCLUSION

In this chapter we have discussed the impact of IoT technology on active learning and more specifically on the use of IoT to enhance the use of remote labs, to enhance fab lab settings and to deal with oral class absenteeism. In the case of remote labs, we have described how IoT can be used to extend the concept into interconnected remote labs. The need for an automated wrapper turned out to be required for a broader acceptance of the concept. In the case of fab lab management, we have shown that the inclusion of an IoT based machine access control system has a quite important impact on the accessibility of the fab lab, the ability to monitor the usage of the machines and the monitoring of students achievements for each type of machine. It also allowed to introduce a pedagogic system in which students can evolve to the level of a fab lab tutor and receive the capacity to guide new students in the fab lab.

We have also discussed an improved fab lab management architecture that is based on a digital services model. Such an architecture has the advantage to offer a better upgradability and scalability towards new services and technologies. This new architecture is still in deployment but has been principally tested on a small size test case with a limited number of machines.

This chapter also discussed a use case in which mobile computing devices in combination with a simulator tool was used to increase the interactivity of an oral class and this way to lower absenteeism.

We also implemented a hedonic tutoring approach in which short term and long-term appreciation for the course was created. That approach had a direct impact on the drop-out which was lowered from more than 70% to a minimum of 6%.

REFERENCES

Bagheri, M., & Movahed, S. H. (2016). *The effect of the internet of things (IoT) on education business model.* Paper presented at 12th International Conference on Signal-Image Technology and Internet-Based Systems (SITIS), Naples, Italy. 10.1109/SITIS.2016.74

Benjamin, L. (2017, Summer). ASPECT: A Survey to Assess Student Perspective of Engagement in an Active-Learning Classroom. *CBE Life Sciences Education, 16*(2), ar32. doi:10.1187/cbe.16-08-0244 PMID:28495936

Burd, B., Barker, L., & Divitini, M. (2017). Courses, content, and tools for internet of things in computer science education. *Proceedings of the ITiCSE Conference on Working Group Reports.* 10.1145/3174781.3174788

Castellani, A. P., Bui, N., Casari, P., Rossi, M., Shelby, Z., & Zorzi, M. (2010). *Architecture and protocols for the internet of things: A case study.* Paper presented at 8th IEEE International Conference on Pervasive Computing and Communications Workshops (PERCOM Workshops), Mannheim, Germany. 10.1109/PERCOMW.2010.5470520

Chen, Y., & Dong, X. (2013). *The development and prospect of new technology in modern distance education.* Paper presented at International Conference on Information Science and Computer Applications (ISCA 2013), Tel Aviv, Israel. 10.2991/isca-13.2013.7

Cheng, H.-C., & Liao, W.-W. (2012). *Establishing a lifelong learning environment using IOT and learning analytics.* Paper presented at 14th International Conference on Advanced Communication Technology (ICACT), PyeongChang, South Korea.

Cornetta, G., Mateos, F. J., Touhafi, A., & Muntean, G.-M. (2019). Design, simulation and testing of a cloud platform for sharing digital fabrication resources for education. *Journal of Cloud Computing, 8*(12). doi:10.118613677-019-0135-x

Elyamany, H. F., & AlKhairi, A. H. (2015). *IoT-academia architecture: A profound approach*. Paper presented at 2015 16th IEEE/ACIS International Conference on software Engineering, Artificial Intelligence, Networking and Parallel/Distributed Computing (SNPD), Takamatsu, Japan. 10.1109/SNPD.2015.7176275

Farahani, B., Firouzi, F., Chang, V., Badaroglu, M., Constant, N., & Mankodiya, K. (2018). Towards fog-driven IoT eHealth: Promises and challenges of IoT in medicine and healthcare. *Future Generation Computer Systems*, 78, 659–676. doi:10.1016/j.future.2017.04.036

Gul, S., Asif, M., Ahmad, S., Yasir, M., Majid, M., & Arshad, M. (2017). A survey on role of internet of things in education. *IJCSNS*, *17*(5), 159–165.

Magrabi, S. A. R., Pasha, M. I., & Pasha, M. Y. (2018). Classroom teaching to enhance critical thinking and problem-solving skills for developing IOTApplications. *J Eng Educ Transform*, *31*(3), 152–157.

Marquez, J., Villanueva, J., Solarte, Z., & Garcia, A. (2016). IoT in Education: Integration of Objects with Virtual Academic Communities. In New Advances in Information Systems and Technologies. Advances in Intelligent Systems and Computing, no. 115 (pp. 201-212). Springer International Publishing.

McKeachie, W. J., & Svinicki, M. (2006). *Teaching Tips: Strategies, Research, and Theory for College and University Teachers*. Belmont, CA: Wadsworth.

Mershad, K., & Wakim, P. (2018). A learning management system enhanced with internet of things applications. *J Educ Learn*, *7*(3), 23. doi:10.5539/jel.v7n3p23

Mohamed, A-B., Gunasekaran, M., Mai, M., & Ehab, R. (2018). *Internet of things in smart education environment: Supportive framework in the decision-making process*. Academic Press.

Robertson, K. (2006). *Increase Student Interaction with "Think-Pair-Shares" and "Circle Chats"*. colorincolorado.org

Shyr, W.-J., Zeng, L.-W., Lin, C.-K., Lin, C.-M., & Hsieh, W.-Y. (2018). Application of an energy management system via the internet of things on a university campus. *Eurasia Journal of Mathematics, Science and Technology Education*, *14*(5), 1759–1766. doi:10.12973/ejmste/80790

Suduc, A.-M., Bizoi, M., & Gorghiu, G. (2018). A Survey on IoT in Education. *Revista Romaneasca pentru Educatie Multidimensionala, 10*(3), 103-111.

Tan, P., Wu, H., Li, P., & Xu, H. (2018). Teaching management system with applications of RFID and IoT technology. *Education in Science*, *8*(1), 26. doi:10.3390/educsci8010026

Touhafi, A., Braeken, A., Tahiri, A., & Zbakh, M. (2018). *CoderLabs: A cloud-based platform for real-time online labs with user collaboration*. Concurrency and Computation Wiley Online Library. doi:10.1002/cpe.4377

Veeramanickam, M., & Mohanapriya, M. (2016). IOT enabled Futurus smart campus with effective E-learning: I-campus. *GSTF Journal of Engineering Technology*, *3*(4), 81.

Wang, Y. (2010). *English interactive teaching model which based upon internet of things*. Paper presented at 2010 International Conference on Computer Application and System Modeling (ICCASM), Taiyuan, China.

Weimer, M. (2015). 10 benefits of getting students to participate in classroom discussions. *Faculty Focus*. https://www.facultyfocus.com/articles/teaching-and-learning/10-benefits-of-getting-students-to-participate-in-classroom-discussions/

Xuemin, C., Gangbing, S., & Yongpeng, Z. (2010). Virtual and Remote Laboratory Development: A Review. *Earth and Space 2010: Engineering, Science, Construction, and Operations in Challenging Environments*, 3843-3852.

KEY TERMS AND DEFINITIONS

Active Learning: Active learning is a method that impacts the learning process on the level of knowledge, skills and attitudes. By actively involving the students in the learning process it is possible to increase students' abilities on the level of knowledge registration, knowledge absorption and knowledge creation.

Cloud Computing: Cloud computing is a method to provide computing, storage and connection resources on demand. The client does not need any knowledge on how to service a server-platform to use the demanded resources.

Digital Twin: A digital twin is a digital replica of a physical object. The digital twin has similar dynamic and time-variant behavior as the physical object.

Edge Computing: Edge computing is a distributed computing paradigm in which the computing resources are located closer to the place where those resources are needed and used.

Fab Lab: A fabrication lab or fab lab is a workshop which typically contains a set of (low cost) machines for digital fabrication of prototypes.

Hedonics: Hedonism is a theory that puts a relation between pleasure and duty.

Remote Lab: A remote laboratory or remote lab is a physical laboratory-system in which telecommunications, electronic sensors and actuators are used to perform the experiments on that laboratory-system from a distant place.

Virtual Lab: A virtual Lab is a simulated lab environment typically implemented as a software program which allows the users to perform their experiments.

Chapter 4
An Unified Secured Cloud System for the Education Sector of India

Kimaya Arun Ambekar
K. J. Somaiya Institute of Management Studies and Research, India

Kamatchi R.
ISME School of Management and Entrepreneurship, India

ABSTRACT

Cloud computing is based on years of research on various computing paradigms. It provides elasticity, which is useful in the situations of uneven ICT resources demands. As the world is moving towards digitalization, the education sector is expected to meet the pace. Acquiring and maintaining the ICT resources also necessitates a huge amount of cost. Education sector as a community can use cloud services on various levels. Though the cloud is very successfully running technology, it also shows some flaws in the area of security, privacy and trust. The research demonstrates a model in which major security areas are covered like authorization, authentication, identity management, access control, privacy, data encryption, and network security. The total idea revolves around the community cloud as university at the center and other associated colleges accessing the resources. This study uses OpenStack environment to create a complete cloud environment. The validation of the model is performed using some cases and some tools.

INTRODUCTION

The transformation in technology has evolved multifold. Different technologies are helping business in various ways. With the progressive nature of businesses and the help of technology, companies started creating a considerable amount of data. Various researchers introduced many computing paradigms to store and process the data. (Garfinkel 2011) in 1961, MIT professor John McCarthy on the day of the centennial celebration declaimed that "computing sooner or later be structured as a telephone system or as a public utility". Primarily researchers developed computing as a utility for businesses. Starting from

DOI: 10.4018/978-1-7998-3817-3.ch004

Copyright © 2020, IGI Global. Copying or distributing in print or electronic forms without written permission of IGI Global is prohibited.

centralized computing and moving towards various other advanced computing paradigms like parallel, distributed, cloud, collaborative computing, etc. are helping organizations to store, process, analyze, and extract the data.

Other than just storing and extracting data, businesses use numerous additional ICT (Information and Communication Technology) resources on everyday transactions. Buying these resources and maintaining them is a gigantic task for businesses. Especially for the organization whose core business value is not IT based, for them having and maintaining the ICT resources becomes a heavy burden. The traditional infrastructure curve for any business will not fulfill the ICT requirement fittingly. Having the apt number of resources for the peak time in the industry is very important but at the same time maintenance of them at the time of the valleys in the business is equally vital and also bothersome.

Cloud Computing is one such crucial technological revolution. Cloud Computing has opened numerous ways in terms of the ICT resources needed for any organization. Cloud Computing is an approach of resource allocation and computing in which the significant characteristics are elasticity and scalability. Organizations can take advantage of the versatility of the number and types of resources from cloud services.

Cloud Computing is a kind of utility computing in where the user needs to pay as per the usage of the resources. Users can accept resources as much as necessary for the period and can release them as soon as the need is satisfied. The total billing will reflect only the used period. This characteristic makes the technique more attractive to users. Also, Cloud Service Provider hosts the Services on their Servers. The CSP (Cloud Service Provider) is responsible for creating the services accessible to the user. The responsibility also includes uploading, maintaining the hardware and software, etc. This feature releases a lot of pressure from the businesses to have an in-house IT department to maintain the ICT resources.

All these striking features have lured organizations into adopting cloud services. Many sectors or domains have started adopting Cloud Computing services linearly. Industries like manufacturing, finance, and banking, healthcare, retailing, marketing, etc. have started using the cloud as their primary infrastructure source. Diverse verticals show great interest in adopting the technology, but still, the percentage rates are meager. If we analyse carefully, one can conclude that the education sector has not progressively adopted the cloud systems. The education sector is one of the most versatile sectors because it needs to adopt new technology to make the student understand the concepts of a new age. The new generations of students are technosavi, and it is a digital generation. Hence the institutes need to adopt more modern technology as fast as possible. Also, with the modern era, the complexity and vastness of the subjects create the need for the corresponding technology to study the issues in detail. It also increases the need for ICT resources. Improvement in ICT is an overhead to educational institutes where funds are already less.

According to Gartner (Gartner, 2018), India's cloud revenue will increase 37.5 percent from USD 1.8 Billion in 2017 to USD 2.5 Billion in 2018. (Rick Martin, 2017) Adoption rates of Cloud Computing in India are still very less. In line with another research agency, in the ranking of cloud readiness index from Asian countries, India is on 9th rank. One of the factors which determine and impact the readiness of adoption to cloud environment is cloud security. (Kim Weins, 2017) The structure of the cloud environment is multifaceted, and the responsibility of the cloud service provider is colossal in it because of which people are hesitant to move their business on the cloud.

Security remains vital in the education field, as well. Here, the marks- sheets of students and their records, financial records of an institute, payroll and HR related records of faculty, researches done by the faculty and students are very confidential and private data. If moving on cloud systems, an educational institute needs specific actions to secure the data.

This chapter addresses the main objectives as:

- Studying the usage of Cloud Computing services in the higher education sector of India and also how community cloud as a deployment model works in this scenario
- Testing the correlation between the ICT needs of the education sector and Cloud Computing services and the security problems. Also, identify the layers of security requirements cloud services for the education sector in India
- Creating a model and framework which can sustain with the requirements of the education sector concerning cloud services
- Creating the actual platform for the cloud, this can accommodate different educational institute as a community cloud and test the model using various use cases and tool.

BACKGROUND

Cloud Computing

Cloud Computing is not the latest technology, but surely is a trend in the market. Much more technologies are surfacing using cloud services as their backbones. Hence Cloud Computing becomes very important to study.

(Buyya et al, 2016) Buyya et al. mention the need for computing in their research. The paper describes computing as the fifth utility after telephone, gas, electricity, and water. The document also discusses the evolutional journey of the technology from data centers and cluster, grids to Cloud Computing. The article also offers a 21st-century vision for Cloud Computing and trends of it. It also specifies the new market-oriented cloud architecture.

(Mell, P., Grance, 2011) The most popular definition of Cloud was stated by NIST(National Institute of Standards and Technology) as "a model for enabling convenient, on-demand network access to a shared pool of configurable computing resources (e.g., networks, servers, storage, applications, and services) that can be rapidly provisioned and released with minimal management effort or service provider interaction".

Cloud Computing in the Education Sector

(Niall Sclater, 2011) Sclater talks about the need for the cloud in education. The report talks about the integration of IT services into the education sector implies the need in a major way. The author also identifies the most probable or primary cloud service uses the educational institutes can start with as email clients, Learning Management Systems (LMS) etc. The report also talks about the advantages of cloud in education as economies of scales, elasticity, and availability. The paper also summarizes the benefits and risks in depth.

(Robert Fogel, 2010) Intel, in the year 2010 launched a concept of delivering education as a service using Cloud Computing. The study started explaining the concept of educational transformation. It has five quadrants as policy, curriculum and assessment, professional development, Information and communication technology, and research & evaluation. The paper further explains the concept of education as a cloud and the user services involved in it. It also talks about the examples and the advantages of the educational clouds. Intel tries to provide a bigger perspective in which the teacher and students can utilize the bigger world of knowledge effortlessly.

Security in Cloud Computing

(Dawei Suna et al., 2011) Suna et al. in their paper mention security, privacy, and trust related issues in Cloud Computing. For Security, they emphasize on security mechanism, confidentiality, transparency, management of the multi-tenant environment, etc. In the context of privacy, the paper talks about what type of data, the user is interested in securing: past, present, or future, how they want the privacy to be maintained, etc. Researchers further elaborate trust with parameters like reliability, confidence, security, belief, etc.

(Martucci et al, 2012) Martucci et al. claim that it is fundamental to adopt cloud technology in the telecommunication industry. It then talks about the challenges faced by this industry. They are legal and regulatory challenges, business and market challenges, and technical challenges. The study categorizes the overall requirements for the above challenges into privacy, security, and trust. For privacy, authors talk about EU data protection rules, PII (Personal Identifiable Information) and PET (Privacy Enhancing Technologies) like obfuscation. Concerning security, loss of data, and control over data, cross authentication, hypervisor vulnerabilities or problems in virtualization, DDoS (Distributed Denial of Service), etc. problems are discussed. For trust, research mentions hard trust, where cloud users make assumptions about security, reliability, and dependability. Users can utilize the certificates, audit reports, and logs to make the assumptions.

After analyzing the possible literature, the research finds that concepts of Cloud Computing, its evolution and benefits are mentioned by many researchers. The researchers also stated the usability of cloud systems in various fields. The majority of them have incorporated the cloud systems in e-learning or higher education systems. But not many have mentioned about the educational cloud systems or education-as-a-service. Hardly any paper was found on higher education as a community cloud. The community cloud can be utilized by the education sector to benefit the learners. It can be exploited to provide better facilities to the students and teachers too. Due to infrastructural deficiency, the students are not getting practical knowledge, which also can be provided by the community cloud approach in the lesser cost. Primarily technical and engineering education needs wide-ranging ICT resources for their practical, projects, etc. By providing these resources to the students, one can enhance the quality of overall training, which in turn can offer more "Industry-Ready" students.

After analysing the literature about Cloud Computing and security in it, it is concluded that none of the frameworks mentions community cloud for higher education domain and specifically for the Indian educational structure. Different threats and attacks on the cloud and also specifically in the cloud for education system is analysed. The specific attacks and threats were acknowledged, and the solutions were scrutinized to make this study more tangible and beneficial for society.

BASICS OF SECURITY

To understand the concept of security in more detail, there are some terms which followed in detail

1. **Vulnerability**: Vulnerability is a weakness in the system which can be exploited by the intruder. The weakness can be encountered in various places in the system like networks, storage, hardware, APIs, etc. But largely vulnerabilities can be perceived because of either Technological or configuration or security policy weaknesses of the organizations.
2. **Threats**: NIAG (National Information Assurance Glossary) states threat as an occasion of having the possibility to adversely impact any administrative processes (including mission, functions, image, or reputation) or any system through unauthorized access, destruction, disclosure, modification of data, and denial of service.
3. **Attacks**: Intruders can use these techniques to abuse the vulnerabilities and generate risks in the form of threats to the system. The impact of the attack can vary depending on the type and intensity of the attack.

CIA (Confidentiality, Integrity, Availability) Triad in Security

(Clark D.D., Wilson D.R., 1987) Clark and Wilson, in their paper, introduced the concept of CIA triad, i.e., Confidentiality, Integrity, and availability of information and IT security. This concept soon became very popular in the securitydomain.CIA model of security is used to measure the majority of security threats attacks and solutions in the IT and ICT.

1. **Confidentiality**: To describe the confidentiality researcher describe it as the information should be accessed by the authorized person only, and it should remain secret to those who are not permitted to receive or see it.
2. **Integrity**: Integrity refers to the completeness and correctness of the information. When a person sends and information to another person, the recipient should get the same information submitted by the sender and nothing else. There are preventive and detective measures to maintain the data integrity
3. **Availability**: Availability refers to the accessibility of the information. The information should be available to the authorized person when needed.

Cloud Threats

As CIA plays important role in security; the cloud is noexception. Cloud Computing has seen many security breaches in the past years. All the threats to Cloud Computing can be categorized into the CIA triad.

Security Levels in Cloud Computing

(Kamatchi R et al., 2016) Various levels of the system encounter multiple types of security threats. The security needs to be tightened into these levels to create a secure cloud environment for the users. These levels also can be used to develop security policies in the organization for maintaining security. The levels are as follows

1. **Physical Level:** Cloud data centers can be far away from the organization. Most of the times, the users don't even actually take a look at the data center before opting for the services. The physical security at the service provider's end becomes a questionable entity. The problems startfrom an

Figure 1. Types of threats under categories of CIA (Confidentiality, Integrity & Availability)

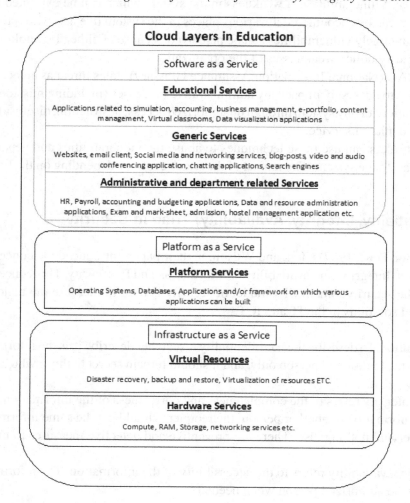

unsafe environment, no logging of guests, the weak security system of the premise, insecure USB ports, insider attacks, natural disaster damage, etc.

2. **Host/virtual Level:** Virtualization is very crucial to cloud services. It helps to create a multitenant architecture in the cloud. Virtual machine manager hence becomes a key player in the environment. Since the underlined infrastructure is the same for many users, the separation between the virtual machines, hardening of them, safety of them and also instance images and templates security becomes essential for any cloud provider.

3. **Network Level:** The essential part of the cloud according to the NIST definition, is the Internet to have universal access to the data. Hence the network becomes the backbone of the cloud environment. All users are connected to the cloud via some networks. All data communication also takes place using these networks. Therefore, security at this level becomes essential.

4. **Interface Level:** Interfaces are the doorways to the services — these need to be equally secured. An attacker can also take advantage of the insecure interfaces to enter into the system. Hence securing these interfaces becomes vital.

5. **Operating system Level:** Host machine hosts the guest machines or virtual machines. The host operating system will handle all the system level calls. It is the operating system which is directly connected to the infrastructure. Hence security breach at the operating system level becomes very crucial. If this is penetrated then complete control over the infrastructure can be lost

6. **Database Level:** CSP stores user's data in some database. As data is an asset to any organization, this becomes a significant area of threat. Data can be at risk in rest or in transit too. Encryption can be used to prevent this problem.

7. **Application Level:** Cloud users use much application as services. Any vulnerability in the application can create a door to an intruder for significant attacks. Access levels in the applications also become a key to control the user access on unauthorized data. It will also reduce intentional and unintentional data thefts.

The security threats in all above mentioned layers, their descriptions and the possible suggestions are tabulated carefully for implementation in the model.

EDUCATION CLOUD MODEL

Education System Transformation in India

(Anonymous, Population of India, 2019) India is a massive country with approximately 1.37 billion population. (Anonymous, India Today Web Desk, Budget, 2018) It ranks 124th in the literacy rate as per many surveys. (Anonymous, India Age structure, 2018) Almost 18% of the total population is between the age group of 15-24. After independence, the government steadily took steps to improve the literacy ratios in the country. (Kothari Commission, 2018) Kothari Commission or National Education Commission (1964-66) was formed to scrutinize the facets of the Indian education system and to counsel the new policies for the development of the education sector. One of the vital thing the commission mentioned about the standardization of the education at all stages ranging from primary to higher education. The major themes of the report talk about the increase in productivity, promotion of social and national integration in education, modernization, and developing social, moral, and spiritual values in students of all ages. After Kothari commission, the enrolment of the students has increased for the 10+2+3 level of education. In turn, the students willing to opt for higher education also increased.

India has seen tremendous evolution in the pedagogy of education system over the years from ancient Gurukul technique to notebook based technique. After industrial devevlopment, with the advancement in the globe, the expansion of education scope and complexity must also increase. ICT has introduced a completely new paradigm shift in the teaching, learning, and research process. Computers at a very early time changed the dimensions of it. Later in the progress, teachers and lecturers started using presentations and whiteboards. With the introduction of various new technologies like Virtual Reality, Artificial Intelligence, Cloud Computing, etc. the learning process has become very interactive and liberal.

Barriers for ICT adoption in Education

ICT technology has penetrated in almost every sector and across the globe. But the acceptance of this technology has not be seen as hundred percent. It is mandatory to address these barriers to understand the difficulties in the process.

- **Lack of Trained Teachers:** An organization which adopts ICT for the advantageous purpose should make the most of it as it is a complex technology. For that, one needs skilled personnel's. In the education sector, getting knowledgeable faculty who are mastered the subjects is itself is a hard task. If any institute implements maximum ICT technology into the organization, then to train the faculty onto the new environment is very difficult. After training them, the faculty or researcher should be able to use that technology to enhance the learning process. If he/she finds any problems in the process, people become reluctant to use the technology. Sometimes in the education field, the resistance to the change or especially resistance for the technology is seen the most. In such a scenario creating a healthy adopting atmosphere for faculty to learn new things is a tricky assignment for any organization. This resistance can be one of the factors to be blamed for low penetration of the ICT in the many sectors like education.

- **Equipment Cost:** Most of the educational institutes are associated with the University. The respective University funds those colleges. There are some institutes which are self-funded. In totality, the capital available to the colleges is meager. Funds available to the institutes are most of the time insufficient. If such institutes want to adopt ICT, it needs a considerable capital investment for it. Buying the equipment like personal computers or laptops, common application, networking, and other connecting devices, setting the infrastructure suitable for the equipment, having skilled people to troubleshoot the problems occur, etc. can be expensive. To accommodate all these things in the allotted budget becomes challenging for the institutes. Some institutes adopt the changes incrementally so that both items are achieved. It can create a shortage of equipment.

- **Unreliability of the Equipment:** All electrical and electronic equipment are very volatile and delicate. They are also highly unreliable. PCs (Personal Computer), projectors, whiteboards, LAN (Local Area Network) cables, adapters, and many more resources can crash or stop working due to many reasons. Reasons can range from low quality of the product, no proper maintenance, no updating on time, no adequate cooling in the rooms, careless handling of the resources to electricity fluctuation, and no cooling environment. With these types of damages,

Digital equipment is highly unreliable. PCs need constant upgrading and patching. These PCs can crash and not work correctly several times which adds to the cost.

- **Inconsistent Power Supply:** India is a vast country with approximately seven lakhs villages. Though the electricity distribution is almost in every village, the power cuts are too often. Some villages get minimal power supply. The uninterrupted power supply is essential to run any electronic equipment. ICT equipment not only needs a power supply to run but also to cool them. When hardware like PCs or servers work, they emit heat. These heat needs to be cooled down to maintain the working of the equipment. Hardware has to be kept in the cold environment to get the maximum benefits from them. It also affects the hardware's lifetime. The places where there is not a constant supply of electricity then those institutes can use the converters to maintain it. But it adds the operational cost for the organization.

- **Insufficient Funds:** As mentioned earlier, the educational institutes are mostly funded by the University/Government or the Trusts. The funds given for the institutes primarily cover the operational costs of it. When a new technology emerges, the absorption of it into the system becomes a costly process. To incur the price, an organization needs an excessive amount. For incorporating ICT flavors into the education system, the institute needs to change the infrastructure. It requires hardware, software, better networks and networking devices, qualified people to assemble the laboratories and other systems, people who can maintain the infrastructure, etc. It doesn't just end with buying the infrastructure (like presentation instruments- projectors, PCs in the classroom, Software which can use to view the resources simultaneously by faculty and student, etc. The maintenance of it includes monthly or yearly hardware maintenance, software updates, and patches, new networking devices according to the more modern standards. Also, it consists of the air-conditioned environment and people with updated knowledge. For such a huge cost getting the grant for the excess amount from the upper management (University/Trust) becomes a prolonged process.

After acquiring the resources, some amount must be spent on the faculty training to get the maximum benefits from the technology.

- **Lack of Technical Support:** To adapt the technology, institutes have to set an infrastructure or change the existing one according to the need. Only specialized skilled people do these tasks. Setting the hardware, installing the necessary operating systems and applications needed by the institute, maintaining the software for patches and updates is highly specialized responsibilities.

Once the infrastructure is in place, one needs to train the employees for the same. All the stakeholders should be comfortable to use the infrastructure. To train the users of different ages, the institute needs well-trained professionals. Finding good people who can teach others is very difficult.

Here Cloud Computing can be a beneficial tool to mitigate the significant problems.

Indian Higher Education Structure

Around 1780s British Government introduced University Structure in terms of Calcutta Madrasa and later Banaras Sanskrit. Then about 1957, three official Universities, i.e., Bombay (Mumbai), Calcutta (Kolkata), and Madras (Chennai) were formed. At present, there are around 821 different Universities, 40000 colleges and 12000 autonomous Institutes in India. Indian Government under HRDM (Human Resource Department Ministry) established a statutory body, namely the University Grant Commission, i.e. UGC. Depending on the type of higher education, further, fifteen statutory institutions are created. (Anonymous, 2019) AICTE (All India Council for Technical Education), BCI (Bar Council of India), NCTE (National Council for Teacher Education) to name the few. There are four major divisions in the types of universities, depending on the difference in authority and legislation. Other than Governmental departments like MHRD (Ministry of Human Resource Department), certain accreditation bodies keep hold on to various streams of Universities like NAAC, NBA, etc.

Cloud Computing in Education

Figure 2. Higher education structure in India

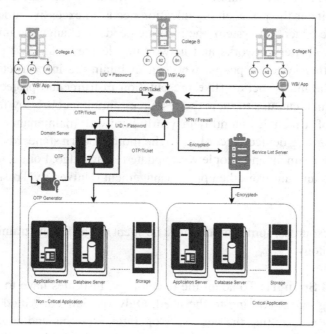

Table 1. Traditional ICT vs. cloud computing

Factors	Traditional approach	Cloud approach
Procurement	Buy infrastructure	Use the architecture as services
Financial model	Need capital investment for the architecture (CAPEX – Capital Expenditure)	Pay only for what has been used (OPEX – Operational Expenditure)
Accessibility	Need high configured PCs and intra-network to access	Can be accessed by any device (Thick/Thin client) using Internet
Resiliency	Traditional data centers are less resilient. If one server fails the recovery of it may take time which can hamper the productivity of the organization	In a cloud environment, if one server fails, then the instances are moved out and kept in a different availability zone to provide better resiliency.
Elasticity	When the organization needs more infrastructure to deal with the demand spikes, it needs to purchase the resources. Resources after peaks become overhead.	Cloud provides more excellent elasticity in terms of getting and releasing new resources as and when needed. The organization only pays for the resources used at the end of the billing cycle.
Technical structure	Single tenant. Only one organization can use the infrastructure. The number of resources should be proportionate to the number of Employees in the organization.	Multi-tenant. Many organizations can use the same infrastructure. In one organization, the number of resources needed is less than the number of employees due to multi-tenancy.
Technical assistance	Need specialized personals to create and manage the infrastructure.	The cloud service provider is entirely responsible for the creation and management of the resources and infrastructure.

Table 2. Types of resources needed in educational institutes

Resources	Description
Stakeholders	
Institute	• Optimized resources and their proper allocation • Resources available 24*7 & as and when required • Maintenance of the data centers. (In terms of power, temperature, updates, and patches of applications, etc.) • Deployment of the software and application is quicker • Lesser IT expert staff • Centralized information system and decrease in information silos across all departments
Faculty/Learner/Parent/Management/Researcher	• Study material/teaching material/data is available from anywhere, from any device and anytime which adds mobility • Applications/software used to learn/ can be available and with lesser infrastructural requirements. • Tests/quizzes/assignment submission and checking should be comfortable and can be accessed from anywhere
System Administrator	• Installation and maintenance of applications/software is reduced • Version control, system updates, system upgrades, patches work reduced • Network monitoring should be efficient and continuous
Study Material	
Notes/Test papers/presentation slides Online databases Books/e-Books Analytical Software Regular applications like an exam, attendance, HR, etc.	• Maximum availability of learning material • Application required is available as a service • Institute doesn't have to worry about the infrastructure needed for the applications • Scheduled tests, assignments, and tutorials can be made available anytime and can be submitted from anywhere • Huge and speedily data saving and sharing capacity • Platforms on which the applications can be created and taught are available as services
Technical Environment	
Infrastructure	• Multitenant architecture which provides better resource utilization and server consolidation Internet-based access from any device • Data storage is theoretically unlimited • More significant system and computing performance because the server capacity can be upgraded in minutes • The time to acquire, install, and maintain any application is reduced tremendously. • Greener environment
Financial Considerations	• Capital investment for setting up the data center will be reduced • Cost of maintenance especially power consumption and cooling of the hardware • Buying cost of licenses for the applications can be reduced and will be paid as per the usage • Cost of upgrades and patches will be reduced

Every Academic institute depending on the type of courses they conduct, need a variety of ICT resources for their day to day transactions. This is considered as a traditional ICT approach for education sector which is mentioned in previous section in detail. But since every state in India is facing some or other adoption barriers mentioned earlier in the chapter, it is challenging to become a complete ICT enabled college or university. Cloud Computing can be used as a bridge to overcome these obstacles. Cloud Computing services are the services which are hosted at a cloud service provider's end or on-premise and can be accessed from anywhere also using any device with the help of the Internet. If the traditional ICT approach with Cloud Computing approach is studied in detail, then the following distinguishing factors are found.

The study tries to accumulate various resources any higher educational institute may need for its regular working. Following table first describes the stakeholders and their needs for the ICT resources. Then it elaborates on the educational material in terms of ICT needed for the stakeholders like teachers, students, etc. In the last part of the table, it explains the technical and financial environment for the educational organizations. The table gives a generalize perspective for the University to understand the requirement of resources college wise. It can help it to understand the overall necessity of the resources. The resources are as follows.

Cloud Service Requirements in Education

Education sector requires many ICT services as mentioned above. All the services can be taken as cloud services. Following figure (Figure 3) describes all the services needed for the educational institutes. This figure also bifurcate the services into Software-as-a-Service, Platform-as-a-Service, Infrastructure-as-a-Service.

Figure 3. Cloud service requirements in the education sector

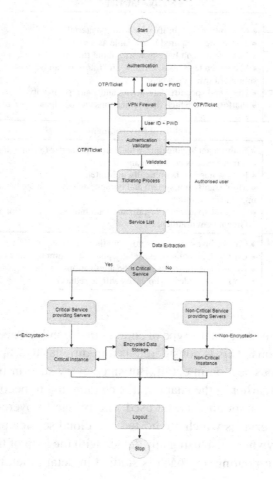

Security Requirements in Cloud Computing for Education sector

Education sector generates a moderate amount of data every year. Data is a very sensitive and vital asset for any organization. There are various aspects of security which remain essential in the education sector when using cloud services. They are as follows:

1. **Identification/ Identity Management:** Identity management is a system of managing identities and authentication and authorizing users in the organization depending on the user's role in the organization. . Identity management is crucial for accessing every resource in the system. Resources include applications, hardware, files, networks, etc. to name a few. The process of the identification makes sure the authorized user is accessing and authenticating resources

2. **Authentication:** Any system should identify the user before entering into the system using some mechanisms like a password, PIN, multifactor authentication, single-sign-on (SSO), biometrics etc. Cloud systems use multitenancy architecture. It infers that multiple users can access a single instance at the same time. According to the user's role, the user can see the application and its parts. For this matter, it becomes imperative to have a proper authenticity mechanism in place to bifurcate the profiles and views appropriately. For example, in the education sector, a teacher should not be able to sign in as an admin of the accounts department.

3. **Authorization:** Theoretically, the cloud environment has unlimited resources. Not all resources are for every stakeholders/user. Every user has some roles and depending on the role, administrator, or cloud service provider can grant the permissions for the resources. A security mechanism which can handle the privileges of each user and can give the access accordingly is called an authorization mechanism.

4. **Access Control:** Authentication and authorization help to create access control in any ICT environment. Access control is the mechanism which is used to enforce the authorization on the users. There are two types of access control; physical and logical. Physical represents the limit controls for physical resources like building, datacentres, finance office, etc. Logical access control represents control over the ICT related resources like data, files, networks, etc.

5. **Asset Management and Control:** Cloud system has numerous assets which are accessed by multiple users simultaneously. On top of it, the Cloud system places the assets in multiple places. The asset location can be many too. It is very significant to understand the total number of assets, used assets, and free assets at any particular time and a specific place.

6. **Privacy:** Data privacy in the education sector is essential. There are many quadrants where privacy of data becomes a vital part like student's data and their marks records, Faculty payments records, institutes financial records, researches done by faculty, etc. Proper virtual machine isolation and segregation can provide privacy.

7. **Data Encryption:** Data is a core element to protect from the intruder in any sector. Here data can be encrypted at rest as well as in transit. It would maintain the privacy, confidentiality, and integrity of the data.

8. **Firewall and Private Network:** The network in which the data and services reside is very significant. So the security of it is equally important. CSP should configure the firewall with proper security conditions. Cloud structure should have such a configuration which will allow only particular IP addresses and block others. It will provide better security.

INTEGRATED CLOUD SECURITY MODEL

Integrated Cloud Security Model is a model developed to address the ICT and security issues hampering Higher Educational Sector of India. The overall ICT requirements of this sector are almost the same. When colleges buy their infrastructure and other ICT resources, it increases the cost enormously. If a University acquires the cloud resources and then distributes them among the affiliated colleges, then due to economies of scale the expense to the colleges reduces. Then the colleges associated with the University can pay-as-per-use basis to the University. Using this model, the University can implement cloud infrastructure, and college can use the abundant resources supplied by the University at a minimal amount.

Proposed Model

Figure 4. Integrated cloud security model

Working Principle

The Integrated Cloud Security model works as follows:

Figure 5. Flowchart for the integrated cloud security model

A University will host the complete infrastructure as a Community Cloud. The associated colleges will be able to use the resources. Any user or stakeholder can access cloud services using login credentials.

A user will log in using the Login ID and the password. The system uses the secured protocol for whole communication. The credentials will be passed through the VPN (Virtual Private Network) Firewall at the University and sent to the Domain Server. It will authenticate the user. If the user Id and password matches, the OTP (One Time Password) Generator is activated, and the system generates an OTP or a ticket.

The System sends this OTP/Ticket to the User via the same secured channel. The User again enters the OTP/Ticket, and then the Domain server will authorize the user.

Once the system authenticates the user, the user will see the list of resources he/she is authorized to access.

All the resources are categorized into two types depending on the User Role – Critical and non-critical. If the user wishes to access the critical application, then the complete transaction is encrypted. As soon as the user requests any resource, the system creates an encrypted instance. The data is encrypted in the transit too. If the resource is non-critical, then the overhead of encryption is reduced, which gives faster access, and the typical instance is created.

The data which is at rest or in storage is by default encrypted to provide better security. Whether a user is accessing the critical or non-critical instance, the data obtained by the instances will always be encrypted.

After completion of the task, the user logs off the system.

Implementation Feasibility

The model is implemented using OpenStack as base software. OpenStack is an open-source and free software platform which allows developers to create cloud infrastructure, especially Infrastructure as a service. Rackspace Hosting and NASA founded OpenStack in 2010. Recently from 2016 onwards OpenStack Foundation, which is a non-profit organization, is now managing the software platform. The advancement in the said software is ongoing, and developers across the Globe are helping and collaborating to make OpenStack more secure and robust. As of now, more than 500 companies from all around are participating in the enhancement. Following is the architecture of the OpenStack (Openstack)

Table 3. Components with their function

Name	Function
Horizon	Dashboard
Nova	Compute
Neutron	Networking
Heat	Orchestration
Swift	Object Storage
Cinder	Block Storage
Keystone	Identity Storage
Glance	Image Service
Trove	Database Server

The components are as follows:

- Hardware requirement for the project:
  - For Production architecture, the following hardware is required
    - Core Components[97]
- Controller node: 1-2 CPU, 8 GB RAM, 100 GB Storage, 2 NIC (Network Interface Card)
- Compute node: 2-4+ CPU, 8+ GB RAM, 100+ GB Storage, 2 NIC (Network Interface Card)
  - Optional Components[98]
- Block storage node: 1-2 CPU, 4 GB RAM, 100+ GB Storage, 1 NIC (Network Interface Card)
- Object storage node: 1-2 CPU, 4+ GB RAM, 100+ GB Storage, 1 NIC (Network Interface Card)
  - For Proof-of-concept environment the following hardware is required
    - Controller node: 1 CPU, 4BG RAM, 5 GB storage
    - Compute node: 1CPU, 2GB RAM, 10GB storage

Security Implementation in the Model

The model is made secured using step by step security on various levels mentioned in chapter 4. The security levels are analyzed for security problems and found the solution concerning OpenStack. Following implementations are done in the model to make it a secured cloud for the education sector

1. **Physical Level:** It is assumed that physical security at the University data center is up-to-date. The university data center has high configuration CCTV cameras. CSP monitor the surveillance diligently. The security log must contain the information of the personals coming and going from data centers. The physical checking of people is done before entering the building for devices like flash drives, cameras, explosives, magnetic material, laptops, eatables, etc. The hardware should be well numbered and checked regularly for theft. The USB ports should be disabled. The anti-virus applications should be well updated and running on all devices. Backup servers should be maintained on a different location to maintain availability as a disaster recovery server. CSP should insure the data centers for the natural calamities. The power generators should be capable enough to support the availability of the resources in the power failure situation

2. Virtual or Host Level

   a. **Virtualization hardening:** It is imperative to harden the virtual level for any types of mischievous activity to secure the virtual level in the model. Virtualization hardening is done as follows

   The virtual driver is a software layer that provides an interface to the virtual machine. QEMU is the hypervisor used and hardens in the model with the following three steps

   i. Code base minimization

   In this, only useful components from the glance, images are kept, and others are disabled

```
$ glance image-update \
--property hw_disk_bus=ide \
--property hw_cdrom_bus=ide \
--property hw_vif_model=e1000 \
f16-x86_64-openstack-sda
```

ii.   MAC (Mandatory Access Control)

It can be seen as a disaster limiting option. If even after code base minimization and some part of compiler hardening, the attacker gets in the system then MAC can help to minimize the damage. It is done using sVirt.

svirt_image_t uniquely identifies the image file of VM. We can uniquely identify according to role, group, user, project and domain based.

b.   **VM isolation:** VM isolation can be done using strict firewall rules and security groups so that VMs cannot have unauthorized communication or interference. Such as follows

```
openstack security group rule create --remote-ip Server_IP
```

This security group will only allow VMs to talk to the server but not to other VMs.

c.   PCI passthrough: PCI Passthrough allows an instance to full access to any PCI hardware resource in the guest VM. PCI passthrough gives enabling the policy. The VM can access the resources which are enabled only.

d.   VNC security Virtual Network Computer is used to give a remote console for desktop access to the guest. This access should be secured using TLS. While configuring the OpenStack cloud infrastructure, the following property is given

```
vnc_port=5900
vnc_port_portal=1000
ssl_only=true
novncproxy_base_url= http://192.168.0.222:6080/vnc_auto.html
vncserver_llsten=192.168.0.222
vncserver_proxyclient_address=192.168.0.222
xvpvncproxy_base_url=http:/1192.168.0.222:6081/console
```

e.   Secure communication between components: All the components in the OpenStack should communicate with each other securely with SSL. Majorly the communication between Nova and Glance should be made secure

f.   Glance image signing: The system uses the image from the Glance while creating a VM. One should validate the images kept in the Glance for security using digital certificate and cryptography.

```
$ glance image-create
--name college#1
--container-format bare
--disk-format qcow2
--property lmg_signature="$college#1_signature"
--property lmg_signature_certificate_uuld="$cert_uuid"
```

```
--property lmg_signature_hash_method='SHA-256'
--property lmg_signature_key_type='RSA-PSS'<college#1image
```

3. Network Level

a. IDS/IPS: To prevent the network from any incidents or if any incident happens then to identify the problem security onion is used as an extension with OpenStack as following

```
kvm -m 4096 \
-drive f ile=./so_test.raw,if=virtio,format=raw \
-drive
file=/home/user/so_create/securityonion-16.04.4.2.iso,media=cdrom,
index= 1\
-net nic,model=virtio \
-net user\
-show-cursor
GRUB_CMOLINE_LINUX_OEFAULT="console=ttySO"
$virt-sparsify --convert qcow2 --compress College#1
_HRMS_Portal.raw College# _HRMS_Portal_CLOUD.qcow2 --tmp .
```

b. Authentication and authorization mechanism: The model uses V3 identity plugin. Following methods are used to create all the user's names and the passwords in the system.

```
>>>from keystoneauthl import session
>>>from keystoneauthl.identity import v3
>>>password = v3.PasswordMethod(username ='Collegel_IT_Admin1', ...
password='pass@123',
...user_domain_name='default')
>>>auth = v3.Auth(auth_url='http://192.168.0.222:SOOO/v3',
...auth_methods=[password],
...project_id='College#1')
>>>sess = session.Session(auth=auth)
```

For authorization purpose, the model contains various projects, roles and security groups to create different access control list

c. Virtual Private Network and IPSec: The communication happening between the networks should be secured to stop the eavesdropping. The best way to do that is to build a Virtual private network. Also, the IPSec protocol is defined and enabled for more security purpose. The protocol should have a policy which is determined by some set of rules

d. Multifactor Authentication: To enable multifactor authentication, the model used a plugin called python based OTP library. It uses the following code in the keystone.

```
"{ "auth": {
   "identity":{
```

```
"methods": ["password", "OTP"],
"password":{
"user":{
"name": "admin"
"domain":{"id":"default"},
"password":"adminpwd"
    }
    },
"OTP":{
"otp_value":"342342343"
    }
}}}'
```

e. Filtering Options: To prevent BGP hijacking, the nova.conf file is changed. In that, following changes are made

```
hash_algorithms = md5 and expiration_time = 600
```

f. ARP Spoofing Prevention: To prevent an address resolution protocol from being targeted for the attack, the reusability of IP address should be prevented. That can be done in the /etc/neutron/plugins/ml2/openvswitch_agent.ini file as follows.

```
prevent_arp_spoofing = True
```

g. Certificate Validation on HTTPS Connections: While making HTTPS connections, certificate validation becomes important to prevent attacks like man-in-the-middle. It is as follows

```
import requests
requests.get('https://www.openstack.org/', verify=CONF.ca_file)
it's a CA trust store which stores certificates coming from trusted authori-
ties
```

4. **Operating System Level:** The operating system in the host and guests plays a critical role concerning the security of the model. Any loose end in the OS can lead to various types of attacks. Research assumes that the Operating system images used in the model for both host and guests are authentic. This OS has heuristic termination analysis as the part in them to defend attacks like exploitation etc. CSP should regularly update the OS copies with the latest upgrades and patches.

   a. OS Hardening: The model uses an ansible-galaxy plugin for Operating system hardening.

   b. Bash History: Whatever commands user fires in the guest operating system will reside in the bash history. An attacker can use the confidential data like IP addresses etc. to create an attack. Bash history should be regularly deleted to maintain the security

5. Data Level: At the data, level to secure the data first and the important thing is data encryption at rest. Swift component in the OpenStack optionally provides object data encryption at data rest. That is performed as follows in the model

```
[filter:keymaster]
use = egg:sqift#keymaster
encryption_root_secret = your_secret --------- openssl rand -base64 32
keymaster_config_path = etc/swift/keymaster.conf
[filter:encryption]
use = egg:swift#encryption
#disable_encryption = False
encryption_root_secret_<secret_id> = <secret value> ---------- A seperate key-
master.config file
```

Generally, the keymaster and data are kept on different servers to maintain the security of keys. The keys data should also be kept encrypted.

6. Application Level: Application level security is paramount because the users are going to use the applications or services extensively. The applications should be well developed and should be authentic versions. The developer of the application should not use hidden fields and query string to manage the state. Instead, session variables should be applied. Some more measures can be as follows
    c. Validating user input
    d. Preparing proper SQL queries
    e. Cookies disabling
    f. Disabling debugging options

ANALYSIS AND RESULTS

A General Overview of the System

The study performs the implementation of the cloud using OpenStack, and the results are as follows. Figure 6 represents the Login Screen for the users. The login screen remains the same for every stakeholder in the system. Figure 7 shows the general dashboard structure shown to the users. The left-hand side panel shows all the possible activities the user is authorized to perform. The right-hand side shows the complete health of the instance in which the user is present. Figure 8 represents the network topology created for the said scenario in the last chapter.

Figure 6. Login screen for user

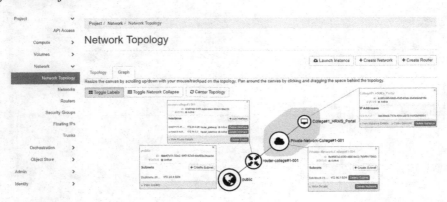

Figure 7. General dashboard structure

Figure 8. The network topology

Identity Module in the Model with Use Cases

1. University Admin
   a. Dashboard
      i. **Projects**: A project is a construct which can possess a virtual machine, container, etc. depending on the type of component. Each project can have multiple users with different roles. A University IT Administrator can view, create, edit, and delete the projects needed for the colleges.

Figure 9. Projects in the model

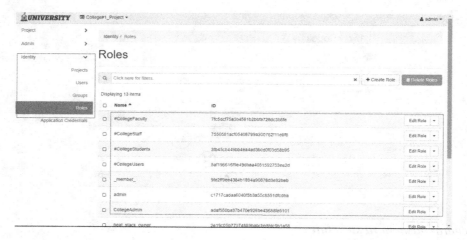

ii. **Users:** A user is an entity which is associated with one or more projects have specific roles with particular security policy. It is used in authentication and authorization. University admin can create, edit, delete, and manage the users from the dashboard.

Figure 10. Users in the model

iii. **Roles:** One user can have multiple roles in multiple projects. Roles restrict the user and can implement access control mechanism in the cloud environment. One user can have various roles in numerous projects. Roles restrict the user and can implement access control mechanism in the cloud environment.

Figure 11. Roles in the model

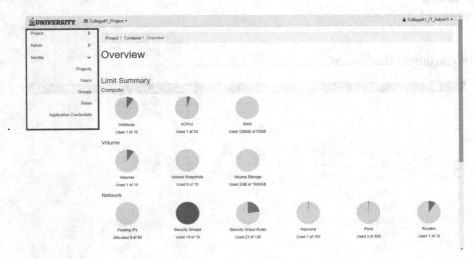

iv. **Groups:** Groups or security groups act as a security constraint for the users. It creates an access control list. OpenStack considers it as a virtual firewall where one can restrict access. OpenStack implements Group-based security policy

Figure 12. Security groups in the model

2. **College Admin**
   a.   Dashboard

Figure 13. College admin dashboard

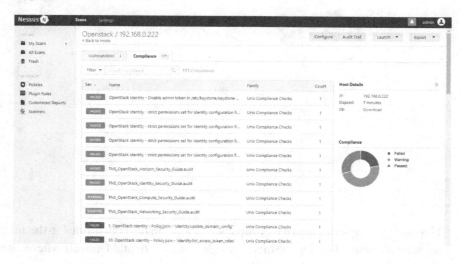

3. **Faculty/Teacher**
   a.   Dashboard

Figure 14. Instances have shown to faculty

Vulnerability Assessment

For the validation and analysis purpose, the research uses a tool called Nessus vulnerability scanner 7.2. (Nessus) The tool is very well designed and developed, especially for cloud vulnerability analysis. The Nessus team works with various technical partners like AWS, CSA, RedHat, Dell, etc. to remain up-to-date in the cybersecurity ecosystem.

The tool has predefined templates for scans like primary network, audit cloud infrastructure, malware scan to name few. Nessus scan generates detailed reports. The reports are easy to understand and in the executive summary format. The summary shows the security problem level, common vulnerability scoring system, a plugin which shows vulnerability and the description.

Results

1. **OpenStack Cloud Infrastructure:** As an analysis, first a complete cloud infrastructure scan specifically for OpenStack clouds is performed. The result is as follows

Figure 15. Vulnerability scan analysis report for OpenStack cloud model

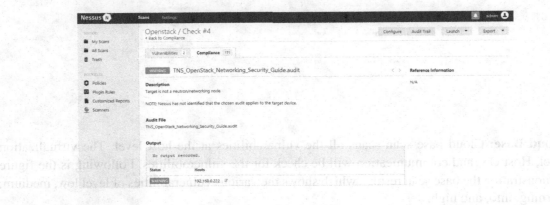

According to the above report, the model passes the majority of the vulnerability tests. Very few are warnings and some tests are failed. The following figure illustrates the description of one of the passed test and the details about it.

Figure 16. A Passed test of OpenStack cloud test

Following is the figure which shows the description of one of the Warnings

Figure 17. Warning description of OpenStack cloud test

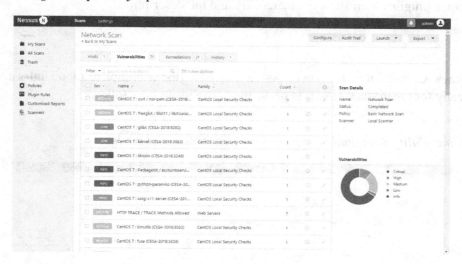

2. **Cloud Base:** Cloud base scan scans all the vulnerabilities at the host level. The virtualization level, Host OS, and communication will be check for the vulnerabilities. Following is the figure demonstrating the base scan results, which shows the various vulnerabilities of level low, medium, warning, info, and high.

Figure 18. Cloud base scan results

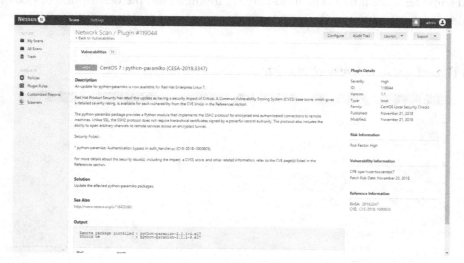

3. **Network Scan:** Network scan identifies vulnerabilities in the network. It also describes various types of vulnerabilities with the explanation as below

Figure 19. Network scan vulnerability result

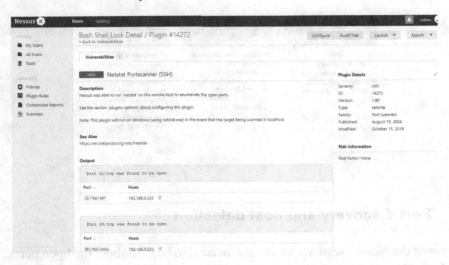

If one tries to discover the high severity vulnerability in network scan then one will realize that it is a problem of a part called Paramiko. Paramiko is an SSHv2 protocol implementation using python. The new update available in the RedHat Enterprise Linux 7 can easily solve the problem.

Figure 20. Demonstrating High severity vulnerability description

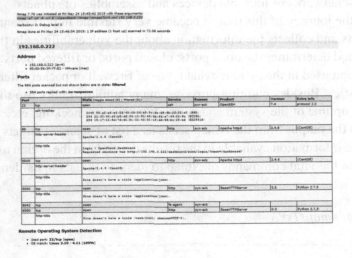

The network scan also provides remediation with the vulnerabilities.

4. **Bash Shell Scan**: Bash shell is a command and text-based shell. This stores all the commands executed by the user. The stored commands can be very harmful if it falls into the wrong hand. Following is the scan for bash shell. The detailed description of the information given in the scan is as follows

Figure 21. Bash shell scan description

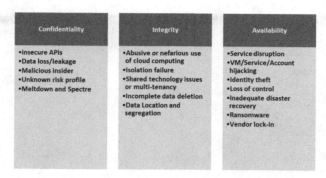

Analysis 2 _ Port discovery and host detection

After completion of the Nessus scan, the study also needed to be sure about the open ports. The research considers the threats Nessus identified scans thoroughly. (nmap) The ports identified by the above scans were scrutinized by this step carefully. For the Port discovery and host detection analysis, the study uses Nmap as a tool.

Nmap is a Network Mapper. The research uses a tool for vulnerability scanning and network discovery. It is also used for network exploration and security auditing. Security experts and network administrators widely use this tool. It is used to detect which devices are running on the systems, which ports are open, which hosts are available, what services they offer, and mainly identifies the security risks. Nmap is used to monitor vast networks of multiple devices and assemblies of subnets.

Over the years of the journey of this tool, it became very flexible in port scanning. It sends the raw packets to system ports and collects the information about the vulnerabilities in the system. It then listens to the responses and determines the open ports, closed ports, or filtered ports. It also checks for the operating system version used in the system, what types of firewall or packet filters are used, and many more such characteristics. Besides auditing purpose, many administrators use this tool for managing upgrades, monitoring uptime of the system and network inventory checking, etc.

The study presents the output from the Nmap scans as a list of scanned targets with necessary additional information. The information available in the results depends on the option used in the commands. The study uses some of the vital commands of Nmap to identify threats to harden the system.

Figure 22. Nmap script nmapsTsVA

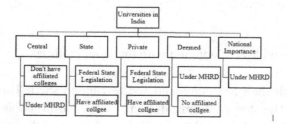

(nmap scripts) Following are the screenshots from the Nmap tool:

```
Command Use: nmap -sT -sV -A -oX E:\OpenStack\Nmap\nmapsTsVA.xml 192.168.0.222
```
Description: Nmap generates output with this command on the host target, i.e., 192.168.0.222 on a specified XML file. Different Scan techniques have been used as below.

Table 4. Parameters used for nmapsTsVA

Sr. No	Command	Method	Description
1	-sT	Scan Techniques	Connect scan
2.	-sV	Service Version Detection	Probe open ports to check service/version info
3.	-A	MiscNmap Options	Enable OS detection, version discovery, script scanning, and traceroute
4.	-oX	Nmap Output Options	Output to XML

- **Command Use: nmap -sT -sV -p22 --script=ssh2-enum-algos -oX E:\OpenStack\Nmap\ nmapsTsVp22scriptssh2enumalgos.xml 192.168.0.222**

Description: In this command Host Target is 192.168.0.222 where the Output file will be generated on a specified XML file. Different Scan techniques have been used as below.

Table 5. Parameters used for nmapsTsVp22scriptssh2enumalgos

Sr. No	Command	Method	Description
1	-sT	Scan Techniques	Connect scan
2.	-sV	Service Version Detection	Probe open ports to control service/version information
3.	-p22	Port Specification and Scan Order	Specify ports, e.g. -p80,443,22 or -p1-65535
4.	-script=ssh2-enum-algos	Script Scan	This command parameter tells the exact number of algorithms that are used in the system or cloud and will also give the type of the algorithms, i.e., which are weak and which are strong. If the client to server and vice versa are typical, then it will give the combined results to the user.
5.	-oX	Nmap Output Options	Output to XML

- **Command Use: nmap -sT -sV -p443 --script=ssl* -oX E:\OpenStack\Nmap\nmapsTsVp-443scriptssl.xml 192.168.0.222**

Description: In this command Host Target is 192.168.0.222 where the Output file will be generated on a specified XML file. Different Scan techniques have been used as below.

Table 6. Parameters used for nmapsTsVp443scriptssl command

Sr. No	Command	Method	Description
1	-sT	Scan Techniques	Connect scan
2.	-sV	Service Version Detection	Probe open ports to control service/version information
3.	-p22	Port Specification and Scan Order	Identify ports, e.g. 1 to 5000, 3389
4.	--script=ssl*	Script Scan	This script will initiate the SSLv3/TSL connection and presents all the cipher suits that the server accepts along with that it will also show some other details which are as mentioned below. 1) SSL certificate expiry, i.e., when the certificate is going to expire. 2) Weak cipher suite which is in the server 3) whether it is affected by Diffiehellman or poodle attack. 4) SSL drown attack is present or not 5) weak hashing algorithms like RC4
5.	-oX	Nmap Output Options	Output to XML

- Command Use: **nmap -sT -sV -p445 --script=smb-security-mode -oX E:\OpenStack\Nmap\ nmapsTsVp445scriptsmbsecuritymode.xml 192.168.0.222**

Description: In this command Host Target is 192.168.0.222 where the Output file will be generated on a specified XML file. Different Scan techniques have been used as below.

Table 7. Parameters used for nmapsTsVp445scriptsmbsecuritymode command

Sr. No	Command	Method	Description
1	-sT	Scan Techniques	Connect scan
2.	-sV	Service Version Detection	Examine open ports to check service/version information
3.	-p22	Port Specification and Scan Order	Identify ports, e.g., 3389, 1 to 5000
4.	--script=smb-security-mode	Script Scan	User-level authentication Share-level authentication Message signing
5.	-oX	Nmap Output Options	Output provided to the XML file

- Command Use: **nmap -sT -sV -p1433 --script=ssl* -oX E:\OpenStack\Nmap\nmapsTsVp-1433scriptssl.xml 192.168.0.222**

Description: In this command Host Target is 192.168.0.222 where the Output file will be generated on a specified XML file. Different Scan techniques have been used as below.

Table 8. Parameters used for nmapsTsVp1433scriptssl

Sr. No	Command	Method	Description
1	-sT	Scan Techniques	Connect scan
2.	-sV	Service Version Detection	Probe open ports to determine service/version info
3.	-p22	Port Specification and Scan Order	Identify ports like1 to 5000 ports
4.	--script=ssl*	Script Scan	Same As Fig 3.
5.	-oX	Nmap Output Options	Output to XML

- **Command Use: nmap -sT -sV -p3389 --script=rdp* -oX E:\OpenStack\Nmap\nmapsTsVp-3389scriptrdp.xml 192.168.0.222**

Description: In this command Host Target is 192.168.0.222 where the Output file will be generated on a specified XML file. Different Scan techniques have been used as below.

Table 9. parameters used nmapsTsVp3389scriptrdp

Sr. No	Command	Method	Description
1	-sT	Scan Techniques	Connect scan
2.	-sV	Service Version Detection	Probe open ports to determine service/version info
3.	-p22	Port Specification and Scan Order	Specify ports, e.g. -p80,443,22 or -p1-65535
4.	--script=rdp*	Script Scan	Determines which The RDP service supports security layer and Encryption level. It does so by cycling through all existing protocols and ciphers. When run in debug mode, the script also returns the protocols and ciphers that fail and any errors that were reported.
5.	-oX	Nmap Output Options	Output to XML

- **Command Use: nmap -sT -sV -p1-65535 -oX E:\OpenStack\Nmap\nmapsTsVp165535.xml 192.168.0.222**

Description: In this command Host Target is 192.168.0.222 where the Output file will be generated on a specified XML file. Different Scan techniques have been used as below.

Table 10. Parameters used for nmapsTsVp165535

Sr. No	Command	Method	Description
1	-sT	Scan Techniques	Connect scan
2.	-sV	Service Version Detection	Probe open ports to determine service/version info
3.	-p1-65535	Port Specification and Scan Order	Specify ports, like 1 to 5000
4.	-oX	Nmap Output Options	Output of an XML file options

OBSERVATIONS

The above analysis and results show the success in the implementation of Secured Cloud Model in Educational sector of India using OpenStack software platform. The model shows various levels of security in different scenarios. The model gives secured access for the academicians from India to different ICT resources. This model can provide flexibility to the educational community for better infrastructure and quality learning. The cost of the infrastructure, platform, and software are divided by cloud economics in the said scenario between different colleges under a University.

CONCLUSION

As a Conclusion, this study presents the modelling of an integrated cloud security system for the higher education sector of India. The chapter first establishes the necessary of a unified secured cloud model for the higher education sector of the India. Then it provides the review of the existing literature of the said topic. Then the chapter provides the structure and ICT need for the higher education sector of India. It also states the security issues in the cloud environment. Chapter provides a distinguished security levels which should be provided in any cloud environment. It lists all the threats and associated solution level wise. It then illustrates a model which then was developed using OpenStack platform. Then it provided the level wise security. It tested using Nessus 5.0 and nMap.

The Model can revolutionaries the ICT sector in higher education sector in India since it provides a secured cloud environment which in turn provides theoretically unlimited ICT resources to any college to associated University.

FUTURE WORK

The study focuses only on cloud services and the security of them in the higher education sector of India. This study exclusively focuses on the higher education sector of India since the educational structure in the said environment is different from other countries. The same research can be tested in other countries using their educational paradigm or structure. Similar work can be done for other communities like finance or healthcare.

The model is implemented as a proof of concept and not on the production scenario. The model was tested using the use cases. Also, the vulnerabilities in the implemented model were checked using tools.

REFERENCES

Buyya, R., & Yeoa, C. S. (2008). *Cloud Computing, and emerging IT platforms: Vision, hype, and reality for delivering computing as the 5th utility.* Elsevier B.V. doi:10.1016/j.future.2008.12.001

Clark, D. D., & Wilson, D. R. (1987). A comparison of commercial and military computer security policies. *Security and Privacy, IEEE Symposium on*, 184–194. 10.1109/SP.1987.10001

Fogel, R. (2010). *White Paper, The Education Cloud: Delivering Education as a Service.* Intel World Ahead.

Garfinkel, S. (2011, Oct. 3). The Cloud Imperative. *MIT Technology Review.* https://www.technology-review.com/s/425623/the-cloud-imperative/

Gartner. (2018). *Gartner Forecasts India Public Cloud Revenue to Grow 37.5 Percent in 2018.* https://www.gartner.com/newsroom/id/3874299

Higher education in India. (n.d.). https://en.wikipedia.org/wiki/Higher_education_in_India

India, T. W. D. (2018). *Budget 2018: Education sector analysis.* https://www.indiatoday.in/education-today/news/story/budget-2018-education-sector-analysis-1172823-2018-02-19

India Age structure. (2018). In *CIA World Factbook.* https://www.indexmundi.com/india/age_structure.html

Kamatchi, Ambekar, & Parikh. (n.d.). Security mapping of a usage based cloud system. *Network Protocols and Algorithms.*

Kothari Commission. (n.d.).https://en.wikipedia.org/wiki/Kothari_Commission

Martin, R. (n.d.). *Japan is Best Prepared to Capitalize on Cloud Computing.* https://www.techinasia.com/japan-cloud-cloud-computing#fnref:1

Martucci, L. A., Zuccatoy, A., & Ben Smeetsk, S. M. (2012). Privacy, Security and Trust in Cloud Computing The Perspective of the Telecommunication Industry. *9th International Conference on Ubiquitous Intelligence and Computing and 9th International Conference on Autonomic and Trusted Computing.* DOI 10.1109/UIC-ATC.2012.166

Mell, P., & Grance, T. (2011). *The NIST Definition of Cloud Computing: Recommendations of the National Institute of Standards and Technology.* https://csrc.nist.gov/publications/nistpubs/800-145/SP800-145.pdf

Nessus. (n.d.). https://www.tenable.com/blog/nessus-50-released

Nmap. (n.d.). https://nmap.org/

Nmap scripts. (n.d.). https://nmap.org/nsedoc/scripts/

Open University. (n.d.).https://en.wikipedia.org/wiki/Open_University

Openstack. (n.d.). https://www.openstack.org/

Population of India 2019. (2019). *India Population 2019, Most Populated States.* http://www.indiapopulation2019.in/

Sclater. (2010). Cloud Computing in Education. UNESCO Institute for Information Technologies in Education.

Suna, Changb, & Suna, & Wanga. (2011). Surveying, and Analyzing Security, Privacy and Trust Issues in Cloud Computing Environments. *Procedia Engineering, 15*. doi:10.1016/j.proeng.2011.08.537

University Grants Commission (India). (n.d.). https://en.wikipedia.org/wiki/University_Grants_Commission

Weins, K., & Trends, C. C. (2017). *State of the Cloud Survey*. https://www.rightscale.com/blog/cloud-industry-insights/cloud-computing-trends-2017-state-cloud-survey

Chapter 5
A Cloud Platform for Sharing Educational Digital Fabrication Resources Over the Internet

Gianluca Cornetta

(iD) https://orcid.org/0000-0001-8614-079X

Universidad San Pablo-CEU, Spain

Abdellah Touhafi

Vrije Universiteit Brussel, Belgium

Gabriel-Miro Muntean

(iD) https://orcid.org/0000-0002-9332-4770

Dublin City University, Ireland

ABSTRACT

Cloud and IoT technologies have the potential to enable a plethora of new applications that are not strictly limited to remote sensing, data collection, and data analysis. In such a context, the IoT paradigm can be seen as an empowering technology rather than a disruptive one since it has the capability to improve the standard business processes by fostering more efficient and sustainable implementations and by reducing the running costs. Cloud and IoT technologies can be applied in a broad range of contexts including entertainment, industry, and education, among others. This chapter presents part of the outputs of the NEWTON H2020 European project on technology-enhanced learning; more specifically, it introduces the concept of fabrication as a service in the context of educational digital fabrication laboratories. Fab Labs can leverage cloud and IoT technologies to enable resource sharing and provide remote access to distributed expensive fabrication resources over the internet. Both platform architecture and impact on learning experience of STEM subjects are presented in detail.

DOI: 10.4018/978-1-7998-3817-3.ch005

Copyright © 2020, IGI Global. Copying or distributing in print or electronic forms without written permission of IGI Global is prohibited.

INTRODUCTION

Formal education, vocational training and lifelong learning play an increasingly important role in society.

These are seen not only as means to providing benefits in terms of enabling future economic development, but also as a way to offer people support for acquiring new skills and knowledge, and to foster personal and professional development. At any moment, worldwide, millions of citizens of all ages benefit from diverse forms of education. This education is mostly *formal* (i.e. in schools, universities), but also *non-formal* (i.e. outside the education system) and *informal* (i.e. individuals are responsible for their education). However, regardless of education type, the interest in pursuing a scientific education is experiencing a negative trend among the younger generations of most developed countries (Murray, 2016). For instance, in Europe alone, the proportion of graduates specializing in science, technology (e.g. computing), engineering and mathematics (STEM) has reduced from 12% to 9% since 2000 and consequently Europe is facing a concrete shortage of scientists (Convert, 2005).

The disengagement starts during secondary education and it is mainly due to two factors:

1. Students perceive scientific subjects as difficult, and
2. they regard science-related careers as little attractive in terms of job quality-pay level balance.

Many efforts are put worldwide trying to reverse this process, including part of large European Union projects such as NEWTON[1]. The goal of the NEWTON project is avoiding early student dropout from the scientific stream; for this reason it is mainly targeted to primary and secondary school students. NEWTON aims at developing student-centered non-formal (i.e. outside the education system) and informal (i.e. based on self-learning) teaching methodologies that leverage the latest innovative technologies to deliver more effectively learning content and make STEM subjects more appealing. In such a context, Fab Labs have been proven to be an innovative and effective teaching tool to attract students to STEM subjects (Gershenfeld, 2012; Blikstein, 2013; Togou, 2019).

A Fab Lab is a novel laboratory concept developed at the Massachusetts Institute of Technology (MIT); it is a small-scale workshop with a set of flexible computer-controlled tools and machines such as 3D printers, laser cutters, CNC (computer numerically controlled) machines, printed circuit board millers and other basic fabrication tools which, usually, are not easily accessible. Fab Lab technology enables the implementation of student-centric teaching and learning techniques based on experimentation and "learning by doing". This is why a Fab Lab attracts students as they can experiment and materialize their ideas in engaging and stimulating ways. Unfortunately, a major limitation of current Fab Labs is their lack of external connectivity and infrastructure flexibility, requiring constant human supervision. Additionally, the costs necessary to deploy a minimum Fab Lab infrastructure compliant with the MIT specifications can be as high as $250,000 and not all the institutions (especially primary and secondary schools) can afford such a huge expense. This is indeed a great barrier to the worldwide diffusion of Fab Labs. In order to overcome this shortcoming, we propose a cloud-based framework that can enable academic institutions which cannot afford to setup their own Fab Labs, to access existing Fab Labs (i.e. Fab Labs deployed in different locations worldwide) through the Internet. We have called this new concept Fabrication as a Service (FaaS). The ubiquitous access provided by the FaaS infrastructure is a necessary evolution of the Fab Lab concept and is necessary to foster the adoption at a larger scale of digital fabrication and experimentation through prototyping as an integral part of the twenty-first-century teaching and learning paradigm. Moreover, FaaS democratises access to Fab Labs by making them available over the Internet. By doing so, academic institutions will not be pressured to invest in expensive equipment to enable their students to benefit from digital fabrication technology.

This chapter provides a thorough review of the FaaS concept and its underlying technologies. The software and hardware architecture and design tradeoffs are extensively analyzed and discussed. The resulting cloud platform has been deployed and stressed in several pilot tests in order to assess both the system performance and the impact of the new technology on the learning outcomes. Experimental data with the system performance as well as detailed statistics targeting user satisfaction are reported, discussed and analyzed in-depth and used as the starting point to propose possible future improvements. Hence, FaaS technology is very complex and embraces several technical and non-technical fields. This chapter offers a comprehensive perspective of the problem by addressing in detail all the aspects of this technology and all the design issues related to the development of the NEWTON Fab Lab platform.

BACKGROUND

The Fab Lab concept is gaining worldwide interest and both governments and the population are starting to recognize the importance of digital fabrication technologies even as early as primary and secondary level education (UK Department for Education, 2013; EU project: FABLAB SCHOOLS EU, 2016-2018; EU project NEWTON, 2016-2019). A direct consequence is that the number of Fab Labs is continuously increasing and to date, there exists a worldwide network of more than 1,750 Fab Labs located in more than 100 countries, which are coordinated by the Fab Lab Foundation[2].

Surprisingly, all the research efforts put to date in the digital fabrication area have been aimed at demonstrating the effectiveness of Fab Labs in education (Martin et al., 2014) and at incorporating digital fabrication in study curricula (Gul & Simisic, 2014; Padfield et al., 2014; Tesconi & Arias, 2014). However, to the best of authors' knowledge, no attempt has been made to address the challenges faced by enhancing the Fab Lab functionality by providing support for pervasive and ubiquitous Internet access.

As mentioned earlier, the main factor that is limiting a wider diffusion of the Fab Lab concept is the laboratory setup cost. Fabrication machines and materials are expensive and not all the educational institutions, especially in primary and secondary education streams, may afford the costs to start and especially maintain a Fab Lab.

Providing a Fab Lab with ubiquitous access is not simply a matter of networking the digital fabrication equipment, but a challenging task that entails rethinking the whole software and hardware infrastructure and that involves the design of an ad-hoc communication stack to manage real time access and control of the networked equipment and address all security issues that might arise by exposing the equipment to the Internet. We call this complex evolution of the Fab Lab concept *Fabrication as a Service* (FaaS). This approach allows remote network access to fabrication services and addresses all software and logistic concerns, including interaction, communication, and security. FaaS addresses a real social and economic need and arises from the application of the technological paradigms behind the Cloud and the Internet of Things in the Fab Lab context.

The Fab Lab FaaS infrastructure is a two-tier architecture deployed both on premises and on the cloud and that requires the interaction and the communication of several subsystems and software services. The interconnected Fab Labs communicate through a centralized cloud hub that is in charge of forwarding the fabrication requests to the selected Fab Lab. Each Fab Lab is accessible through a Fab Lab gateway that implements access and security policies to the Fab Lab infrastructure (i.e. the networked digital fabrication machines). The hardware and software architecture, as well as the inter- and intra-Fab Lab communication protocols, are thoroughly analyzed in (Cornetta et al., 2018). However, NEWTON Fab Lab infrastructure has been designed to scale and to manage several interconnected Fab Labs. The problem of infrastructure design is very complex and entails several challenges. Many of them are related to infrastructure scaling and have been addressed in (Cornetta et al., 2019a). A cloud simulator based on CloudSim (Calehiros et al., 2010) has been developed to assess the performances of the infrastructure as the number of interconnected Fab Labs scales over a wide and distributed geographical area and to detect possible system bottlenecks. Finally, the impact and effectiveness of the FaaS technology on education have been addressed in (Cornetta et al., 2019b).

Cloud and IoT are the technological drivers of the FaaS concept; however, as stated before, they are empowering technologies with the potential for improving almost every standard business process and application. In such a context, *Fabrication as a Service* is just a particular case of a new technological paradigm in which everything can be delivered as a service through the Internet by leveraging cloud technology and infrastructure. There are several examples available in literature reported in Table 1.

Table 1. New service paradigms enabled by cloud and IoT technologies

Service	Description
Fabrication as a Service (FaaS) (Cornetta et al., 2018)	Hardware and software infrastructure to control and monitor digital fabrication machines
Function as a Service (FaaS) (Roberts, 2018)	Serverless paradigm that allows running on demand simple ephemeral containerized functions implementing a simple and atomic business process
Data as a Service (DaaS) (Zaslavsky et al., 2012)	Service that provides ubiquitous access to any kind of data.
Data Base as a Service (DBaaS) (Zaslavsky et al., 2012)	Service that provides interfaces for database management.
NaaS (Network as a Service) (Zaslavsky et al., 2012)	Type of cloud computing model in which the owner of the network infrastructure provides customers with virtualized network functions and services.
Sensing as a Service (SaaS) (Zaslavsky et al., 2012)	Service that provides ubiquitous access to sensor data.
Software as a Service (SaaS) (Zaslavsky et al., 2012)	Type of cloud computing model in which an application is hosted on a cloud infrastructure and licensed to customers on a subscription basis.
Backend as a Service (BaaS) (Roberts, 2018)	Serverless paradigm that provides out-of-the-box server-side managed services such as authentication, data base management, push notifications, etc.
Platform as a Service (PaaS) (Zaslavsky et al., 2012)	Type of cloud computing model that provides development, management tools and runtimes that abstract the complexity of building and maintaining an infrastructure to run an application.
Infrastructure as a Service (IaaS) (Zaslavsky et al., 2012)	Type of cloud computing model that provides virtualized computing and networking resources over the Internet.

The FaaS model provides a software abstraction layer that wraps the underlying digital fabrication machines with REST (REpresentational State Transfer) APIs (Application Programming Interfaces), which allow the NEWTON e-learning platform, as well as any authorized third-party application, to access remote fabrication machines and schedule a fabrication batch.

NEWTON FAB LABS ARCHITECTURE

As already mentioned, FaaS is a natural evolution of Fab Labs, which are small scale digital fabrication facilities equipped with computer-controlled tools. One major limitation of current Fab Labs is their lack of external connectivity and infrastructure flexibility, requiring constant human supervision to carry out any given task.

The architecture provides Fab Labs with an abstraction layer that wraps the underlying hardware infrastructure into a programmatic interface, which consists of a set of REST APIs used for system integration and to expose the Fab Lab as a Web service to third-party applications. The APIs implements the following functions:

1. Fab Lab equipment remote control and configuration.
2. Inter-Fab Lab communication and task synchronization using a publish/subscribe protocol.
3. Intra-Fab Lab communication and task synchronization using a publish/subscribe protocol.

These features allow remote monitoring and automatic synchronization of the machines involved in a fabrication batch with minimum human intervention and enable support for new scenarios in which any complex design can be implemented in a distributed fashion by splitting it among several networked Fab Labs. Moreover, the API approach allows the possibility to develop Web interfaces allowing remote access to fabrication resources, and thus enabling implementation of distance-learning courses and Ed-to-Ed (i.e. Education-to-Education) scenarios in which partner institutions share expensive fabrication equipment for teaching and research.

Figure 1. FaaS infrastructure and Fab Labs internetworking

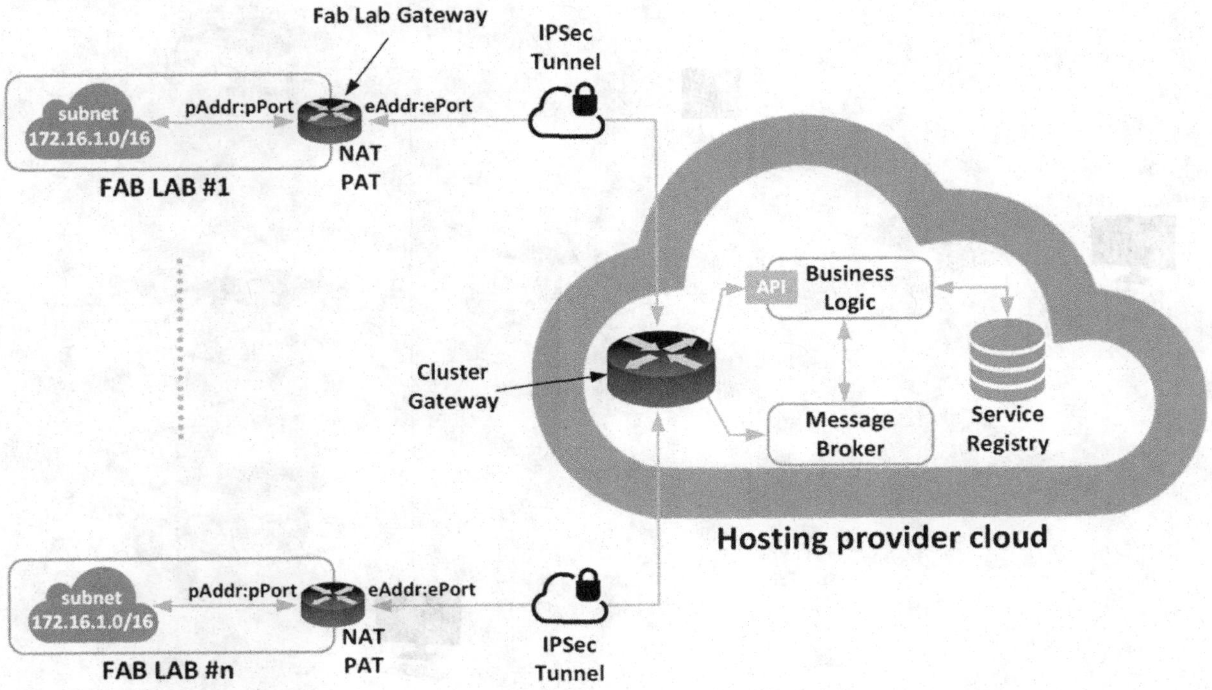

Because of its significant benefits compared to a point-to-point interconnection, the spoke-hub architecture, illustrated in Figure 1, was adopted to interconnect the distributed Fab Labs. In a point-to-point architecture, Fab Labs could directly communicate with each other. This means that the communication overhead and costs increase exponentially according to:

$$\binom{n}{2} = \frac{n(n-1)}{2}$$

where n is the number of interconnected Fab Labs. Thus, 4 interconnected Fab Labs would require 6 connections, 8 Fab Labs would require 28 connections, and so on. Conversely, a spoke-hub model scales better while maintaining a consistent architecture and is more affordable in the long term.

Moreover, the software architecture is organized as a set of loosely coupled microservices deployed both on premises and on the cloud as depicted in Figure 2, and accessible through a set of REST APIs. Each microservice can run and scale independently. In addition, each microservice is relatively small and hence is easier to understand, develop, test and maintain. There are three different microservices, each one responsible for a specific task:

1. The cloud hub microservice.
2. The Fab Lab gateway microservice.
3. The machine wrapper microservice.

Figure 2. NEWTON Fab Labs platform microservices

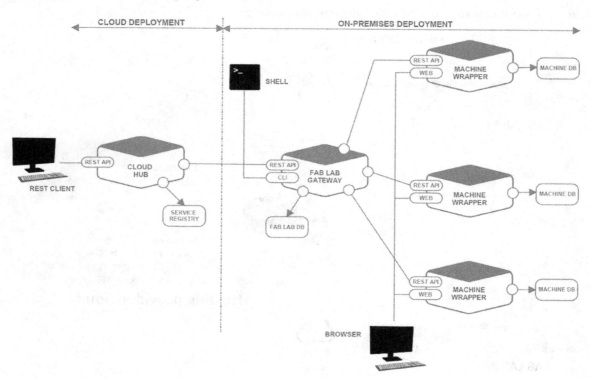

The *cloud hub service* keeps the status of all the interconnected Fab Labs into a registry server; when a client issues a fabrication requests, the hub business logic queries the registry server to detect the Fab Lab that is geographically closer to the client and that has availability of machines and materials and forwards the fabrication requests to it.

The communications among the hub application and the fabrication machines are managed by the *Fab Lab gateway service*. The Fab Lab Gateway decouples the centralized server from the fabrication equipment, controls the inbound traffic among the machines and the outbound traffic to the server on the cloud premises. In addition, the gateway also implements security and API rate limiting policies and share with the cloud servers the responsibility to route the end-to-end traffic between the client application and the remote fabrication machine.

Digital fabrication machines have no network connectivity; thus, in order to make them available over the Internet as web services, we added an extra microservice (the *machine wrapper*) to provide each machine with an abstraction layer that enables external connectivity and with communication protocols to interact with the Fab Lab gateway. Both the Fab Lab gateway and the machine wrapper implementation rely on inexpensive off-the-shelf microcontrollers. The only restriction that applies to hardware choice is the capability to run a Unix-like operating system and **Node.js**[3].

Given that our design is cost-constrained, we tried to find the right balance between affordable costs and acceptable performance. To date, a simulator of our cloud infrastructure was implemented to investigate the cost-performance tradeoffs and to identify potential system bottlenecks as the infrastructure scales (Cornetta et al., 2019a). The appendix at the end of this chapter reports a summary of the system running costs for a typical deployment of Amazon AWS.

Design Goals

The major design goals of the NEWTON Fab Lab platform are as follows:

1. Develop a distributed and modular infrastructure to enable interconnection and communication of several Fab Labs spread over a wide geographical area.
2. Create software and hardware wrappers to expose the fabrication machines to the Internet as web services through a set of REST APIs.
3. Design the communication protocol that enables remote access, monitoring and resource sharing among Fab Labs.

These objectives must be accomplished while:

1. Complying with the security restrictions imposed by the network administrators of the institutions in which the Fab Lab infrastructure is deployed.
2. Limiting the deployment costs by leveraging a minimal cloud infrastructure and inexpensive off-the-shelf micro-controllers to implement machine and Fab Lab wrappers.
3. Limiting the number of vendor-specific cloud services in order to ease the migration to different Infrastructure as a Service (IaaS) providers and to enable the implementation of multi-cloud architectures.
4. Providing software interfaces to easily plug the Fab Lab infrastructure in third-party infrastructure or applications.

System Infrastructure

As mentioned earlier, one of the major limitations of current Fab Labs infrastructure is their lack of external connectivity. This shortcoming is one of the principal barriers to a wider Fab Lab adoption in education, especially at secondary and primary-school levels due to the high start-up costs. The proposed architecture overcomes this limitation by providing a simple but effective way to implement resource sharing of expensive digital fabrication resources allowing remote access through simple web interfaces and seamless integration into third-party applications or infrastructure through a set of REST APIs. The APIs provide Create, Read, Update and Delete (CRUD) methods to manipulate the underlying data model as well as communication primitives to publish and subscribe to services over the Web. The Service Oriented Architecture (SOA) guarantees the inter-operability of the different system components, regardless of the implementation technology and allows easy system scalability.

The NEWTON Fab Lab architecture depicted in Figure 1 employs a two-tier organization composed of a hub and a network of distributed Fab Labs. We leverage cloud technologies to implement a spoke-hub architecture where several Fab Labs (i.e. the spokes) are interconnected through a central hub deployed on cloud premises. The hub keeps the status of all the interconnected Fab Labs into a registry server; when a client issues a fabrication request, the hub business logic queries the registry server to detect the Fab Lab that is geographically closer to the client and that has availability of machines and materials and forwards the fabrication requests to it. However, each Fab Lab does not interact directly with the hub and other labs but relies on a Fab Lab Gateway that also implements filtering and security policies.

The Fab Lab Gateway decouples the centralized server from the fabrication equipment, controls the inbound traffic among the machines and the outbound traffic to the server in the cloud premises. In addition, the gateway also shares with the cloud servers the responsibility to route the end-to-end traffic between the client application and the remote fabrication machine. The communication infrastructure relies on a double message broker architecture which decouples communications in two categories:

1. *Inter-Fab Lab communications*, managed by the centralized broker on the cloud premises, and
2. *Intra-Fab Lab communications*, managed by the Fab Lab Gateway in the Fab Lab Virtual Private Network (VPN).

In order to allow inter-Fab Lab communication, each networked Fab Lab should have at least one public IP address *eAddr:ePort*. The router/gateway maps the inbound traffic into a private address *pAddr:pPort* by means of a Network Address Table (NAT) and a Port Address Table (PAT). Similarly, the router/gateway performs the same task on the outbound traffic by forwarding it to the default gateway or by redirecting the requests for a private address to the private network.

Inter-Fab Lab communications determine the outbound traffic of the Fab Lab network, whereas Intra-Fab Lab communications determine the local network inbound traffic. This architecture drastically reduces the load of the centralized broker, whose task is just to relay simple and short high-level commands from the source to the destination gateway. The gateway acts as a relay for the Fab Lab inbound traffic, routing the incoming command to the target machine according to specific policies that may include machine availability, type and complexity of the fabrication batch, etc. Thus, NEWTON provides the hardware and software infrastructure to enhance the capabilities of a conventional Fab Lab, empowering the pre-existing infrastructure with a message passing interface that, in turn, would allow the networked machines to operate with minimum or no human interaction. The centralized servers in the cloud will particularly benefit from this approach since the number of publishing nodes will be limited to the Fab Lab Gateways and not to all the networked fabrication equipment. In this new context, a NEWTON Fab Lab is a local network of digital fabrication machines. The network connectivity and the ability to control a machine is provided by an external and inexpensive machine wrapper connected to the "slave" digital fabrication equipment. The machine wrapper performs the following tasks:

1.   Decode an incoming message;
2.   Translate the received message in a set of commands understandable by the slave machine.

Spoke and hub nodes form a Virtual Private Network (VPN) in which the Fab lab gateway and the virtual machine instances deployed on cloud premises communicate securely over the Internet using private IP addresses through an IPSec (IP Secure) tunnel. IPsec is a suite of protocols for managing secure encrypted communications at the IP Packet Layer. IPsec also provides methods for the manual and automatic negotiation of security associations (SAs) and key distribution. A security association is a unidirectional agreement between the VPN participants regarding the methods and parameters to use in securing a communication channel. Bidirectional communications require one SA for each direction. Through the SA, an IPsec tunnel can provide the following security functions:

1.   Data privacy (through encryption).
2.   Content integrity (through data authentication).
3.   Sender authentication and—if using certificates—nonrepudiation (through data origin authentication).

Although some novel Internet of Things architectural paradigm exists, in which some data processing is performed at the edge of the network by the devices themselves (Shi & Schahram, 2016), we have preferred a standard approach where all the data must be processed directly in the cloud. This is because the amount of data to be processed (i.e. the Fab Lab status) is not large enough to justify an extra middleware layer between the Fab Labs and the Cloud hub.

System Architecture

The hardware architecture of the FaaS infrastructure is very complex and comprises both a virtualized hardware infrastructure (i.e. virtual machines and virtual network infrastructure) deployed on cloud premises and a simple hardware infrastructure deployed on the Fab Lab premises.

As mentioned earlier, our design is cost-constrained; hence, the resulting architecture is targeted to have affordable deployment and maintenance costs while ensuring acceptable response times. In addition, for this reason, all the infrastructure deployed on premises relies on inexpensive microcontroller boards. More specifically, the Fab Lab Gateway and the Machine wrappers have been implemented using Raspberry Pi III embedded computing boards.

The NEWTON Fab Lab platform has been deployed in production on Amazon AWS public cloud infrastructure. Figure 3 depicts the minimum cloud infrastructure necessary to deploy the cloud hub service.

Figure 3. NEWTON cloud hub hardware architecture

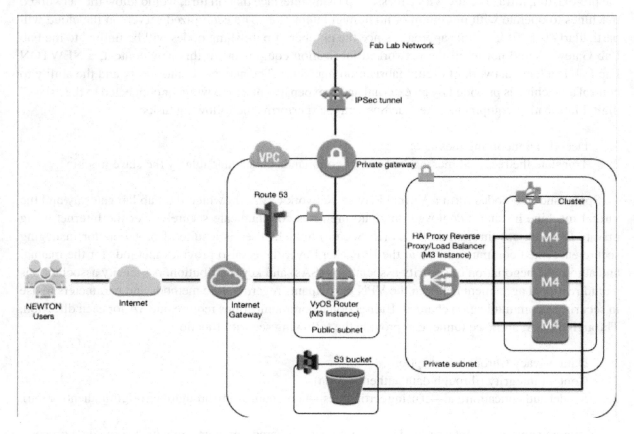

The cloud hub is the centralized communication hub for all the networked NEWTON Fab Labs, and it is tightly integrated into AWS (Amazon Web Services) web services infrastructure. More specifically, the cloud hub infrastructure requires the following AWS managed services:

1. **Route 53** as the Domain Name Service (DNS).
2. **S3** as the back-end storage for the application cluster.
3. **Internet Gateway** to expose to the Internet the underlying public infrastructure.

Table 2 summarizes the characteristics and the target use of the allocated EC2 (Elastic Cloud Computing) instances.

Table 2. Cloud hub EC2 instance allocation

Type	Hardware characteristics	Number	Use
m3.medium	64-bit architecture, 1 Virtual CPU, 3.75 GB Memory, 8GB HD	2	Load balancing and virtual networking functions
m4.large	64-bit architecture, 2 Virtual CPUs, 8 GB Memory, 600 GB HD	3	PaaS (Platform as a Service) infrastructure

A minimum cloud deployment requires five EC2 instances. Two **m3.medium** instances are necessary to deploy the service networking infrastructure, whereas, three **m4.large** instances are necessary to deploy the cluster with the Platform as a Service Infrastructure (PaaS) to manage the Fab Lab cloud services (Cornetta et al., 2019b). The PaaS platform provides a tool to manage and orchestrate containers and runtimes to deploy javaScript server-side applications on cloud premises. The cloud service networking infrastructure is formed by:

1. A VyOS[4] software-defined router to forward the incoming traffic from both the Internet gateway and the IPSec tunnel to the service cluster in the private sub-network.
2. A reverse proxy to route and load balance the traffic forwarded by the VyOS router to the target service running on the service cluster.

The VyOS router is also used to manage the cloud end of the IPSec tunnel that connects the cloud hub to the Fab Labs network. Thus, the cloud hub and the interconnected Fab Labs form a unique VPN in which cloud and on-premise services communicate over an encrypted channel using private IPs.

Figure 4. NEWTON machine wrapper hardware architecture

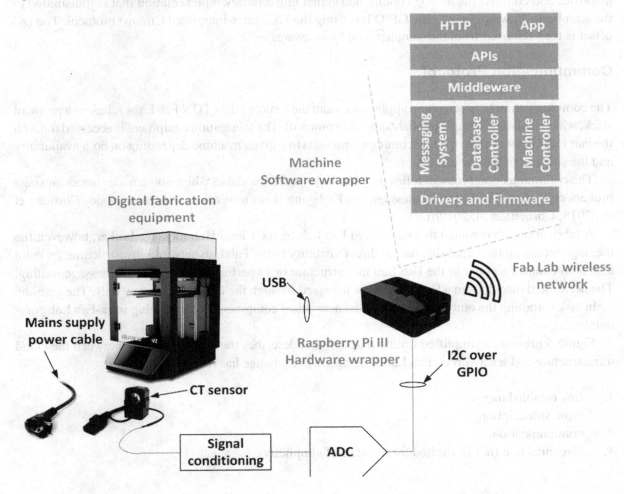

Providing networking support to the Fab Lab infrastructure is difficult because usually fabrication equipment is controlled through USB ports only. In addition, hardware specifications, as well as device drivers, are proprietary, which makes the development of low-level control and monitoring APIs difficult. However, NEWTON FaaS architecture employs an innovative master-slave approach, which enables monitoring and controlling the activity of expensive fabrication equipment through inexpensive external hardware, as shown in Figure 4. The "master" unit is basically an off-the-shelf micro-controller unit (as mentioned before, we use a Raspberry Pi III for this purpose) with basic Ethernet and wireless (802.11) connectivity, as well as an USB and a General-Purpose Input Output (GPIO) port. The application is designed using an API-first approach and communicates with the "slave" digital fabrication equipment through the USB port of the host microcontroller unit and with the other Fab Lab networked equipment through the 802.11 interface. The status of the fabrication equipment is monitored by a non-invasive current transformer (CT) sensor that measures the mains AC current drawn by the equipment. The CT sensor is interfaced to the GPIO digital interface by a high-resolution analog-to-digital converter (ADC) and a simple signal conditioning circuit. This simple configuration allows fast detection of the equipment status (i.e. switched-off, idle or busy)

The signal conditioning circuit performs a current to voltage conversion and adapts the output voltage (just a few mV) to the ADC input dynamic range by adding to the sensed signal a DC offset. The ADC amplifies and converts the analog conditioned signal into a binary representation that is transmitted to the Raspberry Pi wrapper over the GPIO bus using the I2C (Inter-Integrated Circuit) protocol. The DC offset is then removed from the sampled data by software.

Communication Protocol

The communication between client applications and the remote NEWTON Fab Labs relies on a protocol stack, which includes a simple publish/subscribe protocol. The fabrication equipment is accessed through the Fab Lab Gateway that routes incoming commands to a given machine depending on both availability and the specific task to be carried on.

The communication protocol relies on a server-to-server model in which some nodes act as message brokers collecting the incoming messages and relaying them towards a destination node (Cornetta et al., 2018; Cornetta et al. 2019b).

A fabrication job is routed to a networked Fab Lab by the Cloud Hub message broker; however, the message broker on the cloud side has no direct visibility of the Fab Lab network infrastructure. Its main task is to connect a client to the Fab Lab infrastructure or to perform inter-Fab Labs message routing. The networked machines in a Fab Lab can be accessed through the Fab Lab Gateway only. The gateway main task is routing the outbound traffic to the networked equipment and managing intra-Fab Lab communications.

Figure 5 presents a simplified timing diagram that describes the communication between the cloud infrastructure and a networked Fab Lab. The message exchange has four stages:

1. link establishment;
2. topic subscription;
3. communication;
4. disconnection (not illustrated for the sake of simplicity).

Figure 5. Communications timing diagram of the NEWTON Fab Lab platform

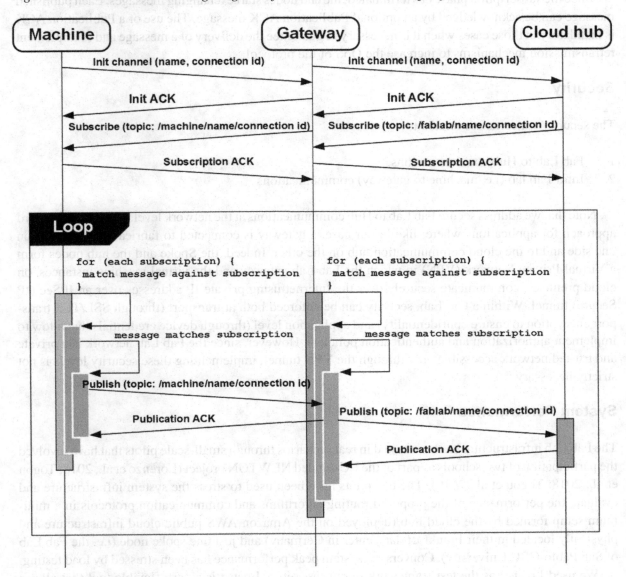

Once the TCP links between the machine and the Fab Lab Gateway on one side, and the Fab Lab Gateway and the Cloud hub broker on the other side, have been established, both the Gateway and the Hub subscribe to topics they are interested in. The topic string is generated using the unique name and connection ID sent by the server that initiates the communications to the destination server during the link establishment. Both the link establishment and the subscription phases are terminated by an ACK message (Init ACK for the link establishment and Subscription ACK for the subscription phase). In other words, the Fab Lab Gateway and the Cloud Hub implement a double broker architecture: the former collects all the incoming messages from the Fab Lab machines, whereas the latter collects all the incoming messages from the networked Fab Lab Gateways. The double broker architecture allows the implementation of Fab Lab access and security policies and custom message filter mechanisms.

Once the subscription phase has terminated, the end nodes start exchanging messages. Each published message can be acknowledged by an optional Publication ACK message. The use of a Publication ACK is mandatory in those cases when it is necessary to guarantee the delivery of a message and to implement retransmission mechanisms to increase the QoS of the protocol.

Security

The security concerns are related to:

1. Fab Lab to Hub communications.
2. Intra-Fab lab (i.e. machine to gateway) communications

Note that we address secure Fab Lab to Hub communications at the network level. This is the standard approach for applications where, like in our case, a gateway is connected to fabrication machines on one side and to the cloud communication hub on the other. Indeed, the Spoke and the hub nodes form a Virtual Private Network (VPN) in which the Fab Lab gateway and the virtual machine instances, on cloud premises, communicate securely over the Internet using private IP addresses over an IPSec (IP Secure) tunnel. Within a Fab Lab, security can be enforced both at transport (through SSL/TLS transport encryption to ensure confidentiality) and application level (through device credentials that allow to implement authorization and authentication policies). However, since the Fab Lab network is a private and trusted network accessible only through the VPN tunnel, implementing these security levels is not strictly necessary.

System Performance

The Fab Lab infrastructure has been tested in real scenarios through small-scale pilots that have involved the participation of two schools as part of the EU-funded NEWTON project (Lorenzo et al., 2018; Togou et al., 2018; Togou et al., 2019). The test pilots have been used to stress the system infrastructure and evaluate the performance of the proposed routing algorithms and communication protocols in a minimum setup formed by the cloud hub (deployed on the Amazon AWS public cloud infrastructure and physically located in their Frankfurt datacenter in Germany) and just one spoke node (i.e. the Fab Lab of San Pablo-CEU University). Conversely, system peak performance has been stressed by load testing.

We used Locust[5] as the test framework in our test setup. Locust is a very flexible tool that allows simulating the user behavior programmatically using a Python script. In addition, Locust is much more than a conventional load-testing tool since it can also be used to test and debug APIs responses. As mentioned earlier, the NEWTON Fab Lab platform is a set of loosely coupled microservices that interact using REST APIs; thus, ensuring that the software interfaces behave as expected is of paramount importance in order to guarantee that the system is production ready.

In order to detect system peak performance, we load-tested it under several realistic load conditions and developed test scenarios that mimic the behavior of a real user and that stress all the system APIs. More specifically, the simulated user behavior is the following:

1. the user GETs the available Fab Lab status;
2. the user POSTs a fabrication job to the available Fab Lab;

3. the user GETs the status information of the submitted job;
4. the user DELETEs the submitted job;
5. the user GETs the information of the jobs running in the available Fab Lab.

In the description of the actions performed by a user, we have highlighted the HTTP verb (i.e. GET, POST, DELETE, etc.) associated with an API call and related to a given user behavior.

The test scenario implements the use cases described in Table 3. These use cases have been translated into a Python script that is parsed by Locust in order to generate the requests for the infrastructure under test. Locust can be further configured so that the user behavior described in that script can be associated with an arbitrary number of virtual users in order to stress the system response under different load conditions.

Table 3. NEWTON Fab Lab modules test cases

Test Id	Test case objective	Test case description	Expected results
1	Check the interface link between the REST client and the Cloud Hub	Authenticate with the JWT token	The user is authorized and can use submission APIs
2	Check the interface link between the Cloud Hub and the Fab Lab Gateway	Send a request to the Fab Lab gateway	The user submits a job, the request is forwarded to the Fab Lab gateway and the all the data bases are correctly updated
3	Check that a fabrication batch is successfully delivered to a machine	Send the request to the machine wrapper	The gateway forwards the requests to the wrapper and all the databases are correctly updated
4	Check that the systems correctly stores all the fabrication requests	The user gets a list of the jobs he/she has submitted to fabrication	The user receives a response with the list of the submitted jobs and the fab lab details
5	Check that a fabrication batch can be cancelled	The user cancels a fabrication batch	The cancellation request is delivered to the machine, the job is cancelled, and all the databases are correctly updated

The Fab Lab test setup has been stressed in the following scenarios:

1. 50 concurrent users with a hatch rate of 5 users per second.
2. 100 concurrent users with a hatch rate of 5 users per second.
3. 150 concurrent users with a hatch rate of 5 users per second.

All the incoming requests are forwarded to the same fabrication machine, each test has a duration of 2 minutes. The most time-consuming operation is the POST request to submit a fabrication job since it involves the following steps:

1. Uploading the image on the cloud hub.
2. Sending the image to the Fab Lab Gateway.
3. Sending the image to the target fabrication machine.
4. Update the jobs queue in the fabrication machine.

Figure 6 shows the load test results for the three scenarios under test (i.e. the cases with 50, 100 and 150 concurrent users, respectively). Figure 6a summarizes the overall results for all the request types, whereas Figure 6b depicts the results only for POST requests. Test results are excellent, considering the Fab Lab infrastructure has been deployed on inexpensive Raspberry Pi III boards. For example, 90% of the incoming requests are served in maximum 680 ms for 50-user scenario, 1,100 ms for the 100-user scenario, and 5,100 ms for 150-user scenario. Of course, as anticipated earlier in this section, the most time-consuming operations are the POST requests whose delay can be as high as 9,141 ms in the case of 150 concurrent users.

Figure 6a. Percentage of requests completed in a given time interval: total requests

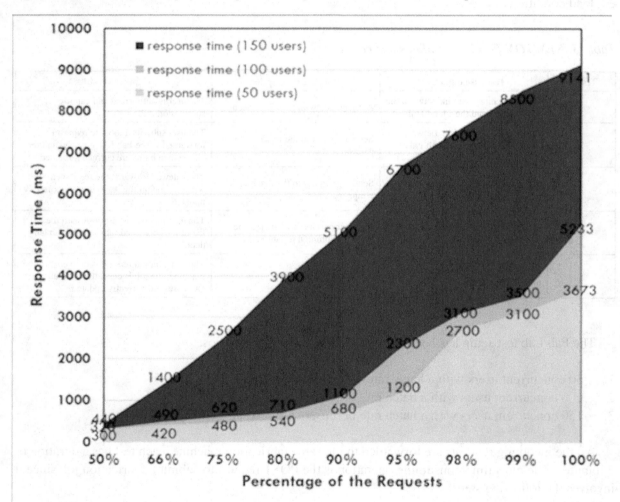

Figure 6b. Percentage of requests completed in a given time interval: POST requests

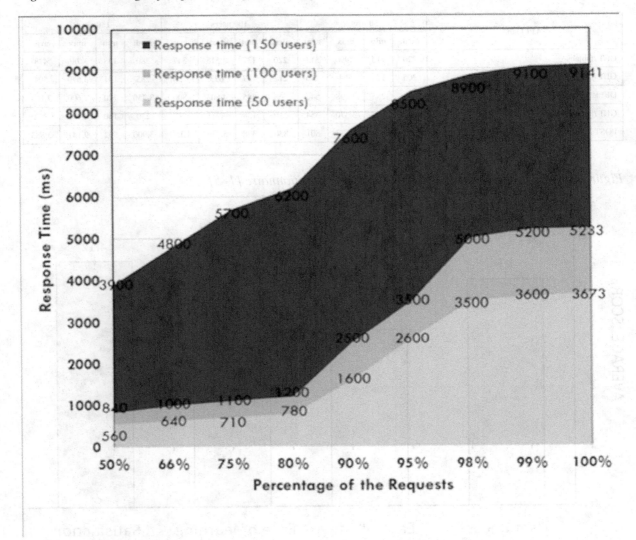

An overview of our findings is summarized in Table 4. The table reports the median, minimum, maximum and average response time in milliseconds for each one of the API called by our simulated scenario for all the test cases studied (namely for the 50-, 100- and 150-user load respectively). The measured values confirm the excellent performance already outlined in Figure 6. From Table 4, the total average response times for the 50-, 100- and 150-user test cases are 452 ms, 568 ms and 1,680 ms, respectively, whereas the maximum average response times are 801 ms, 1,158 ms and 3,883 ms respectively. An average response time of 3,883 ms is acceptable and, according to Fig. 6a and 46b allows, on average, the completion of 100% of the requests for the 50-user scenario, 99% of the requests for the 100-user scenario and almost 80% of the total requests and 50% of the POST requests for the 150-user scenario.

Table 4. Summary of system performance (values are in milliseconds)

API Call	50 users				100 users				150 users			
	med.	min	max	avg.	med.	min	max	avg.	med.	min	max	avg.
GET /fablabs	220	113	2,990	313	220	137	3,515	347	280	138	3,786	478
GET /fablabs/fablab:id/jobs?job=job:id	205	139	664	246	212	137	623	256	285	141	3,679	504
DELETE /fablabs/fablab:id/jobs?job=job:id	438	285	3,508	546	568	285	4,803	800	3,750	320	7,600	3,164
GET /fablabs/jobs	210	139	3,370	354	210	138	3,211	282	230	140	2,948	372
POST /fablabs/jobs?machine=type&lat=. . .	560	374	3,673	801	830	398	5,233	1,158	3,900	502	9,141	3,883

Figure 7. Average scores for the Fab Lab usability questionnaire [1–5]

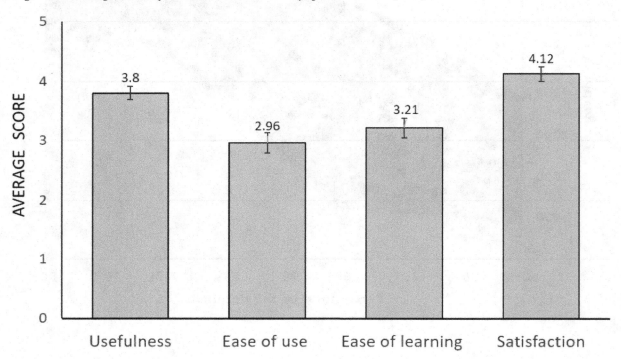

NEWTON FAB LABS IMPACT ON EDUCATION

To validate the effectiveness of the NEWTON Fab Lab Education Initiative, pilot-tests were carried out in two schools. They focused on geometry, perceived to be very difficult by most students in K-12 grades. The goal was to help students to improve their visual imagination and better understand graphic projections. The pilot involved the design and the fabrication of ceramic vases using 3D printers. The goal of these tests was to establish the degree of success of the proposed new learning paradigm based on learning by doing and experimentation in terms of both student learning outcome, and most importantly their degree of satisfaction.

Participants

We carried out our experiments with two schools: Saint Patrick's Boys National School (B.N.S) in Dublin, Ireland and CEU Monteprίncipe School in Madrid, Spain. The former is a primary school while the latter is a secondary school. We worked closely with the schools' principals to identify and suggest the classes to reach out to for participation, based on three criteria: class curriculum, teachers' willingness to participate in the study and students' familiarity with technology (i.e. computers, smartphones, video games). We then reached out to the teachers directly to invite them to participate. The sample drew from 39 6th and 7th-grade students between the age of 10 and 13. 87% of the sample identified as male. 26% of the participants were gifted students. 10% of the sample reported that they have never used a smartphone while 8% stated that they never played games on a gaming console (e.g., PlayStation, Xbox, Nintendo DS).

Pilot Results

The 39 students, aged between 10 and 13, were asked to model 3D ceramic vases using a third-party design software, prepare the digital files and send them over the Internet to the Fab Lab to be printed using the NEWTON platform. Following the usage of the NEWTON Fab Lab technology, the students were asked to fill a usability questionnaire. Figure 7 illustrates the average scores obtained after processing the results of the questionnaire. 87% of the participants from both schools reported that they had fun using the NEWTON Fab Lab technologies and indicated that they would recommend Fab Lab solutions to their friends. This is a great outcome and demonstrates how Fab Lab can have a highly positive impact on student increased satisfaction while learning. Future work will present in detail the results of the deployment of Fab Lab in education.

DISCUSSION

FaaS Lab Deployment

FaaS Fab Lab deployment has been carried out as part of the NEWTON platform. The platform is now in production and includes the Cloud Hub (deployed on an Amazon AWS EC2 cluster) and the on-premises interface infrastructure (implemented with inexpensive Raspberry Pi III boards) that has been deployed and is presently under test at San Pablo-CEU University Madrid, Spain. This deployment has helped in gaining significant insights on several design and implementation aspects and tradeoffs that include hardware design and interfacing, system monitoring and cloud deployment, data security as well as service deployment and orchestration in a multi-cloud environment. Several architectural aspects and implementations have been evaluated and tested so far (Cornetta et al., 2018; Cornetta et al., 2019a; Cornetta et al., 2019b), with particular emphasis on:

1. system replicability and scalability;
2. system costs and maintainability;
3. service availability and auto-discovery in multi-cloud environments;
4. API architecture and design;

5. functional and load test design.

The FaaS design paradigm strongly relies on cloud technologies to implement a centralized communication hub for the networked Fab Labs, and on IoT technologies to transform ordinary fabrication machines into smart objects. This is accomplished by providing a machine with hardware and software wrappers that enable Internet connectivity, implement messaging capabilities using publish/subscribe protocols, and expose REST APIs to access and control the underlying infrastructure. More specifically, a standard fabrication machine is enhanced by wrapping it with software interfaces running on an inexpensive external microcontroller that acts as the machine "master". These interfaces provide a software abstraction layer that enables communication through lightweight machine-to-machine protocols, machine status monitor through current sensors that allow detecting the machine status (either busy, idle or off-line) by measuring the current consumption and machine virtualization through REST APIs. A Fab Lab gateway provides an access point to the machines of a Fab Lab and implements security and rate limiting policies to ensure a fair access to the fabrication resources. The hardware interface design was not difficult and has been accomplished by using standard and inexpensive off-the-shelf components. Conversely, firmware and software development was highly challenging and has involved solving several complex problems related to equipment monitoring and real time communications. A minimum cloud deployment on one AWS region was load tested for different workloads and the results are reported in Table 4.

The deployment of the Fab Lab FaaS infrastructure entails several challenges. Many of them are related to the complexity of the cloud infrastructure. On the one hand, the promise of scalability, redundancy and on-demand service deployment makes a cloud implementation a very appealing solution. On the other hand, all these advantages come at the price of several issues that can make cloud application development and management a difficult task. More specifically, the issues with cloud deployment are related to the following impact factors (Cornetta et al. 2019a; Cornetta et al. 2019b):

1. **Performance:** Disk IO operations can be a serious issue and limit the performance of a cloud deployment. In a cloud infrastructure, the network and the underlying storage are shared among customers. If, for example, another customer sends large amounts of write requests to the cloud storage system, your application may experience slowdowns and its latency becomes unpredictable. Moreover, also the upstream network is shared among customers, so one can experience bottlenecks there too. Unluckily, cloud vendors use to offer to their customers large storage, but not fast storage.

2. **Transparency:** Transparency and simplicity are key factors when debugging either an application or an infrastructure. Unfortunately, cloud services are, in many cases, very opaque and tend to hide underlying hardware and network problems. Cloud infrastructure is a shared service, and, for this reason, cloud users may experience issues that do not occur in dedicated infrastructure. More specifically, cloud infrastructure customers share hardware resources such as CPU, RAM, disk and network; thus the workload of other users can saturate a computing node and heavily affect the performance of your application.

3. **Complexity and scalability:** the complexity of a cloud application can increase very rapidly, especially when it must interact with cloud vendor services whose configuration is not straightforward and require expertise. Moreover, Elastic Load Balancing and scalability are not straightforward in AWS and require the deployment and configuration of additional services that incur extra costs and complexity.

The performance and transparency issues are evident in the results of Table 4. Observe that the distribution of the measured delays has "tail" behavior with large variability between the minimum (namely, 113 ms) and the maximum (namely, 9,141 ms) measured values. As highlighted before, this large variability of the response times is due to the fact that many cloud customers are sharing the same hardware and network infrastructure, which makes a cloud application very sensitive to other users' workloads. However, despite the intrinsic shortcomings of the cloud infrastructure, the measured response times are excellent. Moreover, the FaaS cloud services have been deployed on a PaaS (Platform as a Service) infrastructure that sits on top of the standard cloud infrastructure. The PaaS simplifies application and service deployment in a cloud environment but adds other software layers and additional complexity to the underlying infrastructure, making the application behavior even more unpredictable (Cornetta et al., 2019a; Cornetta et al. 2019b). This unpredictability complicates the infrastructure design, especially when it must be scaled and deployed across several geographical areas. Thus, infrastructure design choices must be assessed with the help of ad-hoc simulator tools in order to timely identify potential system bottlenecks (Cornetta et al., 2019a).

This work describes FaaS deployment in the context of NEWTON next generation Fab Labs; however, the proposed solution is general, hardware-independent and targets all those scenarios which involve collaborative fabrication. We foresee that this capability will have a huge impact not only on education but also on industry helping to develop new business models in which fab-less companies may schedule medium or large-scale fabrication batches hiring third-party remote fabrication services.

NEWTON has been the opportunity for the whole research team to gain particular insight into the impact of the technology on the way we teach and learn. On the one hand we had to investigate new teaching techniques and contents to make STEM subject education more appealing for younger generations; on the other, we had to select those technologies that were more suitable to deliver those contents to a wide audience. We think that Fab Labs are a powerful tool to develop informal teaching activities in which the learning process is based on prototyping and experimentation; however, a Fab Lab is expensive and its deployment costs cannot be afforded by all the institutions, especially the primary and secondary schools that are targeted by the NEWTON project. In this context, cloud and IoT technologies have been proven to be very effective in implementing resource sharing and remote access to distributed fabrication equipment. NEWTON has entailed several challenging tasks for us both as engineers and as educators due to the broad and interdisciplinary nature of the project. However, the whole process from design to development and deployment in production has been productive and enriching and has allowed us to get a better understanding on several cutting-edge technologies (cloud infrastructure architecture and design patterns, IoT technologies, distributed and real time programming, simulation, etc.) and how to integrate them into a working platform that has been battle-tested in several pilot tests. However, the technology developed within the NEWTON project is not an end in itself but serves a well-defined purpose: to foster passion for STEM education in the younger generation through the development of innovative technology-enhanced teaching techniques. Under this point of view, the results obtained so far are very encouraging. The test pilots we carried out (Lorenzo et al., 2018; Togou et al., 2018; Togou et al., 2019) showed a high degree of satisfaction among the surveyed students, which encourages us to follow this path in our future research.

Future Research Directions

The point when designing a cloud application is finding the right balance and tradeoff between target performance and deployment costs. The scalability of the PaaS infrastructure with virtual machines is not limited by the technology, but by the high costs that could arise to provide service to many users. For this reason, we are planning to move to a serverless architecture relying on the BaaS (Backend as a Service) paradigm since it is a completely managed solution where all the services come already integrated and deployed in the platform and can be easily integrated with any web or mobile application. Serverless technologies were still at an early development stage when NEWTON FaaS infrastructure was designed and hence, they were still not stable enough for production deployments. A serverless backend jointly with SPA (Single Page Application) client is a very appealing solution for a cost-constrained design such NEWTON FaaS architecture because such configuration will move great part of the computational complexity to the client, leveraging the cloud services only when strictly necessary.

We are also planning to extend the number of interconnected Fab Labs to stress the system performance and the routing algorithms in more complex scenarios. For this purpose, we will setup a system staging environment that involves networking and interfacing to the cloud hub the Fab Labs at CEU Madrid and Vrije University Brussels in Belgium. This will enable testing the system in a distributed, yet still controlled environment.

CONCLUSION

In this work, we have introduced the concept of Fabrication as a Service (FaaS) in the context of NEW-TON Fab Labs. Although, as stated earlier, this concept is broad and general and has many potential applications in several different areas, we have analyzed its impact in education by implementing a resource sharing mechanism that enables remote access and monitoring of expensive digital fabrication equipment. The impact of this technology on the learning outcomes and students' satisfaction has been assessed through many test pilots (Lorenzo et al., 2018, Togou et al. 2018, Togou et al., 2019). The proposed architecture relies on a complex distributed containerized infrastructure of loosely coupled microservices running both on the cloud and on the Fab Lab premises. The design, deployment and testing of this infrastructure have been thoroughly addressed in (Cornetta et al., 2018).

The results of the load tests reported in Table 4 helped us to gain more insight on platform behavior and performance; however, they were carried out only for a simple deployment (presently in production) formed by the cloud hub and a single Fab Lab in the same AWS region. Those results don't provide information on system performance as it scales over a wider geographical area to interconnect a larger number of Fab Labs. To overcome this limitation, we have used the measured data to build a simulation model that allows estimating system performance under a wide number of configuration and loads. A platform simulator tool is of paramount importance not only to evaluate system performance in a variety of possible scenarios, but also to make the correct design decisions, to detect possible bottlenecks and to allocate the suitable number of cloud resources to cope with users' demand and target response time (Cornetta et al., 2019a).

Cloud, containerization and IoT technologies are enabling a wide range of new applications and business models. FaaS strongly relies on those technologies to implement a novel distributed Fab Labs architecture in which the underlying hardware is wrapped by a software service accessible through APIs.

Distributed systems have been around for decades; however, the main driver for the transition from monolithic to loosely coupled distributed architectures has been the widespread and rapid acceptance of the new containerization technologies. Container technologies have allowed the development and rapid deployment of new stacked distributed design patterns (Burns & Oppenheimer, 2016; Burns, 2018) in which the underlying IT infrastructure is clearly decoupled from the application. In the specific case of the NEWTON Fab Lab platform presented in this work, containerization and cloud technologies have enabled the possibility to deploy a set of loosely coupled microservices that allow seamless communication and interaction of digital fabrication services. On the other hand, IoT technologies provide the possibility to wrap the underlying digital fabrication hardware with a software abstraction layer transforming a conventional machine into a smart object with the capability to interact with other objects of the NEWTON infrastructure through a cloud hub and machine-to-machine communication protocols.

ACKNOWLEDGMENT

The work described in this chapter is part of the NEWTON project, which has been funded by the European Union under the Horizon 2020 Research and Innovation Program with Grant Agreement no. 688503. Gabriel-Miro Muntean acknowledges the support of Science Foundation Ireland (SFI) Research Centres Programme under grants 12/RC/2289 (Insight) and 16/SP/3804 (ENABLE).

REFERENCES

Blikstein, P. (2013). Digital Fabrication and Making in Education: The Democratization of Invention. In J. Walter-Hermann & C. Büching (Eds.), *Fab Labs: Of Machine, Makers and Inventors* (pp. 203–222). Bielefeld, Germany: Transcript Publishers. doi:10.14361/transcript.9783839423820.203

Burns, B. (2018). *Distributed Systems, Patterns and Paradigms for Scalable Microservices*. Sebastopol, CA: O'Reilly Media.

Burns, B., & Oppenheimer, D. (2016). *Design Patterns for Container-based Distributed Systems*. Paper presented at the 8th USENIX Workshop on Hot Topics in Cloud Computing (HotCloud 16), Denver, CO.

Calheiros, R. N., Ranjan, R., Beloglazov, A., De Rose, C. A. F., & Buyya, R. (2010). CloudSim: A toolkit for modeling and simulation of cloud computing environments and evaluation of resource provisioning algorithms. *Software, Practice & Experience*, *41*(1), 23–50. doi:10.1002pe.995

Convert, B. (2005). Europe and the Crisis in Scientific Vocations. *European Journal of Education*, *40*(4), 361–366. doi:10.1111/j.1465-3435.2005.00233.x

Cornetta, G., Mateos, F. J., Touhafi, A., & Muntean, G.-M. (2019a). Modelling and Simulation of a Cloud Platform for Sharing Distributed Digital Fabrication Resources. *Computers*, *8*(2), 47. doi:10.3390/computers8020047

Cornetta, G., Mateos, F. J., Touhafi, A., & Muntean, G.-M. (2019b). Design, simulation and testing of a cloud platform for sharing digital fabrication resources for education. *Journal of Cloud Computing*, *8*(12). doi:10.118613677-019-0135-x

Cornetta, G., Touhafi, A., Mateos, F. J., & Muntean, G.-M. (2018, November). *A Cloud-based Architecture for Remote Access to Digital fabrication Services for Education*. Paper presented at the 4th IEEE International Conference on Cloud Computing Technologies and Applications (Cloudtech), Brussels, Belgium. 10.1109/CloudTech.2018.8713358

EU project. (n.d.a). *FABLAB SCHOOLS EU: Towards Digital Smart, Entrepreneurial and Innovative Pupils*. https://fablabproject.eu/the-project/

EU project. (n.d.b). *NEWTON: Networked Labs for Training in Science and Technology*. http://newton-project.eu

Gershenfeld, N. (2012). How to Make Almost Anything: The Digital Fabrication Revolution. *Foreign Affairs, 91*(6), 43–57.

Gul, L. F., & Simisic, L. (2014, June). *Integration of Digital Fabrication in Architectural Curricula*. Paper presented at the Annual FabLearn Conference Europe, Aarhus, Denmark.

Lorenzo, C., Lorenzo, E., Cornetta, G., Muntean, G.-M., & Togou, M. A. (2018, November) *Designing, testing and adapting to create a distributed learning program in open design and digital fabrication*. Paper presented at the International Conference of Education, Research and Innovation (ICERI), Seville, Spain. 10.21125/iceri.2018.0046

Martin, T., Brasiel, S., Graham, D., Smith, S., Gurko, K., & Fields, D. A. (2014, October). *FabLab Professional Development: Changes in Teacher and Student STEM Content Knowledge*. Paper presented at the Annual FabLearn Conference, Stanford, CA.

Murray, R. (2016, November). *Unlocking Europe's potential via STEM education*. https://blogs.microsoft.com/eupolicy/2016/11/24/

Padfield, N., Haldrup, M., & Hobye, M. (2014, June). *Empowering academia through modern fabrication practices*. Paper presented at the Annual FabLearn Conference Europe, Aarhus, Denmark.

Roberts, M. (2018). *Serverless architectures*. https://martinfowler.com/articles/serverless.html

Shi, W., & Schahram, D. (2016). The promise of edge computing. *Computer, 49*(5), 78–81. doi:10.1109/MC.2016.145

Tesconi, S., & Arias, L. (2014, June). *MAKING as a Tool to Competence-based School Programming*. Paper presented at the Annual FabLearn Conference Europe, Aarhus, Denmark.

Togou, M. A., Lorenzo, C., Lorenzo, E., Cornetta, G., & Muntean, G.-M. (2018, July). *Raising students' interest in STEM education via remote digital fabrication: an Irish primary school case study*. Paper presented at Edulearn 2018, Palma de Mallorca, Spain. 10.21125/edulearn.2018.0756

Togou, M. A., Lorenzo, C., Lorenzo, E., Cornetta, G., & Muntean, G.-M. (2019, June). *NEWTON Fab Lab initiative: a small-scale pilot for STEM education*. Paper presented at EdMedia and Innovate Learning Conference, Amsterdam, The Netherlands.

UK Department for Education. (2013). *National Curriculum in England: Design and Technology Programmes of Study*. Retrieved from https://www.gov.uk/governemnt/publication/national-curriculum-in-england-design-and-technology-programmes-of-study

Zaslavsky, A., Perera, C., & Georgakopoulos, D. (2012, July). *Sensing as a Service and Big Data*. Paper presented at the International Conference on Advances in Cloud Computing (ACC), Bangalore, India.

ADDITIONAL READING

Botta, A., Donato, W., Persico, V., & Pescapè, A. (2016). Integration of Cloud Computing and Internet of Things: A Survey. *Future Generation Computer Systems*, *56*, 684–700. doi:10.1016/j.future.2015.09.021

Buyya, R., & Dastjerdi, A. V. (Eds.). (2016). *Internet of Things. Principles and Paradigms*. Cambridge, MA: Morgan Kaufmann.

Chintan, P., & Doshi, N. (2014). *Internet of Things Security. Challenges, Advances and Analytics*. Boca Raton, FL: CRC Press.

Cirani, S., Ferrari, G., Picone, M., & Veltri, L. (2019). *Internet of Things. Architectures, Protocols and standards*. Hoboken, NJ: Wiley.

Gubbi, J., Buyya, R., Marusic, S., & Palaniswami, M. (2013). Internet of Things (IoT): A vision, architectural elements, and future directions. *Future Generation Computer Systems*, *29*(7), 1645–1660. doi:10.1016/j.future.2013.01.010

Hu, F. (Ed.). (2012). *Security and Privacy in Internet of Things (IoTs). Models, Algorithms and Implementations*. Boca Raton, FL: CRC Press.

Hwang, K., Fox, G. C., & Dongarra, J. J. (2012). *Distributed and Cloud Computing. From Parallel Processing to the Internet of Things*. Waltham, MA: Morgan Kaufmann.

McEwen, A., & Cassimally, H. (2014). *Designing the Internet of Things*. Chichester, UK: John Wiley and Sons.

KEY TERMS AND DEFINITIONS

API: Application programming interfaces (APIs) are a set of functions and routines used as the building blocks of an application and that enable the access to the data and features of an operating system, another application or a service.

IPSec: Internet protocol security (IPSec) is a suite of network protocols used in Virtual Private Networks (VPNs). IPSec includes protocols to support network-level peer authentication, data-origin authentication, data integrity and data privacy through encryption.

Microservices: Microservices or microservice architecture is a software design pattern in which an application is split into a collection of independent and loosely coupled services that can be deployed, scaled and maintained independently.

P2P: Peer to peer (P2P) is a network of nodes working without fixed clients and server where all the nodes behave as peers operating as server and client at the same time.

REST: Representational state transfer (REST) is a software architectural style for developing web services and for defining an interoperability layer among Internet applications.

Serverless: Is an application design pattern that may incorporate third-party backend managed services (Backend as a Service – BaaS) and/or custom code executed on-demand in a managed ephemeral container infrastructure and implementing small atomic functions (Function as a Service – FaaS). Such architecture removes much of the server-side management complexity, speedup development and reduce the application running costs at the price of an increased reliance on vendor infrastructure and services.

SOA: Service-oriented architecture (SOA) is a software design style in which the business logic relies on several independent application components (i.e., the services) accessible over the network through a communication protocol.

SPA: A single page application (SPA) is a kind of web application that interacts with the user by dynamically writing the web page rather than retrieving a new one from the server. In a SPA all the resources (HTML markup, JavaScript code and CSS stylesheets) are loaded just once when the page is retrieved the first time and dynamically added to the web page when necessary or when triggered by the user action. This results in a fluid user experience and in a behavior that resembles the one of a desktop application. In the case of large SPAs, the resources are retrieved in chunks rather that all at once, which may imply a communication with the server under the hood.

XaaS: Is a general term that refers to the delivery of anything (tool, application, or infrastructure) as a service over the internet by leveraging cloud and virtualization technologies.

ENDNOTES

[1]   Project webpage: http://newtonproject.eu
[2]   Fab Lab Foundation website: https://fabfoundation.org
[3]   Node.js platform website: https://nodejs.org
[4]   VyOS website: https://vyos.io
[5]   Locust website: https://locust.io

APPENDIX

Infrastructure Deployment Costs

The problem of infrastructure deployment costs has been thoroughly addressed in (Cornetta et al., 2019b). A deployment necessary to ensure a global coverage must comprise at least four AWS regions: eu-central-1, us-east-1, sa-east-1, and ap-south-east-1. The platform costs depend on the number and type of EC2 instances (i.e. virtual machines) deployed in each region.

The NEWTON infrastructure must comprise four Data Centers to ensure maximum coverage in all the AWS supported regions. The Data Centers implement a spoke-hub architecture being the Frankfurt node (eu-central-1 AWS region) the hub. Spokes must be located in United States (eu-east-1 AWS region), South America (sa-east-1 AWS region) and Singapore (ap-southeast-1 AWS region). The main infrastructure and application (i.e. the registry service, the Fab Lab monitoring service, the Fab Lab connection/routing service) is hosted on the hub, whereas the spokes only run a simple client to query the service registry and the router. With this approach, we limit the more expensive virtual machines (i.e. the **m4.large** instances) to the network hub, whereas the spokes may rely on cheaper virtual machines (i.e. **t2.micro** instances). In its minimum configuration, the NEWTON cloud infrastructure relies on the following Amazon AWS services:

1.   Between five and eight Elastic Cloud Computing (EC2) instances.
2.   Between five and eight EBS volumes allocated for each EC2 instance.
3.   Route53 DNS service.
4.   S3 storage to implement the blobstore for the PaaS infrastructure.
5.   Optionally, the CloudFront content delivery network (CDN) service.

The EC2 instances that form the PaaS infrastructure are configured to be autoscaled, according to the platform load, between three and five instances. This, in turn, requires setting-up other two AWS services:

1.   CloudWatch to monitor platform metrics and trigger the autoscaling.
2.   CloudFormation, to dynamically build and deploy new instances of the PaaS platform.

CloudWatch has a free tier with enough capabilities to support the NEWTON cloud infrastructure. Conversely, CloudFormation is a free service.

Table 5 summarizes the overall monthly costs necessary to run the whole NEWTON Fab Lab infrastructure. Thus, the infrastructure running costs of a minimum deployment may vary between $1,386.33 and $1,811.89 (depending on the number of the deployed virtual machines) per month (VAT not included).

Table 5. NEWTON Fab Labs cloud infrastructure overall monthly running costs

Node	Monthly running costs	
	min.	max.
eu-central-1	$893.98	$1,253.92
us-east-1	$98.41	$115.41
sa-east-1	$263.37	$290.61
ap-south-east-1	$130.57	$151.95
Total:	$1,386.33	$1,811.89

Section 2
Technologies in a Smart City Context

Chapter 6
The Water Cycle in the Smart Cities Environment

Eduardo J. López-Fernández
iD https://orcid.org/0000-0001-9103-3585
Universidad CEU San Pablo, Spain

Francisco Alonso-Peralta
iD https://orcid.org/0000-0002-5095-385X
Technical University of Madrid, Spain

Gastón Sanglier-Contreras
iD https://orcid.org/0000-0002-8981-5622
Universidad CEU San Pablo, Spain

Roberto A. González-Lezcano
iD https://orcid.org/0000-0002-6185-4929
Universidad CEU San Pablo, Spain

ABSTRACT

This chapter analyses the urban water cycle in the smarts cities, describes the current situation, which constitutes a valid but outdated knowledge, adopting the perspective of improving and extending the measures that lead to greater efficiency of the water collection, treatment, supply, sewage, purification, and reuse systems at all stages of the water cycle: the sites, construction, operation, and maintenance of the networks and systems that enable the cycle to be completed effectively. The process of converting a city into smart city includes resources, processes, and services, and all stages of the water cycle are a set of processes, with water as a fundamental resource, which condition the different services to citizens, and therefore, it is necessary to try to establish efficiency improvements in all of them.

DOI: 10.4018/978-1-7998-3817-3.ch006

Copyright © 2020, IGI Global. Copying or distributing in print or electronic forms without written permission of IGI Global is prohibited.

INTRODUCTION

The chapter begins with a necessary examination of the systems and processes developed in the different phases of the water cycle, understood as the system in charge of taking, transporting and bringing water to the point of consumption in correct conditions of quality and quantity. The evacuation, purification, regeneration, reuse and even the treatments associated with the waste generated in these stages are included as part of the sanitation network, which is in charge of returning the water to the riverbed to complete the water cycle in optimal quality conditions. This review shows the unquestionable commitment of the integral water cycle with the measures that lead to optimizing the rational use of the resource, but it also intuits the wide range of possibilities that the water cycle offers in the reduction of emissions and the improvement of energy and hydraulic efficiency, providing even greater effectiveness to the cycle's operations as a whole.

The application of the Circular Economy Strategy promoted by the European Union to operators in the water cycle, focusing on the recycling and reuse of materials, the production, use and saving of energy, the recovery of by-products and reuse, regeneration and water supply, is noteworthy. It also shows the commitment to the corresponding ODS 2030 sustainable development objectives, signed in 2015 under the supervision of the United Nations.

The chapter sets out a series of measures that will undoubtedly help to achieve the fundamental objectives set out by the authors.

First of all the measures aimed at optimising the use of the resource consists of modifying daily habits of our way of life in order to move without excuses towards its moderate and rational use and consumption. The authors believe that this measure requires, fundamentally, a multidisciplinary pedagogical effort aimed at users of all ages.

Emphasis is placed on the paramount importance of monitoring and controlling the operation and maintenance of each stage of the water cycle with the ambitious objective of detecting anomalies, breakdowns and distortions as early as possible to prevent them from causing undesirable losses, inefficiencies and malfunctions in the various processes of the cycle. For some time now there has been an awareness of the fundamental role of each and every one of the automatisms that can be included in the different water networks; as well as the extraordinary contribution of Artificial Intelligence within the vast environment of Internet of Things (IoT).

At all stages, a very high amount of energy is consumed, which is required by hydraulic machines (turbines and pumps of all types), generators and motors which are essential to correctly complete the different physical and chemical processes of the cycle. It is a real challenge to reduce energy consumption without affecting the service of citizens, although it is no less challenging to ensure that all the primary energy source of that operation has a clean and renewable origin.

The authors also address the objectives of saving, recovery and energy production, supported by the necessary reuse of the resource in an efficient way, as well as the treatment of waste from the different processes of the stages of the water cycle (sewage sludge, grease, biogas and phosphorus mainly). In addition, different valid options are considered within the existing regulations, as well as the great possibilities that exist today and the options that future technologies could provide in water regeneration.

The control of irrigation systems is a matter of special interest, to give an example, it is estimated that it represents more than 65% of total water consumption in Spain. It is also important to establish other measures that lead to the hydraulic efficiency of the system such as the correct choice of species for the different plant covers of the buildings.

It also addresses the need to combat climate change, minimizing the carbon footprint, previously calculated, in the different processes of the stages of the cycle.

The chapter ends with the conclusions highlighted by the authors, which arise from the professional experience acquired in the practice of hydraulic engineering and from the study and analysis work carried out during their respective professional careers.

BACKGROUND

Bearing in mind that the integral water cycle is closed, as shown in Figure 1, it is advisable to clarify the different stages through which the resource passes, from the moment of its capture until its return to nature, once it has gone through multiple physical and chemical processes in which, in addition to having consumed significant amounts of energy, some hydraulic inefficiencies have occurred that for a long time were considered inevitable.

Figure 1. Urban Cycle of Water (1.Water collection; 2.Potabilization; 3.Storage; 4.Distribution; 5.Consumption; 6.Sewerage; 7.Wastewater; 8.Water recycling; 9.Return). Source: Aqualia. https://aguaeco-social.com/ciclo-urbano-del-agua/

The first of the stages in the water cycle is the Water Collection and Storage of the resource. Since the first groupings and settlements, man has tried to locate himself close to natural sources of water in order to provide himself with it more easily, making it necessary to try to capture it and store it in order to later dispose of it. It is very important at this stage to distinguish between:

- **surface catchments,** which collect water from different forms of precipitation (rain, snow or ice), especially in the higher areas where these are more abundant once, thanks also to the runoff itself, are collected in natural deposits (lagoons, lakes, etc.) and also artificially in infrastructures created for this purpose. (reservoirs, rafts, etc).
- **underground catchments,** which represent 21% of the total, a figure which confirms their extraordinary contribution in periods of prolonged drought, and which are collected in natural underground aquifers. Logically, the power of underground aquifers is directly related to the perme-

ability of soils which, in turn, contributes to the risk of undesirable percolations that can seriously contaminate groundwater.

Taking the Region of Madrid in Spain as an example, it has a network of 14 reservoirs that store 946 hm3 of surface water, while the groundwater network can contribute in periods of drought with 90 hm3 per year of exploitation. This highlights the substantial importance of the contribution of the groundwater network to date and the urgent need, in the face of the extraordinary events caused by climate change, to preserve the aquifers in perfect conditions of load and service.

After water collection and storage, the water is treated and made drinkable so that it can be consumed without any risk to health. According to the World Health Organization (WHO), water that is intended to be considered potable must not contain biological, chemical or radioactive contaminants, have an adequate proportion of dissolved gases and mineral salts and must be colorless, odorless and tasteless.

The potabilization of water in history situates the Greeks filtering and boiling water, aware of its capacity to transmit diseases.

In 1806 the largest water treatment plant was built in Paris, filtering the water with sand and coal after allowing it to settle for 12 hours.

In 1827, civil engineer James Simpson built a sand filter to purify drinking water, consisting of successive layers of loose bricks, gravel and sand to remove solids from the water, and which today is considered the first effective drinking water system designed to preserve public health.

In the 20th century, water disinfection began using calcium hypochlorite.

The most common processes that constitute the Water Treatment and Potabilization stage can vary significantly, depending on the type of water to be treated, but they can be classified as follows:

1. Preoxidation.

In this process, an oxidizing chemical agent (sodium hypochlorite, calcium hypochlorite, chlorine dioxide, ozone, etc.) is added to the water, capable of eliminating organic and inorganic matter susceptible to oxidation.

2. Coagulation and Flocculation.

They facilitate the grouping of particles responsible for the colour and turbidity of the water.

3. Decanting.

The particles at rest are deposited by the action of gravity together with the groupings of the previous processes, giving rise to a sludge that is removed later.

4. Filtration.

In this process the particles that still remain in the water are passed through suitable filters that retain them.

5.   Neutralization.

The acidity of the water is adjusted with various additives to prevent corrosion of the pipes.

6.   Final disinfection.

In the last of the processes, chlorine and ammonia are added, which eliminates the possible microorganisms that endure from the previous processes and guarantees the correct quality of the water.

All these chemical and physical processes are carried out in suitable facilities which also provide the water with the highest quality for subsequent consumption and which are known as Drinking Water Treatment Plants. The Drinking Water Treatment Plant is so much more efficient that it is capable of treating the largest flow of water, without in any way impairing its quality, with less energy consumption.

In the potabilization of water, the desalination of salt water or brackish water, which is carried out in Desalination Plants, deserves special mention, as it is the only possibility of obtaining drinking water under certain circumstances, in addition to constituting a viable solution in situations of hydric stress such as those currently being considered and which, according to most research on climate change, will become more acute in the future. The most common procedure is reverse osmosis desalination, which can be summarized in three broad phases:

1.   Collection of marine or brackish water.

Raw water is obtained, which may be seawater or brackish water (from surface or underground sources with high saline content). The raw water is piped to the plant site, from where it is pumped by a pumping station to the desalination plant.

2.   Pretreatment.

Before the specific treatment of the salts, a global treatment is carried out in which different physical and chemical processes are included. First, a coagulant is added to the raw water, which adds the particles and causes them to precipitate in the decanter to which this water is to be sent. After the decanting process will proceed to disinfection, to eliminate the biological load, this can be done in different ways, however chlorination is the most commonly used method, since chlorine is a powerful oxidant and disinfectant, it is also cheap and easy to control, but provides an unpleasant taste to the water. After the disinfection treatment, the liquid, with a low pressure, passes through a set of double layer filters (generally sand or natural carbon); after which, most of the suspended matter is retained, obtaining a filtrate of approximately 15 microns. The water obtained will go to a regulating tank that will dose the flow for the next filtration.

Then begins a second filtration stage, in which the water is driven with a higher pressure through multilayer filters (also sand or natural carbon), obtaining a filtration quality of particles less than 10 microns. In a final stage of filtration the water passes through cartridge filters, first through some of 15 microns and then through others of 10 microns. Finally, the water is subjected to a dechlorination process that places the pH of the water below 7, to avoid damaging the osmosis membranes.

3.   Reverse Osmosis.

One or more high pressure pumps drive the water into the reverse osmosis membranes, resulting in the water resulting from this process, as shown in the diagram in Figure 2. In general terms, between 40% and 45% of the resulting water is obtained from raw water, to which a base is added (sodium hypochlorite) which stabilises the pH at around 7 and acts as a disinfectant, thus making it suitable for use or consumption. On the other hand, between 55% and 60% of the impelled water is converted into brine, water with a high concentration of salts that will be sent back to the sea (through a gravity submarine emissary) or, depending on the quantity produced and the possible negative impact, to another disposal area. In medium-sized or large desalination plants, this reject water is passed through a system of turbines where its residual energy is used, thus reducing energy consumption. At present, some desalination plants can go through a second stage of Reverse Osmosis. The resulting water is transferred to a storage tank, where, if necessary, minerals are added in order to improve its quality for human consumption in accordance with current regulation. In Spain, it is REAL DECRETO 140/2003, which establishes the sanitary criteria for water for human consumption.

Figure 2. Reverse Osmosis Water Desalination Process (1.Water collection; 2.Acidification; 3.Storage tank; 4.Dechlorination; 5.Anti-foulings; 6.Disinfection; 7. Coagulant; 8.High pressure pumping; 9.Cartridge filters; 10. Energy recovery; 11.Reverse osmosis; 12.Aeration tower; 13.Cleaning; 14.Alkalisation; 15.Disinfection; 16.Passivating; 17.Rejection to the sea; 18.Intermediate storage). Source: https://www.emagister.com/curso-agua-desalacion-2-4/descripcion-proceso-osmosis

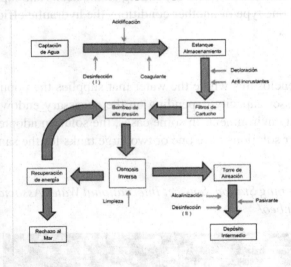

The particularity of the desalination system with reverse osmosis system is that it requires a constant supply of energy to avoid the degradation of its membranes.

The last of the stages that make up the Supply network is the distribution of water to the different points of consumption.

Concern for water storage and distribution is represented by the emergence of significant remains of well transport and distribution infrastructure, first through dug channels and then through hollow pipes in Jérico (Israel) 7000 years ago and also in Mohenjo-Daro (Pakistan).

There are also installations of this type in Greek cities, but it is the Romans who, with great knowledge of hydraulic engineering, have bequeathed millenary constructions. During the Roman Empire dams were built, protected sources of external contaminants and bold aeration systems that purified the water precursors, without any doubt, of the current systems. They developed a water supply system of aqueducts and pipes using cement, rock, bronze, silver, wood and lead.

When the Roman Empire falled, many of these systems ceased to be used, giving way in the Middle Ages to a time when waste was dumped directly into the riverbed, generating serious health problems and diseases. The figure of the water carriers who transport water to the main cities from uncontaminated remote areas is generalized. The first drinking water supply system was built in Paisley (Scotland) in the early 19th century by civil engineer John Gibb. Three years later, filtered water began to be transported to Glasgow.

The increasing price of water in the cities raised the need to improve definitively the water supply. To fulfil the service, from the water treatment stations to the point of consumption, in a general way a series of infrastructures are available that guarantee the supply in quantity and quality. They are detailed below:

1. Large Pipelines.

They are a fundamental element to guarantee the adequate distribution of water. They can be developed in the form of a branched or meshed network, depending on the needs and topographical circumstances of the layout. The choice of one type or another conditions the hydraulic efficiency of the network.

2. Regulatory deposits.

They are waterproofed enclosures where the water that supplies the population is stored. They are designed with greater or lesser capacity depending on the necessary endowment and the availability of space in the geographical environment. In some cases, the solution adopted involves more tanks of smaller capacity, while other solutions have one or two large tanks for the same endowment.

Figure 3. Potable Water Pumping Station. Source: International Water Association https://iwa-network. org/learn/estaciones-de-bombeo/

3.   Pumping stations.

These stations have pumping units, as shown in the image in Figure 3, which take the water from the regulating tanks and raise it to the level necessary to be able to supply it with the appropriate pressure. These are some of the installations where an important energy consumption is carried out, which is completely necessary, but which offers possibilities of optimisation and efficiency.

4.   Distribution network.

This is the network of pipes that carry the water to the point of consumption. Any strategy of renovation, improvement and control of losses in the network, increases the desired efficiency of the cycle.

The Sewage network includes all activities related to wastewater, those from homes, urban centers and those resulting from industrial activity. If untreated wastewater is poured into the riverbed, negative effects are produced, such as: presence of pathogenic microorganisms in the riverbed, appearance of chemical contaminants that eliminate the life of the species, waste on the banks and the floor of the riverbeds, eutrophication of the water caused by high nitrogen and phosphorus contents, bad odours due to the consumption of dissolved oxygen in the process of decomposition of organic matter, etc. It is therefore necessary to subject the water to various treatments before returning it to the riverbed.

Throughout history, remains of sewerage constructions have been found in ancient Crete and Assyria. Also in the ancient Roman cities there are old installations that, to this day, are still erected like the great vault of the "Cloaca Maxima" that can be seen in the city of Rome near its meeting with the Tiber from the Palatine bridge.

In Europe, at the end of the Middle Ages, fecal water was deposited in underground excavations and latrines, the contents of which were used as fertiliser or, in the worst case, thrown into the nearest channel. Later on, it was drained again as in Roman times by means of open pipes and ditches in the streets. Waste was deposited in streams, lakes and rivers, water was polluted by transfer, generating serious public health problems.

During the nineteenth century, wastewater were collected in cities in order to control the transmission of diseases such as cholera. In the second half of the century, the first sanitary systems were established with toilets that encourage the construction of sewage systems. Even so, with these first nets, uncontrolled spillage was reduced but pollution was concentrated in the watercourses, causing unacceptable hygienic and environmental conditions. In this situation, it is proposed for the first time to use the dumping of wastewater as fertilizer, giving rise to the first treatment system that completes the sewage network, adding to the collection and transport of wastewater and its purification.

At the beginning of the twentieth century, the serious problems presented by the elimination of waste through rivers were recognized and the drip-filter septic tank was introduced, which represented the primary treatment of fecal water of domestic origin in rural and urban nuclei.

The purification systems were fundamentally aimed at eliminating solids and soluble organic matter, but it was not until the 70s of the 20th century that the programmed purification of wastewater began, coinciding with the development of the scientific basis of conventional biological treatments.

At present, wastewater treatment focuses on regeneration to allow the reuse of water for various uses not related to human consumption, but which definitively improve the efficiency of the urban water cycle. The system of the sewage network is composed:

1.   Urban drainage networks.

These are the collectors and outfalls in charge of collecting wastewater (domestic, industrial and runoff) and rainwater to be taken to wastewater treatment plants.

2.   Wastewater Pumping Stations.

These are the hydraulic installations that allow water to be transported to treatment plants when it is impossible to do so due to the effect of gravity, for example when the collectors and outfalls are at a lower topographical level than the treatment plant.

3.   Storm tanks.

They are hydraulic structures that manage to regulate the flows in periods of rain; later, to evacuate them in a controlled way, reducing the discharges to the environment and avoiding floods waters under the installation. Thanks to these infrastructures, large volumes of the first rainwater, which are the most polluting, are retained. The image in Figure 4 shows one of the storm tanks on the River Manzanares in Madrid.

Figure 4. Storm Tank in the Manzanares River. Source: Imesapi https://www.imesapi.com/tanques-de-tormenta-del-rio-manzanares-madrid/

4.   Wastewater Treatment Plants.

They are installations designed to eliminate: waste, fats, oils, sands and all the thick elements that water may contain, organic and inorganic materials that can be decanted and biodegradable organic matter dissolved in water. The treatment plants carry out all these actions or only part of them, depending on the size of the populations they serve, the number of inhabitants, the origin of the wastewater, the possibility of producing industrial discharges, etc.

In the treatment plants, the Water Line that collects the residual water that arrives at the installation and the Sludge Line that takes care of the sludge generated in the different purification processes are treated independently.

a.   Water Line.

The following treatments are carried out here:

i.   Pretreatment. It is the phase that happens at the entrance of the installation and consists of eliminating the bulky waste that arrives from the network collectors.

ii.   Primary Treatment. This process reduces suspended solids (controlled by the percentage parameter SS) and part of the biochemical oxygen demand (evaluated by the percentage parameter BOD_5), since suspended solids are composed of organic and inorganic matter.

iii.   Secondary Treatment. In secondary treatment, the organic matter in the wastewater is reduced, through various processes, in biological reactors designed for this purpose, and then subjected to secondary decanting. Figure 5 shows the operating diagram of a wastewater treatment plant without tertiary treatment

iv.   Tertiary Treatment. This is a treatment produced by some treatment plants (which is why they are called waste water regeneration plants), by means of which the water is subjected to certain processes that are even more intense (chlorination, ultraviolet radiation, etc.) than the previous ones, with the aim of obtaining reclaimed water to be reused for non-human consumption uses that require more demanding water quality conditions (irrigation, street cleaning and industrial uses of the plant itself or of other facilities). Thus, reclaimed water is treated wastewater subject to complementary processes that achieve conditions of the resulting water suitable for other uses that do not require drinking water. The use must be indicated through the corresponding Legislation. In Spain, use is regulated by REAL DECRETO 1620/2007, which establishes the legal regime for treated water.

b.   Sludge Line. In this line the sludge is managed as a by-product of sewage treatment plants. These are important quantities of sludge, since those coming from the primary decanting and those that appear in excess in the secondary decanting are joined. In order for the by-product to be put into value or to manage its deposit, it must undergo Thickening, Stabilization, Conditioning and Dewatering processes.

In each and every stage of the cycle and, in particular, in the phases and processes carried out in them, energy consumption is high, which shows a wide margin for improvement in process efficiency. The urban water cycle in Intelligent Cities inevitably depends on all these processes that work with water as a fundamental resource and; therefore, it is necessary to try to establish important improvements in hydraulic and energy efficiency in all of them.

MAIN FOCUS OF THE CHAPTER

Once all the stages of the urban water cycle have been reviewed, the importance of the binomial water and energy is highlighted. This binomial also exerts a bidirectional influence as it works with large volumes of water that make it possible to generate energy; and, at the same time, many of these actions carried out in the cycle require high energy consumption. Critical energy consumption operations, available energy sources, how emissions and consumptions are assessed, and finally, what can be done to improve efficiency in the cycle need to be clearly established.

Figure 5.Treatment Scheme of a Wastewater Treatment Plant without tertiary treatment (1.Degradation of odor; 2.Incoming water; 3. Gauge screens; 4.Sand trap; 5.Primary decanter; 6.Bioreactor; 7.Secondary decanter; 8.Effluent; 9.Float; 10.Biogas; 11.Thickener; 12.Anaerobic digester; 13.Dewatering; 14.Dehydration water; 15.Supernatant treatment; 16.Dehydrated sludge). Source: Canal de Isabel II http://www.madrid.org/bvirtual/BVCM019568.pdf.

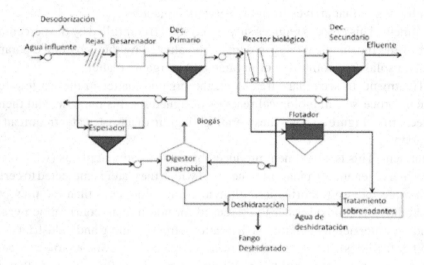

Energy Sources Available - Current and Future Problems

The bidirectional relationship between water and energy is detailed below:

1. **Energy** is needed to carry out the integral water cycle, i.e. to collect, treat and distribute water, desalinate sea or brackish water, treat waste water and also for various domestic, industrial and agricultural uses.
2. **Water** is needed to generate energy, even indirectly. This happens in the necessary cooling of hydroelectric processes of electricity production, in drilling, extraction and production of fuels, in the paper production industry or even in the irrigation of the raw material that gives rise to the production of biofuels among many others.

The current paradox leads to considering water as an energy consumer, when traditionally it was considered an energy source.

In order to be able to apply appropriate criteria for saving energy and for controlling and improving the efficiency of water and energy consumption, the demand, consumption and available energy sources must be clearly established.

Energy efficiency is the set of actions that optimize the relationship between the amount of energy consumed and the final products and services obtained.

Energy sources are generally finite and their proper use is imperative in the present if we are to continue to rely on them in the future. At present, there are some opinions that speak of renouncing a certain degree of well-being and quality of life, although it would probably be enough to adopt responsible habits and take measures of management and investment in the technological field that allow the saving of water and energy.

Energy sources or energy resources are raw materials capable of generating energy and can be classified into renewable and non-renewable energy resources.

Renewable energy sources regenerate naturally and can therefore be considered relatively inexhaustible as well as having a reduced environmental impact. Included as such are hydropower, wind, solar (thermal and photovoltaic), geothermal, biofuel, biomass or marine of various types.

In contrast to these, non-renewable energy sources are considered, which are exhausted over time and have high environmental impacts in obtaining and using them. Energy resources from coal, oil, natural gas, liquefied petroleum gases (LPG) and nuclear energy are non-renewable.

Demand, Consumption and Efficiency

Hydraulic demand is the volume that the end user is willing to purchase in sufficient quantity and quality conditions to meet a given production and consumption target. Usually in the field of hydraulic resources it is measured in hm^3 or km^3, depending on the size of the volume handled. It is conditioned by various factors such as the price of services, the level of income, the type of activity, the technology available, etc.

Within the uses of water subject to demand can be distinguished: supply to populations, agriculture, industrial and energy uses, aquaculture, recreational uses, navigation and transport. It should be clarified that, in the actual exploitation of water resources, it is not always possible to satisfy all the volume required by the different units of water demand. In order to carry out complex estimates of demand in a simplified manner, it is possible to resort to supply data, if this is continuous, and to endowments calculated from a series of variables such as population and its projection, types of crop, climatic characteristics, state of infrastructures, or seasonality. The future expectation is quite negative, due to the fact that the hydraulic demand does not stop growing and this poses a novel scenario, in which the current demand reduction measures are not sufficient.

The final hydraulic consumption is the amount of water that a person has daily for the necessities of cleanliness, cleaning, irrigation and daily activities. It is measured in l/inhab/day or m^3/inhab/year and indirectly reflects the level of economic and social development, when consumption is compared according to income level, showing clearly lower values in areas with low incomes compared to areas with high incomes, as shown in Table 1 which shows water consumption in different areas of the planet.

In the scenario of growing demand mentioned above, the reduction in consumption will play a fundamental role which, at the moment, it does not play.

Hydraulic efficiency refers to the capacity of networks and systems to transport water according to the geometric conditions of the pipes, the materials used and the layout of the networks. Currently, there are inefficiencies caused by unjustified breakdowns and inadequate choices of materials or layout and sizing. There is no doubt that the high technological level of certain areas of engineering offers possibilities for improving hydraulic efficiency that have not yet been explored.

It is necessary to extend the calculation of the water footprint produced in the different available energy sources, in order to be able to quantify the impact of the use of water as energy which, until relatively recently erroneously, was considered negligible. In the current environment with water stress situations becoming more widespread on a daily basis, no data can be dispensed with to help adjust the evaluation of demand. Table 2 shows the water footprint data expressed in m^3/GJ that reveal high water consumption in energy generation.

Table 1. Water consumption in different areas of the earth

Geographical Area	Consumption in l/hab/day
NORTH AND CENTRAL AMERICA	5134
EUROPE	3534
OCEANIA	2430
ASIA	1449
SOUTH AMERICA	1329
AFRICA	685
WORLD AVERAGE	1800
SPAIN	3290

Source: Grupo de Tratamiento de Aguas Residuales. Universidad de Sevilla (2012)

Table 2. Water footprint produced in the generation of energy

	Primary energy source	Water Footprint(m³/GJ)
Non-Renewable	Uranium	0,09
	Natural Gas	0,11
	Coal	0,16
	Oil	1,06
Renewable	Wind	0
	Sun	0,27
	Water	22
	Biomass	70(mean value of range 10-250)

Source: www.waterfootprint.org (2010)

The energy demand can be understood as the amount of energy required by the different elements, machines and systems to carry out the complete operation of the desired task; in the case of the integral water cycle, from the collection of the resource to its return to the environment, going through all the stages described. Currently, energy demand, such as hydropower, is tending to increase due to world population growth and general social and economic development.

Energy consumption represents the cost, in units of energy, necessary to carry out work in a specific activity. In order to evaluate its performance, it must also be quantified economically.

In order to determine the energy consumption of an activity, it is necessary to question the type of energy that is being consumed and the alternatives found in the environment and how this energy is consumed, depending on the available resources and the result obtained, evaluating the performance of the activity analysed. It is also necessary to know how much is consumed in order to correctly dimension the installations that have to provide this energy and, finally, where or who consumes this energy, in order to know the number of applicants and for how long they will have to share part of the energy resources available to carry out the programmed activity.

In order to be able to compare consumption values, ratios calculated from actual energy consumption, i.e. indicators of energy efficiency, are needed. This makes it possible to reduce energy consumption by applying measures, reforms and habits aimed at reducing the energy demand of all processes. In the water sector the energy efficiency indicators are:

1.   Ratio of energy consumption of equipment and installations.

Indicates the specific consumption of the equipment involved in the process and of the installation as a whole, being one of the most significant indicators of the installations. It results from the quotient between the power absorbed and the specific magnitude of the equipment, process or installation evaluated, which may be the flow of water produced, the flow of purified water or the flow of high water. It is measured in kWh/m³.

2.   Ratio of GHG emissions (greenhouse gases).

For integral water cycle activities, it is common to use the indicator gCO_2/m^3 of water supplied (capture, treatment and distribution) or of purified water (sewerage and purification), which provides fundamental information in the process of calculating the Carbon Footprint.

The use of energy in each of the phases of the urban water cycle is reviewed below:

In **water collection**, energy is needed to extract water from the natural environment, with groundwater collection (by means of wells) being more intensive than surface water collection; although, in this case, the origin of the water is a determining factor in knowing how much energy is required to dispose of it, due to the fact that the water may have a specific treatment process associated with a specific energy consumption. Table 3 shows the differences in energy consumption according to the origin of the water and the treatment and distribution systems required.

Table 3. Range of energy consumption according to different water catchments (including distribution) obtained from a study in the Costa Brava, Spain.

Origin of drinking water	Energy consumption (kWh/m³)
Short- distance surface('10 km)	0,0002-0,37
Long distance surface('10 km)	0,15-1,74
Subterranean (aquifers of the zone)	0,37-1,75
Subterranean (distant aquifers)	0,60-1,32
Sea water	4,94-5,41

Source: Sala L. (2007)

Traditional methods of potabilization, consisting of filtration and addition of chemicals, are being replaced by more energy-intensive methods than traditional ones, such as the use of membranes. This is an extraordinary effort when it comes to establishing a balance between the remaining energy consumptions that compensate for this excess.

In the transport and distribution stages, energy is needed to transport the water provided by the pumping stations through pipes and tubes.

90% of water consumption in developed countries is linked to energy consumption, mainly of household appliances and the devices that require it. If you want to optimize the use of water in the final consumption will save water and energy. Currently, especially in large cities, this is being taken into account, but there is still no general implementation of measures and devices for optimizing consumption such as regulating valves, diffusers at points of service, etc.

The energy consumption of drainage systems occurs mainly at points where the water must be raised to higher levels, by means of sewage pumping stations or groups. The rest of the energy consumption is associated with the cleaning, maintenance and rehabilitation of the network, and with the operation of diversion and retention facilities with gates and other electromechanical equipment. There are therefore a number of actions that can lead to significant reductions in energy consumption by improving the performance of equipment.

In the wastewater treatment stage, the process is presented where the greatest amount of electrical energy is consumed from the entire urban water cycle, the biological treatment that leads to the removal of organic matter and nutrients from the wastewater. It is an unprecedented challenge to try to reduce energy consumption at this stage.

Table 4 shows an interval of energy consumption ratios for all stages of the urban water cycle that require energy, estimated from a study in Costa Brava, Spain.

Table 4. Energy consumption ratios of the stages of the urban water cycle

Stages of the urban water cycle	Energy consumption (kWh/m^3)
Collection, pumping and transport	0-3,7
Potabilization	0,03-4,23
Distribution	0,18-0,32
Sewerage and Wastewater Treatment	0,29-1,22
Reuse and transport	0,11-0,32

Source: Sala L. (2007)

Water consumption in urban use, which includes domestic and industrial use, is estimated at 10% and 25% respectively, while agricultural use consumes the remaining 65%; therefore, it makes sense to focus water and energy efficiency efforts on the latter, without ceasing to make management decisions in the other two.

It is also important to identify energy consumption in the uses of water; thus, in domestic use (home, toilets, hygiene, fountains and gardens), sanitary hot water is the water use that reports the highest energy consumption in a domestic environment, since in addition to the own consumption of raising the water is added the necessary to heat it, consuming gas or electricity. The large consumption of water also implies a high energy consumption necessary to supply it (private swimming pools and irrigation of private gardens). Industrial use, which includes refrigeration, product manufacturing, and cleaning, among others, requires energy consumptions that can be very high in certain industries that need specific water treatments, and that involve significant energy consumption to disinfect, remove particles or dissolved salts and to ensure the quality of the necessary water. It also requires techniques with high energy consumption in the process of purification and recycling of industrial effluents without forgetting the industries that consume a high amount of water in their own productive activities (for example, the paper industry). Finally, in agricultural use for intensive irrigation, the consumption largely related to the pumps that move the water from the tanks to the fields is high and usually involves consumption of electricity or diesel, called equivalent diesel consumed.

The inference of the above in the Smart City environment is clear since all the activities, stages and processes analysed condition the different services to the public. For example, the energy behaviour of buildings is favoured by the decisions taken within the study of energy efficiency in the urban water cycle and, in the same way that energy management establishes the standard of Nearly Zero Consumption Building, the possibility of extending the concept to the water cycle in the building is considered, giving rise to what is known as the standard of Zero Consumption Water Building. The Office of Energy Efficiency & Renewable Energy includes, within the United States Federal Energy Management Program, the definition of the Zero Water Consumption Building standard: "A building meets the zero water consumption standard when the amount of alternative water reused plus the amount of water returned to the original source is the same as the amount of water used for consumption in the building itself."

Figure 6. Net Zero Water Building Strategies. Source: https://www.energy.gov/eere/femp/net-zero-water-building-strategies

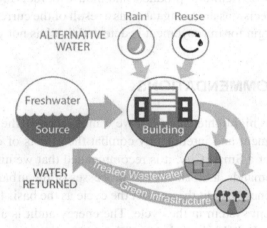

The concept is based on the reduction of the hydraulic demand of the building, the energy demand of the same or both and is outlined in the image of Figure 6 provided by The Office of Energy Efficiency & Renewable Energy. There is therefore a wide range of possibilities within the energy management of the building that so far have not been developed.

To conclude is showed the example of the current situation of the contribution of the water sector in Spain to the circular economy as a line of action within the Circular Economy Strategy, promoted by the European Union, presented at the VI Conference on Water Engineering. From the formulation of the aforementioned strategy, four major sections are recognised in the Water sector: recycling and reuse of materials, production, use and energy saving, recovery of by-products and reuse (regeneration and supply).

Thus, according to data from the Spanish Association of Water Supply and Sanitation (AEAS), in Spain the average annual energy consumption is 0.98 kWh/m^3 and the service energy consumption of the integral water cycle per household is 117 kWh less than the consumption of household appliances when they are on standby.

The energy yield produced by the water sector is around 456 GWh/year, which is equivalent to supplying electricity to a population of 150000 inhabitants for one year. 72% of operators of urban water services have devices for energy use, achieved through the use of renewable energy sources and 40% of that use is for self consumption. The two sources generating the highest percentage of energy use are the production of biogas in wastewater treatment plants and the hydroelectric potential of the water flows used in certain phases of the cycle where the available hydraulic energy is high.

In Spain, approximately 268 hm3 of water has been reused in activities that allow its use in accordance with current legislation; this represents a scarce 7% of the total purified and reclaimed water.

As far as the recovery of by-products is concerned, it is the stabilised sludge or sludge from wastewater treatment plants that is generated in the greatest quantity. Given the legal conditions required for agricultural or forestry use, they enter the distribution chain again as fertilizers and soil conditioners, clearly improving soil properties. The annual production of sewage sludge amounts to a total of 701751 tons of dry matter, approximately 90 kilos of sludge per person per year. 85% of them are used for agriculture, gardening and forestry; 10% for incineration and 5% are deposited in landfills. The possible uses of sand and grease from the pre-treatment and primary treatment of wastewater treatment plants in road pavement layers and as agricultural products and industrial fuels are currently being studied.

In summary, appropriate decisions are being taken as a result of the current incipient energy management policies, but a wide margin for improvement is detected that has not yet been developed.

SOLUTIONS AND RECOMMENDATIONS

In order to tackle the problems highlighted above, if we want to achieve the appropriate level of service while respecting the environment and intelligently combat the effects of climate change in line with the fundamental philosophy of a Smart City, it is recommended that we undertake a strategy aimed at reducing energy and water demands at all stages and processes of the urban water cycle. This involves first carrying out a complete energy audit throughout the cycle as the basis for the subsequent establishment of an energy management system in the cycle. The energy audit is a tool to evaluate the energy performance of an installation. Reliable knowledge of the processes and equipment installed in it makes it possible to determine the factors affecting energy consumption and to propose, if necessary, measures to improve energy efficiency.

Any operator of the urban water cycle has to plan energy audits in all its facilities, especially those with the highest energy consumption, which should also be scheduled every 5-10 years according to the work to which the different equipment of the facility is subject. A valid criterion is the setting of consumption ratios monitored by the operator, which, in the event of a clear change, would lead to a new energy audit.

In order to guarantee the quality and rigour in the preparation of an energy audit, a normative content is established that endorses them. In Spain, these requirements are set out in Standard UNE-EN 16247-5. Auditorías energéticas. Competencia de los auditores energéticos. The complete process of an energy audit in the integral water cycle is detailed below:

1.   Objectives of the energy audit.

The objectives of an energy audit in the urban water cycle are:

a.   Reduce energy consumption.
b.   Improve the energy efficiency of the stages, processes and installations of the water cycle, minimising environmental impact by reducing CO_2 emissions.
c.   Reduce economic expenditure.
d.   Improve the energy behaviour of the installations with greater control of the equipment, detecting opportunities for energy saving in the same.
e.   Improve the level of service and comfort, as determining factors of the process.
2.   Scope of the energy audit.

An energy audit covers the following aspects:

a.   The efficiency of the equipment.
b.   Lighting (interior and exterior).
c.   The air-conditioning of industrial and administrative spaces.
d.   The use of renewable energies.
e.   Energy optimization processes.
f.   The electricity market.
g.   Energy suppliers.
3.   Phases of the energy audit.

The phases of an energy audit form a set of actions that make it possible to establish a reliable and systematic method by which comparable results are obtained. The following are recognized as phases of the energy audit: the pre-diagnosis, the diagnosis, the proposals for improvement and the final report.

a.   Pre-diagnosis.

It consists of collecting the basic information that can then be compared to design ratios, ratios from previous measurements or simply ratios from similar installations that provide a guarantee reference to compare the expected energy consumption. Therefore, in order to carry out an energy audit in the integral water cycle, the first thing to be achieved is to obtain all the information referring to the installation, both the information on the context and location of the installation depending on the activity carried out and that which provides technical data on it.

To check whether the audited equipment is operating in normal energy and economic ranges, reference values are often used in other installations carrying out the same activity. It is common to use reference values for the energy consumption of pumping stations, drinking water supply systems and wastewater treatment.

Table 5 shows an example of the ranges of reference values for energy consumption per cubic metre of water pumped and per metre of elevation in drinking water and wastewater pumps as a function of the installed electrical power (size) of the station. Energy consumption was obtained by taking into account electrical performances of the installation of 90% when the installed power is less than 50 kW,

95% when the power is between 50 kW and 100 kW and 96% when the power is greater than 100 kW, and presenting a hydraulic efficiency between 70% and 80% in the pumping station for drinking water and between 60% and 70% in the pumping station for waste water.

Table 5. Reference values for energy consumption per m³ of pumped water and per m of elevation

Installed power (installation size)(kW)		Energy consumption (kWh/m³/m)
Drinking water from treatment station	P<50kW	0,0038-0,0043
	50kW<P<100kW	0,0036-0,0041
	P>100kW	0,0035-0,0041
Wastewater from pumping station	P<50kW	0,0043-0,0050
	50kW<P<100kW	0,0041-0,0048
	P>100kW	0,0041-0,0047

Source: Sala L. (2007)

b.   Diagnosis.

It consists of analysing the energy and economic data of the installations in order to establish the reference situation that allows comparison of opportunities for improvement in subsequent stages.

c.   Proposals for improvement.

With the current and reference situations perfectly defined, the proposals for improvement are established and those that will be studied in detail and those that will be audited in future visits are selected.

d.   Final report.

A report is drawn up including a detailed description of the current situation and the reference situation used, accompanied by the annexes deemed necessary for the detailed definition of the installation, the proposals for improvement presented and, in addition, a timetable for implementation and follow-up that will facilitate and simplify subsequent energy audits.

On the other hand, together with the necessary awareness of the present and future user, it is important to make use of the possibilities of Big Data fed by the enormous amount of data and measures provided by the different stages of the water cycle. For this reason, all types of automatisms and advanced intelligent systems must be installed that not only feed information into the pre-diagnosis phase of the energy audit, but also contribute to the real-time control of the integral water cycle, making use of the possibilities offered by Artificial Intelligence with the different software already programmed to model and analyse the hydraulic networks and the processes that occur in them.

In this way, all optimization strategies in the different stages of the water cycle, installations and processes would be produced in a more efficient way, since the incorporation of automated control systems would allow, for example, to establish in an appropriate way the operating schedules and provide information on the activity of the same in real time. This information would facilitate immediate decision-making thanks to the management and control of the data received.

The possibilities of improvement that are presented with the help of automatons integrated in the water cycle, would be reflected in the significant reduction of the electrical consumption of the different hydraulic machines and motors necessary for the adequate operation in the different water treatment and pumping stations, through:

1. The optimization of the working schedule of the equipments.
2. A correct choice of the power contracted to the electricity supply company.
3. Improved management of reactive energy consumption by installing capacitor banks that store energy and bring the power factor as close as possible to 1.
4. The simplification of efficiency studies of electric motors that would allow minimizing the different losses in them.
5. Improving the performance of pumping equipment, which currently allows ranges close to 80%, depending on the working point of the machine that can be improved, cutting the impellers and installing frequency variators that control the number of revolutions.
6. Immediate replacement of the elements in which pressure drop is detected.

In all the processes and in the different installations of the water cycle there are possibilities of optimisation of recovery and energy saving, either through the installation of elements such as frequency variators, through the potential for energy recovery that certain phases of the processes present, or even through the potential for the generation of energy and electricity in the same. Tables 6, 7 and 8 present, in a simplified manner, the possible energy consumption or savings and the potential for energy savings in the different stages of the urban water cycle. In the supply network:

Tables 9, 10 and 11 are also presented in a similar way, showing the possible energy consumption or savings and the potential for energy savings in the different stages of the Sewage network of the integral water cycle:

It is evident and quantifiable the high energy and hydraulic consumption that the integral water cycle represents; although, it is precisely this that allows establishing a multitude of energy saving and recovery actions that would optimize the cycle to the point of making it really efficient within the environment of the Smart Cities.

Table 6. Consumption, savings and potential for energy recovery in water collection

Stage of the water cycle	Process	Energy Consumption/Losses	Energy Recovery Potencial
WATER COLLECTION	Gravity water supply	No energy consumption /pressure	Electricity generation with mini-hydraulic energy
	Surface water supply	Pumping	Frequency variators
	Groundwater supply	Pumping from wells/Geothermal energy losses	Geothermal energy recovery

Source: Escuela del Agua. Eficiencia energética en instalaciones de agua. Suez España (2018)

Table 7. Consumption, savings and potential for energy recovery in water treatment

Stage of the water cycle	Process	Energy Consumption/Losses	Energy Recovery Potencial
POTABILIZATION	Removal of iron, carbonate and magnesium	Dosage of reagents	Frequency variators
	Ozonization	Ozone Generation/Ozone Injection/Ozone Destruction (Air heating to 350ºC)	Heat recovery from the air compressor to preheat the incoming airflow
	Flotation, Coagulation and Flocculation	Water Pressurization/Sludge Scratching/Mixing with Barriers or Propellers	Frequency variators
	Sedimentation	Sludge Scraping/Soplant/Vacuum Pump/Sludge Agitation	Heat recovery to heat the steam used for sludge circulation
	Filtration Ultrafiltration/Membranes	High pressure/Cleaning requirements using water or air	Frequency variators
	Chlorination	Dosing pumps	Frequency variators
	Desalination	Reverse Osmosis	Pressure Recovery / Heat Recovery / Solar Desalination

Source: Escuela del Agua. Eficiencia energética en instalaciones de agua. Suez España (2018)

Table 8. Consumption, savings and potential for energy recovery in water transport and distribution.

Stage of the water cycle	Process	Energy Consumption/Losses	Energy Recovery Potencial
TRANSPORT AND DISTRIBUTION	Water storage	Pressure losses at the outlet of the tank if the water comes out by gravity	Electricity generation with mini-hydraulic energy
	Pumping	Heat loss	Heat recovery
	Service Deposits	Pressure and flow losses if the head is greater thannecessary	Electricity generation with mini-hydraulic energy
	Pipes	Presure drop	Installation of microturbines at points of clear overpressure
	Reinforcement pumps	Heat loss	Heat recovery
	Reinforcement Chlorination	Dosing pumps	Frequency variators
	Pressure reducing valves	Pressure drop	Electricity generation with mini-hydraulic energy

Source: Escuela del Agua. Eficiencia energética en instalaciones de agua. Suez España (2018)

Table 9. Consumption, savings and potential for energy recovery in the sewer system

Stage of the water cycle	Process	Energy Consumption/Losses	Energy Recovery Potencial
SEWERAGE	Sewer cleaning	Suction and scraping	Frequency variators

Source: Escuela del Agua. Eficiencia energética en instalaciones de agua. Suez España (2018)

Table 10. Consumption, savings and potential for energy recovery in wastewater treatment and regeneration

Stage of the water cycle	Process	Energy Consumption/Losses	Energy Recovery Potencial
	Gravity sewage inlet	Pressure and flow losses if the head is greater than necessary	Electricity generation with mini-hydraulic energy
	Inlet Pumping	Heat loss and vibrations	Heat recovery
	Inlet tank	Losses of pressure and flow if the inlet is by gravity	Electricity generation with mini-hydraulic energy
	Roughing	Automatic cleaning occasionally under pressure/Rotary mechanism or waterfall	Energy recovery from rotation or waterfall
	Desanding	Occasional mecanical sand extraction/Circular deaerators, rotary mixing, air blowing and sand extraction/Air deaerator with induced flow, air blowing (higher efficiency)	Frequency variators
	Degreasing	Surface scraping	
	Sand filter		
	Processing By-Products (Sand and Grease)	Biological treatment (exothermic process)/Airing	Recovery of energy generated/Use of fats as fuel
WATER TREATMENT AND REGENERATION	Gates	Presure drop	
	Sedimentation	Sludge scraper/Air blower/Vacuum pump/Turbine and agitator for sludge recirculation	Heat recovery to heat the steam used for sludge circulation
	Biological treatment	Blowers for aeration / pressure drop in air transfer	Heat recovery
	Nitrification/De-nitrification	Dosage of reagents	Frequency variators
	Filtration	High pressure/needed cleaning (water or air injection)	
	Digestion	Biogas Generation/Aeration Blowers	Cogeneration
	Flotation, Coagulation and Flocculation	Water Pressurization/Sludge Scratching/Mixing with Barriers or Propellers	Frequency variators
	Ultraviolet (UV) disinfection	UV generation/Heat loss	Heat recovery
	Thickening/Dewatering of sludge	Provision of heat or centrifugation	Heat recovery
	Sludge drying	High energy consumption	Heat recovery for sludge preheating
	Odour control	Fans and blowers	Heat recovery

Source: Escuela del Agua. Eficiencia energética en instalaciones de agua. Suez España (2018)

Table11. Consumption, savings and potential for energy recovery in the return to the riverbed

Stage of the water cycle	Process	Energy Consumption/Losses	Energy Recovery Potencial
RETURN TO THE RIVERBED	Treated water tank	Pressure drop if water is discharged by gravity	Energy recovery from rotation or waterfall
	Pumping of treated water	Heat loss	Heat recovery

Source: Escuela del Agua. Eficiencia energética en instalaciones de agua. Suez España (2018)

To all these measures must be added those related to the optimisation of lighting in installations (use of natural light, use of more efficient lamps, luminaires and auxiliary equipment, installation of presence detectors, implementation of natural light regulation systems, implementation of centralised management by zones, etc.).), the improvement of the efficiency and maintenance of the air conditioning equipment, the construction of the installations, assuming passive architecture criteria that allow absorbing the greatest amount of energy in the most exposed facades and, at the same time, protect them from solar radiation to avoid excessive consumption of air conditioning inside the buildings; as well as the measures of comfort indicated for the personnel who carry out their work in the facilities (adjustment of the temperature to the thermal comfort according to the season of the year, adoption of the appropriate clothing to the time of the year, turning off equipment and lighting when they are not necessary, ensuring the closing of doors and windows, etc.).

In accordance with the above, three examples of real applications already established in the environment of the Smart Cities in Spain are shown below, which are totally comparable in other parts of the world:

1. In the case of Cordoba, in the south of Spain, the Municipal Water Company of Cordoba (EMACSA) controls the water supply of the city, through a SCADA system, which acquires the information from the network through communication with the different field devices (hydraulic instruments), remotely and with radio transmitters, in accordance with the program called SIRETRAC, whose objective is the development of an advanced computer system to improve the management, control and knowledge of the network. With the information handled by the SIRETRAC it is possible to create complete reports of different types. It is a fundamental tool for controlling the volume of unregistered water, defined as the difference between the volume distributed to a system and the volume registered in the system's customer meters, which has traditionally been one of the most important indicators of a system's efficiency. Currently, there are five reports that have been designed by the supervisor in charge, and these can be expanded and/or modified as needed:

    a. Daily report of the sector. Information regarding flows and volumes of the sectors distributed daily. This is generally the most widely used report for observing the operation of each sector.
    b. Report by sector strip. Information of the sectors limited to a time band defined by the user. Useful for the study of night-time minimums.
    c. Sector consumption report. Detailed information on the daily and hourly consumption of each of the sectors.
    d. Daily report of the signals. General information and statistics for each of the signals.
    e. Signal reliability report. Quality of the measurements captured by each of the signals. Useful to detect a malfunction in the hydraulic sensors.

2. In the region of Pamplona, in the north of Spain, a model has been designed to evaluate the energy potential for air conditioning applications in buildings from heat recovery in the supply and sewage networks of the Commonwealth of Pamplona/SCPSA.

In a more practical way, the pre-dimensioning for a residential building has been carried out, in which the energy use in a specific place of the city of Pamplona is evaluated. Under the conditions of this case-study (use of a DN1000 supply pipe or a DN400 collector), with the use of a water-water heat pump, electricity consumption can be reduced in comparison with an air-water heat pump by 24.4% in the case of using the exchanger with the supply network, and by 28.4% in the case of sanitation.

3. One of the main projects developed with the use of this tele-reading system has been carried out in Castellón de la Plana, in eastern Spain. A joint project carried out by IoTsens and its client Facsa where 14,000 meters have been deployed in different areas of the city, working, for the most part, with the LoRaWAN communications protocol. In order to carry out an exhaustive control of the water consumption of the clients, to detect leaks, breakdowns, frauds and manipulations more easily, and to carry out an efficient management of the water resources, Facsa and IoTsens have implemented a project for the intelligent management of the water. Thus, a first proof of concept with 600 smart water meters could be integrated and implemented, paving the way for the current deployment of FACSA consisting of 13,000 water meters connected to the LoRaWAN network. The main results obtained so far are:
    a. Increase in the performance of the supply network by more than 10%.
    b. Adoption of a unified protocol that allows working with different brands and models of meters.
    c. Reading of more than 5,000 meters with a single LoRaWAN Gateway without the need for additional infrastructure.
    d. Installation of 14,000 smart meters.
    e. Extension of Gateway coverage: more than 1 km radius in cities and more than 5 km in open spaces.
    f. Leak detection in 24 hours.
    g. Generation of water balances per hour.

Finally, taking account the importance of green areas in the Smart Cities, a special recommendation is made aimed at optimising the efficient management of water resources in these areas.

Part of the consumption of water resources in urban areas is dedicated to the irrigation of green areas, parks and gardens. In the Region of Madrid (Spain), Canal de Isabel II, the company that manages the integral water cycle in practically the entire region, estimates that close to 20% of the consumption of water resources is for irrigation of green areas. This information in other areas of the planet are significantly lower, yet they highlight the importance of optimizing irrigation management of green areas.

In this way, in areas where water resources are limited, it is very important that public institutions optimise the use of water resources by reusing reclaimed water to irrigate green areas and wash streets. In Spain, this has been regulated in legislation for more than 10 years (BOE 2007 REAL DECRETO 1620/2007, de 7 de Diciembre) and is applied in some cities, with the city of Madrid being a very representative case. Within the management of irrigation water consumption different factors will influence the different stages of the life cycle of the project.

During the project phase, designs that optimise water consumption must be proposed, taking into account the climatic conditions of the area where the project is carried out (rainfall, temperatures, wind speed, radiation and relative humidity), as well as zoning with the species according to water demand. This way of projecting requires multidisciplinary teams in the design of landscaped areas, with specialists in the quantification of water consumption of plant species. Following these recommendations, the WUCOLS (Water Use Classification of Landscape Species) methodology of Costello L.R. et al (2014) has been adapted in many places for several years. With this methodology developed at the University of California it is possible to estimate water consumption in green areas through the reference evapotranspiration (FAO, 2006) corrected with the garden coefficient (K_j).

This coefficient is the product of the crop coefficient (K_c), the coefficient as a function of the planting density (K_d), and the microclimatic coefficient (K_m) of the location of the species within the city. To give a very simple example, the water consumption of a meadow in the middle of an avenue with a high traffic intensity is neither the same nor similar to that within a landscaped area.

Also from the project phase, it is very important to carry out an efficient design of the irrigation installation. In this way, irrigation should be attempted in all areas preferably with localized irrigation systems; and if sprinkler and diffusion systems are needed, these should be low angle and low-medium range to minimize evaporation losses.

In the phase of operation and maintenance of green areas, the day-to-day management of water consumption must be paramount, with monitoring of the installation being essential. In this way, with the help of weather stations, water demands can be calculated on a daily or weekly basis. In order to achieve this, remote management and control systems must be implemented that allow irrigation doses and, therefore, irrigation times to be adapted to real demands, thus optimizing water consumption.

FUTURE RESEARCH DIRECTIONS

In short, the potential for study, development and implementation of measures leading to full energy efficiency of the urban water cycle is high. However, the following are a series of initiatives that, either because they are at an early stage of development or because they have not been investigated in depth, have not yet yielded apreciable results; but they will undoubtedly provide ample room for improvement in the efficient management of the resource and of the waste generated in the water cycle.

1. Intensification and improvement of by-product generation processes (sludge, sand, grease, nitrogen and phosphorus), making them perfectly valorizable and competitive products in various agricultural and industrial applications (fertilizers, industrial fuels, construction materials, etc.)
2. Development of modelling programmes which, aided by the enormous potential of possibilities presented by Artificial Intelligence, facilitate the exploitation of the stages of the integral water cycle, placing special emphasis on those, such as the purification and regeneration of waste water, in which the processes are more complex as they are affected by multivariable operation, which requires exhaustive control of all parameters.
3. Implementation of extraordinary energy efficiency and saving measures that contribute to reducing the greatest possible amount of greenhouse gases and the carbon footprint coming mainly from the electricity consumption of the water cycle, whose mediumterm objective must be to become "carbon neutral".

4. Establishment of programmes for the implementation and development of renewable and clean energies at all stages of the urban water cycle, such as the installation of microturbines at points on networks where overpressure provides excess energy, the installation of thermal and photovoltaic solar panels on all surfaces whose orientation and continuous solar radiation allow energy value to be generated.

5. Intensification of research to improve the current regasification procedures for biogás obtained in wastewater treatment and regeneration plants, allowing the injection of surplus produced in the natural gas distribution network.

The complexity of the urban water cycle makes it possible, without any doubt, to detect many more possibilities for process optimisation, which would make this list of initiatives practically unlimited. Therefore, these are only a representation of these that the authors of the chapter consider to be perfectly feasible.

CONCLUSION

When a city is to become Smart City, resources, processes and services must be included, and all the stages of the water cycle are a set of processes, with water as a fundamental resource, which condition the different services to the citizenry and, therefore, it is necessary to try to establish efficiency improvements in all of them, as has been shown in the development of the chapter. In short, in order to achieve the integration of the necessary urban water cycle in the environment of the Smart Cities, the following conclusions could be emphasized:

1. The analysis of all the stages of the water cycle carried out in the chapter reveals an appreciable margin of control and savings that, without a doubt, are favoured by data management tools (Big Data), by the various automatisms inherent in Artificial Intelligence (AI) and, in short, by the wide range of possibilities provided by Internet of Things (IoT), as shown by the case of the intervention in Castellón de la Plana included in the text.

2. There is an unquestionable certainty in view of the data in Table 1, regarding water consumption on the different continents that, in addition to highlighting the enormous imbalances between them, warns of the obligatory adjustment that the continents with the greatest consumption (North America, Central America and Europe) will have to make in the coming years due to the growing demand from the less consuming continents thanks to the progressive and sustained economic and technological growth that they are experiencing.

3. The water footprint data provided in Table 2 confirm the change of paradigm that places water as an energy consumer in all the processes in which it is involved. The in-depth analysis of these data can be an invaluable aid when choosing, if possible, the energy source that brings the operation of the cycle stages closer to the Smart City concept.

4. If the energy consumption data of the stages of the water cycle are consulted carefully, of which some intervals are given in Table 4, it can be seen that the most intensive stages in terms of energy consumption are Collection, Purification and Regeneration of water; and, therefore, it must be in these stages where the greatest efforts are made to implement measures that lead to greater energy efficiency.

5. The continuous flows of energy that set in motion all the processes of the stages of the water cycle, as reflected in Tables 6, 7, 8, 9, 10, 11 and the real cases included in the chapter, show the great margin of possibilities that heat and energy recovery represent in all these processes.

Finally, the authors hope that reading it will contribute to the awareness of the importance of working with a basic resource in which, first of all, the guarantee of supply must be generalized. Each and every one of the measures already established and the proposals must be directed in this direction. It should not be forgotten that, despite the advances made in hydraulic technology in the last three decades, today more than a third of the world's population does not have adequate access to safe water. This situation depends to a large extent on the efficient management policies developed in the industrialized countries; therefore, an efficient use of the resource will contribute to increasing its availability under appropriate conditions in other areas of the planet where the priority is the resource itself.

REFERENCES

Boletín Oficial del Estado núm. 294. BOE (2007) REAL DECRETO 1620/2007. Ministerio de la Presidencia. Gobierno de España., de 8 de diciembre de 2007.

Boletín Oficial del Estado núm. 162. BOE (2007) REAL DECRETO 907/2007. Ministerio de Medio Ambiente. Gobierno de España., de 7 de julio de 2007.

Costello, L. R., & Jones, K. S. (2014). *WUCOLS IV: Water Use Classification of Landscape Species*. Davis, CA: California Center for Urban Horticulture, University of California. Retrieved from https://ucanr.edu/sites/WUCOLS/

Diario Oficial de la Unión Europea núm. 327. Directiva Marco del Agua (DMA). 2000/60/CE del Parlamento Europeo y del Consejo 22 de diciembre de 2000.

Allen, R. G., Pereira, L. S., Raes, D., & Smith, M. (2006). *Evapotranspiración del cultivo. Guías para la determinación de los requerimientos de agua de los cultivos. FAO Riego y Drenaje, Monografía Nº 56*. Roma: FAO.

Hernández Muñoz, A. (2015). *Abastecimiento y Distribución de Agua. 6ª edición*. Madrid: Garceta Grupo Editorial.

Hernández Muñoz, A. (2015). *Depuración y Desinfección de Aguas Residuales. 6ª edición*. Madrid: Garceta Grupo Editorial.

Hernández Muñoz, A. (2017). *Saneamiento y Alcantarillado. 8ª edición*. Madrid: Garceta Grupo Editorial.

Herrando Mill, E. (2012). *Auditorías energéticas en el ciclo integral del agua*. Barcelona: Presented at Jornada Técnica SMAGUA.

IDAE (2010). *Estudio de Prospectiva. Consumo energético en el sector del agua*. Madrid: Instituto para la Diversificación y Ahorro de la Energía (IDEA). Fundación Observatorio de Prospectiva Tecnológica Industrial (OPTI).

Metcalf & Eddy. (2013). *Wastewater engineering: treatment and reuse* (4th ed.). New York: McGraw-Hill.

Norma UNE-EN 16247-5. (2015). *Auditorías energéticas*. Competencia de los auditores energéticos.

Sala, L. (2007). *Balances energéticos del ciclo del agua y experiencias de reutilización planificada en municipios de la Costa Brava*. Valencia: Presented at Seminario Internacional Agua, Energía y Cambio Climático.

Sensus. (2012). *Water 20/20: Bringing Smart Water Networks into Focus*. Retrieved from https://c.ymcdn. com/sites/www.ncsafewater.org/resource/collection/A0650A28-4C94-471B-B98E-B0DFD4F76C35/ Water_T_AM_09.10_Walsby.pdf

Soto Álvarez, G., Soto Benavides, M., Sáez Abarzúa, C., & Morales Miranda, M. (2013). Desalación de agua de mar mediante sistema Osmosis Inversa y Energía Fotovoltaica para provisión de agua potable en Isla Damas, Región de Coquimbo. Documentos Técnicos del PHI-LAC, N° 33. Montevideo: UNESCO.

Wulf, G. (2010). Agua y energía en California. *Ingeniería del Agua, 17*(3), 201–211.

U.S. Department of Energy. (2019). *Net Zero Water Buildings Strategies*. Retrieved from https://www. energy.gov/eere/femp/net-zero-water-building-strategies

ADDITIONAL READING

Aparicio Guirao, J. M & Páez Clavero, A. (2017). *La digitalización de los servicios de abastecimiento: mejora en la eficiencia de los procesos*. Presented at XXXIV Jornadas Técnicas. Tarragona, Mayo de 2017

Beivide García, A, Jiménez Banzo, A & Campos Gibert, A. (2017) *Swing: Incorporación del concepto Smart city en la ciudad de Burgos*. Presented at XXXIV Jornadas Técnicas. Tarragona, Mayo de 2017

Imbernón Manresa, J. A, Nevado Santos, S & Gonzálvez García, J.M (2017). *Monitorización energética inteligente con Enerlogy Monitoring*. Presented at XXXIV Jornadas Técnicas. Tarragona, Mayo de 2017

Raich-Montiu, J., Peris, R., Gutiérrez, J., Milán, D., & Weingartner, A. (2016). *Importance of hardware and software of on-line monitoring stations for long time day-to-day operation in distribution networks*. Presented at Singapore International Water Week.

Rice, E. W., Baird, R. B., & Eaton, A. D. (2017) Standard Methods for the examination of water and wastewater. Presented at 23rd Ed., AWWA, E.U.A.

Velitchko Tzatchkov. (2012). *Improving efficiency of water utilities: real-time modelling and Scada data assimilation*. Prsented at Smart Water Network Conference. Utrech

KEY TERMS AND DEFINITIONS

Coagulation: Process that consists in adding a chemical product (the coagulant) that causes the destabilization of the dispersed colloidal matter and its agglomeration in flocs.

Crop Coefficient (K_c): Adjustment coefficient that allows the calculation of actual evapotranspiration from potential evapotranspiration or the evapotranspiration of the reference crop. These coefficients depend fundamentally on the characteristics of each crop, so they are specific to each crop and depend on its state of development and its phenological stages, so they are variable over time. They also depend on the characteristics of the soil and its humidity, as well as on agricultural practices and irrigation.

Decanting: Physical process of separating liquids or solids, using the difference in density between the substances that make up a heterogeneous mixture of the wastewater.

Evapotranspiration: It is the sum of two phenomena that take place in the crop-soil relationship, the transpiration of the crop and the evaporation of the soil, which constitutes the fundamental loss of water, from which the water requirement of the crops is calculated.

Flocculation: Chemical process by means of which, with the addition of substances called flocculants, the colloidal substances present in the water are agglutinated, thus facilitating their decantation and subsequent filtering.

Garden Coefficient (K_j): Is the relationship between the evapotranspiration of the reference crop and the evapotranspiration of the garden $ET_c = ET_o \cdot K_j$.

Microclimatic Coefficient (K_m): This is the coefficient that takes into account environmental differences. When the external conditions increase the evaporation of the irrigation zone, there are high microclimatic conditions and $K_m = 1 - 1,4$, when the microclimatic conditions are medium, $K_m = 1$ and; finally, when the microclimatic conditions are low, $K_m = 0,5 - 1$.

Neutralization: A chemical process that consists of adding acids or bases to the waste stream in order to stabilize the pH at a desired value.

Planting Density (K_d): It is the number of crop species per hectare and depends on the separation of the crop lines and the distance between crops in the same line.

Pumping Stations: Facilities that are constructed and equipped to transport water or wastewater from the suction or arrival level to the treatment units, to the upper or outlet level.

Storm Tanks: Storm tanks are elements of the drainage network designed to regulate the flow produced during periods of rain and/or to prevent uncontrolled discharges into the receiving environment (river, sea, etc.).

Chapter 7
Smart City = Smart Citizen = Smart Economy?
An Economic Perspective of Smart Cities

Elizabeth Frank
Universidad CEU San Pablo, Spain

Gloria Aznar Fernández-Montesinos
Universidad CEU San Pablo, Spain

ABSTRACT

With a rapidly growing world population, urban populations are estimated to increase significantly over the next decades. This trend is reason for concern since the planet's resources are limited, and climate change is inherent. This chapter focusses on the question about whether new technologies employed in smart cities can be the answer to current and future needs of a city population. Cutting-edge technological advances are reshaping our ecosystem; transforming society, living, and work environments; transport systems; energy grids; healthcare; communications; businesses; and education. How can cities respond to the multitude of challenges by employing technology and at the same time ensure the public well-being, improve the quality of life of city inhabitants, and make sure that the human is still at the center of decisions?

INTRODUCTION

The world is rapidly changing. In the 1950's, around 1 billion people were living in urban areas around the world. By the year 2018, the urban populations counted for 4.2 billion people. 55% of the cities' population lived in urban areas. These areas account for as much as 70 percent of global GDP nowadays. The United Nations estimates an increase up to 68% of this percentage by 2050. The most urbanized areas are the American continent followed by Europe, Oceania and Asia whereas Africa is the continent with mostly rural residents (United Nations, 2018).

DOI: 10.4018/978-1-7998-3817-3.ch007

Copyright © 2020, IGI Global. Copying or distributing in print or electronic forms without written permission of IGI Global is prohibited.

The increased trend of urbanization brings concerns on how the future generations will live. The actual resources that our planet provides us with are limited and not sufficient, and upcoming generations will see themselves affected. We will face challenges regarding sustainable, socio-economic development, politics and environmental issues.

This chapter focusses on the question whether new technology can be the answer to our future needs. Will Smart Cities be the solution? The main challenge is to recognize needs, interpret digital data and predict changes with the help of technology. It is time to examine technology and think about its implications.

Technological advances are reshaping our ecosystem with cutting-edge technology such as 5G, Internet of Things (IoT), Artificial Intelligence (AI), Machine Learning, Virtual and Augmented Reality, Cloud Computing, Blockchain, Cybersecurity, just to name a few. It transforms everything that surrounds us, beginning with society, work environments, transport systems, energy grids, health care, communications and even relationships. This opens a debate on how the Human is adapting to these new technologies, not only on an individual level, but collectively. Therefore, the next question to ask is how cities can respond to all these challenges. How can we not only adapt and turn our cities into smart cities, but also how can we turn our economy into smart economy and citizens into smart citizens along the way? This is an opportunity that should not only be about technology but also embody the human being.

The objective of this chapter is to review the Smart City discussion by introducing different elements, by illustrating the efforts that have been made so far in this area, the weak links that need to be tied up, the potential Smart Cities have to improve the life of citizens and last, but not least, to provide a perspective for the future.

BACKGROUND

What is a Smart City?

Historically, cities have always been engines of innovation, prosperity and growth (Smith & Lobo, 2019). The Greeks already proved a high degree of innovation when building roads, ensuring water supply through aqueducts or introducing democracy.

Thanks to increasing trade and new trade routes, cities in the Middle Ages where the basis for change in Europe. Up until then agricultural structures and cities had been static for centuries. As living standards in the cities gradually improved, the city population started to grow and cities started to prosper (Mees, 1975).

With the Industrial Revolution in the 18th Century, the transition from a rural to an urban, industrialized society was under way, which again sped up the growth of cities, with the main driver being technological progress.

When looking at the present, the term Smart City is nowadays often used to describe many big cities. As of today, there is no consensus on a common definition of a Smart City (Sánchez-Corcuera et al., 2019). The term was first used in the early 2000s deriving from the term smart phone as a result from the possibilities offered by digitalization and technology. Many claim it is a buzzword, a marketing label or an umbrella term that comprises several different aspects and ideas. The concept itself can be seen as a reaction to the economic, social and political challenges of post-industrial societies, the focus lying on pollution, demographic change, population growth, urbanization, financial and economic crisis and scarcity of resources, amongst others (Angelidou, 2015). Smart City reflects the idea of solving certain problems in a smarter, more intelligent and efficient way than before, like finding parking space in an overfull city center, managing traffic flow or optimizing waste collection and living space.

It also reflects the idea of a city engaging with its citizens in the 21st century, providing a sustainable, modern, intelligent, convenient, competitive and open space for living in a community (Pellicer, Santa, Bleda & Maestre 2013). In their article '*Industry 4.0 as a part of smart cities*', Lom et al. (2016) defend that the term of Smart City was created as a sustainable model that includes technical, economic and human centered as well as legal aspects for improving sustainability.

In the study '*Mapping Smart Cities in the EU*' (2014), the European Parliament provides the following working definition: "A Smart City is a city seeking to address public issues via ICT (*Information, Communication, Technology*)-based solutions on the basis of a multi-stakeholder, municipally based partnership" (p. 9). The same study reveals that in Europe the phenomenon of Smart Cities can be mainly attributed to larger cities. Almost 90% of European Cities with more than 500,000 inhabitants where involved in Smart City initiatives up to 2014, whereas only 43% of cities with inhabitants ranging from 100,000 to 200,000 were undergoing Smart City projects (European Parliament, 2014).

However, there are also voices that advocate that the Smart City is a concept that is mainly driven by the marketing machines of big companies with the idea of making money. The IT industry is at the lead with innovative Smart City solutions that will provide great benefits to the city, to its citizens, but also to the companies selling the solutions and services. Digitalization promises fewer costs, more flexibility and more efficiency and is seen as an improvement of the everyday life of citizens.

MAIN FOCUS OF THE CHAPTER

Smart City Objectives

The main objectives pursued by Smart City initiatives and projects are to increase the public well-being and the quality of life of city inhabitants, driving innovation in the cities to attract businesses in order to enhance economic competitiveness and at the same time focusing on sustainability.

Sub-objectives of these goals are a more efficient and effective decision-making incorporating big data and at the same time enhancing citizen participation and engagement; providing safer communities and improving a city's ecological footprint by rethinking transportation, utility management and infrastructure and developing new economic opportunities and thus increasing a city's overall competitiveness.

It is interesting that according to the European Parliament, most of European cities that had initiated Smart City Initiatives or Projects before 2014 focused mainly on environment and/or on mobility (European Parliament, 2014). This may be a good start, but there is still a long way to go to reach a city's full potential and reach Smart Governance, Smart Living, Smart Mobility, Smart Economy and a Smart Environment.

Outline

In order to respond to some of the before mentioned challenges posed by the 21st century, the Smart City concept aims to implement smarter technology to the critical components of the infrastructure and services of a City (Washburn & Sindhu, 2010). Let us take a closer look at these main components of a city's infrastructure that are affected and their challenges (not ranked by importance):

First, there is the *City Administration*, with its local authorities that need to provide an efficient service to its citizens and at the same time supply an environment in which businesses can thrive.

Second, the *Transportation system* consisting in the road network, public and mass transport, parking grid and mobility in general is another critical and basic component of a city's infrastructure. It plays a key role in modelling a city. Reducing the carbon footprint of cities and citizens is one of the major objectives of the Smart City discussion regarding transport.

In third place, we have the *Utility infrastructure*, consisting in water supply and sewage, energy and power supply, waste management and communication infrastructure. The scarcity of resources, but also pollution and other climate challenges, can directly be linked to the need for a more efficient and greener utility management.

Fourth, *Public Safety and Security* consisting in police, fire departments, first aid and other emergency services are faced with the growing number of people living in the city. Responding quickly to emergency situations becomes challenging. There is a necessity to incorporate the latest communication and surveillance technology, which is essential to be able to fight crime, dispatch the police, ambulance or fire brigade when emergencies require so.

Fifth, the ageing population requires better *Healthcare* solutions. By the year 2070 the life expectancy in Europe will increase to 88.2 years (European Commission, 2017), at the same time the workforce is declining, the number of pensions increasing and the costs for social service and health care grow steadily. But not only challenges of an ageing population are a burden on the health care system of a city, other challenges such as more people suffering from obesity, allergies, cardiovascular diseases, diabetes, cancer or mental health issues have to be addressed.

Sixth, *Real Estate* in terms of public, private, but also corporate dimensions play a detrimental role in any City, not just the Smart City. Being able to offer affordable housing and having residential urban properties are as important as the availability of office spaces and manufacturing sites for businesses. Having green spaces in a City have a number of benefits for inhabitants, ranging from better air quality over social benefits to enhancing safety and public health (European Commission, 2019).

Seventh, *Education* at first glance may be considered a less important area when it comes to city services; however, the access, quality and cost of education do play an important role for the future of our cities.

Following we will be taking a closer look at each of these different elements, the opportunities and challenges that arise when considering Smart City solutions and some illustrative examples of successful Smart City projects that have been implemented around the globe.

Smart Government: How to Involve Citizens Effectively

One of the main objectives of Smart Cities is to ensure that the citizens are at the heart and center of the discussion. It is easy to lose sight of this goal with technology, innovations leading the way, showing up opportunities of what could be achieved by technological progress, and what is feasible. However, it is the responsibility of local city authorities to take decisions that make sense and improve the life of the citizens and in the cities. Therefore, the dialogue with citizens is imperative, to ensure the topics that have to be tackled are relevant to the population. Digitalization does not reduce pollution, promote innovation or improve energy efficiency automatically. Digitalization in itself is not an end, it is a means.

The overall goal is the citizen and the improvement of life in the cities. Hence, citizen participation is not only requested, it is paramount.

In the German city of Tübingen a Smart Citizen App '*Tübinger-Bürger-App*' was developed and tested allowing only registered citizens to participate. It provides the city with a better and more representative basis for decision-making, a higher legitimacy and at the same time activates citizenship. In a referendum about whether to build a new swimming pool or a concert hall in the city, in early 2019 citizens were asked to vote via the app. There was an overall participation rate of 17%, higher than any other citizen survey in the city before (Schwäbisches Tagblatt, 2019). This is representative democracy, getting people involved. However, engaging communities and opening a dialogue with people also raises questions about privacy issues, anonymity and data protection, which we will discuss later on in this chapter.

Another illustrative example on how to reach citizens and get them involved in their communities is the application '*SeeClickFix*' that is currently being used by several hundreds of cities in the United States. This application is based on the direct involvement of citizens that can log information on potholes, broken sidewalks or anything that has to be fixed in the infrastructure of their neighborhood. In Europe, there is a similar service called '*Fix my street*'. Admittedly, gathering data and meaningful information from citizens will enable the city to make better decisions based on real-life data.

Furthermore, digital collaboration between departments and agencies due to improved connectivity should be enhanced. Along this line, the Spanish City of Barcelona has implemented a set of e-government services, aiming for a better transparency and higher efficiency regarding public services (European Parliament, 2014). It makes public data available and supports businesses and the creation of new services and applications (*'Open Data BCN'*). Making local administration more accessible (*'Quiosc PintBCN'*) offers more transparency and a better access to local government, saving time and costs for the citizen and the city administration.

There is no doubt that bureaucracy will be made easier through digitalization. Being able to do your tax declaration online, paying taxes or a parking fine without moving from the couch of your home makes life easier. Costs are reduced, processes are optimized. Cities that can do an online census need not pay for agents that go from home to home to count the population in person.

However, one of the main challenges revealed by the '*Urban Governance Survey (2016)*' and affirmed by half of the city administrators surveyed is the lack of funds in this area (European Commission, 2019). Apart from this, the possibility of scaling e-governance solutions to a wider level of public and, in a further step replicating them to other cities, still needs to be explored in-depth. Another question that is raised is whether citizens using these services are truly representative of a community (in terms of age, gender or ethnicity) (European Commission, 2019).

Smart Transport: Individual or Shared?

When designing a city, planners should not underestimate the need for a basic transport and mobility infrastructure. As most of a city's products, food and natural resources are provided from outside the city, having to transport them into the city strains the environment and increases the ecological footprint, as does the need to commute by the majority of the workforce.

In the last century, transport has been dominated by private means of transportation allowing the individual to be more independent, have a higher level of freedom and providing a higher degree of mobility. At the same time, environmental pollution and traffic congestion have increased and there are negative effects on health and safety (European Commission, 2019).

Several cities have introduced mechanisms to help reduce or limit vehicles accessing the city centers, such as the introduction of the '*Congestion Charge*' for the London City Centre in 2003 that imposes a high fee every time a vehicle enters the city center. Other cities introduce bus lanes, high parking fees or increase the number of pedestrian zones. In the case of Madrid, there are periodic vehicle bans for certain engine types in the city when pollution levels are too high.

Interestingly enough, during the ninth edition of the '*Smart City Expo World Congress 2019*' in Barcelona two topics were dominant on the agenda and both were related to mobility. One was autonomous driving and the other topic was shared mobility.

Some autonomous transport solutions have already been implemented in cities around the word, such as the autonomous electric bus EZ10, produced by EasyMile that can transport up to 15 people. According to the company-website, it is currently "the most deployed driverless shuttle in the world" (EZ10, 2019). In 2017, the automotive manufacturing company Continental acquired a minority share in the company anticipating the growth of the autonomous transport segment (Continental, 2017).

For now, the shuttle is mainly used for transporting individuals, but there is a potential to use the buses for logistical purposes and to transport freight as well. Overall, the use of this type of vehicles reduces traffic and pollution, thus improving the ecological footprint and at the same time, increases traffic safety. (European Commission 2019).

Another example is the pilot project, DGT3.0, that was recently launched in Spain by the Spanish General Traffic Authority together with the car manufacturer SEAT and the telecommunications company Telefónica providing a system that sends out alerts to connected cars via the IoT, thus offering early detection of traffic jams, accidents, construction work or any type of incident affecting traffic and allowing drivers to opt for alternative, less frequented routes according to the article '*La DGT y Telefónica prueban un sistema de IoT que anticipa a los conductores sobre peligros en la carretera*' (2019).

Apart from autonomous driving, there are other, alternative models of transport. We can observe an increasing demand for vehicle sharing, either simultaneously or over time. This concept is known as Collaborative Economy (Gori, Parcu & Stasi, 2015). In this model, the distribution of goods and services differs from the traditional model of corporations selling their products/services. In this model, individuals and businesses rent, co-rent or share assets or spaces, like their cars, homes and time with others (some in a peer-to-peer fashion, others in a business-to-business fashion).

E-bikes, e-scooters or kick-bikes as well as e-cars can be rented short-term in all major cities around the globe and allow for easy access and mobility in the city. The respective web app indicates where you can find the nearest vehicle and paying for the rental via app makes the service easy, user-friendly, exciting and fast. These means of transport help reduce traffic and are a sustainable alternative to cars and even public transport. Examples for companies providing such services are emov, lime, Tier, Bird, Scoot, Spin or Cityscoot, just to name a few of the many and they all have very similar business models. The business with e-vehicles started out as extremely lucrative with many start-ups wanting to take advantage of the hype. However, the company COUP has recently decided to withdraw from the sharing business by removing its roughly 5,000 eScooters from Berlin, Paris and Madrid, due to increased competition and the high cost for maintenance of these vehicles (Spiegel, 2019.1). Having vehicles stolen, disassembled or damaged is one problem for the providers. Another challenge is the short life span, especially with e-scooters, which may range between 3 and 6 months leading to the problem of waste disposal. What was thought to be improving the ecological footprint of the city may actually turn into the opposite, when taking into account the increasing amount of electric waste ending up in landfills. It may well be a question of perspective. If the use of the car is substituted, then the ecological effect may well be positive. If users replace a stroll, bikes, buses or the metro/subway, then the effect may be negative (Wirminghaus, 2019).

As demand for these types of transport increases, so does the demand for more security on the pavements, of the users of these devices but also of the general public. There is a controversy of where certain vehicles should be allowed to circulate. With the growing number of these vehicles in the city, the number of accidents has recently increased and citizens are voicing the need for laws. Should e-bikes and e-scooters be allowed on the same pavement that pedestrians use? Should they be limited to bicycle lanes or should they be allowed to share the road with the cars? Another critical question to clarify is the obligatory (or not) use of helmets. Many of these transport devices are for rent in the cities, but what about the safety of the user and the safety of the by-standers. A lot of work still needs to be done in this area, policy makers need to carefully consider what rules and regulations need to be implemented and enforced.

A further challenge is providing the infrastructure of charging stations for electric vehicles in a city. As the number of vehicles and their use increases, so does the need for a sufficient network of these stations. However, that not being enough, cities have to ensure that technical support is provided as well. Recently a German company offering long-distance coach rides had to shut down its experiment with e-busses since the Chinese provider did not have a technical support network on ground to solve the technical difficulties the busses were repeatedly facing (Spiegel, 2019.2).

There are other models of sharing economy for transportation. Drivers of private vehicles can offer rides to paying customers. Uber, Lyft or Cabify are examples of companies that have developed a business model that allows to match private drivers with nearby commuters. For the commuter this is paradise, since the fares are well below the fares that are usually charged by traditional taxis. However, since transportation services are regulated in almost every city, the arrival of new players has caused controversy about liability, driver protection or fair competition with traditional taxi service (Flores & Rayle, 2016). As a result, an ongoing review of legislation needs to take place.

In order to further improve traffic and reduce pollution, other initiatives are well worth considering. Adapting working hours to alleviate roads and traffic systems during traditional rush hours is a possibility. Encouraging teleworking and the home office frees up expensive office space and reduces the strain on commuters, traffic and the environment (European Commission, 2019).

Within the European Union, we can observe that the environment policy is based on Articles 11 and 191-193 of the "Treaty on the Functioning of the EU". In Article 191, the combat on climate change is an explicit objective of this environmental policy. Furthermore, sustainable development is a principal goal of the European Union. Article 3 of the "Treaty on EU" commits to a high level of protection and improvement of environment's quality.

When it comes to climate change, there are a number of climate policies and strategies that the EU has formulated and implemented, thus ensuring the successful implementation of the Paris Agreement.

The EU makes sure that climate concerns are taken into account in other policy areas such as transport and energy. Promoting and adapting measures to favour low-carbon technologies is just one of many measures taken.

Sustainability combined with environmental activity recognizes the need to balance the resources with climate change. Smart cities are reinventing themselves. The aim of having low emissions brings the right use of resources, energy and infrastructure and improves the environmental situation.

Smart Utilities: The Rise of Data Collection

As previously discussed, the Utility infrastructure of a city consists in a variety of elements, ranging from water supply, drainage and sewage, energy and power supply to waste management and communication infrastructure.

When discussing the utility management, one has to keep in mind that parts of these systems, such as the water systems are the most expensive part of the infrastructure of existing cities in Europe (European Commission, 2019) and at the same time they can be the most difficult to modernize.

When it comes to a city's waste management, we see that many cities already provide effective communication to the public about preventing, reusing, recycling, recovering and disposing of waste. This helps reduce waste generated by each household and its disposal to landfills, which allows for a decrease in emissions, pollution and littering. In recent years, cities have started using sensor technology to generate valuable data.

Trash bins can be equipped with sensors that transmit information about whether or not the bin is full and has to be emptied. This intelligent garbage bin will communicate to the waste disposal center, when the bin has to be emptied and will potentially reduce the frequency of waste removal lorries driving around the city. This will allow for less traffic and less CO_2 emissions, less manpower and a more economical use of resources. Yerraboina et al. (2018) developed such a prototype for India that was called '*Smart Garbage Bin*' (SGB), which evaluated the performance of waste management. Bins provided information on the filling status of the bin. The exchange of information and communication among different devices supports data transfer and connectivity, but the authors acknowledge that there is still room for improvement.

The intelligent light pole has a sensor that will switch on the light when someone passes on the street, thus saving electricity, costs and reducing light pollution. The same intelligent light pole also has a sensor measuring other, environmental factors, such as ozone level, pollen, humidity, temperature, the level of pollutants etc. that could be of critical importance for people with certain allergies or older residents. Via an app citizens are warned during which time of day they should keep their windows closed, or when they should avoid being in the open to minimize health complications. The German City of Munich is implementing this and other Smart City technologies as part of the European '*Smarter Together*' project aiming to reduce harmful CO_2 emissions and increase the use of renewable energy and energy efficiency in the city.

The culmination of this sensor technology is the '*Digital Twin*', a digital replica of the city that represents all streets, buildings, including the height of buildings, detailed infrastructure, including all transport and electricity systems, waterways, simply everything. All real elements being off course equipped with sensors. The City of Rotterdam, the biggest port in Europe, has recently launched the project of creating its Digital Twin.

Smart Safety: How to Keep a City Safe

Taking care of public safety and well-being is an essential objective of the Smart City. When it comes to police work, collecting and analyzing data has always been part of police work (fingerprint or DNA databases, etc.). Nowadays, Smart Cities generate a tremendous amount of data through hundreds of thousands of sensors. This data can and should be used by law enforcement since it is of potential value identifying or preventing crimes (Joh, 2019). However, since manpower to analyze data and view surveillance footage is insufficient, police need to rely on algorithms and AI in order to identify criminal patterns. Automated programs that read license plates are already in use in many countries. Facial recognition software can identify people in crowds and is employed in countries such as China, The Netherlands and the US.

On a more serious note, we can discuss how the police in the UK used Social Networks following the fatal shooting of a 29-year-old local man in 2011. Riots broke out in several major cities in the UK with massive public disorders ending in violence. Various local authorities used Twitter to not only inform, but also control and especially try to reduce the effects of this crisis. A study conducted by Panagiotopoulus (2012) revealed that there is evidence that the use of Twitter by local authorities is an extension of the emergency communication channel towards the public. It shows the importance of having an effective disaster management system in place, backed by technology.

It is essential, that Smart Cities provide a central platform that allows the cooperation between the different City Services, allowing for a more efficient communication and engagement. Traffic lights can be adapted with the objective to reduce time for emergency services to arrive to an accident. Smart Buildings are connected to the fire department and hospitals transmitting real time data through the IoT, reducing response times in emergency situations.

Smart Health: How Can Smart Cities Cater for Healthy Citizens?

Living in big cities can increase health risks. With a great amount of people living and working together on limited space, the city is overcrowded, noise levels and pollution are high, stress levels go up. Physical and mental wellbeing are at risk. It can be argued that living in a big city with many amenities discourages people to be 'active' in the sense of doing sports, cooking, shopping or going out, etc. Fast food is easy to access, supermarkets, shops and restaurants deliver to your doorstep and it is easy to not make any unnecessary move. Companies like UberEats, Deliveroo or Glovo compete in the delivery market, by being ever faster delivering the merchandise. There is no need to go to the cinema anymore, you can watch any movies or series on demand on your smart TV, PC, tablet or smart phone via platforms such as Netflix, amazon prime, HBO or others.

However, one could also argue the opposite. Living in cities can also decrease health risks. Through economies of scale, a better health care can be provided, with a dense infrastructure of health care services at the citizens reach (European Commission, 2019). Having doctors, hospitals and specialists available and in proximity can respond faster to emergencies as opposed to rural regions. The prevention of diseases, vaccination, availability of treatments, better sanitation, overall the access to better health care information and services is provided in cities.

Digital technology and Fitness Apps, Training Apps and Health Apps encourage individuals to be healthier and more active by promoting a healthy and proactive lifestyle. The easy access to medical knowledge thanks to the IoT reduces the need to consult a doctor as frequently and through e-prescriptions and online pharmacies, patient time, doctor time and resources are optimized.

As a byproduct, the monitoring of data generates data. This data can be analyzed and can be the basis for diagnosis and advice. It can furthermore be used for research and is valuable to gather insight on the collective health of a population, how many people suffer from diabetes, how many suffer from heart attacks and so on.

Data is equally important and useful for Smart City planning. Which Health services are necessary and where? Pharmaceutical companies are equally interested in this data to know what drugs are needed, in which areas should there be more research and to be able to produce the necessary vaccines based on real life data. AI helps to analyze the data and provides forecasts, identifies patterns and patients that can be at risk.

Connectivity between different health services, hospitals and insurances provides a global patient history, easily accessible to all health professionals that requires capacity to store the data securely. Blockchain can be the answer to this challenge.

Demographic trends are not the same globally. Though the global population is increasing, in Europe we observe a phenomenon of an overall declining population whereby life expectancy is increasing. This puts a strain on cities, since they are not designed for older people. It can be argued that cities mainly attract a younger working population, providing job opportunities, educational opportunities, leisure and social options, but it cannot be argued that the city population, at least in the Western hemisphere is growing older. As this happens, cities are not yet prepared for the challenges of old age. As one grows old mobility is reduced, sight impaired and an increasing number of older people suffer from dementia, Alzheimer's disease or other cognitive diseases that affect a person's memory, orientation, mobility and often general understanding of things. These groups that are steadily increasing in number are at risk of social isolation. Mental well-being requires specific care.

The town of Motherwell in Scotland is at the forefront of this race, having been declared dementia-friendly in 2012 and being the first town to receive this label. Making life easier for people with dementia and for ageing citizens overall can translate into adapting street signs by making them bigger and clearer, improving lighting, switching from stairs to ramps for easier access, increasing seating areas in public spaces around the city or using different kinds of flooring, such as non-slippery. Some establishments even go so far as to adapt their sanitary equipment by changing the color of toilet seats in disabled toilets, switching from white to another color, so as not to confuse dementia patients and help them differentiate the washbasin from the toilet.

In an article titled '*Wandering Detection Methods in Smart Cities: Current and New Approaches*' the authors Batista et al. (2015) describe how Smart Cities can contribute in detecting wandering dementia patients through sensor technology providing more reliable data as opposed to GPS tracking. This would allow to study and analyze the behavior of dementia patients more efficiently and would permit detection of wandering and disorientation patterns. The possibilities for research provided by data collection seem promising.

According to 'The Silver Economy' from the European Commission (2018), it is overall expected that investments, especially in the area of connected health systems will increase significantly over the next years, including digital systems, software apps, and health devices. The report defines 'Silver Economy' as "the sum of all economic activity that serve the needs of people aged 50 and over, including the products and services (…)" (p. 6). Tapping into this market will provide interesting opportunities for private software and technology companies.

Smart Spaces: Where to House Citizens and Companies?

The people that work in a city need to live somewhere, either in the city or in near enough suburbs. Residential properties that are well connected are of great importance to a city. The current situation regarding residential properties in and around most big cities is a predicament. Access to affordable housing has become challenging over the last decades. Nowadays housing expenses are the highest expense for European households (Eurostat, 2017). Since space in a city is limited, there are boundaries to the real estate market. The market for new housing is very limited, therefore it cannot grow in size and with the shortage of offer, property prices have spiraled and rents have increased. These growth rates in prices and rents have only temporarily been slowed down by the economic/financial crisis (World Economic Forum, 2019).

As a result, new technologies pop up. Online rental platforms or home-sharing platforms are one answer to housing challenges. These platforms allow private homeowners to rent out their apartments. Though homeowners with spare rooms to rent would have also rented their rooms in the past, the costs of renting out have dropped considerably. Individual landlords no longer need to costly advertise their rooms, nor screen the potential tenants. The platform '*PadSplit*' in the US is a great example of sharing economy. It offers members access to private, furnished rooms and the payment covers utility, internet and other bills. Relationships between landlord and tenant are facilitated, which leads to a higher number of people making an effort of renting out spare space.

In Madrid, the program '*CONVIVE*' is an initiative that connects university students with older, mainly lonely people that have a room to rent. Students share an apartment with their elderly landlord/landlady and in return spend time with them, help around the house or do the shopping and pay less rent. A similar idea is pursued by the platform '*Nesterly*' though not limited to students as tenants. Similar platforms exist in other countries and cities.

Companies like Airbnb have developed a successful business model that builds on short-term letting of private property mainly for touristic purposes. The company does not own any of the property listed on its platform, it merely acts as broker.

However, there is a negative effect to some of these models. In the case of Airbnb, the demand for these flats especially in big cities has not only increased property prices, also short-term rental prices go up. It becomes more profitable to rent apartments short term rather than long term, which in turn aggravates the problem of long-term housing shortage.

How can Smart City projects implement affordable and adequate housing on a big scale in a sustainable way that has a long-term positive effect on the housing market?

The city of Barcelona is especially affected by the aforementioned problem. In a joint initiative with New York, both cities have launched a joint '*affordable housing challenge*' that consists in discovering new methods, tools and technologies to battle the problem of housing and affordability. Cities have to be open to new ideas which include innovative aspects such as alternative building materials, module buildings, offsite pre-fabrication, mobile-based solutions, just to name a few (Wray, 2019).

However, one thing remains clear: if there is not enough space in the city, it does not matter how good the technology is. The problem will not be solved purely by technology. It will be up to authorities to review legal protocols on zoning regulations and other policies.

Indeed, there are initiatives of public housing projects that serve as benchmarks for other cities. The Austrian capital Vienna is such an example where nearly 60% of people live in sponsored, city-built properties or council housing (Förster, 2018). One of the housing estates that was created is the '*Car-free Model Estate*' including an outstanding infrastructure of roof gardens, ample parking space for bikes, internet cafes and more. A state-of-the art ecological model has been implemented by employing solar energy, wastewater to recover heat or using recycled material in the construction. But not only sustainability was key, also social aspects were taken into account, such as providing enough kindergardens for child care or flats for elderly people (Förster, 2006). A further project developed in Vienna was the '*Gasometre-City*' that opened in 2001. It converted previously used industrial buildings and monuments, in particular brick buildings that hid iron gas tanks, into mostly subsidized social housing (Förster, 2006).

Looking over the Atlantic, fighting climate change is the number one objective for California. The state is aiming for a clean energy policy and sets a good example in the area of sustainable energy. It is the leading US state in the field of home solar panels, with the objective of completely substituting carbon fueled energy by 2045 (Chediak, Eckhouse & Buhayar 2019).

In terms of individual homes, a further emerging trend are Smart Homes, which consist in the use of sensors and devices throughout a home. These are connected via the IoT to a Smart Home App that can be monitored and controlled remotely, providing comfort, convenience and security to the homeowner at the same time as being more energy efficient. The future will consist in better linking Smart Homes to the other Smart City services such as Smart Utilities, Smart Safety, Smart Health Care, etc.

Businesses are equally affected by the shortage of real estate. Since all space in a city is limited, companies find themselves in similar positions as individuals. Many smaller companies, startups and entrepreneurs tend to share office space in big cities. So-called hot desks, co-working spaces or shared offices allow for agile, flexible and cost-reducing workspace solutions as offered by 'Loom Madrid' or 'Loom Barcelona'. They are used by many companies of all sizes. Startup hubs provide services, resources and sometimes free advice at a reasonable price. Google for Startups Campus, known as 'the Campus' in Spain's Capital Madrid is such an example or the 'Impact Hub' which can be found in over 100 locations worldwide.

When it comes to public spaces, the WHO recommends for cities to provide a minimum of nine square meters of green space per resident (WHO, 2009). According to the European Commission (2019), roughly 40% of European cities consist in green spaces. In general, public spaces should cater for the different citizens and should be accessible, age-friendly and secure. A global trend towards creative usage of public spaces can be observed. In the Dutch city of Utrecht, sedum roofs have been introduced in public spaces such as the roof of bus stops, in order to increase the biodiversity and improve the air quality. The idea is to convert these public areas from merely functional to environmentally sustainable and esthetical spaces. A further trend are 'pseudo-public' spaces, which are private spots that are open to the public, such as restaurants or cafés.

Smart Education: The Future of Learning

Education is essential in a Smart City, not only for younger generations, but also for people that are or have been in the workplace and that need to be IT literates in order to be able to use smart services and participate in e-governance. According to Williamson (2015), "Smart schools are imagined educational institutions that will contribute to urban governance by shaping citizens' capacities to contribute to the management and optimization of the future of the city" (p.2).

Schools and Universities are still adapting to the changes in the learning environment by bringing IT skills and digital education to the classrooms. Online learning, e-textbooks and individual courses provide students with immediate, real time feedback and analysis. Editorial companies like Pearson Education have responded to these trends by introducing new services and products. In order to bridge the skills gap companies like IBM or Microsoft collaborate with Smart Cities by supporting educational infrastructures. Addressing the need of new professional profiles especially in the areas of Big Data, data management, analytics or data mining in order to build technological expertise in the cities is one of the main objectives and biggest challenges.

One can argue that students and teachers are not only recipients in this model, but also provide data as they use the different services. Through analyzing this data, companies can once again develop and adapt products and provide tailor-made services for the education sector.

The cost of education in many countries and cities is currently high. Having access to 5G technology, Internet Services or Wifi enables students to study online which reduces the need to commute which in turn reduces the strain on the transport system of a community and environment and at the same time reduces the cost of education (Washburn & Sindhu, 2010). This is especially valuable to provide access to education to regions and cities that are underdeveloped or difficult to reach. Nonetheless, the education model should not merely rely on digital and online content; it should rather be a hybrid model in which human contact to lecturers and teachers remains a key component.

The Drawbacks Of 'Smart'

The collection of all data has to be handled, stored and above all secured. Data collection is not an isolated goal in itself, but rather a means to improve quality of life for the citizens, improve competiveness of the city and focus on sustainability by being more environmentally conscientious. Much of the criticism of the Smart City model stems from the monitoring and control of the citizen-generated data, as this data can be misused.

Empirical research conducted by Lytras and Visvizi (2018) in Asia, Europe, the Americas, the Arab Peninsula and Australia determined the importance of security, privacy, ethical concerns as well as efficiency and accessibility as main citizen concerns in a Smart City environment. The findings were impacted by the profiles of the citizens that actually use Smart City services. According to their research, citizens with a higher educational background are more likely to use Smart City applications and services. This is probably directly related to their higher level of digital literacy. However, even these individuals, though more prone in using the services, state major concerns. Across all user profiles there were several serious fears listed, amongst which security and protection was the highest concern (45%) followed by data privacy (25%). There is a need for further empirical research in this area.

In his book 'Against the Smart Cities' Adam Greenfield (2013) draws a critical image arguing that urban cities are in the hands of private companies. Mr. Greenfield points out the danger of not having the human in the center. Connectivity, AI and machine learning can have an excessive control over citizens and it raises concerns about having 'a big brother' watching over you, pretty much as described in Orwell's classic novel '1984'. As citizens and consumers, we don´t know what companies actually do with the big amount of data and information collected. Corporations like Philips, Cisco, Google maps or Amazon generate a multitude of data via their data collection, but what do they actually do with it?

In the case of Amazon, which focusses on data-driven marketing, we get a notion of the possibilities that big data provides to companies. They use e-mail campaigns and their web site for high-quality recommendations of related products the user has been previously browsing. The goal is to put products in front of the costumer and turn clicks into sales. The 'frequently bought together' displays recommendations that aim to convince users to purchase more. Up-selling and Cross-selling are clever marketing strategies enabled by collected data.

The Science Fiction movie 'Minority report' tells a story in which algorithms predict the future of a crime yet to be committed and takes action by arresting the yet to be culprit. We need not look to Hollywood to tell us fictional stories. Cathy O'Neil (2016) tells a real life tale in her much-acclaimed book 'Weapons of Math destruction' about a collective of teachers being sacked based on the suggestions of an AI program. Supposedly, these teachers were not performing well enough and therefore got fired. However, by carefully looking at the context, their bad job performance was in comparison to the performance of previous years' teachers, who, owed to an incentive scheme, had inflated grades. Did AI take this into account? Was it intelligent enough to question its own suggestion and see beyond its own algorithm? No, and this is the dark side, a dystopian vision, of relying on big data.

Misinterpreting data or taking wrong decisions is one drawback. The sensitivity of privacy, anonymity and data protection are another. Edward Snowden´s disclosures about privacy breaches or the scandals of Cambridge Analytica with the violation of privacy are examples of the vulnerability of citizens and consumers. Citizen's rights and privacy must be protected. This may lead to a tradeoff between privacy and utility. The more private and secure data gets, the less useful that information will become.

Having AI read and evaluate publicly posted messages to reduce crime in a city seems a noble goal. Nevertheless, we can reach problematic limits. This becomes especially evident in totalitarian regimes. Through the use of facial recognition software to oversee demonstrations or public manifestations, unpleasant activities can be prevented, unwanted behavior sanctioned. Suspicious conduct or suspects can be identified. Where is the line between privacy and public wellbeing? Who is going to control the controllers?

Avoiding privacy issues is one thing, protecting the data is another. Cities have to be able to provide efficient protection in order to block out attacks, avoid system failures and hackers with criminal intentions from getting access to data, services and networks. When the Pentagon issued instructions in late 2018 to restrain US soldiers from using GPS tracking apps when stationed in areas such as warzones, this was an immediate reaction to information retrieved from a fitness app that had revealed where exactly troops had been stationed in Syria. Soldiers going for a jog with their smart wristband and activated fitness tracker unknowingly gave away the positioning of troops. The geolocation capabilities may seem harmless if jogging through Central Park New York, but when stationed in Afghanistan that information in the wrong hands can turn into a security threat for an entire mission.

Another issue are cyberattacks on entire cities that are on the rise (Ledo Iglesias, 2019) and that can be devastating. Once the digital network is paralyzed, it cannot be unlocked without a digital code, which hackers only provide once they have received a handsome ransom. This leaves cities unable to access CCTV camera footage, emergency systems, hospital databases or even water and electricity supply systems. Alone Johannesburg has been hit by at least two cyberattacks against city systems in 2019, leaving many citizens without power for several days. How can this vulnerability be avoided? Cities need to acquire IT knowhow and expertise. The truth is that currently there is a gap between what is needed and what is available in terms of IT knowledge. Specialists in AI, data mining and data analytics are missing in the cities. These need to invest not only in IT systems but also and more importantly in IT professionals. Competence is protection. Adapting education is key, to be able to provide these requested profiles in the near future.

From a scientific and academic point of view, a lot of research still needs to be done. The interconnections between smart devices, data generation, privacy, confidentiality are prevailing issues for citizens, corporations as well as for governments. Gaining the trust of citizens by ensuring transparency and how to safeguard privacy protection is key. So far, data privacy has not been a major topic addressed in most Smart City projects and research thereof (Sánchez-Corcuera et al., 2019). Further fields to investigate are the control of intruders, the threat of data being manipulated or corrupted or the danger of taking wrong decisions based on data.

THE FUTURE OF SMART CITIES

From the economic point of view, the Smart City intensifies the economic and commercial activities and the effects are powerful for the economic potential. It creates favorable conditions for the establishment of creative enterprises and co-creation of professionals. The sharing information favors the creation of technological parks, the revitalization of concentrated zones increasing effectiveness and efficiency. It improves facilities for industry and serves as a boost for economic activity, benefitting production and consumption.

Starting in 2003 the Smart City of Songdo in South Korea was built from scratch in a USD $40 billion project. This ambitious project was designed to minimize the environmental impact, by implementing sensor and solar-equipped buildings, green spaces occupying 40% of the city surface, automated underground waste removal system and more than 25 km of bike lanes. Citywide there are charging stations for electric cars and the city is designed for 300,000 residents that live in smart homes.

This scenario is off course ideal, but rather unrealistic for the majority of regions, where there are no blank spots on the map to create cities out of nothing. Therefore, other impulses and radical changes are required and predicted for the next few decades. Elon Musk (founder of Tesla and SpaceX) is a pioneer when it comes to futuristic visions. SpaceX is currently working on technology to offer economic flights allowing the public to fly anywhere in the world in under one hour, travelling by rocket (Grubb, 2017). This sounds like a Science Fiction fantasy, very much as the Hyperloop transport technology that is currently in its development stage. The idea, first launched in 2013, consists in a means of transport for people and freight in an environmentally friendly fashion. Via pods people can high-speed travel in and between cities that are connected via electro-magnetically impulsed tubes. Hyperloop allows for faster travel times compared to aircrafts, it is also energy efficient and automated. Whether or not this technology is economically viable and indeed safe for human use remains to be seen.

It is likely that our future cities will hold automated vehicles, busses and cars that are connected in a network managed by AI. Delivery drones will be hovering over our cities. Having sensors analyzing the sewage of each household could help police identify whether drugs are being disposed of. Data infrastructure will be at the heart of the Smart City.

It is safe to say that over the next few decades technology will revolutionize everything; the way we live, work, communicate, socialize, commute and learn.

CONCLUSION

Besides the overwhelming amount of positive effects to Smart Cities, to conclude there must be mention of some critical voices.

One of the main difficulties we encounter is the impossibility of finding a homogeneous definition of "Smart City". Though we observe that most definitions rely on technology as main driver, there is still a lack of agreement on a common definition. A further drawback to mention is the difficulty and complexity of replicating Smart City initiatives, experiments and projects between cities that are different in size, regional location, resources (be it natural, demographic or economic) and other aspects. Implying that Smart City initiatives can easily be replicated is a common misconception and highly unrealistic. And finally, let us not forget the challenges of data privacy and data security in Smart City environments which entail rising concerns. Who is using our data and to which purpose? Again it will be the authorities, regional, national and international authorities that will need to make sure to protect the citizen's right on privacy and that need to make sure that these rights will not be undermined, by promptly adapting and deciding on legal regulations and laws in this area.

Tapping into collective intelligence allows businesses and governments to improve the decision-making processes. Thomas Malone, the founder of MIT Collective Intelligence Center, asks: "How can people and computers be connected so that - collectively - they act more intelligently than any person, group, or computer has ever done before?". In his recently published book 'Superminds' (2018) he describes how groups of people collaborating together have been responsible for most of human achievements in business, government and science. He explains furthermore how these groups of people will become smarter through connectivity and by working with AI.

With this in mind, the Smart City discussion does not only include better infrastructures or better transport systems, but goes beyond. As discussed, Smart Cities should include citizens, companies, managers and governments; in short all stakeholders, as part of the process in order to be more connected and collaborative.

In Adam Smith's 'Wealth of Nations' (2003) he describes how and why subjects act in their economic relations. The Smart City is Adam Smith's dream. According to Smith, the success of a company is the success of society, and it should not be measured only via financial criteria but also in terms of dignity, solidarity, justice and democracy.

As the Smart City concept is still being developed, countries like Estonia, Brazil or The Netherlands are leading Nations. The Smart Cities are becoming 'urban sharing' and 'urban collaboration' hubs. It will be key to share best practices and to develop Smart City solutions that have the potential to be replicated and that will be scalable to other cities and other regions.

REFERENCES

Angelidou, A. (2015). *Smart cities: A conjuncture of four forces Cities*. Elsevier Ltd.

Batista, E., Casino, F., & Solanas, A. (2015). Wandering Detection Methods in Smart Cities: Current and New Approaches. *IEEE First International Smart Cities Conference (ISC2)*, 1-2. 10.1109/ISC2.2015.7366175

Chediak, M., Eckhouse, B., & Buhayar, N. (2019). California goes solar. *Bloomberg Business Week*. Retrieved October 26, 2019 from https://www.bloomberg.com/news/articles/2019-10-22/california-prepares-for-a-huge-solar-boom

Continental. (2017). *Press Release: Continental is investing in EasyMile and pushing ahead with the development of driverless mobility*. Retrieved November 20, 2019, from https://www.continental.com/en/press/press-releases/continental-is-investing-in-easymile-70642

EZ10. (2019). Retrieved November 14, 2019, from https://easymile.com/solutions-easymile/ez10-autonomous-shuttle-easymile/

European Commission. (2017). The Ageing Report 2018 – Underlying Assumptions & Projection Methodologies. *Institutional Papers*, *65*. doi:10.2765/286359

European Commission. (2018). *The Silver Economy – Final report*. Luxembourg: Publications Office of the European Union. doi:10.2759/640936

European Commission. (2019). *The Future of Cities – Opportunities, Challenges and The Way Forward*. Joint Research Centre (JRC). doi:10.2760/375209

European Parliament (2014). *Mapping Smart Cities in the EU*. Directorate general for internal policies. Publications Office. doi:. doi:10.2861/3408

European Union. (2015). *Automated transportation in the (driverless) seat*. Research and Innovation. Retrieved November 15, 2019, from https://ec.europa.eu/research/infocentre/converting.cfm

European Union. (2018). *Legislation environment and climate change*. Retrieved March 27th 2020, from https://eur-lex.europa.eu/summary/chapter/environment.html?root_default=SUM_1_CODED=20&locale=en

Eurostat. (2017). *Household expenditure by purpose in the EU, 2017*. Retrieved November 15, 2019, from https://ec.europa.eu/eurostat/news/themes-in-the-spotlight/household-expenditure-2017

Flores, O., & Rayle, L. (2016). *How cities use regulation for innovation: the case of Uber, Lyft and Sidecar in San Francisco*. World Conference on Transport Research - WCTR (2016), Shanghai. Retrieved December 12, 2019 from https://reader.elsevier.com/reader/sd/pii/S2352146517305379?token=BD6F AD1CBDA7F54FEE76091A1897E6AFDA7A9457073DA04C9F9F5F5F7FCEF25199A8DB07F00A-42D332570A3D95B95008

Förster, W. (2006). Housing in the 20th and 21st Centuries: Vienna. Social housing, innovative architecture. Munich: Prestel.

Förster, W. (2018). *The Vienna Model of Social Housing*. Partnerships for Affordable Rental Housing, University of Calgary. Retrieved October 8, 2019 from https://ucalgary.ca/cities/files/cities/forster_the-vienna-model-of-social-housing.pdf

Gori, P., Parcu, P. L., & Stasi, M. (2015). *Smart Cities and Sharing Economy*. Robert Schuman Centre for Advanced Studies. Research Paper No. RSCAS 2015/96. doi:10.2139srn.2706603

Greenfield, A. (2013). Against the Smart City: A Pamphlet. The city is here for you to use, 1. New York, NY: Academic Press.

Grubb, B. (2017). Elon Musk promises 'anywhere in the world in one hour'. *The Sidney Morning Herald*. Retrieved September 28, 2019 from https://www.smh.com.au/technology/elon-musk-promises-anywhere-in-the-world-in-one-hour-20170929-gyrpan.html

Joh, E. E. (2019). Policing the smart city. *International Journal of Law in Context, 15*(2), 177–182. doi:10.1017/S1744552319000107

La DGT y Telefónica prueban un sistema de IoT que anticipa a los conductores sobre peligros en la carretera. (2019). Retrieved October 20, 2019, from https://www.esmartcity.es/2019/09/13/dgt-telefonica-prueban-sistema-iot-anticipa-conductores-peligros-carretera

Ledo Iglesias, A. T. (2019). Analysis of Social and Legal Issues on Critical Infrastructures in Spain. *Sixth International Conference on eDemocracy & eGovernment (ICEDEG)*, 375-377. 10.1109/ICE-DEG.2019.8734451

Lom, O., Pribyl, O., & Svitek, M. (2016). Industry 4.0 as a part of smart cities. *2016 Smart Cities Symposium Prague (SCSP)*, 1-6. 10.1109/SCSP.2016.7501015

Lytras, M. D., & Visvizi, A. (2018). Who uses Smart City Services and What to Make of IT: Toward Interdisciplinary Smart Cities Research. *Sustainability*, *10*(6), 1998. doi:10.3390u10061998

Malone, T. W. (2018). *Superminds*. New York: Hachette.

Mees, A. (1975, December). The revival of cities in medieval Europe: An application of catastrophe theory. *Regional Science and Urban Economics*, *5*(4), 403–425. doi:10.1016/0166-0462(75)90018-6

O'Neil, C. (2016). *Weapons of Math Destruction*. Broadway Books.

Orwell, G. (1949). 1984. New York: Plume. Harcourt Brace Jovanovich.

Panagiotopoulus, P., Ziaee Bigdeli, A., & Sams, S. (2012). *"5 days in August" - How London Local Authorities Used Twitter during the 2011 Riots. In IFIP International Federation for Information Processing 2012* (pp. 102–113). Electronic Government.

Pellicer, S., Santa, G., Bleda, A. L., & Meastre, R. (2013). A Global Perspective of Smart Cities: A Survey. *2013 Seventh International Conference on Innovative Mobile and Internet Services in Ubiguitous Computing*, 439-444. 10.1109/IMIS.2013.79

Sánchez-Corcuera, R., Nuñez-Marcos, A., Sesma-Solance, J., Bilbao-Jayo, A., Mulero, R., Zulaika, U., ... Almeida, A. (2019). Smart Cities survey: Technologies, application domains and challenges fo the cities of the future. *International Journal of Distributed Sensor Networks*, *15*(6). doi:10.1177/1550147719853984

Schwäbisches Tagblatt. (2019). *Klare Mehrheit für ein neues Hallenbad*. Online Ausgabe März 2019. Retrieved October 10, 2019, from https://www.tagblatt.de/Nachrichten/Buerger-App-Rund-12-000-machten-mit-409066.html

Smith, A., & Cannan, E. (2003). *The Wealth of Nations* (6th ed.). New York: N.Y. Bantam Classic.

Smith, M. E., & Lobo, J. (2019). Cities Through the Ages: One Thing or Many? *Front. Digit. Humanit.*, 6, 12. doi:10.3389/fdigh.2019.00012

Spiegel. (2019a). *Mietroller-Anbieter Coup stellt Betrieb ein*. Retrieved October 14, 2019, from: https://www.spiegel.de/auto/aktuell/coup-mietroller-anbieter-stellt-den-betrieb-ein-a-1298185.html

Spiegel. (2019b). *Flixbus stellt E-Bus-Experiment ein*. Retrieved October 11, 2019 from: https://www.spiegel.de/wirtschaft/unternehmen/flixbus-stellt-e-bus-experiment-ein-a-1299697.html

United Nations Department of Economic and Social Affairs. (2018). *68% of the world population projected to live in urban areas by 2050, says UN*. UN DESA. Retrieved November 12, 2019, from: https://www.un.org/development/desa/en/news/population/2018-revision-of-world-urbanization-prospects.html

Washburn, D., & Sindhu, U. (2010). *Helping CIOs Understand "Smart City" Initiatives – Defining The Smart City, Its Drivers, And The Role Of The CIO*. In *Making Leaders Successful Every Day*. Forrester Research.

Williamson, B. (2015, July-December). Educating the Smart city: Schooling Smart citizens through computational urbanism. *Big Data & Society*, 2(2), 1–13. doi:10.1177/2053951715617783

Wirminghaus, N. (2019). Die E-Scooter kommen - und überschwemmen die Städte mit Elektroschrott. *Der Stern*. Retrieved November 29, 2019, from https://www.stern.de/auto/e-scooter--hype-um-elektrotretroller-bringt-jede-menge-elektroschrott-8654792.html

World Economic Forum. (2019). The cost of housing is tearing our society apart. *Global Shapers Annual Summit*. Retrieved November 2, 2019, from: https://www.weforum.org/agenda/2019/01/why-housing-appreciation-is-killing-housing/

World Health Organization (WHO). (2009). *Urban planning and Human health in the European City, Report to the World Health Organisation*. International Society of City and Regional Planners (ISOCARP).

Wray, S. (2019). Smart Cities get their houses in order. *SmartCitiesWorld*. Retrieved November 11, 2019, from https://www.smartcitiesworld.net/special-reports/special-reports/smart-cities-get-their-houses-in-order-

Yerraboina, S., Kumar, N. M., Parimala, K. S., & Aruna, N. J. (2018, June). Monitoring The Smart Garbage Bin Filling Status: An Iot Application Towards Waste Management. *International Journal of Civil Engineering and Technology*, 9(6), 373–381.

ADDITIONAL READING

Nam, T., & Pardo, T. A. (2011). *Smart City as urban innovation: focusing on management, policy, and context*. A paper presented at ICEGOV2011, September 26–28, 2011, Tallinn, Estonia. Retrieved October 9, 2019 from https://dl.acm.org/citation.cfm?id=2072100

Ng, M. K. (2017). Governing green urbanism: The case of Shenzhen, China. *Journal of Urban Affairs*, 1–19.

OECD. (2014). *The Silver Economy as a Pathway for Growth*. Insights from the OECD-GCOA Expert Consultation. Retrieved December 1, 2019, from https://www.oecd.org/sti/the-silver-economy-as-a-pathway-to-growth.pdf

Oxford Economics. (2014). *Future trends and market opportunities in the world's largest 750 cities*. Retrieved December 4, 2019, from https://www.oxfordeconomics.com/Media/Default/landing-pages/cities/OE-cities-summary.pdf

Porter, M. E., & Heppelmann, J. E. (2014). *How Smart, Connected Products Are Transforming Competition*. Harvard Business Review. *Harvard Business Review*, 92, 11–64.

Rode, P., & da Cruz, N. (2018). Governing urban accessibility: Moving beyond transport and mobility. *Applied Mobilities*, *3*(1), 8–33. doi:10.1080/23800127.2018.1438149

Selinger, M., & Kim, T. (2015). *Smart City Needs Smart People: Songdo and Smart + Connected Learning* (D. Araya, Ed.). London: Smart Cities as Democratic Ecologies. Palgrave Macmillan; doi:10.1057/9781137377203_11

KEY TERMS AND DEFINITIONS

Artificial Intelligence: It is a computer system's ability to simulate and imitate intelligent behavior. It can process complex information, perform tasks, interpret data and learn from the data in order to apply the learnings to achieve an established goal.

Big Data: Huge and complex quantities of data sets that can be analyzed to reveal trends, patterns and behaviors. The resulting insights can be used for better decision making or for the development of new products/services.

Smart Citizen: A digitally literate person that takes advantage of technology in order to engage in a Smart City environment, address local issues and take part in decision-making.

Smart City: A City that enhances the quality of life of its inhabitants by taking advantage of the possibilities offered by digitalization and technology in order to solve urban problems and challenges in a more efficient and sustainable manner.

Smart Economy: An economy that is based on technological innovation, resource efficiency, sustainability and high social welfare as engines for success. It adopts innovation, new entrepreneurial initiatives, increases productivity and competitiveness with the overall goal of improving the quality of life of all citizens.

Urban Innovation: This is the essential way forward for smart cities to confront the economic, social, ecological and technological challenges of the 21st century.

Chapter 8
Intelligence Applied to Smart Cities Through Architecture and Urbanism:
Reflections on Multiple and Artificial Intelligences

Guadalupe Cantarero-García
Universidad San Pablo-CEU, Spain

ABSTRACT

Implementation of the smart city concept in architectural school programs is neither evident nor simple. The starting point is a historical heritage of established patterns shaped to different schools of thought that have independently worked on territories at different scales: urban planning and building construction. The Spanish scenario understands the smart city as the ICTs (information and communication technologies) applied to security, data processing, logistics, energy management, among others, but we must not forget the Spanish urban plans born from the architecture discipline and how buildings are positioned within a site. The aim of this study is to highlight some reflections on the need to unite multiple and artificial intelligences so that the latter does not monopolize or gain exclusivity within the smart city design guidelines and listens to the city's demands.

INTRODUCTION

Implementation of the *Smart City* concept in Architectural School programs is neither evident nor simple. The starting point is a historical heritage of established patterns shaped to different schools of thought that have independently worked on territories at different scales: urban planning and building construction. These also share the same basic premise: occupancy and creation of space. However, Urban Planning deals with the external context and Architecture looks both inwards and outwards from that which is

DOI: 10.4018/978-1-7998-3817-3.ch008

Copyright © 2020, IGI Global. Copying or distributing in print or electronic forms without written permission of IGI Global is prohibited.

most precious to the architect: the façade, the building´s appearance and how it relates to the city. What can be said about the disciplinary connection between Architecture and Engineering?

It is a paradox to speak of the city without referring to Architecture or even more so, to Urban Planning. However, in the Spanish scenario the Smart City understands ICTs (information and communication technologies) applied to security, data processing, logistics, energy management among others but it does not understand buildings or how they are positioned within a site. Tectonics is greatly neglected in the Smart field and so is Archeology which provides us with the foundations on which to work through the history of living styles. It is therefore still difficult to find a debate in which Smart City is dealt with assertively.

In order to stablish some kind of parallelism between Spanish architecture schools and other countries, we could point up some interesting ideas launch in technology leading countries as in South Korea by the use of the term: *ubiquitous[1] city*. It is meant to be a new model of sustainable economy based on more efficient use of communication solutions, transportation and natural resources. This city manages information technology ubiquitous.

An interesting report, written seven years ago, about cities all around the world and their longing to devene a *smart city* is describing the following depictive (Essays, 2013):

Helsinki as a Smart city cluster, including also the Helsinki region, in particular focusing on mobile and wireless technologies and applications. Lisbon's ambition as a smart city is to improve the city's liveliness and quality of life, namely through the active involvement of citizens in the city's governance model. Lisbon aims to become an international hub for world scale companies, benefiting from the bridge Lisbon represents between Europe, Africa and America. Manchester is using modern technologies to promote community engagement, capacity building and social capital. New Sondgo is longing the use of ubiquitous computing in the city is the first objective. Osaka is based by ubiquitous information systems in city area.

In the last years Oulu becoming the city of technology and an innovation city. Aim to become the most highly developed city in Finland and Northern Europe. Barcelona had in view to implement of ICT to pursue social and urban growth. Smart City concept was used as a strategic tool and the pillars are infrastructures, open data, innovation service, human capital.

In general terms we could say that the international practice shows that the evolution of *smart city* is based on: Ubiquitous computing, because the *smart city* is firstly based on the physical telecommunications network infrastructure, comprised of the wiring, the wireless, together with any servers and routers required for operating the infrastructure. The second layer constitutes applications that facilitate operations in the city, like traffic control, etc. Such applications will be provided by many vendors, using the provided infrastructure and finally it is based by ubiquitous or connectivity of all.

But in the last three years the *smart city* concept treatment has changed. The conflicting positions between engineering, architecture, archeology, economic sciences, politics and other intervening fields result in us talking of the same concept from different understandings and not concurring in the target´s optimization.

How can we expect not to meet conflicting views when our starting point is a poor translation of the Anglo-Saxon concept of Smart City into other languages? Speaking about Smart City means speaking of urban wisdom. This intelligence is applied exclusively by the citizen who has the capability of conveying the information and imprinting a character tailored to new lifestyles. Smart suggests other nuances such as ready, clever and even elegant. If we keep to the essence, the correct translation would be clever city or ready city. This meaning is far from that of innate intelligence which is lacking in the city. The meaning is however, closer to that of applied intelligence. It is to this end that the study of this research takes us. On the other hand, human intelligence´s evaluating methods have led to suggest emotional intelligence deepening. We could perhaps further evaluate emotional intelligence applied to the city through behavior and new ways to inhabit.

The idea of joining efforts, and reflecting on the optimal way of acting, leads us to think of multidisciplinary teams. Of course, we can design smart cities, combining the efforts of engineers, architects, economists, sociologists, etc... but we have to speak the same language to achieve a global understanding about the final result.

Background Teaching Programs and Intelligences

The aim of this study is to highlight some reflections on the need to unite multiple and artificial intelligences so that the latter does not monopolize or gain exclusivity within the *Smart City* design guidelines and listens to the city's demands.

The city speaks through its dwellers´ claims and accusations. While it can be said that the ICT[2] world should provide for all citizens, it can also be said that currently, less than half of the population understand, practice, have access or include such services as part of their needs to ensure quality of life.

The method employed to demonstrate that *Smart City* requires an assessment from emotional and not merely artificial intelligence, entails interactive work of people with intellectual and physical disabilities and with architecture students in collaboration with students from other engineering, communication and psychology disciplines. To raise global awareness requires acting within academia, where architecture and urban planning act as a link between technology and what is not only technological but also human and emotional.

IMPLEMENTATION OF THE SMART CITY CONCEPT, PAST AND PRESENT

From the Masters of the Past to the Present Moment

If one reflects on ways of living ideals throughout history, examples of innovation, ideation and reverie of the ideal city are found. Starting from precursors of the utopian city lead one to investigate the ideal city and from there, *Smart Cities*. However, at the moment, is it necessary to include the concept of *Smart Cities* in Architecture Schools or is it exclusively part of Telecommunications Engineering?

The term metropolitan area was coined in the United States in 1910 to design heavily populated and urbanized areas under the control of a central city. In Spain, the concept was introduced in the sixties. (Zárate & Rubio 2006).

At present, the concept of *Smart City* or *intelligent city* is shown as a parallel to that dream city of the past but that obviates the emotional intelligence of the citizen who inhabits it. This city is drawn on paper today but may not be supported by the topography or its future materialization.

Therefore, the adaptations that a project undergoes from its conception to its execution takes into account other essential factors before the plans are defined.

Utopian reformers, such as Owen[3] in Scotland and Fourier, Cabet and Godin in France, *enacted models with closed patterns such as family and phalansteries. They were successful for some labor objectives but failed for sociological purposes* (Benevolo, 1974).

An example of this is Owen's own initiative in Harmony[4], Indiana (Fig. 1). This is an example of an ideal, which led to architectural and urban reality in 1825 and exposed the difficulty of moving a theoretical model to physical materialization.

Figure 1. New Harmony design by Owen, "Drawing by F. Bate" (1838)
Source: https://wherearchitectureisfun.tumblr.com/

Society expresses itself through ideals sought after but not always found because there is no way to find all the information necessary to create projects that are both planned well and executed well. What serves us today is obsolete tomorrow. The *ideal city* in Spain may not be ideal in Norway and vice versa. In other words, there are basic factors which dictate that, for a city to be intelligent, it must respond to the needs of its citizens here and now. Therefore, one must bear in mind that this premise has expired. The advance of technology and networks are timeless and citizens' understanding of how to use these technologies depends on the culture in which said society lives (Cantarero, 2018).

Tourism is another delicate concept to be approached in the field of *Smart Cities* because it combines space and time. This is a temporary, non-permanent use of the city and may create a cultural impact created by the tourist. Sharing a unique communication and telecommunication language can make the objective of achieving a *Smart City* for the user more complex. It could even become counterproductive if the use of these technologies is not understood.

How then is it possible to talk about the *ideal city*? What is the use of having a *Smart City* if it is not even *ideal*? If, before trying to plan a *Smart City,* one seeks to develop a suitable plan to offer an *ideal home*, this will awaken the sensitivity required in the arduous process of preparing a preliminary project, which then becomes an integral project to be executed in an urban plan. What is then called *intelligent* is thus inherent from the beginning based on historical, political and social as well as geological and logical principles of the land and the city itself.

To ignore origin and culture, which are the essence of a society, would be clear negligence as planners of the cities of tomorrow. Therefore, looking to the future while understanding the past is an important factor to consider.

Universities, from there point of view of the meaning *universal*, are key in forming multidisciplinary teams that combine engineering, architecture and urban planning with economy, politics, history and geography.

The Figure of the Urban Architect in Spain

The competence of the urbanist in Spain has been achieved through formal education in Architecture studies. This formal training began in 1844 and has not changed substantially. The architect is trained not only in project and urban design but also in engineering disciplines in order to responsibly calculate structures and facilities. This is not the case in other countries, where the urbanist receives a post graduate degree after training in sociology, geography, topography and other humanities sciences as well as technical studies.

Training of the urban planner in Spain, therefore, has been and still is a reference and is very complete as far as urban principles are concerned.

However, response times in urban planning studies are pressing and this plays against the research prior to the ideation phase. Intense data collection about the area itself is required, which should precede urban design. In fact, urban planning projects, whether they are urban action plans, partial plans or other plan modalities, are developed with architects on staff that may not have actually worked on an architectural plan before. Afterwards, the architect plans the building under current regulations developed by a city council technician, who, more than likely, has never executed a project of this type before. Hence, when a plotted design is not situated correctly with the sun in an urban plan or patios are not built according to regulation or the CTE and later crack, it is impossible to even offer the *ideal home*. We can only dream of projects that are not subject to such strict urban regulations. Projects that do not define the delineation of plots or the restrictions on the length of eves, the height of cornices or boundary setbacks [5]. (Figs. 2 and 3).

The problem is that those who make urban plans use broad scales rather than architectural scales or vice versa. Also, when designing a building, the architect does not consider doing a sociological analysis of the person or people who are to inhabit the building, therefore, the question of temporary or permanent occupancy is not taken into account. The design is created with a "one-size-fits-all" concept and not even a single-family home is designed with optimal conditions for the family. This is due to the fact that the concept of time is what sets the standards for defining if a place is habitable or not. Nothing is enclosed and nothing can or should be established.

Study Plans and Teaching Guides

In the current Spanish arena, there are four official study plans (training cycles or university careers) for this profession. They are an Architecture degree [6], an Urban Management Degree [7], an Urban Plan-

Figure 2. Master Plan, Beko Zaha Hadid (https://noticias.arq.com)
Source: https://www.arch2o.com/beko-masterplan-zaha-hadid/

Figure 3. Bionic Tower in Shanghai, 1997 (project not built) Source: https://www.cimentoitambe.com.br/torre-bionica/

ning, Territorial Planning and Sustainability degree[8] and a degree in Civil Engineering, Transport and Urban Services [9].

However, of these four, only a degree in Architecture does not require specialization courses and it has been this way since the 19th century, in other words, for the last 175 years[10]. With the founding of new private universities, the remaining three degrees have been offered with specialized training courses included in their curriculum for the past nineteen years.

"The need to regulate aspects of spatial conformation of cities gave rise to planning systems adopted by different countries. This came about as a result of constantly evolving political, social and economic

processes. Spain has been systematically regulating urban planning since the mid-twentieth century, which is when it adopted a legislative framework that, with successive adjustments, has been directing the development and management of its cities." (Franchini & Raventós, 2018).

Currently, there is a wide range of masters programs and specialized training courses in Urban Planning, many of which are unofficial. Some are online courses while others are face-to-face. Typically, these are the program's own degrees, not necessarily official degrees.

The question is whether this type of training is sufficient and if they are apt to offer an Urban Planning degree.

If we analyze what a degree in Architecture can offer to an urbanist in relation to other methods, the conclusion is quite clear. It is undoubtedly the most complete training offered.

Apart from graphic management, the understanding of the history of architecture, construction, humanities, and the design of a city is very broad. Urbanism within the studies for an Architecture degree in Spain is an introduction to urbanism, which is in the second year. Urban Design is taught in the third year, Urban Planning in the fourth year, and Urban and Territorial Projects[11] in the fifth year.

The first part is an introduction to the territorial analysis of natural and adapted physical environments, landscape elements and socio-demographic characteristics. It also consists of an approach to historical analysis through urban models in history and urbanism.

The second part is attractive to the architect because it focuses on design lines of a city. At this stage, it is essential to analyze elements that make up spatial structure and functional organization. Thus, the first urban planning proposals are born and are created based on the premises of sustainability, universal accessibility, as well as economic, social and landscape aspects.

Proper use of architectural language in courses focused on project creation facilitates the understanding of terminology used in urban planning and vice versa. This is also true with aspects of geometry and scale in urban layouts, spatial composition of volumes, orientation of the sun in relation to a building, etc.

Then, the fundamentals of urban planning or planning come into play. The legal framework and regulations of urban planning [12] affect design features from the beginning of the project, or the general or partially proposed planning[13] phase

Finally, in Urban Planning training, the Spanish architect acquires the tools to execute territorial and metropolitan projects by using a master plan. The complexity of elements used in order to work is multiplied. On this scale it is no longer a partial plan, rather a broader intervention in which the information gathered is greater.

That said, it is true that the concept of a city cannot and should not be determined solely on physical information of the area, rather with adequate knowledge of the normative, economic and social context as well. Hence, the design of a *Smart City* must be carried out with a multidisciplinary or transdisciplinary team.

THE DEBATE BETWEEN A SMART CITY OR AN INTELLIGENT CITY AND HOW TO ADDRESS THE SPANISH CONTEXT

Preparation of the Spanish Capital: Madrid

Madrid is a complex, historical city in terms of topography and orography as well as landscape and urban aspects. The architecture of Madrid, as in other cities with a concentration of historical heritage, is rich in language and culture and therefore its diversity makes this city a complicated area in which to intervene.

In Madrid there are references such as the Spanish Network of Smart Cities RECI, which works from their town halls to integrate *Smart City* concepts and update municipal projects.

However, it is necessary to assess how to intervene in order to create a coherent *Smart City*[14] system. The AENOR[15] and the Ministry of Development are working together to prepare this possible analysis.

This analysis contemplates multiple concepts and encompass both the physical and natural environment, roadways and urban infrastructure networks, socio-economics within the municipality or city, transportation, mobility and citizen security, as well as the implementation of new technologies, or ICTs, and control of demand and energy expenditure.

In proposing a new urban development study, we have to integrate networks in many ways.

According to Avelino Brito, General Director of AENOR,[16] "Spanish cities have shared existing good practices achieved through numerous pilot tests in infrastructure, urban planning, transport, energy etc.". He adds that AENOR has made advances in the matter of Smart City regulations, "… in Spain we have a collective experience that forms an ecosystem, a set of identified and specialized actors. This knowledge is embodied in the technical regulations of AENOR and in the Technical Committee for Standardization CTN 178 "Smart Cities", which are promoted by the Secretary of State for Telecommunications, the Information Society and the Ministry of Industry, Energy and Tourism." (Brito Marquina prologue in: Piñar Mañas, 2017).

Madrid's population has been growing in the outskirts of the city and as well as upwards, as shown in the example of the Four Towers. This trend is changing northern Madrid's skyline. (Fig. 4)

Figure 4. Madrid skyline. The Four Towers built and the fifth tower in progress.
Source: *https://www.expansion.com/empresas/inmobiliario*

The Need to Observe the Past in Order to Design the Future

The eternal question, "Where do we come from and where we are going?" is a key factor in determining whether interventions within an historic, urban environment are consistent or not. Numerous monuments, landmarks and references to the past have been lost as a result of current needs.

The Iron Gate (Puerta de Hierro) and the San Fernando Bridge in Madrid are examples of this because they have been hidden and relegated by traffic[17] (Figs. 5 and 6).

Figure 5. The Iron Gate (Puerta de Hierro). Madrid.
Source: Google Earth / Aerial photograph from the Air Force Historical Archive

Figure 6. The San Fernando Bridge. Madrid.
Source: Google Earth / http://historias-matritenses.blogspot.com

CTE regulations, which have been enforced in Spain since 2006, have been able to help rehabilitation projects in protected and historical heritage buildings.

Traffic dictates the rules of the basic order of a city, much like how the arteries in the body determine blood flow. Extensive use of the car is undoubtedly a main factor in causing our cities to change and adapt. Also, the centralization of industry and business within capital cities has been a decisive point in the configuration of urban layouts and its growth.

Spain is a country that references colonial, military layouts and blends that with international, urban trends. A common denominator for the extensions made in the nineteenth century in Western Europe was the orthogonal layout, otherwise known as a checkerboard or grill.

The grid plan is an European tradition that stems from Roman and military plans.

It has been adopted in America as well, as seen in Nicolás de Fer's plan, which was designed for Mexico (Fig. 7).

An example of these quickly organized, military cities is Carolina (Jaén), which began in 1767 and was finished in 1770. This plan established a perfectly orthogonal road with octagonal and circular points and connecting diagonals.

Figure 7. Mexico City map, Nicolás de Fer (1715)
Source: https://www.pinterest.es

Historical and Urban Heritage in the City of Madrid

Almost a century later, international urbanism arrived in Spain. Ildefonso Cerdá, designer of the extension of Barcelona (1859), wrote a book about roads, channels and ports called *General Theory of Urbanization*, which was published in Madrid in 1867. Both for his theories and for his direct actions, Cerdá played a decisive role in beginning the growth of the capital. This was confirmed by Castro himself in the presentation of the Madrid draft[18]. Thus, Castro (Fig. 8) knew the work of his friend Cerdá both at the governmental and central levels of Spain.

These theoretical - practical plans established in the mid-nineteenth century are studied even today in European urbanism schools[19] .

The continued study of ideas from the past is due to established, general guidelines that continue to endure and show how a city behaves and responds to the basic needs of the moment. Even with new technologies and other advances to mark milestones, these past models are relevant.

Today, when one refers to a city as being intelligent, one associates this concept with a particular intelligent use of mobile applications to expedite orders, postage, mail services, as well as collective measures such as carbon footprint, CO_2 gas emissions, recycling, consumption and energy savings such as urban lighting, parking control and traffic. Nineteenth century designs did not understand these concepts, nevertheless, they already took into account the importance of networks and saving energy. The scale of work encompassed not only the urban area but architectural design as well, treating it as a whole. Therein lies the key to the success of well-understood urbanism, which extensively serves both the city and the citizen.

Orthogonal design plans of Castro, Cerdá and the Linear City of Soria (Fig. 9), take into account the design of communication networks as well as road infrastructure, water supply, sanitation and electricity (Bonet, 1978).

Figure 8. Preliminary plan for the widening of Madrid; Castro Plan (1857) J. Donón (1860)
Source: https://es.wikipedia.org/wiki/Ensanche_de_Madrid

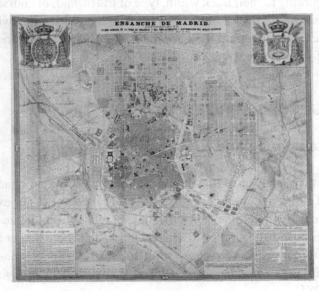

Figure 9. Ciudad Lineal. Arturo Soria's City Urban Project of Ciudad Lineal in 1895; plans and drawings appeared in Madrid Urbanization Company publications
Source: http://www.arteenparte.es/historia-del-interiorismo/el-movimiento-racionalista/

Urban planners of the nineteenth century already considered the scale of vegetation, the sun and shadows produced by surrounding plants in relation to their height and angle of projection on the buildings and the street.

They analyzed street lamps and lumens emitted in order to determine their location. They also planned boulevards and streets according to their track width, type of traffic and, of course, the width was related to the height of the projected building. All of this was taken into consideration while analyzing the most essential aspect, how to achieve maximum light use during the different seasons of the year in order to create an optimal design for the home.

MULTIPLE INTELLIGENCES APPLIED TO A CITY

Applied Artificial Intelligence and Emotional Intelligence

At the end of the 19th century, analysis of how individual intelligence can impact caring for the collective began to take place. Traditional intelligence measurement models are not exhaustive enough since they do not account for the use of intelligence itself. They merely conceptualize its nature and function without observing how it is linked and applied in a real context. Sternberg, father of the Triarchic Theory of Intelligence[20], points out that, "*...the measurement of intellectual capacity has focused solely on one aspect of intelligence while ignoring other aspects of great relevance which form cognitive skills on their own.*" (Sternberg, 1985).

Therefore, it is not enough to see what is done but how it acts and why this action takes place. This concept of mental capacity emphasizes the plurality of actions which denotes intelligence.

For Sternberg, intelligence is any mental activity that guides conscious selection or transformation with the purpose of predicting results, thus actively provoking the adaptation of one with the environment or the environment with the one. It is the set of thinking abilities that are used in solving more or less everyday or abstract problems.

Intelligence is a set of primarily cognitive abilities which allow us to adapt to the environment, solve the problems it poses and even anticipate them.

If the definitions of the psyche are applied to a *Smart City,* what is deemed intelligent can be applied to solve everyday problems in order to find simple solutions, thus providing autonomy for its citizens. Therefore, needs are changing and the ways of responding to them are as well. This is called "service". Technology servicing the human being. However, evaluating ways of living is overlooked. Needs arise from the way of life that each person assumes or acquires from birth to death. Goleman made a point on Payne's theories[21] ten years later about "emotional intelligence" when he talked about, "*...the great power that emotions have over who we are, what we do and how we relate.*

Robert J. Sternberg's[22] (Sternberg, 1985) Triarchic Theory of Intelligence, Howard Gardner's popular theory of multiple intelligences (Gardner, 1983)[23] and Goleman's theory of emotional intelligence (Goleman 1995) have brought to light other factors to consider while evaluating an intellectual quotient.

In relation to a Smart City, one should resort to what Edward L. Thorndike (Thorndike, 1904) called "social intelligence" in his book: *Introduction to the Theory of Mental and Social Measurements.* This term was studied in profundity in 1920. Social intelligence is the basic ability to understand and motivate other people[24]. Twenty years later, David Wechsler[25] pointed out something that is quite logical today when he stated that an intelligence test would not be considered valid if emotional aspects were not previously assessed.

Later, Howard Gardner in 1983 defined the seventh intelligence, or interpersonal intelligence, which is very similar to emotional intelligence. However, Gardner pointed out that the *multiple intelligences* he discovered may not even be the ones he defined. There may be others that he had not taken into account or that were grouped under a single intelligence.

Artificial intelligence imposes itself over our emotional intelligence and seeks a regularization. So who protects us? Are the *open data* accessible to the international network? How to preserve our privacy and how to keep our person whole? Can we be emotionally stable if artificial intelligence is imposed on our being?

Open Data is a young movement. The U.S. Government site: www.data.gov site was launched in 2009 and in 2010 the U.K. Government site: www.data.gov.uk.

These two sites are the most advanced open data sites.

The Australian government published also in 2010 a Declaration of Open Government (AGIMO, 2010), (Huijboom, 2011) in which it supported informing and engaging citizens through increased government transparency.

The Danish government launched an Open Data Innovation Strategy in July 2010 (Danish Ministry of Science, Technology and Innovation, 2010) and in Spain, the Industry, Tourism and Market Minister, launched in 2010 an Open Data Innovation Strategy ('Avanza2'). In this project is highlight that data are crucial for the knowledge economy. By publishing Public Sector Data, more (economic) value can be generated (Huijboom, 2011).

Universal Accessibility in a Smart City: Physical and Cognitive Disabilities of the Citizen

The obsolete concept of "architectural barriers" was replaced by the term "universal accessibility". The motto "Design for All" has also been coined [26] in order to optimize the same concept and open it up to what ultimately affects the entire population.

The "architectural barriers" concept referred specifically to physical problems and solutions but the universal term involves all citizens as users of the city. It is an issue that affects all of us as citizens and opens up avenues for research in order to improve the integration of people with physical and cognitive disabilities within the city that he or she inhabits. It must be taken into account that, throughout life, all people are subject to some disease, temporary or permanent, and even the mere fact of aging is a part of life. Also, someone may be involved in an accident that may or may not have serious consequences. Even using a baby carriage needs to be taken into account. By doing so, this will lead to being more attentive in the way one moves and our surroundings (Boudeguer, & Sepúlveda, 2004).

The European Union has committed itself to providing all citizens with equal opportunities. This means that, in as much as possible, people with different degrees of mobility (the young, the elderly, people with disabilities, people carrying infants or shopping, pregnant women, etc.) should be granted the same comfort, speed and capacity when using public transport. The only way to guarantee this is to ensure that the entire public transport system (railway, buses, taxis and its supporting infrastructure) in the EU becomes universally accessible. (Uniaccess, 2006)

Another important point to take in account is if websites and web tools are properly designed and people with disabilities can use them. However, currently many sites and tools are developed with accessibility barriers that make them difficult or impossible for some people to use.

Making the web accessible benefits individuals, businesses, and society. International web standards define what is needed for accessibility. Recently the north American WAI initiative [27] provides of information about strategies, standards and resources to make the Web accessible to people with disabilities. (WAI, 2019).

WAI also benefits people without disabilities, for example:

- people using mobile phones, smart watches, smart TVs, and other devices with small screens, different input modes, etc.
- older people with changing abilities due to ageing
- people with "temporary disabilities" such as a broken arm or lost glasses
- people with "situational limitations" such as in bright sunlight or in an environment where they cannot listen to audio
- people using a slow Internet connection, or who have limited or expensive bandwidth

In Spain the Urban Rehabilitation, Regeneration and Renovation Law, whose application period ended December 4, 2017, ensured that all buildings improve their accessibility for the elderly and disabled people. This law also established that neighboring communities must obtain a Building Evaluation Report (IEE) in order to prove that their building complies with current regulations.

The extended crisis and its close relation with the unlimited urban growth has led technicians, politicians and academics to take up the interest on the intervention in the consolidated city as well as on urban rehabilitation. That interest, in line with the revival of citizen's demands of public space, has its reflection in the implementation of initiatives for the rehabilitation of buildings or neighbourhoods as well as in the arising of new laws. That is the case of the Urban Rehabilitation, Regeneration and Renovation Law: "Ley 8/2013, del 26 de junio, de rehabilitación, regeneración y renovación urbanas". These interventions are often aimed at introducing new techniques that optimize some aspects, such as energy consumption, or that improve processes or plans. However, in many cases these actions do neither lay on previous experiences nor improve developed processes. (Matesanz & Hernández, 2014).

For web accessibility, the Spanish Accessibility Certification is based on compliance with the UNE 139803: 2012 standard and offers two types of certifications: Certificate of Conformity[28] and an ICT Accessibility Certificate[29] (Asís, Aiello, Bariffi, Campoy & Palacios, 2006). Entities, such as ONCE, issue different certifications internationally for sites and services based on web technology[30]. The e-Administration Portal[31] establishes a meeting point for web portal managers in public administration to share information, experiences and to answer questions.

From this we deduce that the greater the compliance with the regulations, limitations for people in society who are affected by disabilities are greatly reduced.

Requirements for compliance with these normative effects are not reduced to just the spatial or architectural scope (as in the case of "architectural barriers") but have been extended to all areas, specifically to communication and telecommunications.

The Need for Academic Multidisciplinary Teams: Curricular Training Proposals

As it is said in the introduction, the idea of joining efforts, and reflecting on the optimal way of acting, leads us to think of multidisciplinary teams. Of course, we can design smart cities, combining the efforts of engineers, architects, economists, sociologists, etc... but we have to speak the same language to achieve a global understanding about the final result. The idea of integrating a human scale and a human dimension takes center stage when talking about *smart city*.

The research points to the obvious need to implement common, intra-university and multidisciplinary plans. If fluid communication in which the politician understands the architect and the engineer understands the sociologist is expected, advancements must be made in teaching innovative methods that merge professionals, researchers and professors from different disciplines. Urban planning and territorial planning are inserted in the natural and cultural environment. This, in turn, is integrated into an urban environment that is connected to economic development within a functional structure and relevant urban regulations.

Technicians have to deepen their understanding of the human aspects that exist between the walls of the homes where society members reside. In short, it is imperative to understand and listen to the needs of the inhabitant.

However, this is not enough if the politician, the lawyer, the economist and the sociologist do not understand the language of the technician concerning concepts of scale, geology, exposure to the sun, orientation, energy, infrastructure of physical and virtual networks as well as accessibility and sustainability. A predisposition to this kind of mutual understanding is required for the completion of a project.

Therefore, it is essential to have a common language for mutual understanding. This should involve combining the knowledge base and regulations of all disciplines that are involved in the process of defining an action plan within an existing municipality or city as well as for the creation of a new urban plan[32].

To achieve a complete and coherent *Smart City* or *intelligent city* project, it must be based on multidisciplinary cooperation, which requires teamwork with the different actors involved. Politicians, sociologists, economists, lawyers and technicians[33] have to shape the current requirements of the inhabitants of the *Smart City*. Therefore, citizens are presented not only as participants but as protagonists of *Smart City* projects and can dictate the premises that make up the demand.

To ignore the culture and the history, which essentially create the character and the essence of a city, would be clear negligence on the part of the city planners of tomorrow. Therefore, looking towards the future while understanding the past is imperative in the present.

General opinion states that the university is a key factor in the integral formation of multidisciplinary teams. The latest tactics used by professionals and university professors has been to create platforms, observatories and specialized laboratories in order to debate the use of different intelligences and, in particular, artificial intelligence, and how to apply them to a city. The debate concerns observing, preventing and mitigating the challenges of artificial intelligence.

Universities are launching projects and other platforms to study new technologies. They are dedicated to raising awareness among organizations and Spanish society in general about the ethical and social impact of AI through scientific publications, events and training courses. They also advise companies, governments and institutions.

San Pablo CEU University professor, Ricardo Palomo-Zurdo,[34] shows that the university is, "facing an important digital transformation that affects management processes, teaching, as well as work and research groups." It is important to highlight the creation of interdisciplinary work groups lead by teachers with student participation. It is worth citing Blockchain & DLT Lab, Smart Cities Laboratory EPS CEU Lab[35], Observatory of the Impact of Ethics on Artificial Intelligence (ODISEIA) [36] , Google Chair of Privacy[37], Fablab[38] and others. Also, a group of students are analyzing the introduction of cryptocurrency to use in the university in collaboration with a neobank. There are also several Jean Monnet projects that are being requested, as well as the disruptive redefinition project of the university system, called EUuniversiTECH.

SOLUTIONS AND RECOMMENDATIONS

Some of the solutions and recommendations found by analyzing the utopian or dream city from the past and their relation to the ideal, intelligent city of the present are the following:

Society expresses itself through ideals sought after but not always found because there is no means for receiving necessary information to weave together well-thought out and better executed projects.

As noted by researcher and PhD in Fine Arts, Santiago Prieto, (Prieto, 2007) "It is very likely that we only have the resources for imagining our ideal city. We are also sure that man will never stop dreaming. "

Ideals of *Smart Cities* are projected to fulfill the desire to change our chaotic society by trying to submit an artificial planimetric order that plays against unforeseen situations. This creates anxiety as a result of the human condition and dictates ones need to believe that something better is yet to come.

Researcher Manuel Delgado defines the feeling of longing for the dream city as utopian anxiety.

He stated that, "This utopian anxiety about what is perceived as impenetrability of urban life in the city is exacerbated by the intense process of the urbanization of large masses of immigrants, an increase in social agitation and the emergence of metropolitan phenomena. Uselessly contradicting the senselessness of the modern city - ahistorical, sub-social, biotic - the metaphysical and the normativization of the dream of urban planners and architects where a city suddenly clarifies itself, that reproduces, imposing itself, the peace of the planes and the models." (Delgado, 2016).

What served as Fourier's inspiration for Le Corbusier or the Broadacre for Wright is a symptom of how ideas from the past are established in the present. This inspiration occurs even with errors in determining the needs and demands of changing societies in areas now altered by a communication system with previously non-existent infrastructures.

One cannot ignore the past nor our historical roots, but it is important not to make the same mistakes in order not to err like Owen and Cabet.

Thus, it is difficult to avoid looking at the past and trying to understand it in order to discard useless factors, which allows for the creation of new requests and demands through cutting-edge technologies.

In short, multidisciplinary teams are making conclusions from the current debate. They are investigating these concepts and finding ways to answer questions as to how a present city can serve the future.

History shows us examples of innovation, ideation and reverie of the ideal city. Today's concept of a *Smart City* or *intelligent city* is shown as a parallel variable to that dream city of the past. This city is drawn on paper today, but the actual topography for its future materialization may not allow for it to take place.

Therefore, adaptations that a project undergoes from its conception to its execution must take into account various factors before being defined in the actual plans.

The fact that technicians have to deepen their understanding of human aspects is unavoidable. Also, politicians, promoters and managers of the plans must understand, in turn, that spatial construction contemplates the materialization of the project throughout its process. It is essential for a *Smart City* to behave as such.

DIRECTION OF FUTURE RESEARCH

If it is understood and even scheduled into the plans that the services within a city will eventually expire or no longer be useful, does this mean that there is also a scheduled obsolescence of a city? New ways of living would imply new behaviors and therefore a new social and collective intelligence. It is then possible to speak of changing intelligences. As a result, lines of research that open up are:

- Modification of the current urbanism curriculum as a bachelor's or postgraduate degree
- Creation of practical, multidisciplinary teams at the university level
- Study of applied emotional and artificial intelligences.
- Deepen the concepts of "architectural barriers" and "Universal accessibility"

CONCLUSION

Is it necessary to project thinking about the present or an immediate future? Is that feasible? Are those involved aware of the changes that new technologies will bring? Innovative projects, urban and human proposals should work together but this is not the case. In the time in which an urban plan is designed and approved, innovations of all kinds have taken place. Including these recent innovations means working within the same time dynamic. The reflections that arise from the current debate on *Smart Cities* can be applied to new projects, however, when it comes to intervening in an historic city or in a protected heritage context, other relevant aspects must be taken into account. Time factors are, therefore, decisive in the changes that make up a city. This includes ways of assessing the intelligence of a citizen as well as the city itself.

The time it takes tangible aspects to expire responds in part to the quality of the execution, but also how a product is used. In this case the product is a city. "Good practices" are described as good in the present but may not serve as such in the future. Their definition will change as designs and ways of understanding the reality in which one lives also changes. "Useful life" has to be "useful" now. It is possible to foresee in the medium or long term improvements that require technological and logical advances.

Contributions to the state of the matter presented are not presumed as novel but as manifestos that recall forgotten terms and even suggestions for improving the approach that is currently being used in the *Smart City* concept.

The revival of utopian ideals offers a broad vision of us as a society as well as the desires that creative inhabitants of cities may possess, however, this trip to the past may not offer solutions to current circumstances. New technologies dictate how a city may be used as well as changes in the classes offered for a university education. If the intervening participants feel the project is unique and that common goals are shared with global objectives, a positive impact in the quality of life of the citizen will take place. This is when a *smart city* truly becomes an ideal city.

This research project received no specific grants from any funding agency in the public, commercial, or not-for-profit sectors. This research has been translated by Diana Claveria (Architect by the University of Westminster-London-RIBA member and translator: *dyfconsultants.com*).

REFERENCES

Asís, R., Aiello,A.L, Bariffi F., Campoy, I., & Palacios, A. (2006). La accesibilidad Universal en el marco constitucional español. *Derechos y Libertades, 2*(16), 57-82.

Benévolo, L. (1974). *Historia de la Arquitectura moderna.* Barcelona, Spain: Gustavo Gili.

Bonet, A. (1978). *Plan Castro.* Madrid, Spain: Ed. COAM.

Boudeguer, A., & Sepúlveda, F. (2004). Accesibilidad en la edificación. In Manual de Accesibilidad Universal. Cap. III. Santiago de Chile, Chile: Servicio Nacional de Turismo de Chile (SERNATUR).

Cantarero-García, G. (2018). Reflexiones urbanísticas. Referencias del pasado y situación actual de Madrid como ciudad inteligente potencial. In Gestión inteligente y sostenible de las ciudades. Gobernanza, smart cities y turismo. Valencia, Spain: Tirant lo Blanch.

Delgado, M. (2016). La ciudad ideal como derrota finl de lo urbano. In XIV Coloquio Internacional de Geocrítica. Las utopias y la construcción de la Sociedad del futuro, 215-234.

Essays. (2013). *The History Of Smart Cities Concept Information Technology Essay.* Retrieved from https://www.uniassignment.com/essay-samples/information-technology/the-history-of-smart-cities-concept-information-technology-essay.php?vref=1

Franchini, T. (Dir.) & Raventós, T. (Coord.). (2018). Temas de planeamiento urbano. Madrid, Spain: CEU Ediciones.

Gardner, H. (1983). *Multiple intelligences: New horizons.* New York, NY: Basic Books.

Goleman. (1995) *Emotional Intelligence.* New York, NY: Bantam Books.

Huijboom. (2011). The Openness of Government. *European Journal of epractice.eu.* https://joinup. ec.europa.eu/sites/default/files/document/2014-06/ePractice%20Journal-%20Vol.%2012-March_April%202011.pdf

Matesanz, A., & Hernández, A. (2014). *On the improvement of urban regeneration processes from more than thirty years of rehabilitation experiences.* Retrieved from: http://oa.upm.es/33391/1/paper-number577.pdf

Piñar Mañas, J. L. (Dir.), Suárez, M. (Coord.), Cantarero G., Cantó, T., Martínez, R., & Navarro, N. (2017). Smart Cities derecho y técnica para una ciudad más habitable. Madrid, Spain: Editorial Reus.

Ruz Bentué, E. (2007). *Smart. City. Innovación urbana para la sostenibilidad, Efficient Urban.* Madrid: Arnáiz and Partners.

Sternberg, R. J. (1985). *A Triarchic Theory of Intelligence.* Cambridge University Press.

Thorndike, E. (1904). Introduction to the Theory of Mental and Social Measurements. Davenport, 20(519). doi:10.1037/13283-000

Uniaccess. (2006). *Design of Universal Accesibility Systems for Public Transport.* https://trimis.ec.europa.eu/project/design-universal-accessibility-systems-public-transport

WAI. (2019). *Web Accessibility Initiative.* https://www.w3.org/WAI/fundamentals/accessibility-intro/

Zárate Martín, M. A., & Rubio Benito, M. T. (2006). *Glosario y buenas prácticas de Geografía Humana.* Madrid, Spain: Editorial Universitaria Ramón Areces.

ADDITIONAL READING

Larsen, D. R. (1998). *Soldiers of Humanity.* The National Icarian Heritage Society.

López Bustos, C. (1998). *Tranvías de Madrid.* Madrid.

Marchi, A., & Valazzi, M. R. (2012). *La città ideale: l'utopia del Rinascimento a Urbino tra Piero della Francesca e Raffaello.* Milán: Ed. Electa.

Moleón, P., & Berlinches, A. (coords.), (1991). Arquitectura y Desarrollo Urbano. Comunidad de Madrid Zona Centro I y II. Madrid: DGA y COAM.

KEY TERMS AND DEFINITIONS

Accessibility: "Ability to access" and benefit from some system or entity. The concept focuses on enabling access for people with disabilities, or special needs.

Architecture: Knowledge of art, science, technology, and humanity. A general term to describe buildings and other physical structures. The design activity of the architect.

Artificial Intelligence: Is intelligence demonstrated by machines, in contrast to the natural intelligence displayed by humans.

Emotional Intelligence: Capability of individuals to recognize their own emotions and those of others, discern between different feelings and label them appropriately, use emotional information to guide thinking and behavior.

ICT: Information and communications technology. Information technology (IT) that stresses the role of unified communications and the integration of telecommunications (telephone lines and wireless signals) and computers, as well as necessary enterprise software, middleware, storage, and audiovisual systems, that enable users to access, store, transmit, and manipulate information.

Multiple Intelligence: Differentiates human intelligence into specific 'modalities', rather than seeing intelligence as dominated by a single general ability.

Smart City: Is an urban area that uses different types of electronic Internet of Things (IoT) sensors to collect data and then use insights gained from that data to manage assets, resources and services efficiently.

Social Intelligence: Is the capacity to know oneself and to know others. Social Intelligence develops from experience with people and learning from success and failures in social settings. It is more commonly referred to as "tact," "common sense," or "street smarts."

Urbanism: Is the study of how inhabitants of urban areas, such as towns and cities, interact with the built environment. It is a direct component of disciplines such as urban planning, which is the profession focusing on the physical design and management of urban structures and urban sociology which is the academic field the study of urban life and culture.

ENDNOTES

1   Ubiquitous: existing or being everywhere, especially at the same time; omnipresent: (https://www.dictionary.com/browse/ubiquitous).

2   Information and communications technology.

3   Robert Owen (1771-1858). First utopian reformer whose line of thinking is based on a bias-free analysis of economic relations. In 1779, he created his New Lanark yarn company in Scotland.

4   Drawing by F. Bate. Published by "The Association of all Classes of all Nations", at their institution, 69, Great Queen Street. Lincoln's Inn Fields, London, 1838.

5   The Bionic Tower is a vertical city project that is 1228 meters high.
    Spanish Architects Eloy Celaya Escribano, Javier Gómez Pioz and María Rosa Cervera Sardá proposed creating a habitat based on the use of natural resources and saving energy. It consisted of hotels, parks, homes, offices, shops, etc, which were divided into 12 different neighborhoods. Each building was 80 meters high and separated by natural plants to provide security. It was to be built on an artificial island, which had the advantage of reducing movements of the structure in case of earthquakes or strong winds. (https://es.wikipedia.org/wiki/Torre_Bi%C3%B3nica).

6   The Higher Technical School of Architecture of Madrid was founded in 1844 and is the oldest in Spain.

7   A Degree in Urban Management was first created at Camilo José Cela University, a private university, and consists of 180 credits https://www.ucjc.edu/study/degree-in-urban-management/

8   Degree in Urban Planning and Territorial Planning and Sustainability was also created at Camilo José Cela University, a private university, and is similar to the previous one but extended with 240 credits and lasts four years.

9   Degree in Civil Engineering, Transport and Urban Services, born at Alfonso X University https://www.uax.es/grado-en-ingenieria-civil-en-transportes-y-servicios-urbanos.html (currently this website does not work).

10 The legislative framework for urban regulations was started concurrently with the Higher Technical School of Architecture in Madrid.

11 In each course, two parts of each subject are taught and each are worth 3 academic credits.

12 With special emphasis on the municipality management, urban land regime, development, management and execution systems, historical heritage protection and urban discipline.

13 Also, the application of methodological foundations of urban planning with municipal scale management proposals, including urban planning regulations and basic environmental impact studies, are learned.

14 As noted by Mr. Eduardo Gutiérrez, Professor of Political Science and Administration II and representative of SESIAD-MINETAD in CTN 178 "Smart Cities" of UNE and President of CTN 178 / SC6 "Government and Public Services 4.0", in the conference organized by Magdalena Suárez at the UCM Faculty of Law of Madrid.

15 Dª Tania Marcos, Director of Quality, Environment and Risks at AENOR, in the conference organized by Magdalena Suárez at the UCM Faculty of Law of Madrid.

16 Spanish Association for Standardization and Certification.

17 This research stratum belongs to the Project: V Call for Projects CEU-Banco de Santander Bridge 2019-2020 entitled: "The peri-urban landscape of Madrid, visions from memory to the new city" that leads as Principal Investigator Eva Juana Rodríguez .(Proyecto: V Convocatoria de Proyectos

Puente CEU-Banco de Santander 2019-2020 titulado: "El paisaje periurbano de Madrid, visiones desde la memoria hacia la nueva ciudad" que lidera como Investigadora Principal Eva Juana Rodríguez).

[18] Bonet Correa, Antonio, "Plan Castro", *Preliminary study,* p. Madrid, 1978.
"Fortunately for us, sometimes there is a job similar to what we are in charge of. Just refer to the widening of Barcelona. It is so complete, thorough, and full of precious details that there is no doubt when choosing it as a model and applying it to the town (Madrid)."

[19] The Fançais d'Urbanisme Institute, or IFU, offers postgraduate courses to students from various disciplines such as geographers, politicians, economists and architects.

[20] Sternberg approaches the vision of intelligence as a set of capabilities instead of a single, unitary and unmodifiable element. The author established the Triarchic Theory of Intelligence, which derives its name from the consideration of three types of intelligence.

[21] 1985 is when the term "emotional intelligence" appeared for the first time thanks to the doctoral thesis of Wayne Payne, called *A Study of the Emotions: The Development of Emotional Intelligence.*

[22] Sternberg's definition of intelligence is, "mental activity directed toward purposive adaptation to, selection and shaping of real-world environments relevant to one's life".

[23] Linguistics, logical-mathematical, spatial, musical, bodily and kinesthetic, intrapersonal, interpersonal, naturalistic. "Intelligence is not a quantity that can be measured with a number such as intellectual quotient (CI), rather the ability to sort thoughts and coordinate them with actions "

[24] He defined social intelligence as the ability to understand and manage men and women based on a sense of empathy and the ability to live and survive in an individualized world.

[25] The Wechsler Adult Intelligence Scale (WAIS) was first developed in 1939 and was called the Wechsler-Bellevue Intelligence Test.

[26] EIDD. Declaration of Stockholm, 2004. Design for All is a holistic and innovative approach, which constitutes an ethical and creative challenge for all designers, entrepreneurs, administrators and political leaders. http://www.xn--diseoparatodos-tnb.es/Documentacion/bibliograf//Paginas/urbanos.aspx

[27] WAI: (by MIT, ERCIM, Keio, Beihang).

[28] Certifies that the website meets standard reference requirements at the time a certificate is granted but does not involve an annual follow-up audit. Therefore, no trademark license is granted.

[29] AENOR certifies that the website complies with accessibility guidelines of said standard. Also, by performing follow-up audits, it ensures that levels of accessibility are maintained over time. Therefore, the license for the use of the N brand of ICT Accessibility is also granted.

[30] In addition, it also certifies the accessibility of native mobile applications based on iOS and Android operating systems, which are the only systems currently offering basic accessibility features.

[31] https://administracionelectronica.gob.es

[32] Be PAU Urban Action Plan or PP Partial Plan.

[33] Architects, technical architects, engineers, landscape designers, geographers, surveyors, etc.

[34] Ricardo Palomo-Zurdo. Professor of the Faculty of CC. Economics and Business Administration of San Pablo University CEU Madrid CEU San Pablo University, Cardinal Herrera CEU and other educational institutions of the CEU Group: As highlighted in the process for the incorporation of blockchain for the accreditation of university degrees for graduate and postgraduate students, as well as the pioneering project by the CEU, which serves all students, with the introduction of Amazon Echo devices where specific "Alexa" skills are developed. More than 5,000 devices have already

been delivered to students. In addition, traditional management processes are being digitized, thus improving the user experience and use of clouds will be activated shortly in collaboration with Amazon Web Services, Microsoft and other companies. For teaching, an important process of innovation is being addressed in various subjects as well as the introduction of new degrees and postgraduate degrees. Technology and video tutorials are also being incorporated as well as the latest version of the ultra blockboard.

[35] Directed by the author of this chapter.

[36] Directed by Idoia Salazar from the ODISEIA project. This opens an interesting path to knowledge from the university to the company (https://www.odiseia.org/).

[37] Directed by professor and data protection specialist, Dr. José Luis Piñar.

[38] Directed by Covadonga Lorenzo, PhD in Architecture.

Chapter 9
Smart Destinations as a Reconversion Strategy for Rural Areas:
Digital Content Based on Historical Routes to Enhance Tourist Experiences

María Sánchez Martínez

https://orcid.org/0000-0003-1003-2340

Universidad CEU San Pablo, Spain

ABSTRACT

Smart destinations provide value for the tourist experience. Platforms where dialogue arises are important to develop an adequate integration of smart technology as a resource for the cooperative creation of valuable tourist experiences. The incorporation of digital technologies in historical disciplines as a part of humanistic knowledge design is a new paradigm that encourages the creation of innovative content. Taking as a reference the Spanish routes that the war journalists visited during the First Carlista War, it is possible to transform the villages that were protagonists of these historical landmarks as smart tourist destinations. Digital content based on geolocation, GIS developments, apps, audiovisual pieces with videomapping, and augmented reality techniques are the key to bring the traveler the experience in an interactive, personalized, integrative, and participatory environment while the data provided by the different sensors allows measuring their economic and social impact.

INTRODUCTION

The international trend on Smart Destinations is that they grow in geographic spaces where tourism development is planned and implemented. This sort of tourism is based on a technological infrastructure that enhances local sustainability while providing value to the destination itself through the experiences of people who visit it. At the same time, it improves the life of its inhabitants.

DOI: 10.4018/978-1-7998-3817-3.ch009

Copyright © 2020, IGI Global. Copying or distributing in print or electronic forms without written permission of IGI Global is prohibited.

The Smart Cities phenomenon represents the logical and natural development of traditional cities. It is the consequence of the improvement of communication technologies applied to the services they provide on daily operating processes. In the scenario of contemporary strategic communication, the experience of the new patterns shows special and distinctive opportunities for cities and their actual stakeholders, citizens. Technology advances, mainly the development of Internet, have helped citizens access an infinite and varied amount of digital content, developed through not only private initiatives, but also public ones.

The last statistical results from the Ministry of Culture and Sports (CULTURAbase, 2017) based in cultural heritage show an upward trend in cultural tourism. During 2016, the number of foreign tourists who visited Spain exclusively for cultural reasons represented 12.5% of the total. Likewise, the number of Spanish tourists who did local tourism for the same reasons was 5.5%. From an economic point of view, these figures represented a total expenditure of more than 8,500 million euros. In addition, the number of jobs related to cultural activities increased by 5.8%, a number that represents 3% of total employment in Spain.

ICTs have enabled interaction platforms where dialogue arises, promoting personalization and creating relevant experiences (Buhalis, 2002). Consequently, tourists integrate themselves into a new value chain based on their needs and experiences. This change in traveler's behaviour has led the tourism industry to face not only this challenge but also to develop what is known as Smart Destinations. However, what is important is not only technological development itself but rather, creating a strategic and adequate integration of smart technology as a resource for the collaborative creation of valuable tourist experiences (Poupineau, 2016)

This research has been carried out by a group of historians, journalists, communicators, philologists and geographers who used both geolocation possibilities offered by mobile devices (smartphones, tablets) and web applications combined with Geographic Information Systems (GIS) to establish several sustainable routes of a historical-cultural nature.

The aim of these routes is to reflect the itineraries of foreign newspaper correspondents, who were settled in Spain as a consequence of a number of historical events, whilst putting on maps unknown historical points of interest. At the same time, the fact of enriching the routes with digital provides the visitor with a comprehensive display of facts know and understand the historical context. This objective allows, in the first place, bringing the results of the investigation closer to other researchers and to the general public and, secondly, to improve the competitiveness of these destinations compared to others.

The design of the routes has a multidisciplinary and integrative approach, transforming each route into a Smart Tourism Destination. Therefore, the base, in the context of the newspaper foreign correspondents' role in Spain during the early nineteenth century, The value of probable economic impact that these interactive models should be assessed both in rural and national economy.

BACKGROUND

Smart Territories and Rural Communities: An Approach to an Economic Sustainable Development

One of the most worrying problems in the institutional agenda is the depopulation in rural towns, a major issue if we consider that in Spain it represents 72.8% of the territory. However, the costs of dealing with this problem mean the reason why it is not part of the policy definition processes. In the end, it is a circular process since the failure of the primary sector prevents the excess of capital necessary for the investment in the technological advances that are fundamental for economic development.

One of the most important and urgent questions that contemporary societies have to address is how to make communities and their settlements more sustainable. An evergrowing number of aspects are inextricably linked to changes brought forward by technological developments: These are transforming people's everyday routines, perceptions of the environment, access to electricity, food, health, education and many others (Zavratnik, Kos & Duh, 2018).

A village is an ecosystem of a limited size, a community that is driven by specific mechanisms and dynamics that are the product and the outcome of multi-level interaction among all stakeholders. However, the concept of smart villages is adopting insights from the ICT, to engage in conceptually-sound, empirically-focused, and ethically-conscious exploration of problems, challenges, and opportunities for villages and their inhabitants. (Visvizi & Lytras, 2018) From the theoretical point of view, a Smart Village enables its inhabitants to make use of the technological and social achievements while its infrastructures are still being developed. It also offers an opportunity to efficiently deal with issues of local and circular economies. Smart Villages are essentially about people (rural communities) taking the initiative to find practical solutions to challenges and creating new opportunities, based not only in digital but also in smart. Smart implies cooperation and developing new alliances from a thinking outside the box point of view and charting their own path to prosperity and sustainability (EU Rural Development, 2018: 2)

Technology-based infrastructures are contributing to cities becoming more effective in terms of optimizing their citizens' needs and, in addition, to contributing to their socioeconomic development. Therefore, the new economy also finds its place in rural areas through Smart Cities with innovative solutions, which, in turn, bring about a better quality of life for their citizens (Sánchez el al., 2017: 125). Smart City, as a concept, implies a global vision that merges artificial intelligence, big data, decision making ICT and the internet-of-things. Hence, the challenge to transform urban spaces into smart is easier in cities than in rural areas because the economic development in cities provides capital availability for research and investment. Consequently, socio-economic sustainability in a smart village context is one of the key issues that define the prospect of survival of rural communities. Villages need to think beyond themselves to be smart and try to involve the surrounding countryside, groups of villages and small towns and link them to their nearest urban area.

The European Network for Rural Development (ENRD) defines five drivers for Smart Villages:

1. Responding to depopulation and demographic change.
2. Finding local solutions to public funding cuts and the centralisation of public services.
3. Exploiting linkages with small towns and cities.
4. Maximising the role of rural areas in the transition to a low-carbon, circular economy.
5. Promoting the digital transformation of rural areas.

Therefore, achieving sustainability enhanced rates of financing becomes essential for all key components of village development. Encourage sustainable farming, exploring different forms in business organization such as social enterprise or rethinking the spatial organization of production would be important insights of great value to the smart village's debate (Visvizi & Lytras, 2018) In respect of energy provision to villages, the focus has to be put on local generation, in particular solar home systems and mini-grids. In order to be more sustainable also micro-enterprise zones in villages, providing local enterprises with key services, should be expanded more widely to nurture new enterprises and provide a supportive environment in which they can grow. Finally, health and educational developments should not be disregarded to avoid depopulation.

It is important to keep in mind that, in order to implement and use digital services it is necessary to display a good technological and digital infrastructure. In that sense, political agendas must consider their priority to provide rural areas with high-speed digital infrastructure as well as digital education to implement people's digital skills. Both are indispensable to tackle the digital challenge and raise the capacity of rural stakeholders and communities to exploit their digital potential.

The improvement of ICT, based on connectivity, digitalization and infrastructure together, the development of what is known as the Internet of things, the integration of objects into information networks to offer data in real time, has made possible to implement intelligent models to develop more sustainable cities where all the information is found with just one click. The Smart Cities concept refers to those cities that use IT to make both their critical infrastructure, as well as their components and public services offered more interactive and efficient. In addition, citizens can be more aware of them (Fundación Telefónica, 2010). It is not a unique concept, but it is polysemic and multidisciplinary, affecting different areas, not only media related, but also politics, economy, education, health, etc., since cities have a great impact on the economic and social development of countries.

Having a Smart City and transferring its advantages to the rural environment transforming it into Smart Villages, could help the sustainable and efficient management of urban infrastructure and services. The result is the reduction of public spending, the improvement of the quality in the services provided and the improvement of information to citizens. In this way decision-making becomes more effective in order to improve the lives of its inhabitants while stimulating the repopulation of villages and rural areas. A Smart Village itself constitutes a path for innovation, favouring the incubation of new businesses and ideas (Fundación Telefónica, 2010).

There are three perspectives that shape the panorama of the future and the development of cities (Schaffer, Komninos, Pallot, 2011). These perspectives summarize the challenges, infrastructure and the role of the agents involved in the transformation process towards Smart Cities: The first perspective is that of the Internet of the future, where the agents involved must be the researchers and the ICT companies the priorities, technical challenges, resources and facilities for experimentation. In addition, they will also implement the policies aimed at supporting creation of advanced facilities, test and experimental research.

The second perspective is the development of cities and urban planning, where agents must be politicians, citizens' platforms and business associations. Priorities should focus on urban development, essential infrastructure and the creation of new businesses. Other essential priorities are resources, based on the development of urban policy frameworks, organizational assets and development plans and, finally, municipal policies to stimulate innovation together with the creation of new and innovative companies.

The third perspective is the innovation ecosystems, driven by users where the agents involved must be, on the one hand, directors of living labs and, on the other, citizens, governments, companies and researchers as co-creators. The priorities have to be open innovation, fundamentally driven by users and the promotion of citizen participation. It should be possible to have the necessary resources, such as living labs facilities encouraging innovation with tools and physical infrastructure. Finally, policies should be those that drive open and collaborative innovation.

In this environment, digital devices undertake special importance since intelligent platforms, networks or content will be available through mobile phones, televisions and other devices with the aim of interrelating public agents, private agents and citizens.

Considering the ICT aspects, Spain is leading the list of countries with Smart Cities developing and tends to become a Smart Destination (MarcaEspaña, 2017). The benefits and competitive advantages of adopting the intelligent tourist destination model, from an economic development point of view, increase their competitiveness, generate new jobs, promote entrepreneurship, stimulate innovation thanks to public-private collaboration and, as a result, improve the quality of life of the resident (SEGITTUR, 2015). The RECI is the organisation in charge of collecting the different advancements that public-private institutions are doing in terms of the evolution of the Smart Cities. Paradoxical, Spain is also one of the European countries that concentrates a high depopulation level (Eurostat, 2018).

Smart Destinations, E-Tourism and Smart Tourism

The phenomenon of rural tourism has recently acquired new significance, having risen gradually from a marginal to a widespread practice. Traditional locations and rural destinations have raised tourist expectations, encouraging people to travel to less known places and drawing, for this reason, those tourist flows attracted by the authenticity of the experiences visitors are likely to have. The authenticity consist of cultural and social identities, traditions, memories, intangible connections, local peculiarities, and rural landscapes. Therefore communities and local and national governments have to respond to new touristic demands in more complex ways (Garau, 2015).

Buhalis (2000) argues that successful destinations are structured as containing the 6As of tourism destination, which are:

1. Attractions: natural, artificial and cultural ones.
2. Accessibility: Transport systems consisting in routes, terminals and public transport.
3. Activities: Which motivate tourist visitation to a specific place.
4. Available Packages: intermediaries to direct tourist attention.
5. Amenities: services facilitating stay, accommodation, catering and leisure.
6. Ancillary Services: which cover the secondary tourist requirements (i.e. banks, medical, postal, etc)

Smart Destinations are defined as touristic places holding a technological infrastructure that collects information about the tourist activity, analyse and understand its behaviour and needs in real time in order to encourage the interaction between visitors and tourist environment. They are meant to focus both in people and in the economic, social and cultural development. Smart Destinations are growing in geographical spaces were tourism development is planned and executed considering technological infrastructure that allows the increase of local sustainability while providing value for the experiences of visitors and the quality of life for locals. With technology being rooted in all organizations and entities, destinations will exploit synergies between ubiquitous sensing technology and their social gears to hold up the enrichment of tourist experiences (Lopez de Avila, 2015).

Most tourists prefer to enjoy the same comfort they have at home when on holiday. They want to be able to connect to social media, share their photographs and experiences, easily locate relevant sites during their stay, access them without any problems and even expand the information about the place they are visiting, choose the best restaurants and pay by electronic means (Smartcity_lab, 2019). Therefore, the places visited and cultural experiences are connected to tourism by stakeholders, tourist, tourist providers, governments, communities and locals (Wang, 2011).

E-tourism is the digitalisation of all the processes and value chains involved in tourism, travel, hospitality and catering industries that enable organisations to maximise their efficiency and effectiveness (Buhalis 2003). Because of that, tourists integrate themselves into a new value chain based on their own needs and experiences. However, what is important is not only the technological development itself but also the strategic and adequate integration of Smart Technology as a resource for the cooperative creation of valuable tourist experiences (Poupineau, 2016). The prospect of the application to tourism of tremendous amounts of online data has the potential of transforming "big data" into knowledge, dramatically enhancing the touristic experience and providing a deeper understanding of behavioral patterns and the structure of this industry. In this aspect, it marks a clear departure from e-tourism, which was focused in connecting businesses with consumers and consumers with consumers through the Web, collecting information, making information available and searchable, as well as facilitating electronic transactions (Pan, 2015).

Smart tourism is an advanced stage in tourism information. It consists of digital, intelligent, and virtual tourism based on digital, intelligent, and virtual technology (Zang & Yang, 2016) Smart Tourism provides places with unique opportunities to make them preferred choices for the locals and foreign tourists. It aims at increasing the competitiveness of destinations and tourism experience through an inclusive and co-creation process. Smart tourism includes an hybrid eco-system having physical, digital and social communities.

Therefore E-tourism is about digital connections; Smart tourism is about connecting the physical with the digital (Gretzel et Al, 2015: 42). Smart tourism experiences are achieved through personalization, context-awareness and real-time monitoring (Buhalis & Amaranggana, 2014).

Neuhofer, Buhalis and Ladkin (2015) identify information aggregation, ubiquitous connectedness and real-time synchronization as the major drivers of smart tourism experiences. Likewise, cooperative creation brings a new paradigm in business models and economic development due to the capability of Smart Destinations to generate a big amount of data through the continuous feedback with users, both locals and visitors. The priorities of Smart Tourism Destinations structure are to enhance tourists' travel experience; to provide more intelligent platforms to gather and distribute information within destinations; to facilitate efficient allocation of tourism resources; and to integrate tourism suppliers at both micro and macro level aiming at ensuring that benefit from this sector is well distributed to the local society (Rong 2012). Thus, the new systems supporting a variety of travel-related metrics enable tourist destinations to better understand where and how potential and existing visitors live, the nature of information used to plan a trip, as well as with which travellers share their experiences before, during and after the trip. The analytical applications support the design of smart tourism by offering enhanced customer intelligence, improving business processes and, ultimately, enabling the implementation of new strategies for navigating an increasingly competitive environment (Xiang & Fesenmaier, 2017:303).

Integrated governance, comprehensive and participatory planning, productivity gains and a skilled workforce, competitive advantages, an innovation culture, greater mobility, better infrastructure, enhanced quality of life, responsible management and use of natural resources, as well as an inclusive community therefore constitute the major outcomes of smart city development (Gretzel, 2018:174). There are certain areas of action that make the different regions a Smart Destination such as innovation, technology, sustainability and accessibility (Mincotur, 2015). The key focus smart experiences aim at technology-mediated tourism experiences and their enrichment through personalization, concurrent-time and context awareness surveillance (Buhalis and Amaranggana, 2014). Thus, the incorporation of digital technologies in historical disciplines design the paradigm of Digital Humanities. These encourage not only the transference of knowledge but also the creation of innovative content and the developments within digital ecosystems that enhance travel experience and possibly a new value creation opportunity for locals to rise a sustainable economy in rural areas based in their cultural heritage.

MAIN FOCUS OF THE CHAPTER

Issues, Controversies, Problems

Culture is the core of tourism. Indeed, much tourism is built on culture such as historical sites, interesting architecture or cultural centres. Linking people (tourists) to the culture around them enhances their experience of a place. Moreover, with tourism apps and services, they can get acquainted with the culture even before their visit, increase their engagement with it during their stay, and share, review or maintain their experience after the visit. In addition, the more people engaged with the region's culture, the more will visit it, staying overnight, bringing friends and family (Europeana Foundation, 2015). Hence, cultural heritage is not only crucial for tourism but for economic development too. Therefore, the reconversion of the rural territories into Smart Villages or Smart Rural Communities based in the huge heritage Spanish regions own could be the solution since culture can change society for the better, bringing both social and economic change. Cultural and heritage tourism are forms of tourism motivated by an interest in the historical, artistic, scientific and cultural offer of a community, region, group or institution, a desire to seek authenticity and to experience native culture. For this reason, urban destinations are considered inherently of interest to cultural and heritage tourists (Cranmer & Jung, 2014). Spain, with 48 sites declared World Heritage, shows its great historical-cultural legacy around the country. In fact, it is one of the countries that incorporates a greater number of places in the prestigious list of Unesco. Beyond the most remarkable places or landmarks, a number of villages and routes all around Spain that have witnessed the most relevant moments in its History.

In the early years of the nineteenth century, Ferdinand VII resolved to abolish the Salic law. It meant to allow his daughter to be the sovereign with only three years old, propelling Spain into confrontation between the different factions. From the international point of view, this event raised the interest of the foreign press who rapidly sent correspondents to cover the conflict. The appearance of war correspondents is relatively recent, since it requires the existence of large-scale newspapers with huge economic capacity to move professional journalists to the locations where conflicts take place. Nevertheless, the concept of "war correspondent" today constitutes a reference to a specific and perfectly defined type of task within journalism. Most works about war correspondents follow the same pattern. There are authors who discuss about some precursors, but it is most agreed that war journalism started with Russell leaving some of his predecessors in the background. This is what we find in the classic works of Altabella (1945), Mathew (1957), Knightley (1976 and 2000), Bullard (1974), Wilkinson-Latham (1979), Royle (1987), Lande (1995), Roth (1997), Simpson (2002), Moorcraft and Taylor (2008), Brake and Demoor (2009) and Korte (2009), Roth (2010). However, in Spain, it is in the Carlist civil conflict in 1833, when the names of the first journalists appeared and, based on scientific literature, They can be considered as war correspondents like Michael Burke Honan from *The Morning Herald* who spent long periods in the capital, describing the situation of the civil war in his chronicles.

Historically, it seems commonly established that William Howard Russell was the first war correspondent for the coverage he gave to the Crimean War in 1854. However, the study of hemerographic and bibliographic sources has approached a recognized group of correspondents, which cover previous conflicts in Spain during the Carlist civil conflict that began in 1833. Previous research revealed indications that point out that the work done by these correspondents was settle on Spanish territory, responding to the informative criteria required by their editors to generate opinion in their own countries. They were British and French journalists who moved to Spain to cover a war in which their countries were involved because of their support to Isabella II as a consequence of additional articles in the Treaty of the Quadruple Alliance. Therefore, Spain had, for the first time, not an isolated journalist but a group of professional correspondents who moved to the scenes of the conflict and wrote their chronicles from the battlefields. It is known, through their chronicles, the shelters where they hid when the authorities persecuted them; villas, roads or military camps where they were installed or visited to cover their mission. Despite the paradigm that involves the work of these pioneers of war journalism in Spain, their works are virtually unknown.

Certain territories in Spain like Aragón, Burgos, Castellón, Extremadura, Madrid or Navarra were witnesses of the conflict. Ambassadors, diplomats, journalists and correspondents made these locations the main scenery of international negotiations and the point of documentation exchange referring to the army led by the Infante Don Carlos. What was life like in the Court or in the Navarre region? What were the strategic points in the negotiations? How much foreign population did the town have and where were the places of interest in the conflict located? Regarding Madrid, we know that the Carlists undertake the march towards the capital arriving at the gates of Vallecas on September, 12th 1837. Finally they did not attack the city, mainly for political opportunity reasons. That decision changes the course of the war and leads liberals to victory. The Royal Guard, concentrated in Pozuelo and Aravaca, had staged a military uprising demanding that the Regent got rid of the Progressive Government of Calatrava-Mendizábal. Arganda del Rey was also one of the towns that received Infante Don Carlos and where the Royal expedition to Alcalá de Henares to fight with Espartero's troops was planned. Many of the descriptions we know today about the historical context of these regions are based on the memories of the protagonists (Fernández de Cordoba, 1888). Nonetheless, we also have knowledge of what Madrid was like during the first half of the nineteenth century thanks to the information found in the Press of the time and in the chronicles that war correspondents - foreigners and Spaniards - sent to their newspapers from their different destinations. Likewise, Aragon and certain villages such as Villar de los Navarros in the Daroca Region, are witnesses of some battles described in the correspondents' chronicles. There are also chronicles that describe how, in the town of Retuerta near Santo Domingo de Silos, a struggle of the Royal expedition led by Infante Don Carlos, took place during the withdrawal of the Royal troops from Madrid in October, 1837. Some articles relate to the role of the hosts led by the priest Merino in the places of Villodrigo, Castrojeriz and Villafranca Montes de Oca all of them in Burgos.

Hence, taking as a reference these Spanish routes that war journalists visited during the first Carlist war it is possible to identify the villages that were protagonists of these historical landmarks as smart tourist destinations. Digital content based on geolocation, GIS developments, Apps, QR codes, audiovisual pieces with videomapping, augmented reality and virtual reality techniques are the key to offer the traveller this experience in an interactive, personalized, integrative and participatory environment through sustainable contents of historical-cultural character. Besides, the data provided by the different sensors allows the assessment of their economic and social impact.

SOLUTIONS AND RECOMMENDATIONS

Digital Content to Enhance Visitor's Experience

One of the consequences of digitalization, whether it be texts, audio, video or images, either through the transformation of analogical content in a combination of binary digits or through the digital capture of information, means that content can be seen and consumed in different digital devices, leading to a technology and multi-platform convergence (Sánchez Martínez and Ibar Alonso, 2015: 87). Additionally, the emergence of portable devices such as tablets and smart phones has given rise to a universe of apps that help users to access a wide array of content on a daily basis, in fields such as leisure, culture, tourism, health, education or e-commerce (Sánchez Martínez, 2017: 121).

Nowadays touristic experiences are meaningless without digital devices such as smartphones. They are often used not only as a support in their journey but also for planning it. Smartphones facilitate information search, information sharing and information processing. Moreover they enable travellers to learn more about the destination or sharing photos or other "social" activities during the trip (Wang, 2011: 2). As far as travelling is a sense-making process, tourists need to learn, understand and feel the places they are visiting by getting involved with the local culture (Jennings and Weiler, 2006). Smartphones can provide a wide range of information services to support main travel activities. Google published several infographics with the five stages of travels, which are:

1. Dream.
2. Plan.
3. Book.
4. Experience.
5. Share.

All of them involve users in an interactive experience by encouraging visitors in a search-share activity. At present, within the eTourism concept three key factors become the pillars of the travel experience. First, users face the trip planning. It would be the previous stage. Where to go? How to go? What to visit? Once they have made the decision about the destination, appears the second factor appears: It is the information search. Currently, users use both search engines and different websites to find the most valuable information, trying to obtain tips on aspects of the trip such as accommodation, mobility, as well as advice to enjoy of the stay like landmarks to visit, restaurants, facilities, walks or routes. While visitors are enjoying their trip, they share moments and experiences in their networks. Social activity is the third factor: people like to post, review, send their pictures to their contacts in a busy activity to show their leisure. Main users get access to the published information through websites or webpages launched by tour operators, City Halls, business or cultural institutions. Simultaneously apps stores also develop a number of tour guides to enable visitor's experiences merging several types of contents like gourmet routes, cultural plans, city maps, natural routes or landmark's audio guide. Most of these apps

Figure 1. Spanish APP screenshot examples from Madrid, Barcelona and Córdoba (Adapted from [https://play.google.com])

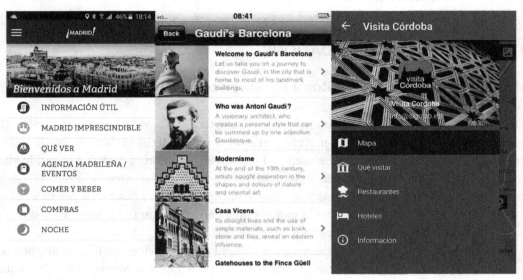

attempt to enhance the user's experience. Some examples in recent developments to increase the content offer in Tourism Apps are:

Therefore, Smartphones can provide a wide range of information services to support not only main travel activities such as planning, reservation, navigation, but also many micro-moments within the travel process (Wang et al., 2011) Micro-moments occur when people turn to a device intending to get an answer to an immediate need. In these moments, the stakes are high for travel brands as preferences are shaped and decisions are made. What happens in these micro-moments ultimately affects the travel decision-making process. As further research is developed in the traveller customer's journey, micro-moments also increase.

Many tourists use apps with the "near me" function to get to know their environment and try new activities. Therefore, location-based marketing becomes even more important for businesses such as restaurants, attractions, and shops which, in turn, means that new strategies need to be developed whereby business embed advertisements into the search results of the apps providing such services. (Wang et al., 2011)

Co-creation is based on participatory design and was already used in organizations and institutions before the emergence of ICT. However, in the tourist sector it is increasingly gaining special importance by integrating both residents and visitors in the process and empowering them. The experiences created must incorporate immersive technological solutions that allow tourists to "become highly involved, participatory and co-create with different stakeholders through the different stages of the trip" (Neuhofer & Buhalis, 2013). According to Buhalis (2013), it is necessary to involve all stakeholders positively to create an experience of Smart Destination. This means local government, local communities, museums in the area, destinations. Tourists and residents together create a system that maximizes both the attractiveness of the destination itself and the satisfaction of the end user achieving a long-term commitment based on sustainability.

Figure 2. Spanish APP screenshot examples from Granada, Navarra and Alcalá de Henares (Adapted from [https://play.google.com])

Today it is essential to design marketing strategies taking into account the participation culture since interactivity encourages learning and, finally, the enjoyment of the experience. The challenge, therefore, is to design personalized experiences that encourage the visitor's commitment to the cultural heritage product in such a way that he learns by doing, that is, learning by doing.

Therefore, and related with the research, some of the developments and proposals in Digital Content in order to spread not only the collected data but to enhance tourist experiences through historical routes are:

Web

A Website is not only a theoretical reference but also an informative tool. It is a site to find historical facts, references and create engagement through the content. A swift swipe of the mouse will connect people to specific topics on the website, and a quick link to a full insight. Corresponsalesdeguerra.com is a site where users can find all the information related not only with the war protagonists but also with the routes, access to videos; how to download the APP as well as researching advances and sources. It provides reliable information to learn more about the history while preparing the trip.

The Site is done with a content management system. Users can scroll the home page to have a complete view of the content maximizing the usability. When users open the site, there is a video embedded from YouTube with a causal explanation to download de APP. Besides there is a navigation bar with the main sections of the content. From the digital marketing point of view there are some features with which content generates engagement with users (Fleming, 2000) Flow, Functionality, Feedback and loyalty. Corresponsalesdeguerra.com has based its content in the three F's. The Site is responsive and users can access to the content in any device.

Figure 3. Web screenshot www.corresponsalesdeguerra.com (© 2018, Instituto Estudios Históricos CEU. Used with permission.)

APP

Studies in Anthropology, Literary Theory, Psychology, Geography, and Organizational Theory also have argued that the narrative is "the closest we can come to experience" (Connelly and Clandinn 1990). According to Wang (2012), about one quarter of the travellers described how the smartphone apps help them to get a good value out of their trips, become more "efficient" in terms of planning and activities, and improve their overall satisfaction. The use of smartphone apps had added delight to their trips, helped them to enjoy a rich experience and visit more places.

The core of the APP is a GIS (Mapbox) that allows the tourist to follow the correspondent's steps through several geolocated routes. Besides, to enhance the content, users can enlarge the information about the battlefields as well as biographies of their protagonist, look for historical facts, take a glance at the cultural heritage or the natural heritage in the territory they are visiting, check battle data and use an advisor of nearby routes. The aim is to allow the user, both tourists and locals, to become the protagonists of the design of their own routes.

The APP allows users to apply different collaboration tools, which provide feedback through the collected data and share the contents in social media channels. These characteristics let new paths open for design and leave the traditional touristic guide pattern, thus moving to an open, transversal and collaborative model, which provides creative and collaborative experiences in which each participant can contribute with their own experience and value. Hence, in this APP, users can discover or share routes with Wikiloc.

Branded Content

An emerging way of using mobile technologies to introduce heritage is to create fun and gamified activities, most of them inspired by urban games or street games (Avouris and Yiannoutsou, 2012). The experience of visiting a destination greatly improves by incorporating GPS services locating users. It can be done by providing global access to heritage through storytelling. Based on people's experiences and reminiscences, involving travellers in a continuous educational process and promoting crowdsourcing are some technological and strategic potentials to enhance tourist experiences (Grevtsova, 2017:67).

Figure 4. APP screenshot www.corresponsalesdeguerra.com (© 2018, Instituto Estudios Históricos CEU. Used with permission.)

Through the creation of relevant content, the user is reached from a personalized approach that not only satisfies his needs but also encourages the content remembrance. It allows to record it into the top of mind and top of heart and, consequently, it generates engagement.

Branded Content is used to build and strengthen ties between destinations and users. For this reason, innovative content must be generated and all social media planning arranged to connect with travellers within participatory platforms. The audiovisual pieces with videomapping and augmented reality techniques are the key to take travellers to their destination in an interactive experience. The main audiovisual piece is a documentary filmed and produced by the researching group based in Charles Gruneisen experience during his stay in Spain as journalist correspondent. Therefore, some content belongs to documentary. Besides, several videos were recorded from battles reenactment that took place near the original battlefield each year and recreated by locals. Furthermore, audiovisual pieces with the correspondents routes and biographies of the main protagonist of the conflict are part of the storytelling to engage users.

CONCLUSION

The relationship between the private sector and the cultural and historic heritage is potentially difficult, since profit-driven corporate activity can sometimes be at odds with the ethics and values surrounding heritage places. Historical preservation is about saving and sustaining historic places, preserving them for future use and protecting them for all to enjoy. It helps us to understand who we are and shapes relationships with neighbours and other communities around the territory. Organizations might preserve or rediscover major historic sites and monuments in order to provide ongoing sustainable access and enjoyment for current and future audiences and include historical landmarks and public spaces.

Figure 5. YouTube Corresponsales de guerra Chanel screenshot (© 2018, Instituto Estudios Históricos CEU. Used with permission.)

Cultural engagement is less about image or about customer loyalty than it is about the central asset of trust. Hence, the idea of cultural engagement has to be rethought. The objective should be that cultural commitment is verifiably correlated with a sustainable economic profit. Art, history and culture have the particular advantage that, on the most part, they generate a basic element of trust. Cultural heritage can introduce the ability to discuss and be reflected into the economy. Thus, cultural heritage adds new meaning to economic structures on territories. It can also provide the means to initiate new economic and sustainable dynamics. Then, the economy can bring structural expertise and practical participation to social and political contexts.

There is a great value in adopting regional perspectives for smart tourism development. Spain needs appropriate adaptation of the smart principles to the territorial level as smart tourism development spreads beyond cities. The sooner it is done, the better for Spanish competitiveness as a Smart Destination.

Tourism is an important component of Spanish national and local economies. Its future success is increasingly reliant upon an understanding of the users´ behaviour in order to mobilize necessary resources to satisfy their needs and wants. User experience, not technology, is a key challenge for the design of content aimed at promoting smart tourism in a framework that attempts to give a holistic view of mobile tourist services from a value-in-use perspective. Creating touristic "micro-moments" that remains in the collective memory as a value for tourism experiences is nowadays mandatory to enhance visitors' knowledge of the region they are visiting.

Finally, the priorities to achieve Smart Tourism Destinations construction in Spain are not only to improve tourists' travel experience by private-public institutions but to provide more intelligent platforms to gather and distribute the information collected from ICT and IoT services as well as Big Data. Likewise being a Smart destination ought to facilitate efficient and sustainable allocation of resources to ensure that benefit from this sector reaches local inhabitants.

ACKNOWLEDGMENT

The results of this research correspond to a study conducted as part of a research project that is supported and financed by CEU San Pablo University and Banco Santander. [Grant number HAR2017-89640]

REFERENCES

Abradelo de Usera, M. I. & Togores, L. (1997). Viajeros románticos por la España isabelina. *Aportes. Revista de Historia Contemporánea*, (12), 119-146.

Alberdi, M. J., & Fleming, P. (2000). *Hablemos de marketing interactivo. Reflexiones sobre marketing digital y comercio electrónico*. Madrid, Spain: ESIC.

Altabella, J. (1945). *Corresponsales de Guerra: su historia y su actuación. De Jenofonte a Knickerbocker, pasando por Peris Mencheta*. Madrid, Spain: Editorial Febo.

Arup. (2010). *Smart Cities, transforming the 21st century via the creative use of technology*. Retrieved November 25, 2019, from https://www.arup.com/Publications/Smart_Cities.aspx

Buhalis, D. (2000). Marketing the competitive destination of the future. *Tourism Management, 21*(1), 97–116. doi:10.1016/S0261-5177(99)00095-3

Buhalis, D. (2003). *Tourism: Information Technology for Strategic Tourism Management*. Gosport, UK: Prentice Hall.

Buhalis, D., & Amaranggana, A. (2014). Smart Tourism Destinations. In Z. Xiang & I. Tussyadiah (Eds.), *Information and Communication Technologies in Tourism* (pp. 553–564). Heidelberg, Germany: Springer. (Original work published 2014)

Buhalis, D., & Licata, M. (2002). The Future eTourism Intermediaries. *Tourism Management, 23*(3), 207–220. doi:10.1016/S0261-5177(01)00085-1

Bullón de Mendoza, A. (2009). Los primeros corresponsales de guerra: España 1833-1840. *Cuadernos de Investigacion Historica, 26*, 345–349.

Calderoni, L., Maio, D., & Palmieri, P. (2012). Location-aware Mobile Services for a Smart City: Design, Implementation and Deployment. *Journal of Theoretical and Applied Electronic Commerce Research, 7*(3), 74–87. doi:10.4067/S0718-18762012000300008

Cranmer, E., & Jung, T. (2014) *Augmented Reality (AR): Business Models in Urban Cultural Heritage Tourist Destinations*. Paper presented at the 12th APacCHRIE Conference 2014, Kuala Lumpur, Malaysia.

CULTURAbase. (2017). *Turismo cultural*. Ministerio de Cultura y Deporte. Retrieved December 12 from http://estadisticas.mecd.gob.es/CulturaDynPx/culturabase/index.htm?type=pcaxis&path=/t7/p7b/a2016/&file=pcaxis

European Network for Rural Development. (2018). Smart Villages Revitalising Rural Services. *Eu Rural Review, 26*. Retrieved December 12, 2019, from https://enrd.ec.europa.eu/sites/enrd/files/enrd_publications/publi-enrd-rr-26-2018-en.pdf

Europeana Foundation. (2015). *Transforming the World with Culture: Next Steps on Increasing the Use of Digital Cultural Heritage in Research*. Education, Tourism and the Creative Industries.

Fundación Telefónica. (2011). *Smart Cities: un primer paso hacia el internet de las cosas*. Madrid, Spain: Author.

Garau, C., Masala, F., & Pinna, F. (2015). Bechmarking smart urban mobility: A study on Italian cities. *Computational science and its applications—ICCSA, 2015, lecture notes in computer science (LNCS)*, 612–623. . doi:10.1007/978-3-319-21470-2

Gretzel, U. (2018). *Tourism and Social Media. In The Sage Handbook of Tourism Management* (pp. 415–432). Sage. doi:10.4135/9781526461490.n28

Gretzel, U., Sigala, M., Xiang, Z., & Koo, C. (2015). *Smart Tourism: Foundations and Developments.* Working Paper, Smart Tourism Research Center, Kyung Hee University.

Hankinson, A. (1982). *Man of war: William Howard Russell of the Times.* Londres, UK: Heinemann.

Hays, S., Page, S. J., & Buhalis, D. (2013). Social Media as a Destination Marketing Tool: Its Use by National Tourism Organisations. *Current Issues in Tourism*, *16*(3), 211–239. doi:10.1080/13683500.2 012.662215

IBM. (2011) *Ciudades más inteligentes para un desarrollo sostenible. Cómo optimizar los sistemas de la ciudad en una economía basada en el talento.* Institute for Business Value. Retrieved November 9, 2019, from https://www.ibm.com/smarterplanet/global/files/es__es_es__cities__ciudades_inteligen-tes_para_desarrollo_sostenible_0622.pdf

Izquierdo, S., & Bartolomé, A. (2019). *Pilares de la divulgación en Humanidades: Geografía, tecnologías digitales y comunicación Historia, pensamiento y humanismo actual. Libro homenaje al profesor Federico Martínez Roda.* Valencia: Universidad de Valencia.

Knightley, P. (1976). *Corresponsales de Guerra.* Barcelona, Spain: Euros.

Lande, N. (1995). *Dispatches from the Front. In News Accounts for the American Wars* (pp. 1776–1991). Nueva York, NY: Henry Holt and Company.

Leguineche, M., & Sánchez, G. (2001). *Los ojos de la guerra.* Barcelona, Spain: Mondadori.

Lopez de Avila, A. (2015). *Smart Destinations: XXI Century Tourism.* Presented at the *ENTER2015 Conference on Information and Communication Technologies in Tourism*, Lugano, Switzerland.

Moorcraft, P. L., & Taylor, P. M. (2008). *Shooting the Messenger. The Political Impact of War Reporting.* Washington, DC: Potomac Books.

Neuhofer, B., Buhalis, D., & Ladkin, A. (2015). Technology as a Catalyst of Change: Enablers and Barriers of the Tourist Experience and Their Consequences. In Information and Communication Technologies in Tourism 2015. Lugano, Switzerland: Springer Verlag.

Pallot, M., Trousse, B., Senach, B., & Scapin, D. (2010). *Living Lab Research Landscape: From User Centred Design and User Experience Towards User Co-creation.* Position Paper, First Living Labs Summer School Inria, París. Retrieved November 9, 2019, from http://link.springer.com/chapter/10.1 007%2F978-3-642-20898-0_31#

PanB. (2015). *E-Tourism.* Doi:10.1007/978-3-319-01669-6_77-1

Pannapacker, W. (2009). *The MLA and the Digital Humanities*. Retrieved November 9, 2019, from https://web.archive.org/web/20120514003204/http://chronicle.com/blogPost/The-MLAthe-Digital/19468

Poupineau, S. (2016). *Which smart tourism experiences are more likely to enhance the destination attractiveness?* Retrieved November 9, 2019, from https://www.researchgate.net/publication/308918443_Which_smart_tourism_experiences_are_more_likely_to_enhance_the_destination_attractiveness

Rong, A. (2012). *China economic net*. Retrieved November 12, 2019, from http://en.ce.cn/Insight/201204/12/t20120412_23235803.shtml

Sánchez, M., Barceló, T., & Cabezuelo, F. (2017). The Smart City Apps as the Core of Place Branding Strategy: A Comparative Analysis of Innovation Cases. *Zer: Revista de Estudios de Comunicación*, *22*(42), 119–135.

Sánchez, M., & Ibar, R. (2015). Convergence and Interaction in the New Media: Typologies of Prosumers among University Students. *Communicatio Socialis*, *28*(2), 87–99.

Schaffers, H., Komninos, N., Pallot, M., Trousse, B., Nilsson, M., & Oliveira, A. (2011). Smart Cities and the Future Internet: Towards Cooperation Frameworks for Open Innovation. In The Future Internet (pp. 66-56). Berlin: Springer.

Secretaría de Estado de la España Global. (2017). *España, referente internacional en Ciudades Inteligentes*. Retrieved November 12, 2019, https://marcaespana.es/actualidad/innovaci%C3%B3n/espa%C3%B1a-referente-internacional-en-ciudades-inteligentes

SEGITTUR. (2015). *Informe destinos turísticos: construyendo el futuro*. Retrieved November 13, 2019, https://www.segittur.es/opencms/export/sites/segitur/.content/galerias/descargas/proyectos/Libro-Blanco-Destinos-Tursticos-Inteligentes-ok_es.pdf

Vasada, M., & Padhiyar, Y. J. (2016). Smart Tourism: Growth for Tomorrow. *Journal for Research*, *01*(12), 55–61.

Visvizi, A., & Lytras, M. (2018). Rescaling and Refocusing Smart Cities Research: From Mega Cities to Smart Villages. *Journal of Science and Technology Policy Management*, *9*(2), 134–145. doi:10.1108/JSTPM-02-2018-0020

Wang, D., Park, S., & Fesenmaier, D. R. (2011). An Examination of Information Services and Smartphone Applications. *Proceedings of 16th Annual Graduate Student Research Conference in Hospitality and Tourism*.

Wang, D., Park, S., & Fesenmaier, D. R. (2011). The Role of Smartphones in Mediating the Touristic Experience. *Journal of Travel Research*, *51*(4), 371–387. doi:10.1177/0047287511426341

Wang, Z. H. (2011). *Smart City Road: Science Governance and Urban Personality / China Telecom Smart City Research Group Compiled*. Electronic Industry Press.

Xiang, Z., & Fesenmaier, D. R. (2017). Big Data Analytics, Tourism Design and Smart Tourism. In Analytics in Smart Tourism Design Concepts and Methods. Springer.

Zavratnik, V., Kos, A., & Stojmenova Duh, E. (2018). Smart Villages: Comprehensive Review of Initiatives and Practices. *Sustainability*, *10*(7), 25–59. doi:10.3390u10072559

Zhang, L., & Yang, J. (2016). Smart Tourism. In J. Jafari & H. Xiao (Eds.), *Encyclopedia of Tourism*. Springer International Publishing. doi:10.1007/978-3-319-01384-8_175

Section 3
Data Privacy and eGovernment

Chapter 10
Consumer Privacy Regulations:
Considerations in the Age of Globalization and Big Data

Martha Davis

https://orcid.org/0000-0001-8756-8616

University of Denver, USA

ABSTRACT

Big data and analytics have not only changed how businesses interact with consumers, but also how consumers interact with the larger world. Smart cities, IoT, cloud, and edge computing technologies are all enabled by data and can provide significant societal benefits via efficiencies and reduction of waste. However, data breaches have also caused serious harm to customers by exposing personal information. Consumers often are unable to make informed decisions about their digital privacy because they are in a position of asymmetric information. There are an increasing number of privacy regulations to give consumers more control over their data. This chapter provides an overview of data privacy regulations, including GDPR. In today's globalized economy, the patchwork of international privacy regulations is difficult to navigate, and, in many instances, fails to provide adequate business certainty or consumer protection. This chapter also discusses current research and implications for costs, data-driven innovation, and consumer trust.

INTRODUCTION

Big data and data analytics are still evolving fields of study. Thus, an agreed-upon and fully comprehensive definition is yet to be established (Uthayasankar, Muhammad, Zahir, & Vishanth, in press). It is also debatable whether big data is a disruptive technology (Frizzo-Barker, Chow-White, Mazafari, & Ha, 2016). However, we do know that it is changing how businesses understand, connect with, and ultimately profit from their customers. Manyika and Brown (2011) state that big data has the potential to increase business operating margins by up to sixty percent. Data is becoming crucial for companies

DOI: 10.4018/978-1-7998-3817-3.ch010

Copyright © 2020, IGI Global. Copying or distributing in print or electronic forms without written permission of IGI Global is prohibited.

in decision-making, relationship-management, production, and maintaining an overall competitive advantage. It is particularly valuable once turned into digital intelligence.

The overall amount of data collected is doubling every two years, with an estimated 44 zettabytes of data by the end of 2019. That is equal to 99 billion years of music files, 686 billion 64GB tablets, or 1.4 billion years of HD video. Businesses can monetize all this data in several ways, including use for advertising revenue (Facebook, Google, etc.), marketplace transactions (Amazon, eBay, Alibaba, Uber, etc.), production optimization (Rolls Royce, Caterpillar, etc.), and the selling or renting of cloud services (AWS). Users often pay for seemingly free services, such as downloadable white papers and e-books, by signing up with their data.

Big data and analytics have changed not only how consumers interact with businesses, but also how they interact with the larger world. Smart cities, IoT, cloud, and edge computing technologies are all enabled by data and have the potential to provide significant societal benefits through efficiencies and the reduction of waste. While digitization has the potential to benefit both businesses and society at large through new intelligence, innovation, and profits, the primary challenges are that of privacy and security (Frizzo-Barker et al., 2016). In the age of big data and business analytics, concern over privacy and data protection is increasingly at the forefront of consumers' minds. Massive data breaches have caused severe economic, social, and psychological harm to customers by exposing personal information. Data breaches have also severely damaged the consumer-trust relationship with the companies at issue, often reducing firm market valuations and forever tarnishing brands (Choong, Hutton, Richardson, & Rinaldo, 2017). A simple Internet search shows the scale of this problem, with massive data breaches involving even high-profile companies, such as Equifax, Marriot, Yahoo, and Uber, to name just a few examples. It is also worth mentioning that consumer privacy concerns can extend beyond unauthorized data breaches. For example, there was significant consumer backlash in the United States related to the Facebook sale of personal data to Cambridge Analytica for political purposes (Meredith, 2018). With the proliferation of big data, there are also numerous new policy questions relating to data ownership, a concentration of large companies that control this data, and data flows across international borders.

The objectives of this chapter are to:

- Provide an overview of the various international data privacy regulations, including GDPR;
- Discuss the pros and cons of the different data privacy regulations and lessons learned;
- Discuss the implications of data privacy regulations on data-driven innovation, the economics of privacy, and consumer trust; and
- Suggest potential solutions and recommendations.

BACKGROUND

Information privacy is the ability to control personal data and associated identities, and it is now widely regarded as one of the most vulnerable aspects of online use (Nissenbaum, 2011). Privacy regulations are concerned with how businesses handle data and information privacy. While privacy regulations have existed for many years, the number of proposed government regulations have been increasing as a result of the growing number of data breaches and associated consumer backlash. One of the more well-known regulations is the General Data Protection Regulation (GDPR) in the European Union (EU). Globally, the current position of consumer data privacy regulations is not ideal. Many jurisdictions have no regulations, and the regulations that do exist are not uniform in nature. The status quo is quite a challenging environment for businesses to operate under and has had the practical implication of global companies voluntarily rolling out GDPR-type controls as a global baseline.

Given the recent trend of digitization, the number of data privacy regulations will undoubtedly continue to grow in the future. This trend also links privacy policy to innovation policy, which means that privacy regulations have the potential to impact the direction of innovation. There are also other significant implications of data privacy regulations affecting the cost of doing business and overall consumer trust.

DATA PROTECTION REGULATIONS

General Data Protection Regulation (GDPR)

Before the passage of GDPR in 2016, data privacy regulations in the European Union (EU) were inconsistent across countries, which was a complicated situation for multinational businesses to navigate. This difficulty, combined with the increased use of new technologies, created the impetus for a more uniform and broad approach to data privacy protections (Tankard, 2016). GDPR became effective on May 24, 2018, and applies to all personal data across various industries within the EU (Albrect, 2016). This regulation is among the most stringent data protection laws in the world and has very high fines for non-compliance.

The GDPR gives individuals greater control over the use of their data, provides a single regulatory environment across all EU member countries, and places businesses on an even playing field. The GDPR defines personal data as any information that relates to an identifiable living individual. Individual pieces of information that can collectively lead to the identification of a person are also considered personal data. Companies must notify consumers about the use of their data, and consumers must also provide affirmative consent for the use of their data (i.e., opting in rather than opting out of a program).

Table 1. Key attributes of the General Data Protection Regulation (GDPR)

General Data Protection Regulation
• A legal compliance issue, not a technology issue
• Impacts any company, regardless of location
• Appointment of Data Protection Officer
• Requires a robust compliance framework
• Affects businesses that collect or process personal data
• Requires data retention and destruction policies and procedures
• More significant data processor obligations or accountability
• Effective May 25, 2018

Source: (FitzPatrick, 2017)

The GDPR has 11 chapters and 91 articles. The key points are summarized below:

Article 4: A new concept of "pseudonymization" refers to the processing of personal data in a manner that the data can no longer identify a specific person without the use of additional information. Such additional information is to be stored separately to ensure that personal data is not attributable to an identifiable person. Organizations that implement pseudonymization have various benefits under GDPR, including a reduced risk of fines in the event a data breach does occur. Companies should only use identifiable personal data if anonymous or pseudonym data is not an option (DLA Piper, 2020).

Article 17: Consumers have the right of erasure, also known as the "right to be forgotten." The right of erasure means that third parties must remove the personal data of an individual upon request if there are no real business reasons to store the information.

Article 18: Consumers also have the "right to portability," which is the right to transfer their data between different service providers more easily (EU, 2016).

Articles 23 and 30: Require companies to implement reasonable data protection measures to protect consumers' data.

Article 31: Consumers have a right to know if a breach involves their data, and companies may be fined up to €10 million or two percent of worldwide revenues, whichever is higher, for noncompliance. Data breaches must be reported to supervising authorities (SA) within 72 hours of learning about the breach.

Article 32: Requires data controllers to notify data subjects as quickly as possible.

Article 33: Requires companies to perform data protection impact assessments to identify risks to consumers.

Article 35: Requires certain companies to appoint data protection officers (DPO). Any company that processes data about a subject's genetic data, health, racial or ethnic origin, religious beliefs, and so on, must designate a DPO. DPOs serve to advise companies about compliance with the regulation and act as a point of contact with SAs. Some companies fall under these guidelines due to the personal human resources information that is collected about their employees.

Articles 36 & 37: Discusses the data protection officer position. It still is somewhat unclear what a DPO is and precisely what qualifications someone in this position should possess. There is also a shortage of experts in this field because the DPO requirement is new outside of Germany.

Article 45: Extends GDPR to international companies. Even if a company is not in the EU, they are still subject to GDPR if they market goods or services and collect information belonging to individuals within the EU. Thus, this law captures many other international organizations. If a company's website is not GDPR-compliant, it will be inaccessible within the EU. Well-known examples of this include the Chicago Tribune and the Los Angeles Times.

Article 79: Outlines the penalties for GDPR non-compliance, depending on the nature of the violation. There are two tiers of fines with up to €10 million or two percent of worldwide revenues for less severe infractions, and up to €20 million or four percent of global revenues, whichever is higher, for more severe offenses (EU, 2016; De Groot, 2019).

Practical Implications of GDPR for Businesses

The potential for hefty fines means that compliance with GDPR is necessary for businesses. The European Data Protection Board (EDPB) released a preliminary report in 2019, examining the first nine months of the implementation of the GDPR. According to the EDPB, there had been a total of 206,326 cases, comprised of 94,622 complaints and 64,684 data breach violations. The fines issued thus far have been at pre-GDPR levels, except for a noteworthy penalty assessed to Google. The total penalty issued was €55,955,871, with nearly ninety percent of that amount (€50 million) fined to Google by the French Data Protection Supervisory Authority, CNIL (EDPB, 2019).

In terms of other practical implications for businesses, GDPR also requires companies to review supply chains and current contracts to ensure compliance. Additionally, insurance policies should have cyber, and data protection coverage added (DLA Piper, 2020).

GDPR After One Year

The creation of many of the GDPR enforcement frameworks are still in progress, but enough time has passed to assess how it is going thus far. There are a few key takeaways regarding the level of compliance uncertainty, business impact, regulatory enforcement, and potential loopholes.

Companies are still coming to terms with what it means to be compliant, and there are several areas of uncertainty. For example, GDPR's applicability to facial recognition technologies is somewhat unclear, and Facebook has recently reimplemented this technology. Previously, facial recognition technology was not allowed by the EU due to the potential to track consumers without consent (De Groot, 2019).

It has been much harder for companies to build out consumer mailing lists with GDPR opt-in requirements (De Groot, 2019). See the previous discussion of ways to monetize consumer data in order to fully understand the financial and competitive impacts this higher standard of informed consent has on businesses, particularly media companies.

Most fines have been below the maximum amount. After removing the Google outlier, the average GDPR fine was approximately €66,000. See previous discussions about the penalties that have been assessed thus far for additional information (GDPR, 2019). The regulatory leniency observed thus far is expected to end after GDPR's first anniversary, and companies should expect more GDPR penalties in the future. Just as businesses have needed time to understand GDPR, many regulatory bodies spent 2018 staffing up and finalizing their frameworks. Also, only 52 percent of the 2018 cases have been resolved (GDPR, 2019).

Businesses can likely receive reduced fines by cooperating. One of the penalties assessed was against a German social media provider, Knuddels.de, for a data breach in September 2018 that exposed 330,000 email addresses. Knuddels immediately informed its users of the breach, temporarily deactivated accounts, reported the violation to the German data protection agency, LfDI; and took steps to increase security. The LfDI issued a fine of €20,000, saying it was a proportionate punishment and cited the company's "exemplary cooperation" (GDPR, 2019).

A potential loophole for businesses is related to where companies locate their data controller. Under GDPR, the lead regulator is assigned based on where companies have their data controller. Most companies are selecting Ireland, which has failed to bring forth any data enforcement actions. This loophole practically enables technology companies to continue to collect massive amounts of consumer data. The loophole also opens the door for corruption by other countries that may also wish to attract technology companies in the same manner (De Groot, 2019).

Consumer Data Privacy in the United States

The United States does not have comprehensive data privacy regulations, similar to GDPR, but has passed limited laws in some areas. For example, the State of California recently passed its stringent consumer protection legislation, called the California Consumer Privacy Act (CCPA) of 2018. The United States also has some industry-specific protections, such as the Health Insurance Portability and Accountability Act (1996), which applies to the healthcare field, and the Gramm-Leach-Bliley Act (1999), which applies to financial institutions. Author's note: These examples simply illustrate the fragmented nature of consumer data protection in the United States; a more comprehensive list of data protection laws in the United States is in Table 2.

The fragmented approach taken with data privacy laws in the United States is called a *sectoral approach*, in which data privacy laws are targeted to a single industry (in contrast with an *omnibus approach*, like GDPR). This sectoral approach to data privacy in the United States gets very little respect abroad. In fact, trust for respecting privacy rights in the United States ranks behind even China and Russia, according to a survey by Ovum (2014).

Globally, sectoral approaches are becoming less common due to the proliferation of data use across multiple industries, and one can anticipate the effectiveness of this type of model to be worse in the future. Additionally, these regulations tend to not keep up with changes in technology, and enforcement gaps still exist. Fewer than a dozen countries still have a sectoral approach to data protection like the United States does, while close to a hundred countries have a more comprehensive or omnibus approach, like GDPR.

The sectoral approach in the United States has caused many businesses to fall under multiple and overlapping data privacy regulations. A dozen or more data protection regulations regulate some countries. Similarly, the sectoral approach does not offer much confidence to consumers regarding the protection of their data. This patchwork approach to data privacy in the United States makes legal compliance very difficult, inconsistent, costly, and uncertain. The United States has been reluctant to join international data privacy initiatives (more on these later) and is unlikely to do so in the future because of this conceptual difference. A summary of the patchwork system of data-protection laws in the United States is in Table 2.

Consumers are increasingly discussing data privacy rights in the United States, and this issue has recently taken a high-profile turn due to Congressional hearings with the founder of Facebook, Mark Zuckerberg. Comprehensive legislation has been proposed in the United States. Many predict that comprehensive legislation will be passed within the next three to five years, particularly if the technology giants do not straighten up. Many believe that it would be wise for the United States to move toward having an omnibus data-protection law to avoid unnecessary complexity, avoid overlap, close gaps, and eliminate inconsistency. According to an Ovum report, two-thirds of companies in the United States may already be reconsidering their data strategies as a result of GDPR. Many companies expect an increase in data-privacy regulations in the United States; therefore, some are voluntarily implementing more stringent data-protection measures across the board (Ovum, 2014). Voluntarily implementing GDPR is also known as the "Brussels effect," which is the process of regulatory globalization caused by the EU externalizing its laws outside its borders.

International Data Protection Regulations

There are hundreds of international data protection regulations, and the number is quickly increasing due to digitization. Table 3 summarizes key international data protection laws.

According to the United Nations Conference on Trade and Development (UNCTD), several other countries are looking to adopt comprehensive GDPR-type laws, including Brazil, India, Japan, the Republic of Korea, and Thailand. Many developing economies do not have any consumer data privacy laws. There is no data for approximately 67 countries that do not address online consumer protection. There is data for 125 countries, and 97 of those have adopted consumer protection legislation related

Table 2. United States data protection laws

United States
• Privacy Act of 1974 • Federal Trade Commission Act • Electronic Communications Privacy Act of 1986 • Judicial Redress Act • Cybersecurity Executive Order • Data breach regulations • Health Insurance Portability and Accountability Act of 1996 (HIPAA) • Health Information Technology for Economic and Clinical Health Act (HITECH) • Children's Online Privacy Protection Act (amended in 2012) • Trans-Pacific Partnership Agreement (TPP) • Regulated industries (government, financial, and critical infrastructure) • State privacy laws, i.e., California Consumer Privacy Act of 2018 • Privacy Shield

Source: (FitzPatrick, 2017)

Table 3. Regional data protection regulations

GDPR	Asia-Pacific	Canada	Latin America
• ePrivacy directive • Country-specific laws • Cloud computing directive • Data sovereignty obligations • Cybersecurity directive • Antispam laws • Healthcare privacy laws • Data breach regulation	• Country-specific privacy laws • Healthcare privacy laws • Asia-Pacific Economic Cooperation (APEC) cyber privacy code • Cross- border Privacy Rules • Restrictions on marketing activities • Restrictions on cloud computing • Data breach regulations	• Privacy Act • Personal Information Protection and Electronic Documents Act • Digital Privacy Act (2015) • Provincial or sovereignty laws • Medical records laws • Cybersecurity regulations • Canada Anti-Spam Law (CASL) • Data breach regulations	• Cross-border transfer restrictions • Country-specific privacy laws • Personal health information privacy laws • Cloud computing regulations • Organization of American States cybersecurity guidelines • Data breach regulations

Source: (FitzPatrick, 2017)

to e-commerce. The prevalence of data protection laws is particularly low in Africa and Asia, with less than 40 percent of countries having a law in place (UNCTD, 2020).

In addition to the GDPR in the EU, there are a few other notable regional data protection initiatives, including the Asia-Pacific Economic Cooperation (APEC), African Union (AU), Commonwealth Initiative, and various trade agreements such as the Trans-Pacific Partnership Agreement (TPP). An overview of the strengths and limitations of these initiatives is in Table 4 (UNCTAD, 2016).

Several global initiatives have addressed data protection. The following organizations have addressed the main initiatives: The United Nations (UN), Council of Europe (CoE), Organisation for Economic Cooperation and Development (OECD), and the International Data Protection Commissioners (IDPC). The United States has been reluctant to join any international initiatives on data privacy and likely will not in the future. An overview of the various strengths and limitations of these initiatives is in Table 5 (UNCTAD, 2016).

Table 4. Strengths and limitations of regional data protection initiatives

Initiative	Strengths	Limitations
Asia-Pacific Economic Cooperation (APEC)	• Broad membership • One of the few data protection agreements that involve the U.S. • Flexibility in implementation	• Voluntary participation • Business registration and annual fees • Other privacy laws may trump APEC rules.
African Union (AU)	• High-profile body • Targets developing countries	• New • Lack of political support • Implementation is complex. • There are severe resource constraints in this region related to implementation.
Commonwealth Initiative	• Large membership made up of 53 countries • Technical assistance available • Targets such regions where there are limited data protection regulations (i.e., Caribbean and Pacific)	• Non-binding • Does not address cross-border data transfers • Does not apply to the private sector, only the public sector
Trade Agreements	• Potential for a wide range of countries to participate • Agreements are binding.	• Negotiations are complex, with consumers often excluded. • Complex disputes about terms can occur.

Source: (UNCTAD, 2016)

Table 5. Strengths and limitations of global data protection initiatives

Initiative	Strengths	Limitations
United Nations (UN)	• Global Coverage • Long History of Protecting Human Rights • Recognition of Privacy as a Fundamental Right	• Too High Level • UN Resource Constraints
Council of Europe (CoE)	• Comprehensive Coverage • Wide Acceptance • Any Country May Join • Collaborative Process • Binding • Endorsed by IDPC	• Focus is on Europe • Challenging to Implement in Other Countries
Organization for Economic Co-operation and Development (OECD)	• Long and Respected History • Wide Acceptance • Achieves Balance	• Absence of a Proportionality Principle • Non-Binding
International Data Protection Commissioners (IDPC)	• Global Influence • Real-World Experience • Emphasizes the CoE Initiative.	• Lack of Formal Structure • Non-Binding

Source: (UNCTAD, 2016)

IMPLICATIONS OF DATA PRIVACY REGULATIONS

Data-Driven Innovation

Given the recent trend of digitization, the number of data privacy regulations will undoubtedly continue to grow in the future. The growth in regulations also links privacy policy to innovation policy, which means privacy regulations have the potential to impact the direction of innovation. Regulations, such as

GDPR, seek to give consumers more control over their data; however, it isn't yet clear if these regulations will change how firms use big data and innovate. The academic literature is ambivalent regarding the impact of regulation on innovation. An overview of the literature provides additional context.

Traditionally, economists consider regulation to be a coercive force that limits firms' profitability (Van de Broek, 2018). Regulations impose a cost burden on firms, causing them to reallocate their spending away from investments in innovation (Stewart, 2010). However, some studies argue that economic efficiency is a necessary sacrifice for improved social welfare (Posner, 1981). Other studies go even further, such as the Porter hypothesis (discussed in greater detail below), and have shown that environmental regulations, in particular, may actually trigger innovation. However, characterizing a single economic theory of privacy is difficult because the issues occur in different contexts. Much of the literature on this topic is not based on formal economic models but rather on general economic arguments (Acquisti, Taylor, & Wagman, 2016).

Measuring the effects of regulation on innovation has been given little attention, and much of what we do know now is quite dated (Jascow & Rose, 1989). Thus, the research surrounding privacy regulations and innovation is especially scarce. However, there is research on the effect of regulations on innovation in the context of specific industries, such as regulations impacting the advertising, manufacturing, energy, healthcare, telecommunications, finance, and agricultural sectors. These studies have produced mixed results that have proven to be very case-specific (Stewart, 2010; Goldfarb & Tucker, 2012).

Stewart (2010) and the Organisation for Economic Cooperation and Development (OECD) (1997) distinguish between the theoretical basis of economic, social, and institutional regulations, which is somewhat helpful in describing the ambivalence of the relationships between regulation and innovation. Economic regulations generally are believed to suppress innovation, social regulations tend to show a mostly positive relationship with innovation, and the relationship between innovation and institutional regulation is uncertain for the most part (Blind, 2012).

Generally, economic regulations inhibit innovation, but this often is based on anecdotal evidence (Blind, 2012). Joscow and Rose (1989) found little evidence related to economic regulations on innovation beyond anecdotes, case studies, and a few econometric studies. What little we do know now is dated. They also find it distressing that so little effort has been devoted to measuring the effects of regulation on innovation and believe that further research is essential.

Recent research on social regulations tends to show mostly positive innovation, especially regarding environmental regulations, which spurred the environmental industry. Concerning environmental regulations, Porter (1991) found that regulations increased domestic firm innovation compared with foreign competitors. Lanjouw and Mody (1996) examined the increase in environmental compliance costs in the patenting of environmental technologies. He found that with a one to two-year lag, environmental compliance cost increases led to increases in the patenting of new technologies. Porter and Van der Linde (1995) found that well-designed environmental regulations may stimulate firms to improve their technology and may even trigger innovation, also known as the Porter hypothesis. Jaffe and Palmer (1997) found that increased regulatory compliance costs increased research and development (R&D) investments, but only by a small amount. There was no correlation between R&D expenditures and patent activity. Additionally, the results were mixed in terms of regulatory stringency compared to increased innovation. Even today, findings show conflicting results regarding the Porter hypothesis described above (Ambec, Cohen, Eligie, & Lanoie, 2013).

The Economics of Privacy

Economists such as Posner (1981) and Stigler (1980) found that limiting the disclosure of information may render markets less efficient in the allocation of scarce resources. Fuller (2018) shows that digital privacy regulation "fails to simulate the market, stifles entrepreneurial discovery, and creates opportunities for superfluous discovery." He suggests that policymakers gain a more holistic view of market costs before imposing additional privacy regulations.

Additionally, Campbell (2015) found that regulatory attempts to protect information privacy through consent-based approaches cause compliance costs for all firms. For example, companies that do not comply with GDPR or experience data breaches are subject to substantial penalties of up to 4 percent of their worldwide revenue (EU, 2016). According to Ovum (2014), as cited by Tankard (2016), 52 percent of organizations believe that GDPR will result in fines for their business, and 68 percent of organizations feel that it will dramatically increase the cost of doing business in Europe. Some studies have shown that these compliance costs have disproportionate and adverse effects on the competitiveness of data-intensive firms that offer a smaller scope of services (Campbell, 2015). The introduction of new laws and regulations also has created new opponents, such as the Online Privacy Alliance (OPA), in the United States, which claims that additional legislation would diminish national competitiveness and weaken the economy.

It is challenging to incorporate privacy into economic models because it often deals with consumer emotion. Regulators must balance consumers' apprehension of data collection with the consequences of regulation on innovation (Hui & Png, 2006). Goldfarb and Tucker (2012) state that privacy regulations will have to balance the trade-offs between data-driven innovation and potential consumer harms due to the collection of digital information. The U.S. Department of Commerce's National Institute of Standards and Technology (NIST) Cybersecurity for the Internet of Things (IoT) program articulates in its mission statement the importance of balancing these interests: "Cultivate trust in the IoT and *foster an environment that enables innovation* on a global scale through standards, guidance, and related tools." (emphasis added)

Digital Privacy and Trust

A primary challenge of big data is that of consumer privacy (Hann, Hui, Lee, & Png, 2002; Frizzo-Barker, Chow-White, Mozafari, & Ha, 2016). While a great deal of literature exists across multiple disciplines about privacy in general, research on the impact of consumer data privacy regulations on innovation is scarce. The U.S. Public Interest Research Group (2000) also stated that the primary barrier to the growth of e-commerce is a lack of consumer trust. Consumers worry that companies will take advantage of them and capture personal information for marketing or other purposes without their informed consent.

Acquisti, Taylor, and Wagman (2016) found that consumers are often unable to make informed decisions about their digital privacy because they are in a position of asymmetric information regarding what information is collected and why. Asymmetric information occurs in circumstances in which two actors have different amounts of information. This asymmetry creates an imbalance of power, which can even cause market failure. The theory of asymmetric information is especially relevant when one party is not wholly aware of the characteristics and the behavioral intentions of the other actor (Moss, Neubaum, & Meyskens, 2015). While the seminal research on asymmetric information was in the context of the used car market (Akerlof, 1970), other markets with asymmetry include the insurance market (Rothschild &

Stiglitz, 1976), credit market (Stiglitz & Weiss, 1981), and retail market. These problems are considerably more significant in e-commerce because of the lack of opportunity for face-to-face interaction, which reduces people's ability to detect deception (Ben-Ner & Putterman, 2003 as cited by Lee, Ang, & Debelaar, 2015).

Signaling theory emerged from the study of information economics and deals with the notion of information asymmetry of buyers and sellers facing a market interaction (Boulding & Amna, 1993). According to Lee, Ang, and Debelaar (2015), a signal is an action taken by the more informed party to communicate its actual characteristics credibly to the less knowledgeable party. They go on to show that there are three types of signals of trustworthiness with B2C web merchants, including branding, presence of a privacy policy, and a money-back guarantee. The literature is silent as to whether consumer data privacy regulations serve as a signal to increase consumer trust.

The literature also examines the negative impact of privacy concerns on trust in electronic health records (Malhotra, Kim, & Agarwal, 2004; Eastlick, Lotz, & Warrington, 2006; Van Dyke, Midha, & Nemati, 2007; Kim, 2008; Angst & Agarwal, 2009). Prufer (2018) also studied the issue of privacy and trust in cloud computing and found it to be a primary obstacle to fully deploying the economic potential of these new technologies.

Milberg, Smith, and Burke (2000) point out that when firms are not managing information privacy issues competently, individuals are more likely to prefer government regulation over industry self-regulation. As a result of the increase in data breaches, proposed governmental rules to address consumer data privacy have also increased (Hann, Hui, Lee, & Png, 2002). In fact, as of 2017, 120 countries had data privacy regulations, with legislation also being introduced for consideration in thirty or more additional countries. At that time, data privacy regulations had increased by 10 percent since previously being studied in 2015 (Greenleaf, 2017). As of 2019, 134 countries now have data protection laws.

SOLUTIONS AND RECOMMENDATIONS

With the increase in digitalization, there is a view that consumers have lost control over their personal data. It should be evident through the review of this chapter that data privacy regulations are not equally protective in all parts of the planet. There are several related issues in this regard: 1. What is the form of consumer protection in the event of bankruptcy in the custody of personal data; 2. The transfer of international data between countries that do not have the same level of consumer protection; and 3. Cybercrime. The answers depend on the laws of the countries related to both the consumer and the business. The consumer protections could range from nothing at all to an omnibus structure, such as GDPR. Therefore, it is reasonable that both companies and consumers insist on an omnibus legal system for comprehensive data privacy protection. Finally, I would also recommend that known loopholes within data privacy regulations be corrected as soon as possible. Such a loophole exists in GDPR and opens the door for corrupt countries to court technology companies to reside in their country, and practically allow those companies to operate in an unregulated manner concerning consumer privacy.

It is worth noting that we may be close to a time where all consumer protection solutions don't necessarily have to come from a governmental body. Unfortunately, while precautions exist to protect consumers from cybercrime, practically speaking, illegal activity knows no borders. Another emerging technology, blockchain, also has the capabilities of predictive analytics and real-time data analysis.

Through the use of a decentralized ledger that cannot be manipulated or leaked, the quality associated with blockchain technology also has the potential to help maintain consumer trust and deter bad actors. Blockchain technology may even be able to support frameworks for global-citizenship or a sovereign digital identity, giving consumers more authority over the distribution of their data.

FUTURE RESEARCH DIRECTIONS

In the age of big data, the area of consumer data privacy regulation is ripe for further research. As discussed previously, the literature is ambivalent as to the impact of regulation on innovation. This author also questions whether data privacy regulations appropriately fit within the existing theoretical frameworks of economic, social, or institutional regulations. For example, data privacy regulations certainly have economic impacts on businesses, including compliance costs and fines. However, this economic impact is admittedly dissimilar to other economically regulated industries, such as the highly regulated monopoly public utility industry in which a regulatory commission sets the rates paid by consumers as a proxy for competition. Moreover, data privacy laws also arguably exist for the good of society as a whole, similar to other societal regulations like environmental regulations. The appropriate placement of regulation within this framework may drive its theoretical effect on innovation. The author believes there is an opportunity to clarify specifically where data privacy regulations fit within the existing theoretical framework, including if there may be new or "hybrid" types of regulations and their associated effects on innovation. The passage of more comprehensive data privacy legislation may also provide new opportunities to empirically measure the regulatory effects on innovation, or the effects on consumer trust, as was also previously discussed. Implications for business practitioners are numerous and may inform their assessment of competitive and regulatory risk. There are also implications for policymakers, which may inform the appropriate balancing of interests for both consumers and businesses.

CONCLUSION

As previously discussed, big data is changing the way businesses understand, connect with, and ultimately profit from customers. However, consumers are often unable to make informed decisions about their digital privacy because they are in a position of asymmetric information regarding what information is collected and the rationale for doing so. Trust is central to the issues of asymmetric information, and lack of trust can cause consumers not to transact or a market not to develop at all. Trust and privacy are also primary obstacles to fully deploying big data technologies.

Consequently, individuals prefer government privacy regulations when they believe firms do not adequately self-regulate. Thus, an increasingly complex patchwork of international data protection regulations exists to balance the interests of both consumers and businesses, with GDPR taking its place as the global baseline. Countries still using a sectoral approach to data protection laws, including the United States, are in the minority and are not adequately protecting consumers. This patchwork system also confuses businesses. These countries will likely move to a more omnibus approach to data protection in the near future due to consumer demand. Compliance with data privacy regulations is not optional for businesses due to the heavy penalties assessed under GDPR, which has shifted the focus of companies away from the firm and toward the consumer. GDPR is creating opportunities not only for new professions but also for corruption by countries seeking to court technology companies to relocate. While GDPR is still in its infancy and uncertainties remain, one certainty is that it has caused consumers to view their data protection rights quite differently. Businesses seeking to monetize big data must adhere accordingly.

ACKNOWLEDGMENT

The author thanks the two anonymous reviewers for their helpful suggestions. This research received no specific grant from any funding agency in the public, commercial, or not-for-profit sectors.

REFERENCES

Acquisti, A., Taylor, C., & Wagman, L. (2016). The economics of privacy. *Journal of Economic Literature*, *54*(2), 442–492. doi:10.1257/jel.54.2.442

Akerlof, G. (1970). The market for lemons. *The Quarterly Journal of Economics*, *84*(3), 488–500. doi:10.2307/1879431

Albrecht, J. (2016). How the GDPR will change the world. *European Data Protection Law Review*, *2*(3), 287–289. doi:10.21552/EDPL/2016/3/4

Ambec, S., Cohen, M., Eligie, S., & Lanoie, P. (2013). The Porter hypothesis at 20: Can environmental regulation enhance innovation and competitiveness? *Review of Environmental Economics and Policy*, *7*(1), 2–22. doi:10.1093/reep/res016

Angst, C., & Agarwal, R. (2009). Adoption of electronic health records in the presence of privacy concerns: The elaboration likelihood model and individual persuasion. *Management Information Systems Quarterly*, *33*(2), 339–370. doi:10.2307/20650295

Ben-Ner, A., & Putterman, L. (2003). *New economy handbook: Trust in the new economy*. New York, NY: Academic Press.

Boulding, W., & Amna, K. (1993). A consumer-side experimental examination of signaling theory: Do consumers perceive warranties as signals of quality? *The Journal of Consumer Research*, *20*(1), 111–123. doi:10.1086/209337

Campbell, J., Goldfarb, A., & Tucker, C. (2015). Privacy regulation and market structure. *Journal of Economics & Management Strategy*, *24*(1), 47–73. doi:10.1111/jems.12079

De Groot, J. (2019). *What is the general data protection regulation? Understanding and complying with GDPR requirements in 2019*. Retrieved from https://digitalguardian.com/blog/what-gdpr-general-data-protection-regulation-understanding-and-complying-gdpr-data-protection

Eastlick, M. A., Lotz, S. L., & Warrington, P. (2006). Understanding online b-to-c relationships: An integrated model of privacy concerns, trust, and commitment. *Journal of Business Research*, *59*(8), 877–886. doi:10.1016/j.jbusres.2006.02.006

EU approves GDPR. (2016). *Information Management, 50*(4), 7. Retrieved from https://search-proquest-com.du.idm.oclc.org/docview/1805460371?accountid=14608

European Data Protection Board. (2019). *First overview of the implementation of GDPR and the roles and means of the national supervisory authorities*. Retrieved from https://www.europarl.europa.eu/meetdocs/2014_2019/plmrep/COMMITTEES/LIBE/DV/2019/02-25/9_EDPB_report_EN.pdf

FitzPatrick, S. M. (2017). *Data privacy and sovereignty changing legal landscape*. Retrieved from https://fr.slideshare.net/tealium/digital-velocity-london-2017-data-privacy-and-sovereignty-sheila-fitz-patrick/6

Frizzo-Barker, J., Chow-White, P. A., Mozafari, M., & Ha, D. (2016). An empirical study of the rise of big data in business scholarship. *International Journal of Information Management, 36*(3), 403–413. doi:10.1016/j.ijinfomgt.2016.01.006

Fuller, C. S. (2018). Privacy law as price control. *European Journal of Law and Economics, 45*(2), 225–250. doi:10.100710657-017-9563-6

GDPR. (2019). *GDPR fines after one year: key takeaways for businesses*. Retrieved from: https://gdpr.eu/gdpr-fines-so-far/

Goldfarb, A., & Tucker, C. (2012). Privacy and innovation. *Innovation Policy and the Economy, 12*(1), 65–90. doi:10.1086/663156

Greenleaf, G. (2017). Global tables of data privacy laws and bills. *Privacy Laws & Business International Report, 5*, 14–26.

Hann, I., Hui, K., Lee, T., & Png, I. (2002). *Online information privacy: Measuring the cost-benefit trade-off*. Paper presented at the International Conference on Information Systems, Barcelona, Spain.

Hui, K., & Png, I. P. L. (2006). The economics of privacy. *Economics and Information Systems, 1*, 271–293.

Jaffe, A. B., Newell, R. G., & Stavins, R. N. (2002). Environmental policy and technological change. *Environmental and Resource Economics, 22*(1-2), 41–49. doi:10.1023/A:1015519401088

Jaffe, A. B., & Palmer, K. (1997). Environmental regulation and innovation: A panel data study. *The Review of Economics and Statistics, 79*(4), 610–619. doi:10.1162/003465397557196

Jascow, P. L., & Rose, N. L. (1989). The effects of economic regulation. Handbook of Industrial Organization, 2, 1450–1498.

Kim, D. J. (2008). Self-perception-based versus transference-based trust determinants in computer-mediated transactions: A cross-cultural comparison study. *Journal of Management Information Systems, 24*(4), 13–45. doi:10.2753/MIS0742-1222240401

Lanjouw, J. O., & Mody, A. (1996). Stimulating innovation and the international diffusion of environmentally responsive technology: The role of expenditures and institutions. *Research Policy, 25*(4), 549–571. doi:10.1016/0048-7333(95)00853-5

Lee, B., Ang, L., & Dubelaar, C. (2015). Lemons on the web: A signaling approach to the problem of trust in Internet commerce. *Journal of Economic Psychology, 26*(5), 607–623. doi:10.1016/j.joep.2005.01.001

Malhotra, N. K., Kim, S. S., & Agarwal, J. (2004). Internet users' internet privacy concerns (IUIPC): The construct, the scale, and a causal model. *Information Systems, 15*(4), 311–416.

Manyika, J., Chui, M., Brown, B., Bughin, J., Dobbs, R., Roxburgh, C., & Byers, A. (2011). *Big data: The next frontier for innovation, competition, and productivity*. Retrieved from https://www.mckinsey.com/business-functions/mckinsey-digital/our-insights/big-data-the-next-frontier-for-innovation

Meredith, S. (2018). *Facebook-Cambridge Analytica: A Timeline of the Data Hijacking Scandal*. Retrieved from https://www.cnbc.com/2018/04/10/facebook-cambridge-analytica-a-timeline-of-the-data-hijacking-scandal.html

Milberg, S., Smith, J., & Burke, S. (2000). Information privacy: Corporate management and national regulation. *Organization Science, 11*(1), 35–37. doi:10.1287/orsc.11.1.35.12567

Moss, T. W., Neubaum, D. O., & Meyskens, M. (2015). The effect of virtuous and entrepreneurial orientations on microfinance lending and repayment: A signaling theory perspective. *Entrepreneurship Theory and Practice, 39*(1), 27–52. doi:10.1111/etap.12110

Nissenbaum, H. (2011). A contextual approach to privacy online. *Daedalus, 140*(4), 32–48. doi:10.1162/DAED_a_00113

OECD. (1997). The OECD Report on Regulatory Reform: Volume 1: Sectoral Studies. OECD.

Ovum. (2014). *Data privacy laws: Cutting the red tape*. Retrieved from https://www.intralinks.com/resources/analyst-reports/ovum-report-data-privacy-laws cutting-red-tape#

DLA Piper. (2020). *EU general data privacy regulation*. Retrieved from https://www.dlapiper.com/en/us/focus/eu-data-protection-regulation/home

Porter, M. E. (1991). America's Green Strategy. *Scientific American, 6*(3), 168. doi:10.1038cientifica merican0491-168 PMID:1925488

Porter, M. E., & Van Der Linde, C. (1995). Toward a new conception of the environment -competitiveness relationship. *The Journal of Economic Perspectives, 9*(4), 97–118. doi:10.1257/jep.9.4.97

Posner, R. A. (1981). The economics of privacy. *The American Economic Review, 71*(2), 405–409.

Prufer, J. (2018). Trusting privacy in the cloud. *Information Economics and Policy, 45*, 52–67. doi:10.1016/j.infoecopol.2018.10.003

Rothschild, M., & Stiglitz, J. (1976). Equilibrium in competitive insurance markets: An essay on the economics of imperfect information. *The Quarterly Journal of Economics, 90*(4), 629–649. doi:10.2307/1885326

Stewart, L. A. (2010). *The Impact of Regulation on Innovation in the United States: A Cross-Industry Literature Review*. Information Technology & Innovation Foundation.

Stigler, G. J. (1980). An introduction to privacy in Economics and Politics. *The Journal of Legal Studies, 9*(4), 623–644. doi:10.1086/467657

Stiglitz, J. E., & Weiss, A. (1981). Credit rationing in markets with imperfect information. *The American Economic Review, 71*(3), 393–410.

Tankard, C. (2016). What the GDPR means for business. *Network Security, 2016*(6), 5–8. doi:10.1016/S1353-4858(16)30056-3

United Nations Conference on Trade and Development (UNCTAD). (2016). *Data protection regulations and international data flows: Implications for trade and development*. Retrieved from https://unctad.org/en/PublicationsLibrary/dtlstict2016d1_en.pdf

United Nations Conference on Trade and Development (UNCTAD). (n.d.). *Online consumer protection legislation worldwide*. Retrieved from https://unctad.org/en/Pages/DTL/STI_and_ICTs/ICT4D-Legislation/eCom-Consumer-Protection-Laws.aspx

U.S. Public Interest Research Group. Public comment on barriers to electronic commerce, Response to call by U.S. Department of Commerce (65 Federal Register 15898), April 25, 2000.

Uthayasankar, S., & Muhammad, M. K., Zahir, I., & Vishanth, W. (in press). Critical analysis of big data challenges and analytical methods. *ScienceDirect. Journal of Business Research.*

Van Dyke, T. P., Midha, V., & Nemati, H. (2007). The effect of consumer privacy empowerment on trust and privacy concerns in e-commerce. *Electronic Markets, 17*(1), 68–81. doi:10.1080/10196780601136997

ADDITIONAL READING

Greenleaf, G. (2019). Global tables of data privacy laws and bills. *Privacy Laws & Business International Report (PLBIR)*. Retrieved from https://ssrn.com/abstract=3380794

DLA Piper. (2020). *EU general data privacy regulation*. Retrieved from https://www.dlapiper.com/en/us/focus/eu-data-protection-regulation/home

United Nations Conference on Trade and Development. Data protection and privacy legislation worldwide. Retrieved from https://unctad.org/en/Pages/DTL/STI_and_ICTs/ICT4D-Legislation/eCom-Data-Protection-Laws.aspx

KEY TERMS AND DEFINITIONS

Asymmetric Information: Asymmetric information occurs in circumstances in which two actors have different amounts of information. This asymmetry creates an imbalance of power, which can cause market failure.

Brussels Effect: The process of regulatory globalization caused by the European Union externalizing its laws outside its borders.

Data Protection Officers or DPOs: GDPR requires DPOs for any company that processes data about a subject's genetic data, health, racial or ethnic origin, religious beliefs, etc. DPOs serve to advise companies about compliance with the regulation and act as a point of contact with Supervising Authorities (SAs).

General Data Privacy Regulation or GDPR: This regulation went into effect on May 24, 2018 and applies to all personal data across various industries within the European Union.

Information Privacy: Information privacy is the ability to control personal data and associated identities.

Omnibus Approach: The omnibus approach to data privacy regulations describes when there is one overarching law across multiple industries, like GDPR.

Privacy Regulations: Regulations that are concerned with how businesses handle data and information privacy.

Pseudonymization: Pseudonymization is defined in Article 4 of GDPR as the processing of personal data in a manner that the data can no longer be attributable to a specific person without the use of additional information. Such additional information shall remain separate to ensure that the personal data cannot identify the individual.

Right of Erasure: The right of erasure, also known as the "right to be forgotten," is a GDPR provision that means third parties must remove the personal data of an individual upon request if there are no real business reasons to store the information.

Right to Portability: A GDPR provision that gives consumers the right to transfer their data between different service providers more easily.

Sectoral Approach: The sectoral approach to data privacy regulations is applied when laws only apply to specific industries, such as with consumer privacy laws in the United States.

Signaling Theory: A theory that emerged from the study of information economics and deals with the notion of information asymmetry of buyers and sellers facing a market interaction. A signal is an action taken by the more informed party to communicate its actual characteristics credibly to the less knowledgeable party.

Chapter 11
Privacy in Cloud-Based Computing

Monjur Ahmed
Waikato Institute of Technology, New Zealand

Nurul I. Sarkar
iD https://orcid.org/0000-0003-2770-8319
Auckland University of Technology, New Zealand

ABSTRACT

Cloud computing, internet of things (IoT), edge computing, and fog computing are gaining attention as emerging research topics and computing approaches in recent years. These computing approaches are rather conceptual and contextual strategies rather than being computing technologies themselves, and in practice, they often overlap. For example, an IoT architecture may incorporate cloud computing and fog computing. Cloud computing is a significant concept in contemporary computing and being adopted in almost every means of computing. All computing architectures incorporating cloud computing are termed as cloud-based computing (CbC) in general. However, cloud computing itself is the basis of CbC because it significantly depends on resources that are remote, and the remote resources are often under third-party ownership where the privacy of sensitive data is a big concern. This chapter investigates various privacy issues associated with CbC. The data privacy issues and possible solutions within the context of cloud computing, IoT, edge computing, and fog computing are also explored.

INTRODUCTION

The emergence of few recent computing approaches bring new paradigm to computing world. Examples of such computing approaches are Cloud Computing, IoT, Edge Computing and Fog Computing. With numerous benefits and advantageous features, all these computing approaches come with a severe downside – that is, security. Security is a major concern for the above computing approaches from perspectives of business strategy as well as technological and Human Factors. These computing approaches use and/or transfer an organisation's digital assets (i.e., digital information) off-site for various purposes.

DOI: 10.4018/978-1-7998-3817-3.ch011

Copyright © 2020, IGI Global. Copying or distributing in print or electronic forms without written permission of IGI Global is prohibited.

Cloud Computing, IoT, Edge Computing and Fog Computing have become a hype. Organisations are submerging themselves in this hype and – in some cases, discussed later in this chapter– handing over digital assets to third parties. Using computing techniques like Cloud Computing may incorporate moving data into remote computers that are geographically dispersed and crossing political geographic boundaries. Besides, the aforementioned computing techniques use latest technologies, computing devices and gadgets (e.g., smart phone). Electronic end-user gadgets, when become part of a network as an end-user terminal or node, may pose security and privacy concerns. The infrastructural settings of recent computing approaches in terms of location of various elements (e.g., computers, data storage, processing) are crucial factors in information security and privacy. Based on the locations of architectural/infrastructural elements, Cloud Computing, Fog Computing and Edge Computing may introduce a very complex scenario for organisations in terms of Governance, Risk and Compliance (GRC).

Cloud Computing incorporates numerous security concerns (Ahmed & Hossain, 2014; Ahmed, Litchfield & Ahmed, 2014; Ahmed & Litchfield, 2016; Khalil, Khreishah & Azeem, 2014; Aljawarneh & Yassein, 2016; Kar & Mishra, 2016). From an information security and privacy viewpoint, this chapter investigates the computing techniques that use Cloud Computing. Cloud Computing, Fog Computing, Edge Computing, IoT – these are few recent computing techniques/approaches considered in this chapter.

All kinds of CbC uses remote resources and infrastructure that are owned and managed by third party vendors. This results in a situation where customers (individual or organisation) hand over their data to the vendors. Customers' data and information reside in the vendors infrastructures and servers dispersed geographically around the globe. This results in various complex scenario that are considered as threat to information privacy and security in cyber space. The focal point in this chapter is how CbC may have an impact on the privacy of an organisation's digital assets.

Cloud, Fog, Edge Computing, and IoT

Location of the users as well as the computing and networking devices & elements, and the types of devices used in a computing setting are significant contributing factors in information privacy and security. This section presents the concept of Cloud Computing, Fog Computing, Edge Computing and IoT, with a focus on the locations of various infrastructural elements involved in these computing settings.

Cloud Computing means using remote computing resources or infrastructure for computing and/or data storage purposes (Ali & Haseebuddin, 2015; Birje, Challagidad, Goudar & Tapale, 2017; Cardoso & Simões, 2011; Jadeja & Modi, 2012). Such remote computing infrastructures are normally 'borrowed' or 'rented'. The provider and owner of such infrastructures are third parties known as Cloud Service Provider (CSP). The end-users (individuals or organisations) utilise the CSPs computers (i.e., Cloud servers) or infrastructure to store data or for computing purposes. Figure 1 illustrates the concept of Cloud Computing.

When it comes to IoT, an infrastructure implementing IoT may incorporate Cloud Computing, Fog Computing and Edge Computing. To explain this, Figure 4 portrays the conceptual architecture and the core layers of an IoT infrastructure.

IoT has three conceptual layers – Application Layer, Network Layer and Perception Layer (Goyal, Garg, Rastogi & Singhal, 2018; Sethi & Sarangi, 2017; Shouran, Ashari & Priyambodo, 2019). Referring to Figure 4, the end-users' devices form the Application Layer, the communication network through which data traverses between the Application Layer and Perception Layer, and the Perception Layer is where data collected through devices in Application Layer are stored or processed or both. The Percep-

Figure 1. Cloud computing concept

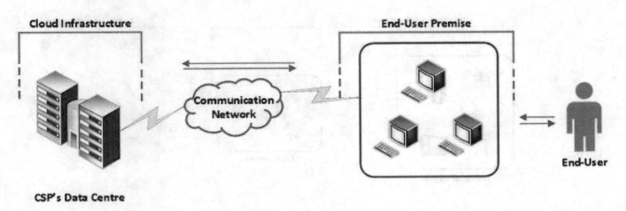

Figure 2. Cloud computing, fog computing and edge computing

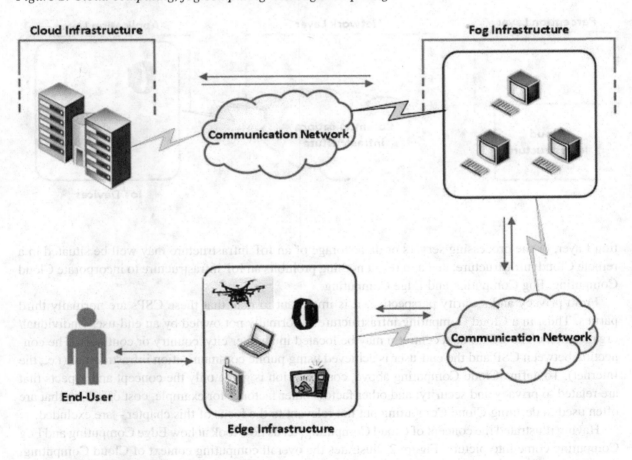

Figure 3. Edge computing

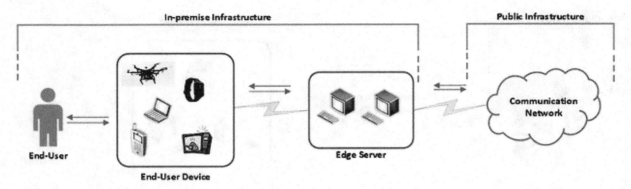

Figure 4. IoT infrastructure and its layers

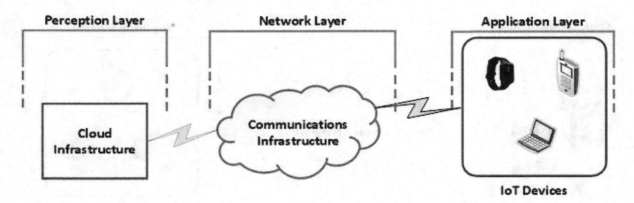

tion Layer, or the processing servers or data storage of an IoT infrastructure may well be situated in a remote Cloud infrastructure; and as a result nothing prohibits an IoT infrastructure to incorporate Cloud Computing, Fog Computing and Edge Computing.

From privacy and security perspective, it is important to note that these CSPs are normally third parties. Thus, in a Cloud Computing infrastructure is normally not owned by an end-user (individual/ organisation). The CSP's data centre(s) may be located in another city, country or continent. The connection between CSP and the end-user is achieved using public communication infrastructure (i.e., the Internet). To define Cloud Computing above, consideration is given only the concept and aspects that are related to privacy and security; and other factors other factors - for example, cost or billing that are often used in defining Cloud Computing but not relevant to the focus of this chapter – are excluded.

Having illustrated the concept of Cloud Computing, let us now look at how Edge Computing and Fog Computing come into picture. Figure 2 illustrates the overall computing context of Cloud Computing, Fog Computing and Edge Computing. As mentioned earlier, a CSP (to be more precise, a CSP's data centre) may be located remotely. The distance between end-user's premises and the CSP's data centre may introduce performance issue (e.g., latency) or bottlenecks. To combat this, an intermediary infrastructure could be used for faster performance. This concept of using an intermediary infrastructure, as illustrated in Figure 2, is known as Fog Computing.

Figure 2 also illustrates edge computing. in edge computing, the processing intermediary infrastructure is even closer (compared to that of Fog Computing) to the end-users. To be precise, the processing infrastructure in Edge Computing situates in the end-users' premises. In Edge Computing, the processing may actually happen in the end-users' devices. While Edge Computing generally means moving the processing into the end-users' end, it may not necessarily mean that the processing is happening in the end-users' devices. Rather, there might be another layer, an intermediary infrastructure located in the end-user's premises – this is termed as Edge Computing.

Edge Computing is further illustrated in Figure 3, showing the proximity of end-users' premises and public infrastructure that comprises Edge Computing architecture. The concept of Edge Computing and Fog Computing is also discussed by other researchers, for example, Anwar, Wang, Muhammad, Jadoon, Akram & Raza (2018), Hajibaba and Gorgin (2014), Kitanov and Janevski (2019), Rahman and Wen (2018), More (2015), and Saharan and Kumar (2015).

Cloud-Based Computing

The term CbC refers to all computing techniques/approaches that use the concept of Cloud Computing to any extent. Cloud Computing itself is a CbC. If we consider Fog Computing or Edge Computing, it is apparent that these computing techniques are introduced as performance boosters for Cloud Computing, and thus they are certainly CbC.

Cloud Computing itself is more of an architectural concept or computing approach rather than being a technology. The core concept of Cloud Computing is that, it uses remote computing resources for computing and repository purposes. Any technology may come to aid to achieve such approach that would collectively be called as Cloud Computing. Virtualisation is one example of such technologies used in Cloud Computing context. While virtualisation is a technology, Cloud Computing is an architectural approach using virtualisation (and a lot other technologies) to actualise itself. In the same way, since Fog Computing and Edge Computing are mere virtual and additional layers for Cloud Computing, they are rather more of an architectural concept or computing approach – they are not computing technologies.

Having said the above, any kind of computing that reflects the Cloud Computing approach may be considered as CbC. According to our above proposed definition, we consider Cloud Computing, Fog Computing, and Edge Computing as CbC. In addition to that, there may be other computing techniques or technologies that are CbC. For example, IoT and IIoT infrastructures using Cloud Computing techniques are considered as CbC. The architectural extent for IoT is much wider than Cloud Computing. However, since Cloud Computing may well be part of an IoT infrastructure – which is normally the case – IoT may be considered as CbC.

Privacy in CbC

Privacy and security are biggest concerns in CbC and these will ever remain so. In our opinion, the root cause for CbC to ever be a cautious computing approach is due to two reasons – geographic dispersion of the infrastructural elements, and housing digital assets in infrastructures under third parties' ownership and management. In addition, all traditional privacy and security concerns from all other computing technologies and techniques are applicable to CbC. Human Factors play significant role in cybersecurity

Figure 5. Major factors affecting privacy in CbC

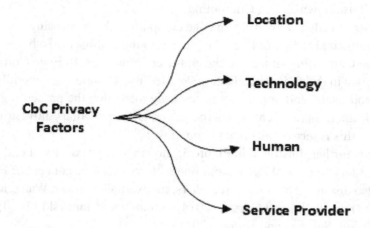

and thus is applicable to security contexts of CbC too. Figure 5 shows major factors that might associate with the emergence of privacy concerns for digital assets of an organisation.

Location of the infrastructural elements of CbC and the manner in which third parties (e.g., CSP) are involved in CbC make the privacy aspects of a CbC context fairly complex and notoriously concerning. Human Factors and technological factors are concerning, but an organisation may practice greater control over these factors. Organisations (as CbC user or as a CSP's customers) have very little control on the factors related to geographic dispersion and service providers.

Location and Service Provider

Since the focus of this chapter is privacy in CbC context, and since relative geographic location is a focal factor that defines CbC; it is important to investigate how different geographic location of various elements of CbC architecture and privacy are inter-related. For any CbC, different parts (e.g., Cloud infrastructure, end-users' premises) are geographically dispersed. Reconsidering generic Cloud Computing architecture in Figure 6, the end-users and their infrastructure may be located in one country or continent while the data-centre is located in another, and the data traversing between these two may have to go through another continent/country depending on the location of the data-centre and the end-user's premises. One of the biggest privacy concerns arise for such geographic dispersion.

The geographic dispersion of infrastructural elements in a cross-border manner introduces severe complexity for an organisation in terms of GRC. Unfortunately, there is no standard list of issues and resolutions for security and privacy concerns that arise due to geographic dispersion. The related issues and concerns should be figured out on a case-by-case basis. The following are some highlights of the issues that may arise duo to geographic dispersion in CbC, all of which eventually may lead to compromised privacy of digital assets and/or digital information for an organisation:

1. Jurisdiction – If an organisation's digital assets and digital processes are stored or taking place in a remote place, different jurisdiction may apply to the digital assets. An organisation may not assume that their local jurisdiction is applicable with their CSP. It is imperative that an organisation

Figure 6. Geographic dispersion of elements of a CbC infrastructure

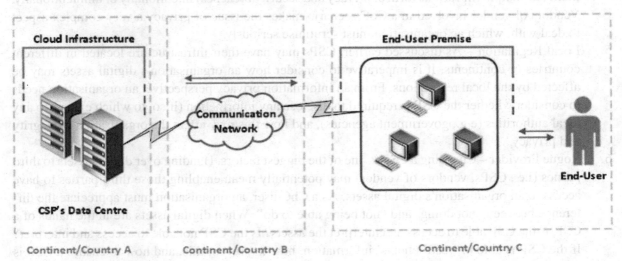

clearly seeks information on the location where their digital assets will be held and how jurisdictions are applicable for that location. An organisation also needs to work out the impact of this on their business. For example, the medical records and histories of patients of a hospital in country A could be stored in country B by their CSP. Now, if the data (i.e., patients' history and personal records) is breached and leaked, what measures are in places to revive business goodwill, and how the responsible parties could be held accountable for such malpractice, which location's jurisdiction is application – all these requires concrete answers. It is also important to note that, A CSP's business office's location and data centres' location may not necessarily be the same. A CSP could have their business operation in country A, and the data centres in country B, country C and so on. An organisation must consider all the scenarios and insist on detailed information to understand the implication of such location dispersion on privacy and security of their digital assets.

2. Governance – Adapting CbC literally means handing over data to CSPs. In other words, CbC for an organisation as an end-user means transfer digital assets to third parties who own and manage the infrastructure where the digital assets are housed. Some real-time business processes may also be carried out on CbC infrastructure. This directly results in less control on digital assets and business processes for an organisation. While the severity of consequence can only be decided on a case-by-case basis, an organisation certainly loses control to some extent over its digital assets or business processes when housed in CbC infrastructure. This reduced level of governance may potentially emerge as a reason for breach of privacy.

3. Risk Management & Compliance – Migrating to a CbC infrastructure associates creating dependency on the CSPs. The dependency not only comes from service provisioning but also from risk management and subsequent compliance (or lack of compliance thereof) viewpoint. Such dependency may affect the integrity of an organisation's standard risk management procedures – a consequence of this could be breach of privacy in various forms (e.g., organisation's own information or its clients' information breach).

4. Vendors of Vendor – For service provisioning, a remotely located vendor (i.e., CSP) may use third parties which in turn are located in a different location. These vendors of vendor may introduce

malicious output (in various form of privacy and security breaches) intentionally or unintentionally. Vendors of vendor involved in a CbC scenario makes the issue of privacy a very complex aspect to deal with, which an organisation must scrutinise seriously.

5. Local Regulation – As discussed earlier, CSPs may have their infrastructure located in different countries or continents. It is imperative to consider how an organisation's digital assets may be affected by the local regulations. From an information privacy perspective, an organisation needs to consider whether the CSP is required to disclose any information (if so, to which extent) to any local authorities (e.g., government agencies), and how this may affect the organisation's integrity and privacy.

6. Rogue Provider – Choosing a CSP is one of the biggest factors. Handing over digital assets to third parties (i.e., CSPs, vendors of vendor) may potentially mean enabling those third parties to have access to an organisation's digital assets. As a CbC user, an organisation must appreciate the difference between "not doing' and "not being able to do". When digital assets are in the hands of a CSP, is the CSP able to access and interpret the assets? Is the CSP not able to access and interpret? If the CSP is able to 'read' clients' information, how to prevent this, and how to ensure a CSP is not sneaking into its clients' digital assets?

Technology and Human Factors

In a CbC scenario, privacy may be compromised for technological or human related factors. Ahmed and Litchfield (2016) propose a threat taxonomy for Cloud Computing, which is equally applicable for any CbC context. Referring to the taxonomy cited above as a baseline, technological and Human Factors pose privacy concerns in CbC. Among technological factors, issues related to software may lead to breach of privacy. In a Cloud-based context, different parties are involved – CSP, end-user and probably other third party intermediary vendors. The technological infrastructure of all involved parties are potential source of privacy issues. The software and tools used in Cloud infrastructure as well as end-users or other parties involved may contain bugs or other kinds of potential security loopholes that may result in data leakage and subsequently breach of privacy. The security related issues may emerge from the operating systems or from any other software/tools used within the infrastructures of the parties involved in CbC.

In a CbC scenario, data travels through communication networks where different communication software, communication protocols, web services, and security mechanisms work collaboratively for successful communication and secure data transfer and processing. It is no surprise that any of these key players in digital communication may potentially have weakness or loopholes that can be exploited resulting in information exposure and breach of privacy.

Human Factor is an all-time biggest concerns in computing security and privacy. A study by Ahmed, Kambam, Liu and Uddin (2019) shows Human Factors play a crucial role in security breaches in Cloud Computing. Human Factor in relation to computing security is also mentioned in Colwill (2009), Goel, Williams and Dincelli (2014), Hadlington (2018), and Palega and Knapinski (2018). People are often labelled as the weakest link in information security. The biggest challenge for Human Factor-centric privacy concerns is that, there is no defined roadmap or structure that fit into protecting Human Factor centric breaches – the ways of social engineering is unlimited in numbers and an attacker may always find innovative ways exploit human aspects to get into a system. CbC are no exception in this regard.

One of the areas that require further attention is the use of smart gadgets, for example, smart phones, tablets, wearable smart devices and other forms of gadgets. These gadgets have the capability to turn themselves into a powerful sneaking device and may potentially 'hear' everything around it. For example, an application may access an user's all data held in the device where the application is installed, or may record audio or video – and the reason for an app in doing so may always not be justified. Inadvertently accepting license agreement to install apps on smart gadgets may lead to undesired consequences in terms of security and privacy.

This section is kept relatively short due to the fact that, it is nearly impossible to list all the technological and Human Factors that may contribute in data and privacy breach. Every organisational CbC context is different and the privacy & security concerns are unique to each different context – it depends on the technologies being used within a CbC architecture, the geographic location, local legislation and culture, the level competence of the people involved, and the robustness of the information security policy enforced and in practice.

Privacy in Cloud, Edge, Fog and IoT

Privacy is a significant concern in Cloud Computing (Aldossary & Allen, 2016; Kar & Mishra, 2016; Rajarajeswari & Somasundaram, 2016). All privacy factors discussed above are applicable to Cloud Computing, Fog Computing, Edge Computing and IoT, since all these computing approaches are CbC. The privacy concerns are overlapping in these computing approaches and thus they are discussed earlier in this chapter under one umbrella (i.e., CbC). In this section, some generic and indirect factors that pose threats to privacy in any kinds of computing settings, including CbC are explored.

While end-user devices form part of IoT, the others have provision to include end-user devices as part of their infrastructure. The inclusion of smart gadgets (e.g., smartphones, tablets, smart wearable gadgets, smart TV and so on) takes the level of privacy related complexity to a whole different higher level compared to the scenario where these devices are not involved. The rise of Social Networking Sites (SNS) is a direct threat to information privacy when combined with ultra-portable smart gadgets like smartphones or smartwatches. SNSs that come with live streaming and other information sharing (e.g., audio, images) capability, and are used in ultra-portable smart devices as apps, may help anyone to make confidential information publicly available in the blink of an eye by sharing them on SNSs – a smart gadget user may let their smart gadget do it intentionally or unintentionally. Human Factors play a very big role in such scenario where people are not aware enough the importance of reading license agreement to install tools on smart gadgets. A user must be aware of the permissions they have given to their smart gadgets whether to record and transmit information or not.

Interestingly, a breach in privacy may not appear as a security breach and may even go unnoticed. For example, consider a confidential board-of-directors' meeting – everyone in the 'confidential' meeting room with their smart gadgets that are recording the meeting and transmitting to unauthorised parties even without the knowledge of the participants of the meeting. The consequence is not only breach of privacy but may also lead to corporate sabotage and more.

It is important for an organisation to understand all the stakeholders and key players within a CBC scenario. The control of data as well as the ability to delete the data are important factors to scrutinise. For any CBC approach, Service Level Agreement (SLA) plays a crucial part. As CbC users, an organisation must work with the service provider to develop a robust and integrated SLA to ensure all the provisions (e.g., service, location, control of data, bindings of information disclosure in all possible scenario, deletion of information upon exit, to name a few) are clearly and unambiguously mentioned and agreed by both parties.

Information security is to be ensured both in transition and at storage. As discussed, privacy of data for the CbC (e.g., Cloud Computing, Edge Computing, Fog Computing, IoT) depends both on technological and strategic business factors. The provision of technologies and their related risks, vulnerabilities and loopholes may play a detrimental part of breach of privacy. In the same way, the strategic and legal aspects (e.g., location, control, information disclosure) are equally important to design and enforce an integrated security and risk programme in CbC scenario.

Comparative Severity of Privacy Factors

As mentioned earlier, Location, Technology, People, and Service Provider as key factors in privacy within a CbC context. This section explores the severity of these factors in Cloud Computing, Fog Computing, Edge Computing and IoT. For any CbC, none of the factors can be low. Generally, the severity for any kind of CbC is High to Very High; though in some cases it can be Moderate depending on the context. Ideally, in our opinion, all the factors should be treated as at least High by an organisation – this is a safe and proactive practice. Table 1 lists few CbCs (i.e., Cloud Computing, Fog Computing, Edge Computing and IoT) and the severity of the key factors among those CbCs.

Table 1. Comparative Severity of Privacy Factors among few CbCs

	Cloud Computing	Fog Computing	Edge Computing	IoT
Location	Very High	Very High	Moderate	Moderate to Very High
Technology	High	High	High	Moderate to very High
People	Very High	Very High	Very High	Very High
Service Provider	Very High	Very high	Very High	Very High

For Cloud Computing, the authors rate the severity for Location as Very High. Geographic dispersion is one of the core reasons and motivations of writing this chapter from a data privacy context – earlier discussion in this chapter explores how geographic dispersion may notoriously affect privacy in cyber space. When it comes to Fog Computing, Location remains with a Very High rating in our table, for the same reason that the Fog Computing infrastructure is off-premise (for the users) and is just another form of Cloud Computing infrastructure but at a closer location to the end-user – thus, Cloud Computing and Fog Computing would have same severity rating for any threat factors related to privacy and security. In Edge Computing infrastructure, Location may be Moderate severity factor but not regardless. If the Edge infrastructure is located within the same premise with the end-user devices, it may pose a moderate risk; but having dispersed infrastructure by the end-user organisation and connecting among own different remote sites (via public network) within an Edge infrastructure would increase the severity level to High.

Technology for Cloud Computing has high severity as a threatening factor to privacy – this is from an end-user's perspective. A customer may not know what specific technologies are being used within a CSPs infrastructure. Besides, the technologies used by CSPs may contain vulnerabilities or other security loopholes. For example, virtualisation is a key technology used within a Cloud Infrastructures.

Virtualisation – as a technology – comes with its own security loopholes. It is not only what technologies are used within a CSP's premises, but also the technologies embedded in communications networks and the end-users' premises that collectively creates the Cloud Computing scenario. A CSP may not control the technologies used in end-users' premises and vice versa – the same applies to the providers or the communications infrastructure too. This creates a complex scenario of potential security threats that may emerge from technologies used within a Cloud Computing infrastructure. Technology is a High severity factor for Fog Computing and Edge Computing too. For IoT, Technology could be of a Moderate severity factor only if it is not a Cloud-based one, which is hardly the case any longer.

As discussed earlier, Human Factors play a crucial role in computing security; and People is often marked as a significant factor in relation to privacy. In cybersecurity, human being is termed as the 'weakest link'. People are the most challenging element for any computing scenario, CbC is no exception. Human Factors-centric threats that may lead to breach of privacy are literally limitless. Social engineering is the dark art to unveil unlimited ways to compromise a system and thus perhaps privacy too.

Service Provider is a very high severity factor for data privacy in Cloud Computing – so is in Fog Computing. We may extend the notion of Service Provider beyond just being CSP – a service provider may be any vendor who is providing infrastructure, software, hardware, communication networks or infrastructures. The vendors of software (e.g., operating systems or any other software), hardware (e.g., keyboard, tablet, computers, smartphones), communication devices and infrastructures (e.g., routers. switches, wireless access points) – all these are potential sources of threats with risk of breach of privacy. A rogue vendor may embed malicious piece of code in their software (or in the firmware of the hardware) to carry out unauthorised tasks. This is a matter of serious concern in CbC, since a CbC end-user may simply have no idea of the vendors that are serving their CSP (and thus acting as an indirect service provider for them). Based on this, Service Provider may be considered as a factor with Very High severity for all kinds of computing scenario, whether it is CbC or not.

Table 1 gives us one bottom-line in short – when it comes to data privacy, there is little room to allow deviation from standard and ongoing resilience. It is important to note that, the factors for one computing approach may have different level of severity when combined with other computing approaches. For example, referring to Table 1, the factor Location may have Moderate to very High Severity only when it is not a Cloud-based one. The severity rating of Cloud Computing is applicable to all CbC.

CONCLUSION

The future of any CbC is questionable from privacy perspective. The feasibility of CbC technologies requires more scrutiny. The apparent benefits of CbC often wins over its long-term effect on organisations. It is a very complex task to develop a plan to use CbC to rip its benefits off while not compromising with privacy and security. The privacy and security concerns in CbC applies to Cloud Computing, Edge Computing, Fog Computing and IoT. Without a doubt, these computing approaches bring great flexibility and benefits, but the security and privacy concerns may very well outweigh all the benefits that these computing approaches have in offer.

Current trend to computing privacy is vague and not well structured. The scenario of privacy concerns are severely complex in computing scenario, and are not being address adequately. For example, an end-user with a smart mobile phone may have applications installed on the phone that the user have given permission (knowingly or by inadvertently agreeing to end-user license agreements) to record audio or video (or both). If the user takes the phone to any public event where the phone keeps recording – a severe breach to privacy that most often goes unnoticed regardless of whether the above end-user or the vendors of the recording applications of the end-user's phone is liable for such breach. Scenario like the above could be just the tip of an iceberg. Further and massive investigation is required within computing privacy & security context to better structure and formulate integrated policy and laws around the globe.

CbC will undoubtedly create more problem than flexibility in the area of privacy and security. Can we then just exclude CbC from our life? Due to current computing trends, the industry 4.0 revolution through CbC and IoT, and due to the competitive edge of current business environment – it may not be possible to just exclude CbC from scenario. CbC is inevitable. Organisations need to carefully design information architecture, information security policy, and risk programme for resilience in the age of CbC.

REFERENCES

Ahmed, M., & Hossain, M. A. (2014). Cloud computing and security issues in the cloud. *International Journal of Network Security & Its Applications*, *6*(1), 25–36. doi:10.5121/ijnsa.2014.6103

Ahmed, M., Kambam, H. R., Liu, Y., & Uddin, M. N. (2019, June). Impact of Human Factors in Cloud Data Breach. In *International Conference on Intelligent and Interactive Systems and Applications* (pp. 568-577). Springer.

Ahmed, M., & Litchfield, A. T. (2016). Taxonomy for identification of security issues in cloud computing environments. *Journal of Computer Information Systems*, *58*(1), 79–88. doi:10.1080/08874417.20 16.1192520

Ahmed, M., Litchfield, A. T., & Ahmed, S. (2014). *A generalized threat taxonomy for cloud computing*. ACIS.

Aldossary, S., & Allen, W. (2016). Data security, privacy, availability and integrity in cloud computing: Issues and current solutions. *International Journal of Advanced Computer Science and Applications*, *7*(4), 485–498. doi:10.14569/IJACSA.2016.070464

Ali, M. M., & Haseebuddin, M. (2015). Cloud Computing for Retailing Industry: An Overview. *International Journal of Computer Trends and Technology*, *19*(1), 51–56. doi:10.14445/22312803/IJCTT-V19P110

Aljawarneh, S. A., & Yassein, M. O. B. (2016). A conceptual security framework for cloud computing issues. *International Journal of Intelligent Information Technologies*, *12*(2), 12–24. doi:10.4018/IJIIT.2016040102

Anawar, M. R., Wang, S., Azam Zia, M., Jadoon, A. K., Akram, U., & Raza, S. (2018). Fog computing: An overview of big IoT data analytics. *Wireless Communications and Mobile Computing*, *2018*, 1–22. doi:10.1155/2018/7157192

Birje, M. N., Challagidad, P. S., Goudar, R. H., & Tapale, M. T. (2017). Cloud computing review: Concepts, technology, challenges and security. *International Journal of Cloud Computing*, *6*(1), 32–57. doi:10.1504/IJCC.2017.083905

Cardoso, A., & Simões, P. (2011, July). Cloud computing: Concepts, technologies and challenges. In *International Conference on Virtual and Networked Organizations, Emergent Technologies, and Tools* (pp. 127-136). Springer.

Colwill, C. (2009). Human Factors in information security: The insider threat–Who can you trust these days? *Information Security Technical Report, 14*(4), 186–196. doi:10.1016/j.istr.2010.04.004

Goel, S., Williams, K., & Dincelli, E. (2017). Got phished? Internet security and human vulnerability. *Journal of the Association for Information Systems, 18*(1), 22–44. doi:10.17705/1jais.00447

Goyal, K. K., Garg, A., Rastogi, A., & Singhal, S. (2018). A Literature Survey on Internet of Things (IOT). *International Journal of Advanced Networking and Applications, 9*(6), 3663–3668.

Hadlington, L. (2018). The "Human Factor" in cybersecurity: Exploring the accidental insider. In Psychological and Behavioral Examinations in Cyber Security (pp. 46-63). IGI Global.

Hajibaba, M., & Gorgin, S. (2014). A review on modern distributed computing paradigms: Cloud computing, jungle computing and fog computing. *CIT. Journal of Computing and Information Technology, 22*(2), 69–84. doi:10.2498/cit.1002381

Jadeja, Y., & Modi, K. (2012, March). Cloud computing-concepts, architecture and challenges. In *2012 International Conference on Computing, Electronics and Electrical Technologies (ICCEET)* (pp. 877-880). IEEE. 10.1109/ICCEET.2012.6203873

Kar, J., & Mishra, M. R. (2016). Mitigate threats and security metrics in cloud computing. *J Inf Process Syst, 12*(2), 226–233.

Khalil, I., Khreishah, A., & Azeem, M. (2014). Cloud computing security: A survey. *Computers, 3*(1), 1–35. doi:10.3390/computers3010001

Kitanov, S., & Janevski, T. (2019). Introduction to fog computing. In *The Rise of Fog Computing in the Digital Era* (pp. 1–35). IGI Global. doi:10.4018/978-1-5225-6070-8.ch001

More, P. (2015). Review of implementing fog computing. *International Journal of Research in Engineering and Technology, 4*(06), 335–338. doi:10.15623/ijret.2015.0406057

Palega, M., & Knapinski, M. (2018). Threats associated with the Human Factor in the aspect of information security. *Scientific Journal of the Military University of Land Forces, 50*(1), 105–118. doi:10.5604/01.3001.0011.7364

Rahman, G., & Chuah, C. W. (2018). Fog computing, applications, security and challenges [review]. *IACSIT International Journal of Engineering and Technology, 7*(3), 1615–1621. doi:10.14419/ijet.v7i3.12612

Rajarajeswari, S., & Somasundaram, K. (2016). Data confidentiality and privacy in cloud computing. *Indian Journal of Science and Technology, 9*(4), 1–8. doi:10.17485/ijst/2016/v9i4/87040

Saharan, K. P., & Kumar, A. (2015). Fog in comparison to cloud: A survey. *International Journal of Computers and Applications, 122*(3), 10–12. doi:10.5120/21679-4773

Sethi, P., & Sarangi, S. R. (2017). Internet of things: Architectures, protocols, and applications. *Journal of Electrical and Computer Engineering, 2017*, 1–25. doi:10.1155/2017/9324035

Shouran, Z., Ashari, A., & Priyambodo, T. (2019). Internet of Things (IoT) of Smart Home: Privacy and Security. *International Journal of Computers and Applications*, *182*(39), 3–8. doi:10.5120/ijca2019918450

KEY TERMS AND DEFINITIONS

Application Layer: In an IoT infrastructure, application layer is the part of the network where data is collected through applications residing in devices used by end-users (e.g., smart phones), or the devices that are deployed in environment (e.g., CCTV, sensors).

Cloud-Based Computing: Any computing settings where cloud computing forms part of the infrastructure.

Cloud Computing: An architectural computing approach where users use remote computing resources (e.g., remote computers or computer networks) to carry out their computing needs.

Cloud Infrastructure: The network infrastructure used in a cloud computing architecture. This is the remote infrastructure from a user's perspective.

Cloud Service Provider: Third parties who provide cloud computing infrastructure and rents the infrastructure to various users (individual or organisation).

Edge Computing: An architectural CbC approach where part of the processing is carried out within the end-users' premises.

End-User Premise: The users' own perimeter or organisational boundary where the users' own infrastructure (owned and managed by the end-users) is situated.

End-Users' Devices: Devices used by the end-users or deployed within the end-users' premises. Examples of such devices are users' computers, CCTV, various sensors, smart phones.

Fog Computing: An architectural computing approach that adds an extra intermediary cloud infrastructure for faster computing performance.

GRC: The aspects of information security that deals with integrated governance, risk manage, and compliance for an organisation from information security perspective.

Human Factor: In information security, human factors refer to those factors potential to result in information privacy and security breach due to human action/error/incompetence.

IoT: IoT refers to an architectural computing concept where every devices (smart phones, CCTV, sensors, household gadgets, TV, washing machine, microwave) have computational and communication capability and connected to the Internet to form a network of everything.

Latency: Delay in computational processing due to various factors. Example of factors are distance data needs to travel, or excessive amount of data compared to processing capability of a computer resulting in processing bottlenecks.

Network Layer: In an IoT architecture, network layer is the part of network that connects and transmits data back and forth between the end-users' devices and the servers that processed the data collected from the end-users' devices.

Perception Layer: In an IoT architecture, perception layer is where the computer servers reside that processes the data collected from end-users' devices to interpret for various purposes.

Vendor: Normally a third party, vendor is an entity that provides (rents or sells) hard/software/infrastructure/service to customers.

Chapter 12
Privacy Preserving in Digital Health:
Main Issues, Technologies, and Solutions

Zakariae El Ouazzani

Rabat IT Center, Smart Systems Laboratory ENSIAS, Mohammed V University, Rabat, Morocco

Hanan El Bakkali

Rabat IT Center, Smart Systems Laboratory ENSIAS, Mohammed V University, Rabat, Morocco

Souad Sadki

Rabat IT Center, Smart Systems Laboratory ENSIAS, Mohammed V University, Rabat, Morocco

ABSTRACT

Recently, digital health solutions are taking advantage of recent advances in information and communication technologies. In this context, patients' health data are shared with other stakeholders. Moreover, it's now easier to collect massive health data due to the rising use of connected sensors in the health sector. However, the sensitivity of this shared healthcare data related to patients may increase the risks of privacy violation. Therefore, healthcare-related data need robust security measurements to prevent its disclosure and preserve patients' privacy. However, in order to make well-informed decisions, it is often necessary to allow more permissive security policies for healthcare organizations even without the consent of patients or against their preferences. The authors of this chapter concentrate on highlighting these challenging issues related to patient privacy and presenting some of the most significant privacy preserving approaches in the context of digital health.

DOI: 10.4018/978-1-7998-3817-3.ch012

Copyright © 2020, IGI Global. Copying or distributing in print or electronic forms without written permission of IGI Global is prohibited.

INTRODUCTION

Nowadays, thanks to recent advances in Information and Communication Technologies (ICT), healthcare related data is more and more collected, recorded, processed and shared electronically allowing a significant enhancement in the health care sector or, let's say, its digital transformation towards the "Healthcare 4.0".

In this context, digital health solutions could offer to the patient better quality of care benefits in terms of both cost and time. However, these solutions increase also the risks of data breaches and privacy violation. In fact, digital health systems involve different technologies and various stakeholders (healthcare providers, Cloud providers, intermediate services such as laboratories, pharmacies...) increasing the number of potential attack vectors with new chances for intruders to gain unauthorized access to personal and sensitive healthcare data.

As stated in (The biggest healthcare data breaches, 2018), e-health systems are a profitable target for hackers. Attacks exploiting ransom ware, human errors and spear phishing emails seem to be the most dominating the last few years. In August 2019, phishing attacks continued to pose serious problems for US healthcare organizations such as with the largest breach on Presbyterian Healthcare Services, which involved more than 150,000 healthcare records breached (Healthcare Data Breach Report, 2019). Such statistics show clearly that more efforts are needed to secure and protect personal healthcare data.

Moreover, healthcare related data require stronger security measures than other types of data. This is due to the nature of the health information that may contain sensitive and private information such as sexual or mental health data, etc. Such measures should prevent disclosure of this sensitive data to any third party without prior and explicit consent of the patient (Gilson, 2012).

But, for the healthcare patricians' point of view, the security policies of the health care organizations should give them the ability to access or to share sensitive patient information(even if it is against the patients' security preferences) in order to make well informed decisions particularly, in critical emergency cases. In this context, it is clear that privacy preserving solutions should take into account all these different and sometimes conflicting needs.

It is also very important to share and publish patients' related data (including, genetic, imaging, patient-centered, etc.) to allow innovation in the healthcare sector. For example, more than 10,000 labeled images on Image Net (Department of Biomedical Informatics, 2018) were shared publicly to allow the training of deep neural networks for image recognition tasks.

Generally, such publicly shared healthcare data is anonymized before being shared, but, it is widely admitted that mitigating the risks of re-identification is still a challenging issue. Other challenging issues are raised regarding the data sharing among different health providers. For instance, the use of mobile apps and IoT devices to collect patients health data, which are then stored on the cloud, etc.

In this chapter, the authors aim to give a clear picture of privacy concerns in digital health. They focus particularly on highlighting the challenging issues related to patient's privacy and present some of the most promising privacy preserving approaches.

Thus, the proposed chapter will be organized in 5 sections. Section 2 presents some related privacy concepts and definitions particularly in the context of digital health. The description of the main e-health stakeholders and the technologies behind the rise of digital health is given in Section 3. Section 4 shows the impact, on the patient's privacy, of potential attacks that could exploit vulnerabilities inside these technologies. Section 5 discusses three kinds of privacy-preserving approaches and techniques that have been proposed recently to mitigate such risks and still need deeper research work.

The chapter will end with a conclusion and some future research directions in this hot and challenging topic.

PRIVACY BACKGROUND

This section gives some definitions of privacy, privacy policy, privacy preferences and major related concepts. It particularly highlights the gap that often exists in the digital world between the desire of preserving privacy (that itself requires privacy awareness and a certain level of IT literacy) and the ability of achieving this desire (that requires to have some means of control).

Privacy Definitions

From the very early ages, researchers and philosophers indicated the importance of understanding the meaning of privacy concept. For instance, Solove (2002) argued that the most striking thing about the right to privacy is that nobody seems to have any very clear idea what it is. Thus, privacy awareness of the privacy concerns he may encounter while consuming any internet service. But first, and before talking about privacy protection, this concept has to be properly understood by users and any organization willing to use or disclose personal data on the internet.

Explicitly, Information security means protecting information and information systems from unauthorized access, use, disclosure, disruption, modification or destruction so that the confidentiality, integrity and availability of information are maintained (Feruza & Kim, 2007). In contrast, privacy ensures that user's data are stored, used and disclosed fairly according to the data owner's preferences.

In the healthcare field, the National Committee for Vital and Health Statistics (National committee on vital and health statistics, 2006) describes the differences between and among privacy, confidentiality, and security this way:

"Health information privacy is an individual's right to control the acquisition, uses, or disclosures of his or her identifiable health data. Confidentiality, which is closely related, refers to the obligations of those who receive information to respect the privacy interests of those to whom the data relate. Security is altogether different. It refers to physical, technological, or administrative safeguards or tools used to protect identifiable health data from unwarranted access or disclosure".

Hereafter, some privacy definitions are given for better understanding:

Definition 1: Privacy is a fundamental human right, enshrined in numerous international human rights instruments. It is central to the protection of human dignity and forms the basis of any democratic society (The Right to Privacy in Singapore, 1999).

Definition 2: The concept of privacy relates to individual autonomy and each person's control over their own information, this includes each person's right to decide when and whether to share personal information, how much information to share, and the circumstances under which that information can be shared (Seastrom, 2011).

Definition 3: "Privacy" means controlling all information about oneself, including protecting identity (anonymity), personal information, and information about personal activity (Burmester, Desmedt, Wright & Yasinsac, 2002).

These definitions link privacy with the person's desire of keeping his sensitive information secret, safe and under control without the interruption of others. Therefore, owing to its strong impact on individuals' behaviors, privacy is considered a fundamental right that must be accorded to all people from all ages. Each one has the right to keep his personal information private and control the disclosure of that information. Patient's medical histories, family secrets, shopper preferences, votes' results are all examples of sensitive data that require a high-level of privacy protection.

The way to ensure such right and desire of privacy is far from being simple. Thus, each organization storing or processing personal data should make public its privacy policy to allow verification of compliance with related laws and regulations.

Privacy Policy

The term privacy policy is well known by researchers, the computer science community and anyone who has ever browsed the internet. But, what is the real explanation of this term, particularly, in e-health? Does it indicate how the sharing, collection and management of medical data is done to reassure patients? Or is it just used to show how the privacy policy is compliant with privacy laws and regulations? Hence, and in order to clarify the real meaning and purpose of this concept and its importance in e-health, the authors selected the following three definitions:

Definition 1: A privacy policy is a written, published statement that articulates the policy position of an organization on how it handles the Personally Identifiable Information (PII) that it gathers and uses in the normal course of business. PII is any information that can be used on its own or with other information to identify, contact, or locate a single person, or to identify an individual in context (Parimala, 2017).

Definition 2: A Statement that declares a firm's or website's policy on collecting and releasing information about a visitor. It usually declares what specific information is collected and whether it is kept confidential or shared with or sold to other firms, researchers or sellers (Cavoukian & Tapscott, 1997).

Definition 3: A privacy policy is a statement or a legal document (in privacy law) that discloses some or all of the ways a party gathers, uses, discloses, and manages a customer or client's data. It fulfills a legal requirement to protect a customer or client's privacy (Baumer, Earp & Poindexter, 2004).

Referring to the above definitions authors can conclude that ensuring data privacy requires that the sharing, collection and management of sensitive information are regulated using privacy policies. These statements or legal documents contain some or all the ways a party manages users' data i.e. what information is collected, how it is collected and under what circumstances this information is used or stored.

In the health context, there is a need of privacy policies that allow healthcare providers to access all the relevant information (generally, in a more permissive and timely manner than other contexts) and to share patient health information with other health providers or relevant stakeholders to make well informed decisions. In critical situations, a healthcare provider should even be able to override the patients' preferences with regards to data sharing.

Privacy Preferences

Patients have the right (as a human right) to decide on themselves to whom disclose their data and under what circumstance and healthcare providers should normally show in their privacy policies that they respond to their patients' preferences.

Fortunately, with the recent advance in privacy preserving solutions and the new important updates made in some privacy laws, more and more healthcare providers in developed countries use innovative ICT solutions that allow a patient to manage access to his personal data or to specific types of sensitive information. Therefore, he is gradually moving away from a passive to an active role. Yet, even with these patient-centric solutions in place, more efforts are needed to make patients more active regarding the decisions made concerning the usage, disclosure and management of their sensitive medical information.

It is also important to give patients the means to verify if their privacy preferences will be taking into account when exchanging or divulgating their private health information to other health actors. At least, they would be able to easily verify if the privacy policies of these actors are both convenient (according to their preferences) and compliant with relevant privacy laws.

Hence, authors believe that patients have all the right to express their privacy preferences and since their health conditions or IT literacy do not always allow them to perform this task, researchers and policy makers have to help patients expressing their privacy preferences in a simple way.

Privacy Laws

The terms of "privacy law", "privacy regulations", "privacy directive" and "privacy act" could be used differently according to the concerned country or region. Yet all of them aims to assure that citizen's PII is properly protected. In the healthcare sector, the privacy laws play an important role in protecting patients' privacy while allowing the flow of health information needed to provide and promote high quality health care and to protect the public's health and well-being (Barth, Mitchell & Rosenstein, 2004).

A privacy Law could be defined as a statute that protects a person's right to be left alone, and governs collection, storage, and release of his or her financial, medical, and other personal information (Cavoukian & Tapscott, 1997).

A privacy Regulation is a kind of rule regulating how certain activity, behavior or data should be protected. Regulations can define two things; a process of monitoring and enforcing privacy legislations and a written instrument containing rules that have privacy law on them (Naish, 2014).

A privacy Act is an act that protects a person against the unauthorized use of personal data by any government agency.

For instance, the United States, unlike many other countries, does not have an overarching data privacy law that applies to all types of personal information, including health information. However, it does have a general health privacy law with broad application that may be extended to e-Health. One of the most important federal laws is the Health Insurance Portability and Accountability Act (HIPAA) which were created to improve the efficiency and effectiveness of the health care system, by encouraging the development of a health information system by establishing requirements and standards and for the electronic transmission of certain health information.

In the European Union, the Data Protection Directive 1995/46/EC sets up a regulatory framework aiming to strike a balance between a high level of protection for the privacy of individuals and the free movement of personal data within the EU by setting strict limits on the collection and use of personal data (Data Protection Laws of the World, 2019).

DIGITAL HEALTH STAKEHOLDERS AND ENABLING TECHNOLOGIES

In the process of seeking well-being and health recovery, patients often interact with multiple healthcare providers. In the context of digital health, this diversity of actors involved in patients' care, is enriched with additional actors due to the use of new ICT technologies to collect, store, share or process patients' electronic health records (EHR). Thus, all these actors should be concerned by the protection of their privacy.

Authors of (Shaw et al., 2017) have interviewed many e-Health practitioners and policy makers to develop a 3-domains-based conceptual model for e-Health (see Figure 1). This model and its domains highlight the importance of the use of digital technologies to monitor, inform and facilitate communication and data exchange among health stakeholders in order to enhance health services quality.

Figure 1. E-health conceptual model (Shaw et al., 2017)

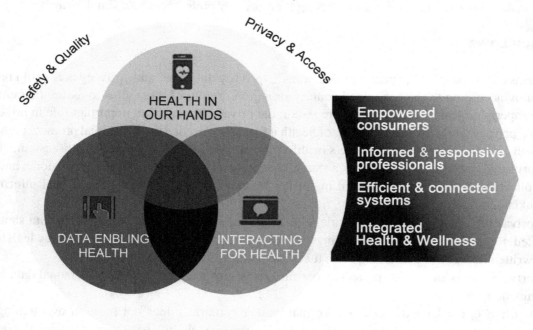

In this section, the authors show the diversity of the actors involved in patients' care in the context of digital health and their interactions. In addition, the authors will focus on the advanced technologies that are behind the rising of digital health applications and initiatives and show how they could be used by the main actors of digital healthcare to provide useful services for the patients.

At this level, patients seem to be the most vulnerable and passive actor since they usually do not have the ability to control the disclosure restrictions of their data once shared with one of the other actors and often do not understand how the advanced technologies used in e-health could be harmful for their privacy.

Main Digital Health Stakeholders

Nowadays, it is current for patients to treat with multiple actors, even directly, like with hospitals, doctors, laboratories, radiology centers, pharmacies and insurance institutions or indirectly, like with IT providers (cloud computing, IoT, Web and mobile applications providers), research centers and governmental agencies (for study and research purposes).

Each of these actors has their own IT system storing some information related to patient records. Thus, data about the patient's health condition is scattered throughout different systems governed by different security and privacy policies.

This plethora of systems, duplicated or even fragmented health records have a negative impact on patient's well-being (risks of medical errors, conflicting prescriptions, increased costs, etc.) and also its privacy preserving.

Unfortunately, this lack of coordination among the actors gives rise to the complex interoperability issue that still needs additional research work. In fact, better interoperability will create a propitious environment for better privacy preserving solutions. However, this issue is beyond the scope of this chapter.

Figure 2. Adapted stakeholders and advanced technologies (Vimarlund, 2011)

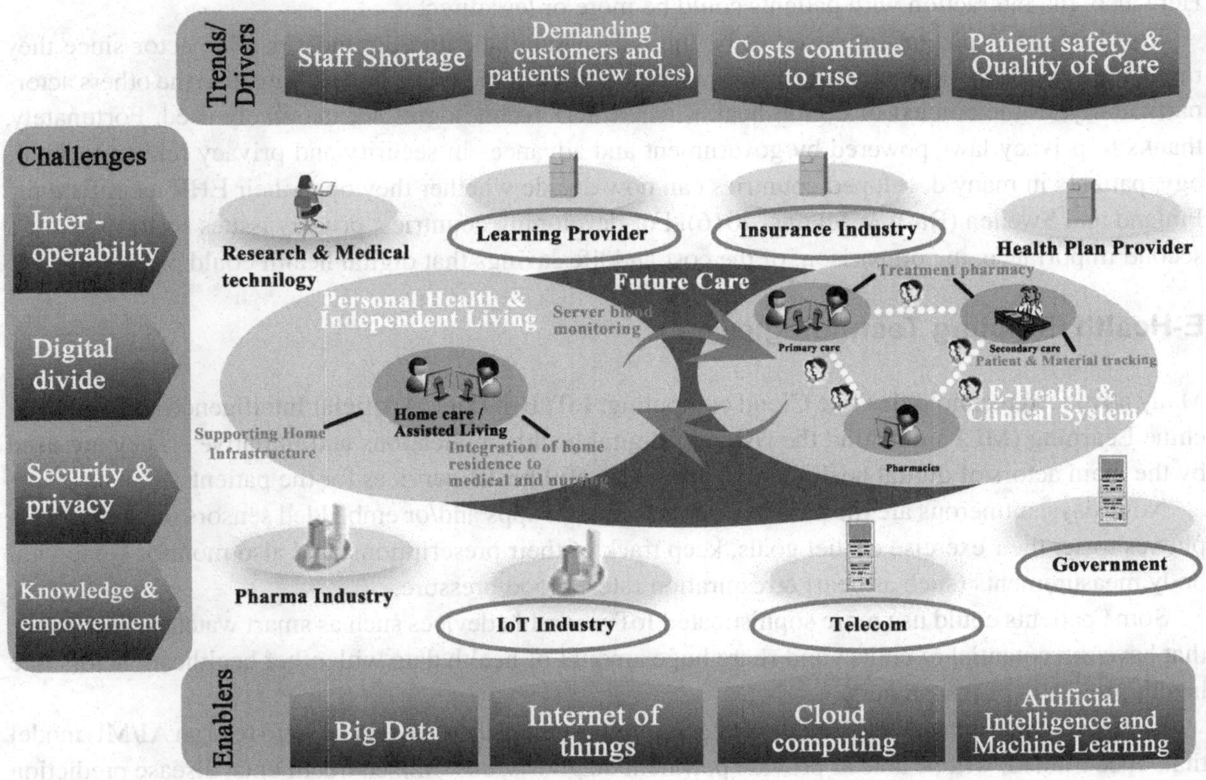

The figure 2 (Vimarlund, 2011) shows the multitude of actors in the digital health, the main challenges they face and how some innovative ICT advances like IoT could act as enablers.

Hospitals, recovery centers and clinics with their medical staff (including doctors, radiologists, nurses, etc.), generally called **Healthcare providers**, are the most interacting actor with patients and thus, the most susceptible to collect and store their data. With the advance in the health sector and the availability of health information (medical web sites, health apps, etc.), the interaction between patients and Healthcare providers seems to move towards a more collaborative relation where the patient could have a more active role.

All Researchers and their organizations that are interested in studying health related issues (like in the "*Data enabling health* domain") and that collect or process patients' EHR are also important actors with regard to digital health and underlying privacy issues. The relationship between Patients and Researchers, is often mediated by a Healthcare provider but fortunately due to the advances in digital health this relationship also tends to become more direct as with the recent trend of patient-centered outcomes research (PCORI, 2019). Besides these two main actors there are the **Insurance institutions** or other funding sources that could have access to patient data via interactions with healthcare providers, researchers or directly with patients.

Governments and policy makers are without doubt important actors in health in general and in e-health in particular, that could be viewed as a way for them to make better health decisions as it facilitates data collection and analytics. Besides, as highlighted above, governments play a crucial role in the privacy laws enforcement.

ICT providers (such as Cloud providers, IoT industrials, Telecom operators, Software and Mobile apps developers,) play a crucial role in the digital health particularly, in preserving patient's privacy. Here also, the interaction with patients could be more or less direct.

To summarize, patients are used to be the most vulnerable and the most passive actor since they rarely have the ability to control the disclosure restrictions of their data once divulged to the others actors particularly, in the context of digital health, where ICT technologies are massively used. Fortunately, thanks to privacy laws powered by government and advances in security and privacy related technology, patients in many developed countries can now decide whether they open their EHR as in Estonia, Finland and Sweden (Basu & Munns, 2016). For developing countries, privacy issues seem to be for a second importance, in comparison, of the cost and life savings that digital health could offer.

E-Health Enabling Technologies

Many advanced technologies like Cloud computing, IoT, Big Data, Artificial Intelligence (AI) and Machine Learning (ML) are behind the rising of digital health applications and initiatives. They are used by the main actors of digital healthcare to provide useful health services for the patients.

Nowadays, numerous are the patients who use mobile apps and/or embedded sensors on their smartphones to set their exercise or diet goals, keep track of their prescriptions, and also monitor some vital body measurements (such as heart &respiration rates, blood pressure, ...).

Some patients could use more sophisticated IoT-wearable devices such as smart watches, headbands that have the potential to collect and share huge amount of health data with other healthcare actors like health providers or researchers.

These collected data, or let's say Big Data, is often stored in the Cloud in order to feed an AI/ML model that, once trained, will be able to provide pertinent diagnosis, customized treatments, disease prediction and prevention, etc. that are appropriate for each patient. Moreover, advanced sensors allow healthcare providers to observe patient's health condition and to be notified in real-time if some abnormalities occur.

In fact, thanks to integration of these advanced technologies into the healthcare sector, health providers, researchers, insurances institutions and governments can provide more efficient and tailored health services, which then contribute in enhancing public health while saving costs.

However, such advanced technologies introduce also new threats on the privacy and security of patients' health data.

PRIVACY ISSUES IN DIGITAL HEALTH

In this section, the authors show how the recent and advanced ICT technologies and AI have created new privacy risks in the digital health landscape. Moreover, the fact that different actors have access to patients' data (pharmacies, laboratories, the medical stuff of the hospital, Insurance, Cloud providers, etc.) makes even harder the protection of patient's sensitive data from inside and outside breaches.

The possible federation of a large amount of patient health data collected from different sources (EHR stored on hospitals databases, data collected from IoT devices and stored in the Cloud, genomic data stored in research centers, etc.) allowed by modern digital health solutions, has a negative impact on patients' privacy which is much greater than classical e-health systems within the boundary of few health organizations.

Several kinds of attack scenarios could be imagined: attacks on mobile devices and IoT sensors (generally, less secured than hospital servers), attacks on wireless communication channels (which are more vulnerable than wired channels), attacks on devices manufacturers and Cloud providers, attacks on AI/ML models (by feeding them with wrong data), etc.

Digital Health stakeholders should be aware that the use of technologies like IoT and cloud computing in healthcare create new vulnerabilities and threats that will require a design of new security models and privacy preserving solutions in order to protect their information systems and their patients' data.

Table 1. New threats in digital health introduced by recent technologies

Used Technology	Introduced Threats and Vulnerabilities
IoT	- Mobile devices and IoT sensors are generally less secured than hospital servers or cloud provider systems, which introduces new attack vectors. - Wearable devices for Digital Health (manufacturers rarely respect security by design principle) make patients more vulnerable and put their privacy at risk.
Wireless communication channels	- Wireless networks are generally more vulnerable than wired channels. - Often patients are not able to deal with security aspects of the connection configurations of the used devices.
Big Data and Cloud computing	- New vulnerabilities and bigger attack surface due to the diversity of Digital Health stakeholders and extensive data sharing. - More complexity due to the co-existence of different privacy policies and different privacy laws which introduces compliance issues and potential conflicts.
Artificial intelligence	- AI/ML models used for health data analytics could be attacked by feeding them with biased data. - AI techniques could be used to perform inference attacks against patient privacy (like attacks that are based on generative adversarial networks).

Moreover, when data sharing implies different jurisdictions with different laws the privacy issue becomes more challenging (Biswas, Mazuz & Mendes, 2014). In Table 1, the authors present possible threats in digital health of recent technologies.

In such context, classical security solutions like encrypted transmission and storage is not sufficient, privacy enhancing techniques must be considered to allow patient health data protection like anonymization techniques and dynamic negotiation of privacy policies among actors, etc.

Main Privacy-Preserving Solutions in E-Health

Solutions that are specifically designed to protect privacy are often referred to as Privacy Enhancing Techniques (PETs). According to (Borking & Raab, 2001), PETs can be described as "A coherent system of ICT measures that protects privacy by eliminating or reducing personal data or by preventing unnecessary and/or undesired processing of personal data, all without losing the functionality of the information system".

Privacy protection is a shared responsibility between all the stakeholders of e-health: patients, healthcare service providers and any organizations involved in patients' care. As was previously stated, privacy policies and preferences play a crucial role in ensuring patients' privacy. These policies have to be compliant with local laws and regulations. Yet, privacy policies on their own are not sufficient to ensure patients' privacy. Anonymization techniques are widely used to hide the identity of patients and therefore to protect their privacy.

In what follows, the authors will discuss three categories of privacy-preserving approaches that have been proposed recently to deal with privacy issues in e-health systems:

- Approaches that focus on privacy policy management in e-health, with regards to patient's preferences concordance and policy laws compliance.
- Anonymization techniques which aim to guarantee anonymity of patients while making their EHR available for other health actors mainly for research purposes.
- Recent Blockchain based approaches that aim to make patients more active and aware with regards to the processing of their health records by the other stakeholders.

The authors present in Table 2 the benefits of three recent privacy-preserving approaches ensuring privacy in e-health systems.

In the following, the authors will present a number of recent approaches in each of these categories while highlighting major limitations related to their adoption.

Policy-Based Privacy Preserving Approaches

In this section, the authors show the importance of considering patients' privacy preferences when exchanging, using or divulgating their private health information. To achieve this, they present a number of recent patient-centric works illustrating how privacy policies of different actors should take into account patients' preferences regarding their sensitive data. Indeed, the authors tackle, on one hand, the issue of conflicting privacy policies of third parties with patient's preferences where a number of research work is presented. On the other hand, the authors emphasize the crucial role that privacy laws and regulations for healthcare could play in protecting patients' privacy by verifying the compliance of

Table 2. Privacy-preserving approaches and benefits

Privacy-Preserving Approaches	Benefits
Privacy policy management	- Correct handling of the collection, exchange and disclosure of patient data - Retaining data quality and accessibility - Avoiding conflicts among different healthcare stakeholders. - Ensuring data transparency. - Improving the healthcare industry's ability to protect patient information. - Enhancing patient's quality of care
Anonymization techniques	- Enhanced information security against attacks. - Ensuring privacy in big data - Preserving the data utility - Minimization of risks regarding the disclosure of information. - Possible re-use of the information - Application of automated Big Data techniques
Blockchain	- Improving patients' trust in their healthcare providers thanks to transparency. - Ensuring an easy and efficient access to patients' data. - Permit Data verifiability - Enhancing patients' engagement and Health data ownership - Allowing a decentralized management

third parties' privacy policies. Indeed, due to the fact that multiple actors are involved in patients' care, the policies of these actors may be in conflict. Finally, authors link this part to the formalization issue explaining why next to patients' privacy preferences and third parties policies these privacy laws and regulations need to be formalized and understood by all the involved parties to facilitate the compliance verification operation. In what follow, the authors distinguish between two main type if conflicts: 1) Conflicts between third parties' privacy policies and 2) Conflicts between third parties' privacy policies and patients' privacy preferences.

Conflicts Among Patients' Privacy Preferences and Third Parties' Policies

With the development in technology, patient consent of their right to privacy increases. For this, researchers start to investigate patients about their opinions of electronic and mobile technology used for healthcare. In this regard, Breaux and Rao (2013) performed a study about patients' attitudes and perceptions concerning e/m-Health technology and also to address their concerns regarding e/m-Health privacy. The study shows that patients' are highly concerned about their privacy depending on the type of information being communicated, where and when the information is being accessed, who is accessing or seeing the information, and for what reasons (Gawanmeh & Alomari, 2015). In the same context, a study about patient's privacy preferences for e-health data sharing was conducted by Baumer et al. (2004). The study confirmed that people's sharing behavior depends on the type of information being shared and the sharing recipient. Also, Gandomi and Haider (2015) showed the importance of understanding the impact of privacy preserving enforcement on patients on improving the user acceptance of personalized E-Health Services.

Taking into account patients' privacy preferences, many privacy-preserving solutions have been suggested. In this regard, Gandomi and Haider (2015) studied the problem of user preferences prediction and proposed a distributed anonymization scheme allowing patients to individually anonymize their own data without accessing each other's data. In the opportunistic computing, based on an attribute-based access control and a new privacy-preserving scalar product computation (PPSPC) technique (Nargundi & Phalnikar, 2013) suggests user-centric privacy access control framework that allows a medical user to decide who can participate in the opportunistic computing process. By including patient in the decision making process authors are actually giving him an active role. In the same context, a patient-centric privacy measurement method was suggested by Canadian Nurses Association (2003). This solution quantifies privacy risks based on privacy user preferences in participatory sensing systems. In addition, Sadki and EL Bakkali (2016) suggest an approach that aims to resolve the problem of conflicting privacy policies in Cloud-based mobile environments based on negotiation technique. This is achieved by including the patient in the decision making process. In addition to these works, Yang et al. (2018) propose a privacy-preserving e-health system, which is a fusion of Internet-of-things (IoT), big data and cloud computing storage. This work allows a flexible policy update while preventing privacy leakage. Hence, and for many reasons, patients can prefer to keep their sensitive information private and also limit the access to only minimum-necessary information. For instance, an employer may decide not to hire someone with psychological issues, an insurance company may refuse to provide life insurance when aware of the disease history of a patient.

Conflicts Among Third Parties' Policies and Their Impact of Patients' Privacy

Even if some recent works start to consider patients' preferences, some challenges and issues still remain. On one hand, multiple service providers might have different privacy policies that apply to their services, so patients become confused about which privacy policies should apply (Kaplan, 2014).

On the other hand, the diversity of actors involved in patient' scare can lead to conflicts among privacy policies defined by these actors. Furthermore, these policies are expressed using mainly natural languages and more rarely formal languages such as eXtensible Access Control Markup Language (XACML), Enterprise Privacy Authorization Language (EPAL) or Platform for Privacy Preference (P3P). In this regard, Khurat et al. (2017) extend the P3P and propose a formal semantics for P3P to facilitate reasoning about semantic ambiguities in P3P policies. By eliminating these ambiguities conflict among third parties policies are reduced. Similarly, and based on an XACML engine, Seol et al. (2018) suggest a prototype, that a conflict resolution strategy following the negotiation mechanism. The question is, how can third parties' privacy policies be expressed using formal languages? Also, wouldn't patients' data be more protected with the existence of a common and a standardized privacy language that simultaneously formalize service providers' privacy policies and patients' privacy preferences? In this regard, Sadki and EL Bakkali (2016) propose a solution to resolve the issue of conflicting policies where both patients' privacy preferences and service providers' policies are expressed using the same language.

In a nutshell, the first step of patients' implication is protecting his data is by allowing the expression of his privacy preferences in an easy and formal way and the non-taking into account his opinion and decision in case a conflicting situation takes place. Above patients' privacy preferences formalization issue, another serious concern threatening patients' privacy and needing a particular attention need to be adequately treated: conflicts among privacy policies. Indeed, the fact that privacy policy is generally created by the data owner and can offer more semantics compared to access control policies, make the privacy policy more complex and much easier to produce conflicts (Alpert, 2003). Afterwards, since data gathered and exchanged via computers or mobile devices can be issued from different sources, it is necessary to standardize services providers' privacy policies and patients' privacy preferences to facilitate the conflict detection and resolution tasks. Above this, owing to the importance of regulations and standards in ensuring patients' privacy protection, compliance of these privacy policies to local privacy laws and principles should also be considered.

ANONYMIZATION-BASED PRIVACY PRESERVING TECHNIQUES

In this section, the authors will show that e-health big data could be very profitable: for example, for health care scientists to achieve greater understanding and make useful health discoveries and for policymakers and states, it could be a way to make better decisions, etc. At this purpose, several techniques were proposed in the literature in order to ensure privacy in big data while keeping the utility of the shared data.

In order to ensure privacy in big data, many anonymization approaches were proposed in the literature including cryptography, randomization and generalization. However, the use of cryptographic approach degrades the system's speed and the use of randomization approach involves removing or aggregating variables. Then, the use of generalization approach is more preferable when anonymizing the data in order to both ensure privacy and preserve the data utility.

Anonymization Techniques Related to Generalization Approach

It is widely known that there exist two major types of attributes in the literature which are quasi-identifier (QI) and sensitive attributes. The first type constitutes a set of information containing individual details other than identifiers such as age and gender (Hassan, Domingo-Ferrer & Soria-Comas, 2018). The second type constitutes private individual attributes; for instance, in a healthcare data set, "Disease" attribute is viewed as a sensitive attribute (Sei, Takenouchi & Ohsuga, 2015). In this section, the authors present three main anonymization techniques belonging to generalization approach.

K-Anonymity Technique

For many years, k-anonymity has been handled as an anonymization technique ensuring privacy in big data when treating QI attributes. The k-anonymity is achieved when each value is similar to at least k-1 other values within each bucket in the data set (Anushree & Rio, 2019). Divers algorithms based on the k-anonymity principle were proposed in the literature. This technique is used in various domains. For instance, Förster et al. (2015) suggested a common way to decentralize the k-anonymity of location data throughout a cryptographic algorithm using distributed secret sharing. Besides, Jain et al. (2019) proposed an ameliorated k-anonymity algorithm applied to a considerable candidate election data set. However, the majority of researches consider that the privacy parameter k of k-anonymity must be set to an exact value before applying the k-anonymity algorithm and since the more the value of the threshold k is high, the more the probability of re-identification is low. El Ouazzani and El Bakkali (2018a) assume that the best way of using the k-anonymity principle consists on not setting a fixed value to the threshold k of k-anonymity. The proposed algorithm in (El Ouazzani & El Bakkali, 2018a) is original because it deals with both numerical and categorical QI attributes. Moreover, it works on unfixed number of rows belonging to the data set, which gives the possibility to apply the algorithm on large data sets.

L-Diversity Technique

The l-diversity technique addresses some of the weaknesses in the k-anonymity technique where the protection of identities at the level of k individuals is not equal to the protection of the corresponding sensitive values that were generalized. Among the anonymization techniques based on the principle of l-diversity, distinct l-diversity is the most used technique. This method guarantees that each bucket in the data set includes at least l "well-represented" distinct sensitive values (Canbay, Vural & Sagiroglu, 2018). Generally, l-diversity technique is applied while the privacy parameter l is set to a fixed value. Besides, Abouelmehdi et al. (2018) find that dummy data must be inserted into the data set in the case it does not contain as much as different values. However, this dummy data will enhance the privacy but may cause problems during the analysis and lack of data utility. Thus, El Ouazzani and El Bakkali (2019b) propose an algorithm treating sensitive attributes and using the principle of l-diversity without a prior value of the threshold l of l-diversity in order to ensure maximum privacy without adding dummy data to the data set. Furthermore, since sensitive attributes are in general separated, the correlation between these different attributes is lost. Thus, El Ouazzani and El Bakkali (2019b) apply the distinct l-diversity algorithm only on highly correlated attributes based on a vertical partitioning in order to preserve the data utility.

T-Closeness Technique

T-closeness is considered as an improvement of l-diversity technique. It aims to measure the distance between the distribution of a sensitive attribute in each bucket and the global distribution of the same attribute in the data set (Wang et al., 2018). The distance could be measured based on a distance metric like Earth Mover's Distance (EMD). This distance metric is involved by El Ouazzani and El Bakkali (2017) in their proposed algorithm. Many researches have been made using t-closeness principle. Wang, Zhu, Chen and Chang (2018) proposed an algorithm treating multiple sensitive attributes and make the published anonymized data set satisfying the t-closeness principle. Moreover, Wang, Jiang, and Yang (2018) develop an algorithm called t-closeness slicing (TCS) in order to protect transactional data against the possible attacks. In addition, an algorithm is proposed in (El Ouazzani & El Bakkali, 2017) using the t-closeness principle without setting a prior value to the threshold t of t-closeness when treating sensitive numerical attributes in order to efficiently ensure privacy. This algorithm is ameliorated to become more general and able to treat multiple sensitive numerical attributes as done in (El Ouazzani & El Bakkali, 2019a). In another side, the treatment of categorical attributes is different from the treatment of numerical ones. For instance, in the medical field, diverse identifying data exists in the data set as categorical attributes, such as diagnosis methods, disease and treatment. El Ouazzani and El Bakkali (2018b) proposed an algorithm treating categorical sensitive attributes by using the permutation process and t-closeness principle without considering any threshold. Besides, the algorithm addresses the l-diversity weakness by breaking the semantic similarity of categorical values within each bucket.

Although l-diversity is a good anonymization technique, it does not resist against the similarity attack. Thus, a technique combining l-diversity and t-closeness principles is essential to address the l-diversity technique limitation (El Ouazzani & El Bakkali, 2018b). Moreover, k-anonymity technique must be combined with the previous ones to deal with QI and sensitive attributes and to make a balance between ensuring privacy and preserving data utility. Next, the authors present various possible attacks to the anonymization techniques already mentioned before.

Attacks Against Anonymization Techniques

In this subsection, the authors highlight four main attacks against the anonymization techniques including background, Singling Out, Inference and proximity attacks.

Background Knowledge Attack

Actually, various background knowledge data like well-known facts, public records and demographic information can be available to adversaries. However, it is quite hard to know the exact background knowledge that will be used by an adversary before publishing the anonymized data set. Therefore, background knowledge attack arises to be one of great challenges for anonymization-based privacy preserving techniques (Dong, Xianmang, LongBin & Huahui, 2016). This attack is generally done based on the attacker's background knowledge obtained through an investigation or logical reasoning. So, such attacker knowledge should be taken considered in the anonymization process since both sensitive and categorical attributes are included in the data set (Rajendran, Jayabalan & Rana, 2017). Among the anonymization techniques existing in the literature, k-anonymity fails to resist against background knowledge attack; however, l-diversity technique addresses the k-anonymity limitation and resists against such (Rajendran et al., 2017), (Shouling, Prateek & Raheem, 2017). Moreover, a technique called (c, k)-safety technique is proposed in (Shouling et al., 2017) to resist against background knowledge attack, where the threshold "k" represents the background knowledge and the desired privacy level is characterized by the threshold "c".

Singling Out Attack

In cases where an adversary knows some background knowledge from the QI attributes existing in the data set, it will be easy to deduce information about the sensitive attribute values. Singling out attack is realized when there is a chance to isolate some or all the records that identify an individual in the data set (Križan, Brakus & Vukelić, 2015), (Hu, Stalla-Bourdillon, Yang, Schiavo & Sassone, 2015). Such attack may occur even if all the buckets existing in an anonymized data set include distinct values with respect to sensitive attributes since those distinct values within buckets are corresponding to a specific category that may provide a single meaning. Permutation technique alone is insufficient to reasonably mitigate the singling out risk (Hu et al., 2015). The l-diversity technique is unable to resist against this type of attacks. However, K-anonymity is considered robust against singling out attack (Hu et al., 2015).

Inference Attack

An Inference Attack is a data mining technique achieved by analyzing the data in order to gain a significant knowledge about an individual. The term inference indicates the possibility to know with remarkable probability, the values belonging to an individual from the values of other attributes (Hu et al., 2015). Therefore, data can be traced to individuals based on the logical deductions (Toledo & Spruit, 2016). By applying k-anonymity technique, the inference attack remains a risk. However, by applying the permutation technique, the inference attack is no more a risk (Hu et al., 2015). Furthermore, l-diversity technique is able to mitigate the risk of inference to a probability of no more than 1/L.

Proximity Attack

Also called semantic similarity attack, it occurs when some or all records are semantically similar within buckets in the anonymized data set (Saeed & Rauf, 2018), (Toledo & Spruit, 2016). Existing diversity models especially those for hierarchical data are unable to capture the semantic similarity between sensitive values within buckets in the data set. Thus, a technique based on l-diversity principle may cause serious similarity attacks (Wang, Han, Wang & Wang, 2014). Although k-anonymity is a good anonymization technique ensuring privacy in big data, it cannot resist against proximity attack. Even if the distinct l-diversity technique is robust against inference attack, it fails to resist against semantic similarity attack. Thus, many improvements of k-anonymity and l-diversity techniques have been proposed with t-closeness being one of the strictest privacy models (Wang, Zhu, Chen & Chang, 2018). El Ouazzani and El Bakkali (2018b) proposed a new way to resist against proximity attack when treating hierarchical categorical data.

Blockchain-Based Privacy Preserving Solutions

Blockchains are generally defined as tamper resistant and distributed ledgers (i.e., without a trusted third party or a central repository) to enable a community of participants, organized as a p2p (peer-to-peer) network, to record transactions (and possibly other kind of data) in this shared ledger, such that no transaction can be changed once published as shown in Figure 3 (NIST, 2019). Thus, it allows parties without prior trust or knowledge to collaborate securely (and pseudo-anonymously) via the use of a permanent, immutable, verifiable and transparent ledger that records all data exchanges or transactions processing without a need of a central authority. Each node of the p2p network maintains a copy of the block chain where each block (corresponding to a transaction) is linked to the prior block (by containing its hash) until the first one.

Figure 3. Blockchain transactions (NIST, 2019)

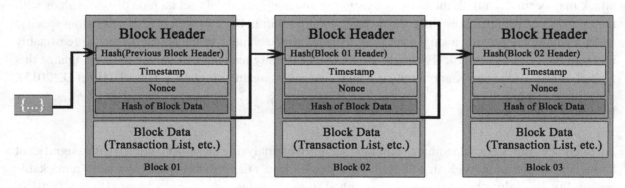

In addition to distribution and replication, the security features of the blockchain technology rely on the use of cryptographic algorithms like ECDSA (Elliptic Curve Digital Signature Algorithm) and hash functions (like SHA256). Generally, the ECDSA private key of a participant is used to digitally sign transactions while the public key is used to derive its address. For more technical details, interested readers could refer to (NIST, 2019.

Recently, blockchain technology has been applied to different domains, extending beyond the financial and banking sector (for which Bitcoin was the first use case), and ranging from Supply-Chain industry, Transport, Energy… to Education and Governance. Particularly, blockchain technology seems to be tailored to the Digital health sector due to its potential to offer an effective and transparent way to protect patient privacy while using, sharing, and processing e-health records by different healthcare stakeholders. Moreover, using blockchain technology in e-health increases transparency and trust in the means used to preserve patients' privacy, while allowing them to be active actors.

The majority of blockchain-based privacy preserving solutions in the e-health sector privileges the use of a consortium permissioned blockchain which is a kind of a hybrid model between private (all the nodes pertain to the same organization and no access to the blockchain is given to the public) and public blockchains (as the original bitcoin's blockchain where access is open to the public). In fact, in a consortium permissioned blockchain each participant is known in advance by the others and already have been authorized.

In this section, some recent work on the use of blockchain technology in e-health context will be presented to show how this technology could provide a secure environment for healthcare data sharing and allows patients to participate in managing access to their data. For example, each patient could set his medical record so as to require a number of credentials before allowing access (that could be total or partial) to healthcare actors.

At this purpose, Hirtan et al. (2019) propose a blockchain-based system where a patient' critical information regarding his medical analyses is shared between hospitals, medical laboratories and research institutes based on access policies defined by the patient. Indeed, and in order to protect confidential data, this solution deploys two types of chains: a private that gives information about real ID of the patients, and a public that stores information about patients' health data using a temporary ID.

Another interesting blockchain and IoT based solution (Griggs et al., 2018) is a system based on a permissioned consortium blockchain that stores all transactions and events among IoT sensors and smart devices. This solution is intended for medical interventions and real-time patient monitoring by allowing automatic notification –via the use of smart contract- of the responsible physician when his patient is in critical situation. The use of the blockchain allows a secure and transparent recording of health information under the control of both the patient and his doctor.

Another solution based on a permissioned blockchain that includes healthcare providers, insurance companies, and patients is proposed in (Bhuiyan et al., 2018). The authors start from the assumptions that each participant will find a value in sharing data with the others and that the patient controls who has access to his data and when. They then propose a three-tier architecture that consists of 3 distinct layers: the application layer (for user access management), the blockchain layer and the encrypted database layer (that stores all the health records). The blockchain layer interacts with the other layers, the nodes and a key authoring entity (responsible for generating the public/private key pairs for all the nodes)in order to ensure data privacy and security. This work has not yet proposed a proof of concept or a prototype of their solution.

There exist also some interesting surveys and reviews on the use of blockchain technology in e-health. Alonso et al. (2019) presented a review of the existing blockchain-focused research works in the literature, from which 18 are applied in e-Health. They particularly present the possible research trends related to the adoption of this technology in e-health. According to this review, challenges such as scalability, security, privacy and profitability of blockchain technology will require more research before large-scale production implementations. In the same line, an interesting survey of a wide applications area (with a particular attention given to e-health) and its implementation challenges was presented in (Mohanta, Jena, Panda & Sobhanayak, 2019). The main focus of this survey is on security and privacy concerns that arise from the adoption of blockchain technology in e-health. Yet, some researchers such as Feng et al. (2019) focused only on privacy. Other surveys such as (McGhin, Choo, Liu & He, 2019) while exposing a number of advantages related to the adoption of blockchain in e-health, it addresses specific issues such as: scalability, mining incentives, blockchain specific attacks, and key management/key leakage.

All the aforementioned work show the promising potential of blockchain technology in preserving privacy particularly in the e-health domain, however it is important to be aware that blockchain (specially, the permissioned type), has many limitations as that all smart contracts are executed sequentially by all the nodes. In this context, the trust model is not flexible, the difficulty to add other participants and many performance and scalability challenges. By passing such limitations seems to be a prerequisite to take really advantage of the blockchain technology in preserving privacy in the e-health sector.

The authors hope that this section will help interested researchers to try to overcome these limitations and build new approaches based on efficient architectures allowing a consent-based patient data sharing and usage. This way the patient becomes more and more engaged with his care and more reassured about his privacy.

FUTURE RESEARCH DIRECTIONS

The expansion of e-health information systems, platforms and mobile applications will certainly continue to be a way to offer more reliable, up-to-date and easily exploitable health data, for serving the interests of not only healthcare providers, but also, research centers, governments and, above all, patients.

To maintain this expansion without scarifying patient privacy, researchers in the security field should try to propose more efficient and innovative ways of preserving his privacy.

Some of the promising and interesting research directions in this context are:

- Proposition of means to verify if Access Control policies of healthcare providers correspond to their privacy policies while allowing fine grained access control and respect of "Need to know" principle. In fact, each healthcare actor needs to know only a part of the patient health data (for example, for a doctor, the policy will give only data that is significant to his specialty)
- Proposition of more efficient and resistant anonymization techniques that preserve data utility in order to enable to open more health data sets to feed AI algorithms and allow more research innovation in the health sector.
- Proposition of blockchain-based solutions that could provide granular and real-time access to health data while being able to verify automatically the conformance to both privacy policies and patient preferences, this could also improve coordination among the different actors and resistance to privacy and security attacks.

For researchers from the cryptography field, cryptographic-based research directions include efficient processing of encrypted data, encrypted search and so on.

To summarize, it is clear that the road to an "ideal" privacy preserving solution for digital health applications is still scattered with many challenges which will need the effort of many researches from the security field.

CONCLUSION

Due to the explosive amount of sensitive health data generated by digital health applications and devices, patients are more and more becoming the most vulnerable actor among the different stakeholders. In fact, recent digital health systems developments seem to contribute directly in the aggravation of patient's privacy violation risks. In this chapter, the authors presented first some related privacy concepts and definitions, especially in the digital health context. In addition, they described the main e-health stakeholders and the technologies behind the rise of digital health. Moreover, the authors highlighted the negative impact of these technologies on the patient's privacy. Since the healthcare organizations privacy policies could allow the sharing of patient's data even without its consent in order to allow research innovation in the healthcare sector.

In this context, the chapter focused on presenting three categories of privacy-preserving techniques that have been proposed recently to make a balance, on the one hand, between privacy policies and patient preferences (powered by privacy laws), and on the other hand, between patient data anonymity and its utility for researchers and other stakeholders.

REFERENCES

Abouelmehdi, K., Hssane, A. B., & Khaloufi, H. (2017). Big healthcare data: Preserving security and privacy. Springer. *Journal of Big Data*, 5(1), 1–18. doi:10.118640537-017-0110-7

Alonso, S., Basañez, J., Lopez-Coronado, M., & De la Torre Díez, I. (2019). Proposing New Blockchain Challenges in eHealth. *Journal of Medical Systems*, 43. PMID:30729329

Alpert, S. (2003). Protecting medical privacy: Challenges in the age of genetic information. *The Journal of Social Issues*, 59(2), 301–322. doi:10.1111/1540-4560.00066

Anushree, R., & Rio, G.L.D. (2019). Big Data Anonymization in Cloud using k-Anonymity Algorithm using Map Reduce Framework. *International Journal of Scientific Research in Computer Science, Engineering and Information Technology*, 50-56.

Barth, A., Mitchell, J. C., & Rosenstein, J. (2004).Conflict and combination in privacy policy languages. In *Proceeding of the workshop on Privacy in the electronic society (WPES)* (pp. 45-46). ACM. 10.1145/1029179.1029195

Basu, S., & Munns, C. (2016). *Privacy and Healthcare Data "Choice of Control" to "Choice" and "Control"*. Routledge. doi:10.4324/9781315602202

Baumer, D., Earp, J., & Poindexter, J. C. (2004). Internet privacy law: A comparison between the United States and the European Union. *Journal of Computer Security*, 23(5), 400–412. doi:10.1016/j.cose.2003.11.001

Bhuiyan, M. Z. A., Zaman, A., Wang, T., Wang, G., Tao, H., & Hassan, M. M. (2018). Blockchain and Big Data to Transform the Healthcare. *Proceedings of the International Conference on Data Processing and Applications*, 62–68. 10.1145/3224207.3224220

Biswas, S., Mazuz, K., & Mendes, R. A. (2014). E-Healthcare Disparities Across Cultures. *International Journal of User-Driven Healthcare, 4*(4), 1–16. doi:10.4018/IJUDH.2014100101

Borking, J., & Raab, C. (2001). Laws, PETs and Other Technologies for Privacy Protection. *Journal of Information, Law and Technology.* Available at SSRN: https://ssrn.com/abstract=3034261

Breaux, T. D., & Rao, A. (2013). Formal analysis of privacy requirements specifications for multi-tier applications. In *Proceeding of the 21st IEEE International Requirements Engineering Conference (RE).* (pp. 14-23). Rio de Janeiro: IEEE. 10.1109/RE.2013.6636701

Burmester, M., Desmedt, Y., Wright, R., & Yasinsac, A. (2002). Security or Privacy, Must We Choose? In *Proceeding of the Symposium on Critical Infrastructure Protection and the Law* (pp. 1-8). Academic Press.

Canadian Nurses Association. (2003). Privacy and Health Information: Challenges for Nurses and for The Nursing Profession. *Ethics in Practice for Registered Nurses.*

Canbay, Y., Vural, Y., & Sagiroglu, S. (2018). Privacy Preserving Big Data Publishing. In *International Congress on Big Data, Deep Learning and Fighting Cyber Terrorism (IBIGDELFT)* (pp. 24-29). Ankara, Turkey: IEEE. 10.1109/IBIGDELFT.2018.8625358

Cavoukian, A., & Tapscott, D. (1997). *Who Knows: Safeguarding Your Privacy in a Networked World.* McGraw-Hill Professional Publisher.

Data Protection Laws of the World. (2019). *Technical report. DLAPIPER.* https://www.dlapiperdata-protection.com

Department of Biomedical Informatics at Harvard Medical School. (2018). *n2c2 builds on the legacy of i2b2.* Available from https://dbmi.hms.harvard.edu/programs/healthcare-data-science-program/clinical-nlp-research-data-sets

Dong, L., Xianmang, H., LongBin, C., & Huahui, C. (2016). Permutation anonymization. *Journal of Intelligent Information Systems Archive, 47*(3), 427-445.

El Ouazzani, Z., & El Bakkali, H. (2017). New Technique Ensuring Privacy in Big Data: Variable t-Closeness for Sensitive Numerical Attributes. In *The 3rd International Conference on Cloud Computing and Technology Application (CloudTech'17),* (pp. 1-6). IEEE.

El Ouazzani, Z., & El Bakkali, H. (2018a). A new technique ensuring privacy in big data: K-anonymity withoutprior value of the threshold k. In *Proceeding of The First International Conference On Intelligent Computing in Data Sciences.* (pp. 52 - 59). Elsevier. 10.1016/j.procs.2018.01.097

El Ouazzani, Z., & El Bakkali, H. (2018b). Proximity Test for Sensitive Categorical Attributes in Big Data. In *Proceeding of the 4th International Conference on Cloud Computing Technologies and Applications (Cloudtech).* IEEE, 10.1109/CloudTech.2018.8713359

El Ouazzani, Z., & El Bakkali, H. (2019a). Privacy in Big Data Through Variable t-Closeness for MSN Attributes. In M. Zbakh, M. Essaaidi, P. Manneback, & C. Rong (Eds.), *Cloud Computing and Big Data: Technologies, Applications and Security (CloudTech 2017). Lecture Notes in Networks and Systems. 49* (pp. 52–59). Elsevier.

El Ouazzani, Z., & El Bakkali, H. (2019b). Variable Distinct L-diversity Algorithm Applied on Highly Sensitive Correlated Attributes. In *The Fifteenth International Conference on Wireless and Mobile Communications (ICWMC),* (pp. 47-52). Rome, Italy: ThinkMind.

Feng, Q., He, D., Zeadally, S., Khan, K., & Kumar, N. (2019). A survey on privacy protection in blockchain system. *Journal of Network and Computer Applications, 126,* 45–58. doi:10.1016/j.jnca.2018.10.020

Feruza, Y., & Kim, T.-H. (2007). IT Security Review: Privacy, Protection, Access Control. *Assurance and System Security., 2*(2), 17–32.

Förster, D., Löhr, H., & Kargl, F. (2015). Decentralized enforcement of k-anonymity for location privacy using secret sharing. In *Vehicular Networking Conference (VNC)* (pp. 279 - 286). Kyoto, Japan: IEEE. 10.1109/VNC.2015.7385589

Gandomi, A., & Haider, M. (2015). Beyond the hype: Big data concepts, methods and analytics. *International Journal of Information Management, 35*(2), 137–144. doi:10.1016/j.ijinfomgt.2014.10.007

Gawanmeh, A., & Alomari, A. (2015). Challenges in Formal Methods for Testing and Verification of Cloud Computing Systems. *Journal of Scalable Computing: Practice and Experience, 16*(3), 321–332. doi:10.12694cpe.v16i3.1104

Gilson, L. (2012). *Health Policy and Systems Research: A Methodology Reader.* Alliance for Health Policy and Systems Research and World Health Organization. Retrieved from https://www.who.int/alliance-hpsr/alliancehpsr_reader.pdf

Griggs, K. N., Ossipova, O., Kohlios, C. P., Baccarini, A. N., Howson, E. A., & Hayajneh, T. (2018). Healthcare Blockchain System Using Smart Contracts for Secure Automated Remote Patient Monitoring. *Journal of Medical Systems, 42*(7), 130. doi:10.100710916-018-0982-x PMID:29876661

Hassan, F., Domingo-Ferrer, J., & Soria-Comas, J. (2018). Anonymization of Unstructured Data via Named-Entity Recognition. In V. Torra, Y. Narukawa, I. Aguiló, & M. González-Hidalgo (Eds.), *Modeling Decisions for Artificial Intelligence. MDAI 2018* (pp. 296–305). Springer International Publishing. doi:10.1007/978-3-030-00202-2_24

Healthcare Data Breach Report. (2019). *HIPAA Journal.* Retrieved from https://www.hipaajournal.com/august-2019-healthcare-data-breach-report/

Hirtan, L., Krawiec, P., Dobre, C., & Batalla, J. (2019). Blockchain-Based Approach for e-Health Data Access Management with Privacy Protection. In *Proceeding of the 24th International Workshop on Computer Aided Modeling and Design of Communication Links and Networks (CAMAD).* (pp. 1-7). IEEE. 10.1109/CAMAD.2019.8858469

Hu, R., Stalla-Bourdillon, S., Yang, Mu., Schiavo, V., & Sassone, V. (2017). Regulation, and Practice? A Techno-Legal Analysis of Three Types of Data in the GDPR. In Data Protection and Privacy: The Age of Intelligent Machines. Academic Press.

Jain, P., Gyanchandani, M., & Khare, N. (2019). Improved k-Anonymity Privacy-Preserving Algorithm Using Madhya Pradesh State Election Commission Big Data. In A. Krishna, K. Srikantaiah, & C. Naveena (Eds.), *Integrated Intelligent Computing, Communication and Security. Studies in Computational Intelligence, 771* (pp. 1–10). Singapore: Springer. doi:10.1007/978-981-10-8797-4_1

Kaplan, B. (2014). *Patient health data privacy.* Available at: https://papers.ssrn.com/sol3/papers.cfm?abstract_id=2510429

Khurat, A., Boontawee, S., & Dieter, G. (2017). Privacy policies verification in composite services using OWL. *Journal of Computer Security, 67,* 122–141. doi:10.1016/j.cose.2017.02.015

Križan, T., Brakus, M., & Vukelić, D. (2015). In-Situ Anonymization of Big Data. In *Proceeding of the 38th International Convention on Information and Communication Technology, Electronics and Microelectronics (MIPRO)* (pp. 292-298). Opatija, Croatia: IEEE.

McGhin, T., Choo, K.-K. R., Liu, C., & He, D. (2019). Blockchain in healthcare applications: Research challenges and opportunities. *Journal of Network and Computer Applications, 135,* 135. doi:10.1016/j.jnca.2019.02.027

Mohanta, B., Jena, D., Panda, S. & Sobhanayak, S. (2019). Blockchain Technology: A Survey on Applications and Security Privacy Challenges. *Journal of Internet of Things,* 100-107.

Naish, M. (2014). *Implementing Public Key Infrastructure (PKI) Using Microsoft Windows Server 2012 Certificate Services.* Digital Certificates.

Nargundi, S., & Phalnikar, R. (2013). Data De-Identification Tool for Privacy Preserving Data Mining. *International Journal of Computer Science Engineering and Information Technology Research, 3*(1), 267–276.

National committee on vital and health statistics. (2006). Functional Requirements Needed for the Initial Definition of a Nationwide Health Information Network (NHIN). *Report to the Secretary of the U.S. Department of Health and Human Services.* Retrieved from https://ncvhs.hhs.gov/wp-content/uploads/2014/05/061030lt.pdf

NIST National Institute of Standards and Technology Us Department of Commerce. (n.d.). *Blockchain.* Retrieved from https://www.nist.gov/topics/blockchain

Parimala, S. (2017). A Survey on Security and Privacy Issues of BigData in Healthcare Industry and Implication of Predictive analytics. *International Journal of Innovative Research in Computer and Communication Engineering, 5*(4), 8130–8134.

PCORI Patient-Centered Outcomes Research Institute. (2019). *Improving Outcomes Important to Patients.* Retrieved from https://www.pcori.org

Rajendran, K., Jayabalan, M., & Rana, M. E. (2017). A Study on k-anonymity, l-diversity, and t-closeness techniques focusing Medical Data. *International Journal of Computer Science and Network Security*, *17*(12), 172–177.

Sadki, S. & EL Bakkali, H. (2016). Resolving conflicting privacy policies in m-healthbased on prioritization. *Journal of Scalable Computing: Practice & Experience*, 17.

Saeed, R., & Rauf, A. (2018). Anatomization through generalization (AG): A hybrid privacy-preserving approach to prevent membership, identity and semantic similarity disclosure attacks. In *The International Conference on Computing, Mathematics and Engineering Technologies (iCoMET)* (pp. 1-7). Sukkur, Pakistan: Academic Press.

Seastrom M. (2011). *Data Stewardship: Managing Personally Identifiable Information in Electronic Student Education Records*. Technical/Methodological Report. National Center for Education Statistics (NCES 2011-602).

Sei, Y., Takenouchi, T., & Ohsuga, A. (2015). (l1, ...,lq)-diversity for Anonymizing Sensitive Quasi-Identifiers. *IEEE Journal of Trustcom/BigDataSE/ISPA*, 596-603.

Seol, K., Kim, Y., Lee, E., Seo, Y., & Baik, D. (2018). Privacy-Preserving Attribute-Based Access Control Model for XML-Based Electronic Health Record System. *IEEE Access : Practical Innovations, Open Solutions*, *6*, 9114–9128. doi:10.1109/ACCESS.2018.2800288

Shaw, T., Mcgregor, D., Brunner, M., Keep, M., Janssen, A., & Barnet, S. (2017). What is eHealth (6)? Development of a Conceptual Model for eHealth: Qualitative Study with Key Informants. *Journal of Medical Internet Research*, *19*(10), e324. doi:10.2196/jmir.8106 PMID:29066429

Shouling, J., Prateek, M., & Raheem, B. (2017). Graph Data Anonymization, De-Anonymization Attacks, and De-Anonymizability Quantification: A Survey. *IEEE Communications Surveys and Tutorials*, *19*(2), 1305–1326. doi:10.1109/COMST.2016.2633620

Solove, D. J. (2002). Conceptualizing privacy. *California Law Review*, *90*(4), 1087–1155. doi:10.2307/3481326

The biggest healthcare data breaches. (2018). *Healthcare IT News magazine*. Retrieved from https://www.healthcareitnews.com/projects/biggest-healthcare-data-breaches-2018-so-far

The Right to Privacy in Singapore. (1999). *Privacy International*. Technical report.

Toledo, C. V., & Spruit, M. R. (2016). Adopting Privacy Regulations in a Data Warehouse A Case of the Anonimity versus Utility Dilemma. In *The 8th International Joint Conference on Knowledge Discovery, Knowledge Engineering and Knowledge Management (IC3K 2016)* (pp. 67 - 72). Porto, Portugal: Academic Press.

Vimarlund, V. (2011). Capturing the Value of IT investments in Health and Social Care. *International conference in e-Health*.

Wang, H., Han, J., Wang, J., & Wang, L. (2014). (l, e)-Diversity-A Privacy Preserving Model to Resist Semantic Similarity Attack. *Journal of Computers*, *9*(1), 59–65. doi:10.4304/jcp.9.1.59-64

Wang, M., Jiang, Z., & Yang, H. (2018). T-Closeness Slicing: A New Privacy Preserving Approach for Transactional Data Publishing. *INFORMS Journal on Computing*, *30*(3), 1–34. doi:10.1287/ijoc.2017.0791

Wang, R., Zhu, Y., Chen, T., & Chang, C. (2018). Privacy-Preserving Algorithms for Multiple Sensitive Attributes Satisfying t-Closeness. *Journal of Computer Science and Technology*, *33*(6), 1231–1242. doi:10.100711390-018-1884-6

Wang, X., Chou, J., Chen, W., Guan, H., Chen, W., Lao, T., & Ma, K. (2018).A Utility-Aware Visual Approach for Anonymizing Multi-Attribute Tabular Data. *Proceeding of The IEEE Transactions on Visualization and Computer Graphics*, *24*, 351-360. [Doi:10.1109/TBDATA.2018.2829886]. 10.1109/TVCG.2017.2745139

Yang, Y., Zheng, X., Guo, W., Liu, X., & Chang, V. (2018). Privacy-preserving fusion of IoT and big data for e-health. *Journal of Future Generation Computer Systems*, *86*, 1437–1455. doi:10.1016/j.future.2018.01.003

Chapter 13
Public Services and Evolution of Smart Cities:
The Public Administration at the Service of the Citizenship

Magdalena Suárez
Universidad Complutense de Madrid, Spain

ABSTRACT

The smart city is a concept that began to take shape at the end of the last century, emerging as a consequence of the real evolution of urban requirements. Whilst in bygone eras the need arose to equip cities with elements such as security, public health services, and public adornment, which were primordial for development of said cities, nowadays the—increasingly demanding—citizenry calls for a type of services related to the introduction of information and communications technology (ICT), aside from the cities' own evolution, as well as growth of the social and environmental capital. A smart city could be defined as a city which uses information and communications technology to ensure that both its critical infrastructure and the public services and components it offers are more interactive and efficient and that citizens can become more aware of them.

INTRODUCTION

Smart cities have taken up the latest efforts of doctrine to shape an all-encompassing concept of the phenomenon. The work of public administrations, international consultancy firms, business schools and the private sector have shown themselves to be diligent in this task. But above all, the intense work of standardisation entities has given it a structure endowed with a technical and organisational nature that was hitherto unknown. The fundamental interest of public interest was associated to the criteria of the Digital Agenda, and therefore the crucial point for us to be able to speak of smart cities is precisely the utilisation of ICTs in the management of public services. Regulation, which is basically focussed on promotion activity, centres on giving greater prominence to smart territories, after the calls for tenders of smart cities.

DOI: 10.4018/978-1-7998-3817-3.ch013

Copyright © 2020, IGI Global. Copying or distributing in print or electronic forms without written permission of IGI Global is prohibited.

SMART CITIES AND INTELLIGENCE APPLIED TO CITIES

Utopia, Dystopia, E-Topia

One could say that a reflection on smart cities once again includes new utopian elements in the discourse of urbanization, elements based on the Platonic city, Aristotelian discourse when in *Politics* he refers to the urban utopia of Hippodamus, and naturally the great reflection on *Utopia* by Thomas More or Saint Augustine's *The City of God*. Also Rabelais', *La Città del Sole* by Tomaso Campanella and *The New Atlantis* by Francis Bacon. One may well say that the ideal city as a basic element of relations between subjects has been the object of permanent analysis, given the importance of the human being within the space he inhabits and the condition of territoriality which forms the basis of his decisions.

Today we are faced with complex, confused societies which do however demand public services and are avid when incorporating new technologies into cities in such a way that the efficiency attained has a direct and indirect influence on improving citizens' quality of life.

On the one hand, this leads to complexity in management. There are two elements of progress in relation to the functioning of public administrations: the introduction of elements of town planning information allowing feedback on public actions to be obtained from the citizenry (one example is the Think Tank Platforms) and other elements designed to make public management more dynamic by applying the principles of governance or the incorporation of open data.

Contemporary society is contradictory: it wishes to include technology immediately, but at the same time human activity becomes useless and in turn generates dependence with regard to electronic systems, leading to a permanent feeling of dissatisfaction.

The Concept and Evolution of Smart Cities

The smart city is a concept that began to take shape at the end of the last century, emerging as a consequence of the real evolution of urban requirements. Whilst in bygone eras the need arose to equip cities with elements such as security, public health services and public adornment, which were primordial for development of said cities, nowadays the - increasingly demanding - citizenry calls for a type of services related to the introduction of information and communications technology (ICT), aside from the cities' own evolution, as well as growth of the social and environmental capital.

A smart city could be defined "as a city which uses information and communications technology to ensure that both its critical infrastructure and the public services and components it offers are more interactive and efficient and that citizens can become more aware of them".

In a broader definition, a city may be deemed "smart" when the investments in human and social capital, and in communications infrastructure, promote precisely a sustainable economic development and a high quality of life, with judicio us management of natural resources through a participative government" (Telefónica: 2011).

The discussion on how we should define a smart city has caused rivers of ink to flow and given rise to intense debates. There were several questions: whether a city could be smart or its authorities and inhabitants truly were smart; whether cities that are not digitally adapted could not be smart; whether the designs of classical cities (Athens, Rome, Paris, London…) or "ideal cities" were not living examples of talent in spite of having introduced new technology, because obviously, these did not exist.

Without doubt, all this holds great meaning and at the very least deserves some careful reflection. What is clear today is that when we speak of smart cities, we are referring to a phenomenon that occurs as a consequence of the technology revolution[1] which, at a given time, translates – as is to be expected – into the city. ICTs leave their natural spaces of data management and the astonishing boost of the communications media and over time, technological development and perfection begin to give responses to the events and services that take place in cities.

Of the many definitions that exist[2], I propose that offered by the CNT 178 (Technical Standardisation Committee of the Association of Standardisation of Spain), "A smart city is the holistic vision of a city that applies ICTs to improve the quality of life and accessibility of its inhabitants and ensures sustainable economic, social and environmental development which improves permanently. It allows citizens to interact with it in a multidisciplinary manner and adapts in real time to their needs in a way that is efficient in terms of quality and costs, offering open data, solutions and services geared towards citizens as people".

In this way, what smart cities seek is to provide a response to social needs, employing the new technological instruments available, but it is not an absolute category, since cities still have the same environmental, historical, tourism-related and ethnographical commitments or any other commitments that may be present in their everyday reality. As a result, we are faced with terminological clarifications such as those made by UN-HABITAT[3], introducing the concept of resilience (*smart and resilient cities*), i.e. cities that are prepared for change and capable of overcoming situations of crisis or adversity (environmental tragedies or extreme violence).

In any case, technology applied to cities must also fulfil a role that integrates and generates common places of social dialogue. The utilisation of the space and time in everyday life can be positively amplified by using ICTs. There are already numerous examples of this (apps for people with disabilities, think-tanks, etc.)[4]. In addition, they can serve as a lever for circular economy and participatory economy initiatives.

Analysing the evolution of smart cities we can find two phases, from a scientific viewpoint.

1. A general reflection on the growth of cities, their sustainability and the participation of citizens when detecting town planning problems and resolving them. The North American studies in this area are worth mentioning in this regard (*Getting to Smart Growth*, University of Michigan, SHAPIRO: 2005). All of which is included within a process whereby new town planning strategies are generated to attain a higher level of wellbeing and the increased environmental integration of urban spaces.
2. Secondly, specific measures for action are on the increase, so that proposals manage to integrate the different town planning and building factors that are completed by ICT. The category of "The Internet of Things" is also included, creating a system to connect the different elements of the city. And open data elements are adopted by citizens.

Currently, the outlines of smart cities are diffused, but three basic lines of action can be profiled:

1. Energy efficiency and buildings
2. Energy supply networks
3. Mobility and transport

The Current Challenges of Smart Cities

Without a doubt, over recent years smart cities have been one of the most publicly relevant issues on a political level (although perhaps not on a dissemination level). On this occasion, the private sector and the public administrations have driven a model supported by three fundamental pillars: standardisation, industry and governance. As a consequence of this, several calls for subsidies of smart cities were made, as part of the Digital Agenda and the numerous standards produced within the UNE[5]. Because of all this, it is understood that Spain and Dubai represent the two successful all-inclusive conceptual models for smart cities. Those whose influence may apparently attain the greatest development[6].

Currently, the provision of innovative public services has had to deal with questions such as:Overcoming the understanding that services cannot be understood unequivocally, but that there is a relation between them: as a result, the "vertical concept" had to be transformed into a "platform" model.

- Cities are similar to living organisms, but they also have a unitary dimension. The IoT – the Internet of Things – leads one to look at buildings in an individualised manner, with the possibility that the information they transmit is highly valuable for the city as a whole, within which there are emblematic points (football stadia, airports, metro stations, department stores, to give some examples).
- As we will see later, the current problems have passed from smart cities to smart territories
- Smart islands pose singularities because they are particularly attractive and environmentally fragile.Smart tourism destinations have had a special impact given that 12% of Spain's GDP comes from tourism income. There can be no doubt that the tension between the stable population and the fluctuation of people of 20%40% in certain periods cannot be dealt with using an ordinary local management system.

The implantation of the new formulae proposed by smart cities force the transformation of structures as well, as with any situation of change. In our country at present, and having overcome the initial phases, we are faced with the following challenges:Adoption of common information systems so that the efforts employed in the implementation of models may serve as a model within the strategy of digital and research.

- Reaching consensus in the common naming of actions and objects in order to facilitate the flow of data.
- Utilisation of standardised, open services for the purpose of propitiating interoperability between the same.
- Management capacity of big data and possibility of offering Rich Communication Services (RCS).

THE PROPOSALS OF THE EUROPEAN UNION

The European Union Policies

European policies on smart cities are expressed through the search for environmentally sustainable surroundings, in an attempt to improve quality of life in view of the quest for energy efficiency and the reduction of carbon emissions. In harmony with the Green Digital Charter. The European innovation partnership on smart cities and communities (EIP-SCC) is an initiative supported by the European Commission that brings together cities, industry, small business (SMEs), banks, research and others.

In this regard, the initiative is included in the current EU and national policies and programmes, such as CIVITAS, CONCERTO and Intelligent Energy Europe. It will also be based on the other SET-Plans of industrial initiatives, in particular the solar grill and electricity. Influence will also be brought to bear on the EU initiative which unites public and private initiatives for green vehicles and buildings established in the European Economic Recovery Plan (Communication of 29 October – COM(2008) 706) adopted to minimize the effects of the crisis on citizens. These measures will work in harmony with the principles established in the Covenant of Mayors (4388 signatories) in its commitment to local sustainable energy, which will foreseeably allow for its impact to be expanded.

The goals of the proposals are:

- To activate sufficient assimilation in citizens (reaching 5% of the EU population) of efficient energy and lowcarbon technologies and to unlock the market.
- To reduce greenhouse gases from emissions by 40% by the year 2020, demonstrating not only the benefits in terms of energy and environmental safety, but also in order to create social and economic advantages in terms of quality of life, local employment and companies and citizen empowerment.
- To favour a system of improved European practices of the concepts of sustainable energy on a local level, driven, as we mentioned, by the Covenant of Mayors.

The European Union Action Measures Applied to Smart Cities

The theory on smart cities is crystallized in a series of specific action measures.

Within the scope of the European Union, the aim is to attain the following goals:

1. Buildings: Establish a trial system on 100 new homes and 100 new non-residential buildings for different design options for zero energy buildings in different climate zones. Test and assess, through programmes, the strategies for renovation of at least 50% of current public buildings (including social housing buildings, non-residential buildings, etc.). Apart from the technologies, innovative financing systems and rehabilitation techniques will be developed and tested, along with strategies for the complete renovation of 50% of all existing buildings (for example residential buildings, public buildings, non-residential buildings, etc.).
2. Energy Networks
   a. Heating and Air Conditioning: To introduce demonstration programmes for widespread deployment of renewable energies for heating and refrigeration in cities, supplying 50% of the heat and demand for cooling.
   b. Electricity: The priority consists of testing the intelligent network concept in collaboration with local distribution companies, and to do so the development and deployment programme will be prioritized focussing on high-efficiency lighting devices and intelligent measuring. The cooperation of all the pertinent information of the ESET Plan will also be promoted, as will priority access for local generation and renewable electricity, smart meters, storage and response to demand.

3. Transport: The goal is to set in motion test programmes for the large-scale deployment of alternative fuel vehicles, ranging from public road transport and municipal fleets to private passenger vehicles (electric, hydrogen and fuel battery vehicles, low-consumption vehicles, natural gas and biofuel vehicles, etc.), including the fuel / energy supply infrastructure.

Moreover, the development and trial programmes centred on sustainable mobility, including the advanced mode of smart public transport, intelligent traffic management and prevention of congestion, management of demand, information and communication, distribution of goods, on foot and by bicycle.

If we examine the set of measures developed in the international sphere in detail, the series of initiatives could be summarized as:

- The area of mobility; the aim is to establish criteria of sustainability, safety and efficiency of infrastructures and transport systems, including local, national and international accessibility. To achieve this formulae can be established such as realtime traffic information, areas where building work is going on, the introduction of timing in traffic lights, etc. With regard to public transport, dynamic information systems have been introduced. On motorway the "telepayment" toll system and in private transport, media used for electric vehicles or initiatives such as i Car you (vehicle-pooling establishing communications from mobile devices).
- Environmental measures: energy efficiency, bringing instant consumption monitoring devices into homes, connected to the network (Home energy monitoring) with the aim of introducing citizens to the concept of responsible consumption. There are also initiatives to improve the treatment of urban solid waste (capacity sensors) and improve the automation system for watering parks and gardens. The measuring of environmental parameters and information in real time (isochronics, taxi movements, pollen concentration, air quality, water, humidity, temperature, etc.).
- Management of infrastructures and public buildings (immotics).
- Steps tending to establish measures for transparency and participation in decisionmaking. One fairly popular initiative is eAdministration (*Web services Pilot* digital access to different administrative procedures), and the elements of eParticipation. As well as the growing tendency towards using open data as a formula for placing information in the hands of citizens.
- Improving public safety and health. With regard to the first point, the aim is to improve the response of the emergency services and introduce elements of telemonitoring and telemedicine (GPS bracelets, electronic clinical histories and electronic prescriptions). With regard to safety, the initiatives have been developed in the area of videosurveillance and crowd detection in mass events.
- Introduction of several services through the development of eCommerce (payments by mobile phone introducing NFC technology).

FROM SMART CITIES TO SMART TERRITORIES

Evolution of Smart Cities

City planning has always awoken fierce controversy and undoubtedly fruitful philosophical, scientific and cultural analysis. At present, moving beyond city analysis in a morphological way has given way to the generation of other paradigms such as social differences, segregation, ethnicity or criminality, propelled to a large extent by the Chicago School[7]. At the current time, cities are becoming important in themselves, because there is a clear tendency to adopt binding decisions for citizens at a supranational or international level; but also at a subnational level. It is clear that decisions of a regional nature largely shape the rights of citizens, which are decisively defined by said policies. But the role represented by municipalities in people's lives, their day-to-day business and the way in which their primary needs are absorbed, is not a lesser one.

In the issue of smart cities, the question appears to be posed in a strictly local way; that is to say, in principle the implantation of ICTs is heavily determined by the political decision itself; technical and economic capacity; the number of inhabitants and the effective signal reception. That is to say, it would appear that the perfect candidates are provincial capitals or medium-sized or large cities.

Evidently, with the phenomenon of globalisation, a real competitiveness has been established between cities, boosted by the constant production of rankings.

In this way, when the impetus of smart cities begins, what we are thinking of is large towns, cities. Particularities are established when we are dealing with tourist municipalities.

Beyond these initiatives, smart cities received a boost from government when they were included as a strategy within the Digital Agenda and the National Plan for Smart Cities was approved and subsidies began for projects for cities with certain adaptation characteristics, according to criteria of population or technological development through the public business entity Red.es.

But right now, the policies go further, having detected the situation in which many areas will never reach sufficient ratios in order to satisfactorily implement sustained policies in a digital environment. Which is why the Ministry of Energy, Tourism and Digital Agenda has approved the National Plan for Smart Territories[8], the strategic lines for which are as follows:

- Territorial actions: comprised of six areas: internal objects of cities (buildings, stations, ports and airports), 5G, Virtual Interoperability Laboratory, Smart Rural Territories, Smart Tourism and Public Services 4.0 in rural world and city platforms.
- Support actions: encompasses the actions that facilitate the territorial actions: boosting of Standardisation, actions of an international nature, governance of National Plan, communication, dissemination, instruction and training.
- Complementary actions: IoT for the provision of public services in Smart Territories and Mobility.

The Need to Find New Approaches for The Rural World

One of the questions which arouse the greatest concern and interest at present is that of offering a solution to ensure that the rural world can enter the digital world.

On occasions, we may not be entirely aware of the weight of the rural world on the national scene. The situation is as follows:

Using techniques derived from Geographical Information Systems (GIS) and in line with recent European literature, the need to integrate at least two other dimensions is defended: the intensity of human information on the territory — measured by the type of ground cover that prevails — and the degree of accessibility from rural municipalities to cities.

The result is a typological proposal that considers six different types of municipalities: open and closed urban and intermediate municipalities (according to the ground cover), and remote and accessible rural municipalities. The classification according to the uses of land is not discriminatory for rural municipalities, in the same way that, by definition, the dimension of accessibility does not affect urban municipalities.

The results indicate that 77.6% of municipalities are rural and open, whilst only 2% are urban and closed, and 58% of rural municipalities may be considered accessible. Remote rural municipalities represent the remaining 42.2% of rural municipalities, housing 30% of the total population of the latter (around two million people). The duration of travel from them to the closest city is 66 minutes. It was found that there is an appreciable level of heterogeneity on a provincial scale in terms of the more or less remote nature of the corresponding rural areas."

As well as this important significance, the measures adopted must be in accordance with Law 45/2007, of 13th December, for the sustainable development of the rural environment[9]. In this setting, several different challenges are posed, including that of achieving suitable methodological guidelines, based on:

- Establishing a measuring system based on the principles of efficiency, interoperability and transferability
- Determining "empathy maps" in order to discover real needs
- Determining strategies in terms of sustainability

It is extremely important to bear in mind that the rural medium is not susceptible to the flat application of the same norms as those established for smart cities. Rural communities suffer – at times severely – from depopulation and aging of their inhabitants. Therefore, the establishment of public services 4.0 demands a personalised format on the part of the authorities, bringing the provision of said public services closer; instead of moving large numbers of people, the services move, since the public administration is aware of the circumstances of this population because it has numerous administrative data.

The rural world needs to obtain the following from the application of ICTs to its territory: the possibility of fixing the population, attracting talent and generating opportunities without forfeiting identity.

The success of the policy on smart territories is based on a determining factor, the possibility of access to broadband and signal reception which, as can be seen, drops visibly when we find a place with a low population density or far from somewhere where network coverage is acceptable.

Undoubtedly this question brings with it the need to apply public funds; let us hope that the commitments of public policies move forward in this way and the new satellites (particularly Hispasat 30 W6) can satisfy broadband demands in remote locations. Together with this, it is imperative that some appropriate norms and criteria for assistance and training in the rural world be established in order to face up to these challenges. There do, however, appear to be some rays of hope: one valid example applied to date are the digital communities of Castilla y León whose lines of action are agreements with municipal entities and provincial governments[10].

The European Union: Territorial and Cohesion Policies and Environmental Policy

It is highly likely that the implantation of smart villages will not have a happy ending if it is not accompanied by a decisive stance on and application of energies on attempting to alleviate territorial, economic and social differences, along the lines established in the Treaty of Lisbon (articles 174 et seq.), which reads as follows:

"In order to promote its overall harmonious development, the Union shall develop and pursue its actions leading to the strengthening of its economic, social and territorial cohesion. In particular, the Union shall aim at reducing disparities between the levels of development of the various regions and the backwardness of the least favoured regions. Among the regions concerned, particular attention shall be paid to rural areas, areas affected by industrial transition, and regions which suffer from several and permanent natural or demographic handicaps such as the northernmost regions with very low population density and island, cross-border and mountain regions."

Therefore, the policies of the EU have also focussed on alleviating the deep income diversity found within the territory of the Union. This is due to different reasons, such as; improving the coordination of the different policies, moving forward in the integration process and strengthening the development of depressed regions for the purpose of consolidating and improving the functioning of the internal market[11].

As can be seen in the image, the differences in income between the different regions is notable, as a result of which logically enough the satisfactory implantation of smart territories will be more costly in general terms in a significant part of the European Union.

At present, a formula is being studied to allow for deployment of suitable public policies, acting on the different territorial levels. One of the criteria that can be followed is the delimitation employed by EUROSTAT which defines the territories of the EU in the categories NUTS 2 (which will coincide with Autonomous Communities) and NUTS 3 (Provinces).

Thus we shall see that this territorial policy is reconciled with the smart villages; until now, the ERDF (European Regional Social Development Fund) has been a relevant financier for the subsidies that Spain has allocated to the implantation and improvement of smart cities.

We must bear in mind that these smart cities will, in any case, be green cities, by the imperative logic of European community policies which establish as fundamental objectives of urban development that initiatives should maintain principles of environmental sustainability[12], directed at three strategic points:

1. Sustainable Urban Mobility, through utilisation of alternative energies, public transport, efficient logistics and correct planning.
2. Sustainable districts and constructed environment: improving the energy efficiency of buildings and districts, increasing the proportion of renewable energy sources used and the habitability of communities.
3. Integrated infrastructures and processes in Energy, ICT and Transport, connecting infrastructure assets to improve the efficiency and sustainability of cities.

The Digital Impulse on a National and International Level

As we have already pointed out, the implantation and use of technology is unavoidable if we are dealing with smart cities. It is no news that Spain is a leader in the boosting of standardisation systems through UNE[13]; there are now 23 standards that have been approved in all the areas imaginable which respond to the different needs for implantation of smart systems in cities. These standards are not compulsory and the proposal can come from the private sector. In this regard, the CTN 178 on smart cities has certainly been hard-working and dynamic[14]. This good work has had repercussions in the national leadership when it comes to proposing lines of action in international bodies.

Recently the ITU approved a series of document, outstanding from among which is the generation of KPIs, based on three large analysis blocks: an environment dimension, an economy dimension and a society and culture dimension.

More recently, Spain was a model in terms of adoptions of the ITU recommendations: ITU-T Y.4200: Requirements for the interoperability of smart city platforms, and ITU-T Y.4201: High-level requirements and reference framework of smart city platforms, based on UNE standard 178104 "Smart cities. Infrastructures. Integrated smart city management systems"[15].

SMART CITIES, ANTIDISCRIMINATION POLICIES AND UNIVERSAL ACCESIBILITY

The concept of Smart Cities has been defined, but we must find out how to create Smart Cities that are inclusive, accessible and friendly. The key to discovering the strategies we need to apply for the creation of these cities lies in guaranteeing all people's right to use these cities, promoting Universal Accessibility and Design for All, and boosting equal opportunities for all in terms of employability, training, health, etc…

This situation is achieved through the permanent collaboration of the technological community and citizens, with the common objective of improving the lives of people with disabilities and elderly people, and guaranteeing the fulfilment of the internationally-recognised rights of this group.

To achieve this, it is necessary to create new applications, improve existing ones and apply the concepts of universal accessibility and design for all. One emerging need is to fulfil the objectives of the United Nations Convention on the rights of persons with disabilities and contribute to reinforcing the world network of smart cities, guaranteeing the inclusion of all citizens. It is critical that we join the criteria of designers and citizens in order to share ideas and develop services and applications that are accessible for everyone, based on the opinion of people with disabilities and elderly people, as a guarantee of inclusion in cities and usability of the services, environments and products created.

Recently "Apps for All" was created, aimed at experts in web and mobile applications who work on creating accessible support tools for everyone. Amongst other objectives the challenge, which came into being coinciding with the 10th anniversary of the United Nations Convention on the rights of persons with disabilities, set those of removing barriers and improving ICT accessibility; moving towards the concept of universal accessibility; guaranteeing people with disabilities and elderly people an independent life that is not conditioned in terms of decision-making; facilitating people's rights through universal design and contributing to eliminate stigmas.

All of this is aimed at removing existing barriers, improving physical accessibility and accessibility to ICT, committing to the concept of universal accessibility and design for all, guaranteeing the improvement of the lives of people with disabilities and elderly persons, guaranteeing their full independence and social inclusion with dignity.

This is to say, it is a question of joining forces in a common project of mutual interest which improves the lives of everyone and in particular of one of the most vulnerable groups in society, people with disabilities and elderly people, with the aim of attaining universal technological solutions which are accessible for all citizens.

If we analyse the opinions of people and politicians regarding the decision-making and proposals made in the new idea of the city, we are shown how, amongst the main drivers behind Smart Cities, the citizen is the conspicuously absent figure, when citizens should occupy the place of the main agent.

The most essential points we must consider in the creation of the new cities of usage for all can be summed up in the following aspects.

- Smart spaces must be characterised by their accessibility, respect for the environment and integrate transport that facilitates the mobility of all.
- The inclusion and accessibility of smart cities must be achieved jointly, with the participation of both citizens and politicians, taking into consideration equality of conditions for the group of persons with disabilities and elderly people.

The full integration of people with disabilities and elderly people into the new city and the implications of incorporating new technology, as the base for the smart city, must assess the problems this entails for elderly people.

- The design of the new smart spaces must take into consideration the opinion of adults, placing particular value on the elderly.
- The public authorities must organise the city, taking into consideration the proposals and suggestions of citizens, which will serve as a starting point for making decisions which will determine the design of the new cities.

On important factor in smart cities is the conception of the application of information and communication technology in regions, which needs to be similar between all cities – useful, easy to use and accessible for all citizens. The goal is for the data citizens have available to be correct, so that the proposals they make for their cities are interesting and applicable. The channels used for making proposals for access to information in cities must be intuitive, user-friendly channels, so as to prevent knowledge or training hindrances which make it impossible for some citizens to access said information, taking the group of people with disabilities and elderly people specifically under consideration.

Finally, we should point out the importance of adapting autonomous community regulations, which are currently very disperse and have different criteria, to the United Nations Convention on the rights of persons with disabilities and the needs of the elderly.

Accessibility Measures: The New Proposal in European Union and Analysis of New Solutions Applied to Smart Cities

If smart cities are to place their intelligence at the service of citizens, they must understand them in all of their functional diversity. In this sense, tthe future adoption of the European Act on disability (Directive) will be decisive in order to clearly specify the application of Community policies on accessibility[16].

In the proposal, the chapter on access to goods and services, the directive will include parameters for unification of accessibility criteria, which enables common norms to be established for all companies, which must act with uniform requisites in terms of accessibility. The objective is to improve the functioning of the internal market, facilitating the provision by companies of accessible products and services. Common accessibility criteria will also be applied in the contracting standards of the EU and the utilisation of European funds. It will have significant repercussions on the rights of people with disabilities in the European community, enabling them to carry out actions in areas in which they hitherto had some limitations, such as communications, banking services, telephony, audiovisuals, e-commerce, transport and computers.

The number of people with disabilities, which makes for ten percent (10%) of the world's population, and the people over 65 in Europe are 19% of the population we can understand the need to plan smart cities considering the basic principles of universal accessibility and design for all, and apply accessibility parameters as a guarantee that ensures the inclusion of all users. In this way, we will have accessible urban environments and information and communication technologies that can be used by all users, facilitating the utilisation of the services and applications placed at the disposal of users.

Moreover, in today's cities, an increase in the average age of the population can be detected, which implies a high number of elderly people who use and enjoy them, but some of them have mobility problems. This situation calls for the development of innovative projects related to smart management of mobility, social architecture and new urban uses, integrating one essential factor: the accessibility of cities.

Many cities have worked on this aspect. If we analyse what has occurred on a European level, and point out cities that stand out for their accessibility, we must consider Nantes, Stockholm or Krakow or Lyon. The cities that have received the most recognition are:

Berlin (Germany) It is important to highlight this city, which won the "Access City Award" in 2013 – the European prize that recognises the work of the most accessible cities for persons with disabilities and elderly people. It promotes universal accessibility and the inclusion of all and allows for the dissemination of actions on the removal of barriers in the cities of the European Union and the sharing of solutions.

The city of Berlin has committed to accessibility in its innovation in the city, paying special attention to the integration of people with disabilities. This city has established strategic inclusion policies, joining forces to eliminate barriers, showing special interest in guaranteeing the mobility of people with disabilities. It has spacious avenues which allow for easy movement, highlighting the principle they have championed of "Unrestricted Travellers", installing adapted bus stops.

Gothenburg (Sweden) "City for All" is the motto of this Swedish city. Its inclusive focus and strategic policies earned it the Access City Award 2014.

Salzburg (Austria). Winner of the Access City Award 2012. It performed significant adaptation in tourism; all the museums and cultural spaces are adapted, and have ramps and itineraries for wheelchair users. Its old town has pedestrianised streets which improve mobility. Tourism spaces and counters are adapted, and guides indicate adapted routes. It is another of the cities that stand out for their interest in including people with disabilities in the city, relying on their participation in the process of transforming the city as a guarantee that it adapts to their needs. The improvements achieved have been significant in the transport, communication and information technology systems. We should highlight the information system incorporated that is aimed at tourism, providing tourists with disabilities with highly useful information via the website "Infoplatform for Accessible Tourism" (IBFT), which includes all the accessible places in the city. The information is specified for wheelchair users and people with visual and auditory disabilities, but intellectual and developmental disabilities have not been included.

The comprehensive progress in this city has earned high recognition and interventions have been carried out in architecture, town planning, transport, information and communication, surroundings, installations and public services.

Ávila (Spain) is a town that has received several awards due to its accessibility plans. In 2010 the European Commission gave it the Access City Award, after competing with more than sixty-six (66) municipalities, "for its defence of accessibility for people with disabilities". An Urban Development Plan has been generated that has improved the accessibility of public buildings, and has been implemented since 2002 "in collaboration with organisations representing people with disabilities and the elderly". Emblematic spaces in the city have been adapted, such as the City Wall, considered a World Heritage Site, which was adapted so that wheelchair users and people with reduced mobility can gain access, by installing a lift and an adapted bathroom. In this case, all of the studies and adaptations have been carried out with the participation of disabled persons.

Lyon (France). Winner of the Access City Award 2018. The public buses in Lyon are 100% accessible and access to culture is also guaranteed, thanks to the inclusion of accessible equipment in libraries, such as reading machines, audiobook readers and amplifying screens. Likewise, the city has developed digital tools for people with disabilities and, in terms of work integration, 7.8% of staff members are people with disabilities, a percentage significantly higher than the 6% minimum legal quota required by French legislation.

Other examples of good practices are the cities: Boras (Sweden) 2015, Milan (Italy) 2016, Chester (United Kindom) 2017, Breda (Netherlands) 2019, Warsaw (Poland) 2020, and they have also obtained the corresponding recognition.

All of the cities we have cited as examples establish that innovation in inclusive cities is an essential tool, which not only corresponds to the use of more advanced technology allowing citizens to be aided, but that there is another essential factor, i.e. the humanisation of cities as an essential element that allows for the co-existence side by side of everyone, with everyone and for everyone. Useable, friendly spaces must be created, and we should not understand technology as an element of innovation in the city alone. At present, ICT is understood as a means for improving the quality of life of users. But it has been established that technology can be a cause of discrimination, when its usability and adaptability for all people are not guaranteed. Which is why technologies must be created on the basis of accessibility, to ensure their universal usability.

The Incorporation of New Information Technology into the Management of Cities and its Eventual Effect of Excluding Some Citizens

We had not yet overcome the traditional differences between countryside and city, or the impact of the socio-economic differences in the urban environment, when we were faced with a new challenge. Smart cities will incorporate factors of exclusion for the population who are not "digitally illiterate", possibly (although not in generalised fashion) including elderly people.

In principle, ICT has functioned as an inclusive mechanism that has enabled a large number of people with disabilities to access goods and services they would otherwise have had limited access to, or access to which would have been difficult for them. But smart cities can also be turned into a motive for exclusion if imposed as the only mechanism of interlocution with citizens.

In the case Indiana versus IBM (Court of Appeals, Indiana, 13th February 2014), the State of Indiana decided to suppress the direct relationship of social workers with the marginalised population who benefited from food stamps and a basic health service. Funds the federal states had to distribute satisfactorily as they were responsible for managing funding that formed part of the US budget. To do so it put the welfare system out to tender, with IBM winning and proceeding to implant a hardware-software system to answer the users of the service via an automatic telephony system or website. In the face of the strong criticism received, some rectifications were made but the matter ended up in the courts, as the State of

Indiana deemed the contract to have been breached. IBM, for its part, reacted judicially by claiming an amount for compensation for the equipment installed. Both the first instance judgement and the appeal judgement eventually established mutual compensation systems e fixing different amounts, in the midst of legal controversy as well (the appeal sentence was published, and included a dissenting vote).

The comments that emerged on the right in the US as a result of the publication of the sentence were quick in coming, many of them highlighting the failure of both parties, and going beyond the political criteria that justified this decision.

This leads us to reflect on the issue that the evaluation of the budget item would presumably save thousands of trips, but perhaps the implantation of the decision in question did not take the social base of the population it was aimed at sufficiently into account; both because their ability to access technical resources was probably severely limited, and because, in pressing social issues such as the one in hand, doing away with direct, personal dialogue with the public services does not seem to be the right move.

SOLUTIONS AND RECOMMENDATION

In Spain and in other countries of similar political structures; the public administration, the private sector and standardization have been drivers of smart cities in a good scenario of harmony and collaboration. This has led to the approval of numerous UNE standards which have been a global model and source of inspiration for several recommendations published by the ITU.

The Digital Agenda fulfils an important role in the promotion of smart cities, and now of smart territories too.

Numerous challenges remain: the application of the IoT, application of ICTs in rural areas, smart rural destinations and smart islands, in the main.

DIRECTION OF FUTURE RESEARCH

The Framework of the Europe 2020 Strategy promotes the creation of a Digital Agenda by each Member State, who must detail a number of concrete plans and lines of action to enable them to achieve the agreed objectives. The Digital Agenda for Spain defines, among others, the National Plan of Smart Territories, from which the main fields of action are being coordinated divided into three types, based on the experiences and results derived from the implementation of the National Smart Cities Plan.

On March 16, a new European Standardization Technical Committee called CEN / TC 465, entitled "Sustainable and intelligent cities and communities" will be established in Brussels. Most likely this circumstance leads to greater reflection at European Community level of reflection are the common guidelines that should be adopted regarding environmental policies and ICT in regard to smart cities

Socio-economic systems, from the point of view of solving the problems that arise both internally and in relation to the rest of the systems, especially with the administrative political system, require the definition of their own space and model of political-administrative territorial organization. The economic and social phenomena that have been observed since recent decades suggest that they are social phenomena more structural and territorial in nature than only economic, social or demographic. They appear to refer to the transit of local industrial spaces (regional and/or national) to a planetary urbanization (global urbanization), where both the free movement of goods and capital and the concentration of investment/

employment/wealth, and a conception of economic growth versus development, are the bases of operation of the system. These issues, necessarily, require (re)rebuilding a new territorial political-administrative model that accommodates past rural versus urban conceptions of past decades.

It is important to note that in processes of economic, sociological and political transformation as deep as the current one, societies must build new spaces and space functions through models of territorial, political and social organization/planning appropriate to contemporaneity. The planning instruments, management systems and administrative delimitations available correspond to an organization of the territory arising from the industrial revolution and which therefore find no answer to current situations.

CONCLUSION

In conclusion, from a scientific viewpoint we are once again faced with the eternal reflection on the balance between humans and their surroundings, and the capacity to generate an ideal city, attempting to create a holistic vision of the urban medium.

The initiative to promote smart cities has been the promotion activity. The State has managed through the European Social Fund (FSO) in a main way the costly initiatives to incorporate ICTs to cities that already have a good level of services and a population number of around one million people. But without a doubt, a more accurate solution is missing for those larger cities or little towns with the notes of masculinity, aging and dispersion existing today.

On the other hand, many small municipalities have tried to establish services of the smart cities without taking into account the disconnection that global management of services that could have on different platforms without connection between them the collection of garbage and the cleaning service, to put An example. Therefore, it is necessary that the interventions that take place at the local level be carried out in an integrated service platform.

Basically the introduction of smart cities is an initiative aimed at efficient management of urban services and infrastructures; the desired consequences are a reduction in public expenditure, improvement in the quality of public services and in citizens' information and an improvement in decision-making.

This new step forward involves the incorporation of new formulae developed technologically for the realm of cities, and there can be no doubt that this is a logical, necessary evolution. Until now smart city initiatives have been growing exponentially but we cannot assert that they are general practice, so we must take precautions against the danger of a deepening of the digital breach and the creation of urban segregation as a result of their introduction. In particular, care must be taken over the setting and fulfilment of universal public service conditions. On this point, we can observe progress which exceeds political ideologies as lower expenditure and efficiency are a basic element of any structural and organisational design.

ACKNOWLEDGMENT

This research was supported by Thematic Network of Urban Development: From Greencities to Smartcities (SUMANET) Financed from the own plan of the University of Málaga action D-6, and to action B-3, research project in Social and Legal Sciences, (CIMA) Environmentally accessible Cities; both funded from the University of Malaga's Own Research Plan.

REFERENCES

Brito Marquina, A., Cantarero García, G., Piñar Mañas, J., Suárez Ojeda, M., Cantarero García, G., Piñar Mañas, J., & Suárez Ojeda, M. (2017). Smart cities: Derecho y técnica para una ciudad mas habitable. Madrid: Reus.

Chen, H., & Liu, X. (2006). Adoption of low mobility services: 'Little-Smart' in China as a case. *Info*, *8*(6), 69–78. doi:10.1108/14636690610707491

Freilich, R., & Popowitz, N. (2010). The Umbrella of Sustainability: Smart Growth, New Urbanism, Renewable Energy and Green Development in the 21st Century. *The Urban Lawyer*, *42*(1), 1–39.

Ganapati, S., & Schoepp, C. (2008). The wireless city. *International Journal of Electronic Government Research*, *4*(4), 54–68. doi:10.4018/jegr.2008100104

Getting to Smart Growth II. (2003). *100 more policies for implementation/ Smart Network*. Washington, DC: International City/County Management Association.

Harding, A., Blokland-Potters, T., & Blokland, T. (2014). *Urban theory: A critical introduction to power, cities and urbanism in the 21st century*. Los Angeles: SAGE.

Hawkins, C. (2011). Smart Growth Policy Choice: A Resource Dependency and Local Governance Explanation. *Policy Studies Journal: the Journal of the Policy Studies Organization*, *39*(4), 679–707. doi:10.1111/j.1541-0072.2011.00427.x

ICMA. (2003). Getting to Smart Growth II: 100 more policies for implementation. Smart Network International City/County Management Association.

McCann, E., & Paddison, R. (2014). Cities & social change: Encounters with contemporary urbanism. Los Angeles: SAGE.

O'Connell, L. (2009). The Impact of Local Supporters on Smart Growth Policy Adoption. *Journal of the American Planning Association*, *75*(3), 281–291. doi:10.1080/01944360902885495

Portney, K. (2005). Civic Engagement and Sustainable Cities in the United States. *Public Administration Review*, *65*(5), 579–591. doi:10.1111/j.1540-6210.2005.00485.x

Quadra-Salcedo y Fernández del Castillo, T., Piñar Mañas, J., Barrio Andrés, M., & Torregrosa Vázquez, J. (2018). Sociedad digital y derecho. Madrid: Ministerio de Industria, Comercio y Turismo.

Resnik, D. (2010). Urban Sprawl, Smart Growth, and Deliberative Democracy. *American Journal of Public Health*, *100*(10), 1852–1856. doi:10.2105/AJPH.2009.182501 PMID:20724685

Shapiro, J. (2005). *Smart cities: Quality of life, productivity, and the growth effects of human capital (Documentos de trabajo, 11615)*. Cambridge, MA: National Bureau of Economic Research.

Staley, S. (2004). Urban Planning, Smart Growth, and Economic Calculation: An Austrian Critique and Extension. *The Review of Austrian Economics*, *17*(2), 265–283.

Sun, L. (2011). Smart Growth in Dumb Places: Sustainability, Disaster, and the Future of the American City. *Brigham Young University Law Review*, *2011*(6), 2157–2201. doi:10.2139srn.1918386

Telefónica, F. (2011). *Smart cities: un primer paso hacia el internet de las cosas*. Barcelona: Ariel.

Tomalty, R., & Curran, D. (2003). Living it up: The wide range of support for smart growth in Canada promises more livable towns and cities. *Alternatives, 29*(3), 10–18.

Walters, D. (2011). Smart cities, smart places, smart democracy: Form-based codes, electronic governance and the role of place in making smart cities. *Intelligent Buildings International, 3*(3), 198–218. doi:10.1080/17508975.2011.586670

ADDITIONAL READING

López, C., & Teresa, M. (2017). Administración Pública y participación activa del ciudadano en la gestión de la ciudad inteligente. In *Smart cities, derecho y técnica para una ciudad más habitable* (pp. 33–51). Madrid: Reus.

Mañas, P., & Luis, J. (2017). *Derecho, técnica e innovación en las llamadas ciudades inteligentes. Privacidad y gobierno abierto in Smart cities, derecho y técnica para una ciudad más habitable* (pp. 11–31). Madrid: Reus.

KEY TERMS AND DEFINITIONS

Accessibility: The concept includes the transport, the work of the microenterprises that provide services, the household appliances. In the case of the urbanism, the accessible buildings and infrastructure and the environment where people spend most of their time.

Cohesion Policies: Cohesion policy is the European Union's strategy to promote and support the 'overall harmonious development' of its Member States and regions.

Public Administration: The public administration serves the general interests objectively and acts in accordance with the principles of effectiveness, hierarchy, decentralization, deconcentration, and coordination, with full submission to the law and the Law.

Smart Land: The rural development policy aims to achieve the following objectives: fostering the competitiveness of agriculture; ensuring the sustainable management of natural resources, and climate action; achieving a balanced territorial development of rural economies and communities, including the creation and maintenance of employment.

Sustainable Development: Sustainable development give recognition to its economic, social and environmental dimensions that should be tackled together. Development must meet the needs of the present without compromising the ability of future generations to meet their own needs. A life of dignity for all within the planet's limits and reconciling economic efficiency, social inclusion, and environmental responsibility is at the essence of sustainable development.

ENDNOTES

[1] All inventions of humankind have been applied immediately to everyday life; indeed, since the era of the great inventions, the tension of improvement of cities has been evident. This was the case of street lighting, running water supply to homes or railways, to give some examples.

The impact of innovation encourages an attractive dialogue between tradition and modernity, which is highly productive. *See* EDGERTON, David. Innovación y tradición. Historia de la tecnología moderna. Barcelona, Crítica, 2007

[2] Another correct definition is that provided by the ITU: "A smart sustainable city is an innovative city that uses information and communication technologies (ICTs) and other means to improve quality of life, efficiency of urban operation and services, and competitiveness, while ensuring that it meets the needs of present and future generations with respect to economic, social and environmental aspects".

[3] UN-Habitat, "World Cities Report 2016" (2016) http://wcr.unhabitat.org/

[4] LAHOZ PALACIO, Carlos F. "La influencia de las tecnologías de la comunicación sobre la sociabilidad en los espacios públicos" III Congreso Ciudades Inteligentes, Madrid, Tecmared, 2017, pp. 47-52. Navarro Cano, Nieves. "Ciudades inteligentes inclusivas y accesibles, diseñar para la diversidad" in Smart cities, derecho y técnica para una ciudad más habitable, Reus, Madrid, 2017.

[5] SUAREZ OJEDA, Magdalena. "De las ciudades inteligentes a los territorios inteligentes. Especial referencia a la discapacidad". Tirant lo Blanch, 2018.

[6] ".... standards (future UIT recommendations) are also being developed at present on external systems such as smart airports, ports or stations, smart buildings, rural systems and tourism intelligence, which will allow for the development of solutions that have a strong impact on cities and create new business models. In collaboration with the national standardisation organism, UNE, there has been contact with the main representative entities that are taking part in the generation of interfaces and models for standardised data, such as CENELEC (European Committee for the Electrotechnical Standardization), ETSI (European Telecommunications Standards Institute) and others." Red.es: https://www--red--es.insuit.net/redes/es/actualidad/magazin-en-red/espa%C3%B1a-logra-el-consenso-internacional-en-la-estandarizaci%C3%B3n-de-la

[7] PADDISON, Ronan and MCCANN, Eugene. "Introduction: Encountering the city-Multiple Perspectives on Urban Social Change" pp.3-14. Cities & Social Change. Encounters with contemporary urbanism. Sage publications, London, 2014.

[8] Plan Nacional de Territorios Inteligentes (2017), Ministerio de Energía, Turismo y Agenda Digital, SESIAD. https://avancedigital.gob.es/planes-TIC/agenda-digital/DescargasAgendaDigital/Planes%20espec%C3%ADficos/Plan-ADpE-11_Plan-Nacional-Territorios-Inteligentes.pdf

[9] "Article 10. Delimitation and classification of rural areas.

[1.] In order to apply the Sustainable Rural Development Programme, the Autonomous Communities shall carry out the delimitation and classification of rural areas defined in article

3 b) in their respective territory, in accordance with the following types:

a) Rural areas to be revitalised: those with low population density, elevated relevance of agricultural activity, low levels of income and significant geographical isolation or difficulties of regional structuring.

b) Intermediate rural areas: those with low or medium population density, with employment diversified between the primary, secondary and tertiary sector, low or medium levels of income and distant from the direct area of influence of large cities.

c) Peri-urban rural areas: those with a growing population, with a predominance of employment in the tertiary sector, medium or high levels of income and located in the environment of urban areas or densely populated areas".

[10] Digital Communities Castilla-León: https://rmd.jcyl.es/web/jcyl/MunicipiosDigitales/es/Plantilla100/1274785626082/

[11] Eurostat: http://ec.europa.eu/eurostat/statistics-explained/index.php/Urban-rural_typology#The_OECD_methodology

[12] European Innovation Partnership on Smart Cities and Communities: https://ec.europa.eu/eip/smartcities/files/sip_final_en.pdf

[13] "Smart cities. In 2015 the former Ministry of Industry, Energy and Tourism set in motion the National Plan for Smart Cities as part of the Digital Agenda for Spain. Making cities and human settlements inclusive, safe, resilient and sustainable is one of the 17 sustainable development goals of the United Nations Agenda 2030. Smart cities go a long way to contributing to attaining this goal, by allowing for optimisation of resources, reduction of greenhouse gas emissions and improvement of people's lives and mobility.

For the construction of open and accessible smart cities, the complexity of the urban environment calls, amongst other factors, for a solid body of standards. Which is why in April of 2016, collaboration began between the then-State Secretariat of Telecommunications and the Information Society, AENOR and the International Telecommunication Union, which has enabled Spain to drive forward the development of twenty standards which will contribute to setting in motion the recommendations for standardisation published by the ITU. The result of all these efforts has materialised in the recognition of the Spanish model s an international reference model in the field of smart cities, as indicated in the report of the UN Broadband Commission for Sustainable Development." Pag 111
http://www.minetad.gob.es/es-ES/IndicadoresyEstadisticas/Informes/InformesMITYC/Informe%20Anual%202016.%20S.G.%20de%20Estudios,%20An%C3%A1lisis%20y%20Planes%20de%20Actuaci%C3%B3n/Informe%20Anual%20(SG%20Estudios).pdf

[14] CTN 178 - SMART CITIES
UNE 178104: 2017
Comprehensive Smart City Management Systems. Interoperability requirements for a Smart City Platform.
CTN 178 / SC 1 INFRASTRUCTURES
UNE 178108: 2017
Smart cities. Requirements of smart buildings for consideration as IoT node according to Standard UNE 178104.
CTN 178 / SC 1 INFRASTRUCTURES
UNE 178301: 2015
Smart cities. Open Data.
CTN 178 / SC 3 MOBILITY AND TRANSPORT PLATFORMS
UNE 178201: 2016
Smart cities. Definition, attributes and requirements
CTN 178 / SC 2 INDICATORS AND SEMANTICS

UNE 178202: 2016

Smart cities. Management indicators based on management dashboards city.

CTN 178 / SC 2 INDICATORS AND SEMANTICS

UNE-ISO 37120: 2015

Sustainable development in the cities. Indicators for urban services and the quality of lifetime.

CTN 178 / SC 2 INDICATORS AND SEMANTICS

UNE 178401: 2017

Smart cities. Exterior lighting. Degrees of functionality, zoning and management architecture

CTN 178 / SC 4 ENERGY AND ENVIRONMENT

UNE 178105: 2017

Universal Accessibility in Smart Cities.

CTN 178 / SC 1 INFRASTRUCTURES

UNE 178402: 2015

Smart cities. Management of basic services and water and electricity supply in smart ports.

CTN 178 / SC 4 ENERGY AND ENVIRONMENT

UNE 178101-1: 2015

Smart cities. Infrastructures Public Services Networks. Part 1: Networks of waters

CTN 178 / SC 1 INFRASTRUCTURES

UNE 178101-5-1: 2015

Smart cities. Infrastructures Public Services Networks. Part 5-1: Networks of Energy. Electricity.

CTN 178 / SC 1 INFRASTRUCTURES

UNE 178101-4: 2015

Smart cities. Infrastructures Public Services Networks. Part 4: Networks of telecommunication.

CTN 178 / SC 1 INFRASTRUCTURES

UNE 178303: 2015

Smart cities. Asset management of the city. Specs.

CTN 178 / SC 3 MOBILITY AND TRANSPORT PLATFORMS

UNE 178503: 2019

Smart tourist destinations. Semantics applied to tourism.

CTN 178 / SC 5 TOURIST DESTINATIONS

UNE 178504: 2019

Digital, intelligent and connected hotel (HDIC) to tourist destination platforms smart / smart city. Requirements and recommendations.

CTN 178 / SC 5 TOURIST DESTINATIONS

UNE 178109: 2018

Smart cities. Smart station and connection to the city platform intelligent.

CTN 178 / SC 1 INFRASTRUCTURES

UNE 178405: 2018

Smart cities. Environmental sensing Smart irrigation system

CTN 178 / SC 4 ENERGY AND ENVIRONMENT

UNE 178502: 2018

Indicators and tools of intelligent tourist destinations.

CTN 178 / SC 5 TOURIST DESTINATIONS

UNE 178501: 2018 UNE

Management system for smart tourist destinations. Requirements

CTN 178 / SC 5 TOURIST DESTINATIONS

UNE 178101-2: 2018

Smart cities. Infrastructures Public Services Networks. Part 2: Networks of waste.

CTN 178 / SC 1 INFRASTRUCTURES

UNE 178101-3: 2016

Smart cities. Infrastructures Public Services Networks. Part 3: Networks of transport.

CTN 178 / SC 1 INFRASTRUCTURES

UNE 178107-6: 2016 IN

Guide for Smart Cities infrastructures. Access and transport networks. Part 6: Radio links

CTN 178 / SC 1 INFRASTRUCTURES

UNE 178107-5: 2015 IN

Guide for Smart Cities infrastructures. Access and transport networks. Part 5: Mobile Safety and Emergency Networks, SSE.

CTN 178 / SC 1 INFRASTRUCTURES

UNE 178107-4: 2015 IN

Guide for Smart Cities infrastructures. Access and transport networks. Part 4: Sensor Networks, WSN.

CTN 178 / SC 1 INFRASTRUCTURES

UNE 178102-1: 2015

Smart cities. Infrastructures Telecommunication systems Part 1: Network Municipal Multiservice.

CTN 178 / SC 1 INFRASTRUCTURES

UNE 178102-3: 2015

Smart cities. Infrastructures Telecommunication systems Part 3: SystemUnified Communications, SCU.

CTN 178 / SC 1 INFRASTRUCTURES

UNE 178107-1: 2015 IN

Guide for Smart Cities infrastructures. Access and transport networks. Part1: Fiber Optic Networks.

CTN 178 / SC 1 INFRASTRUCTURES

UNE 178107-2: 2015 IN

Guide for Smart Cities infrastructures. Access and transport networks. Part 2: Wide area Wireless networks, WMAN.

CTN 178 / SC 1 INFRASTRUCTURES

UNE 178107-3: 2015 IN

Guide for Smart Cities infrastructures. Access and transport networks. Part 3: Wireless local area networks, WLAN.

CTN 178 / SC 1 INFRASTRUCTURES

UNE-EN ISO / IEC 17025: 2017

General requirements for the competence of testing and calibration laboratories.

UNE-EN ISO 9001: 2015

Quality Management Systems. Requirements

UNE-EN ISO 14001: 2015

Environmental management systems. Requirements with guidance for use

15   European Union EU (2019) "Urban Agenda for the Smart Cities of Tomorrow" https://www.slideshare.net/ashabook/urban-europe. Marcos Paramio, Tania (2019) "El modelo de normalización español de Ciudades Inteligentes (UNE, CTN 178) y su impacto internacional" https://www.esmartcity.es/comunicaciones/comunicacion-modelo-normalizacion-espanol-ciudades-inteligentes UIT (2019): https://www.itu.int/en/publications/Documents/tsb/2017-U4SSC-Collection-Methodology/index.html#p=18

16   Policies of integration European Union https://ec.europa.eu/social/main.jsp?catId=1137&langId=en

Compilation of References

Abbasi, A. Z., Islam, N., & Shaikh, Z. A. (2014). A review of wireless sensors and networks' applications in agriculture. *Computer Standards & Interfaces*, *36*(2), 263–270. doi:10.1016/j.csi.2011.03.004

Abouelmehdi, K., Hssane, A. B., & Khaloufi, H. (2017). Big healthcare data: Preserving security and privacy. Springer. *Journal of Big Data*, *5*(1), 1–18. doi:10.118640537-017-0110-7

Abradelo de Usera, M. I. & Togores, L. (1997). Viajeros románticos por la España isabelina. *Aportes. Revista de Historia Contemporánea*, (12), 119-146.

Acquisti, A., Taylor, C., & Wagman, L. (2016). The economics of privacy. *Journal of Economic Literature*, *54*(2), 442–492. doi:10.1257/jel.54.2.442

Ahmed, M., & Hossain, M. A. (2014). Cloud computing and security issues in the cloud. *International Journal of Network Security & Its Applications*, *6*(1), 25–36. doi:10.5121/ijnsa.2014.6103

Ahmed, M., Kambam, H. R., Liu, Y., & Uddin, M. N. (2019, June). Impact of Human Factors in Cloud Data Breach. In *International Conference on Intelligent and Interactive Systems and Applications* (pp. 568-577). Springer.

Ahmed, M., & Litchfield, A. T. (2016). Taxonomy for identification of security issues in cloud computing environments. *Journal of Computer Information Systems*, *58*(1), 79–88. doi:10.1080/08874417.2016.1192520

Ahmed, M., Litchfield, A. T., & Ahmed, S. (2014). *A generalized threat taxonomy for cloud computing*. ACIS.

Akerlof, G. (1970). The market for lemons. *The Quarterly Journal of Economics*, *84*(3), 488–500. doi:10.2307/1879431

Akyildiz, I. F., Su, W., Sakarasubramaniam, Y., & Cayirci, E. (2002). A survey on sensor networks. *IEEE Communications Magazine*, *40*(8), 102–114. doi:10.1109/MCOM.2002.1024422

Akyildiz, I., Wang, P., & Lin, S. (2015). SoftAir: A software defined networking architecture for 5G wireless systems. *Computer Networks*, *85*, 1–18. doi:10.1016/j.comnet.2015.05.007

Alberdi, M. J., & Fleming, P. (2000). *Hablemos de marketing interactivo. Reflexiones sobre marketing digital y comercio electrónico*. Madrid, Spain: ESIC.

Albrecht, J. (2016). How the GDPR will change the world. *European Data Protection Law Review*, *2*(3), 287–289. doi:10.21552/EDPL/2016/3/4

Aldossary, S., & Allen, W. (2016). Data security, privacy, availability and integrity in cloud computing: Issues and current solutions. *International Journal of Advanced Computer Science and Applications*, *7*(4), 485–498. doi:10.14569/IJACSA.2016.070464

Al-Emran, M., Malik, S. I., & Al-Kabi, M. N. (2020). A Survey of Internet of Things (IoT) in Education: Opportunities and Challenges. In Toward Social Internet of Things (SIoT): Enabling Technologies, Architectures and Applications (pp. 197-209). Springer.

Ali, M. M., & Haseebuddin, M. (2015). Cloud Computing for Retailing Industry: An Overview. *International Journal of Computer Trends and Technology, 19*(1), 51–56. doi:10.14445/22312803/IJCTT-V19P110

Aljawarneh, S. A., & Yassein, M. O. B. (2016). A conceptual security framework for cloud computing issues. *International Journal of Intelligent Information Technologies, 12*(2), 12–24. doi:10.4018/IJIIT.2016040102

Allen, R. G., Pereira, L. S., Raes, D., & Smith, M. (2006). *Evapotranspiración del cultivo. Guías para la determinación de los requerimientos de agua de los cultivos. FAO Riego y Drenaje, Monografía Nº 56*. Roma: FAO.

Alonso, S., Basañez, J., Lopez-Coronado, M., & De la Torre Díez, I. (2019). Proposing New Blockchain Challenges in eHealth. *Journal of Medical Systems, 43*. PMID:30729329

Alpert, S. (2003). Protecting medical privacy: Challenges in the age of genetic information. *The Journal of Social Issues, 59*(2), 301–322. doi:10.1111/1540-4560.00066

Altabella, J. (1945). *Corresponsales de Guerra: su historia y su actuación. De Jenofonte a Knickerbocker, pasando por Peris Mencheta*. Madrid, Spain: Editorial Febo.

Ambec, S., Cohen, M., Eligie, S., & Lanoie, P. (2013). The Porter hypothesis at 20: Can environmental regulation enhance innovation and competitiveness? *Review of Environmental Economics and Policy, 7*(1), 2–22. doi:10.1093/reep/res016

Anawar, M. R., Wang, S., Azam Zia, M., Jadoon, A. K., Akram, U., & Raza, S. (2018). Fog computing: An overview of big IoT data analytics. *Wireless Communications and Mobile Computing, 2018*, 1–22. doi:10.1155/2018/7157192

Angelidou, A. (2015). *Smart cities: A conjuncture of four forces Cities*. Elsevier Ltd.

Angst, C., & Agarwal, R. (2009). Adoption of electronic health records in the presence of privacy concerns: The elaboration likelihood model and individual persuasion. *Management Information Systems Quarterly, 33*(2), 339–370. doi:10.2307/20650295

An, N., Kim, Y., Park, J., Kwon, D.-H., & Lim, H. (2019). Slice Management for Quality of Service Differentiation in Wireless Network Slicing. *Sensors (Basel), 19*(12), 2745. doi:10.339019122745 PMID:31248088

Antonovic, M. P., Cannata, M., Danani, A., Engeler, L., Flacio, E., Mangili, F., Ravasi, D., Strigaro, D., & Tonolla, M. (2018). ALBIS: Integrated system for risk-based surveillance of invasive mosquito Aedes albopictus. *PeerJ PrePrints, 6*, e27251v1.

Anushree, R., & Rio, G.L.D. (2019). Big Data Anonymization in Cloud using k-Anonymity Algorithm using Map Reduce Framework. *International Journal of Scientific Research in Computer Science, Engineering and Information Technology*, 50-56.

Article 29. (2014). *Opinion 8/2014 on the recent developments on the Internet of Things*. Data Protection Working Party.

Arup. (2010). *Smart Cities, transforming the 21st century via the creative use of technology*. Retrieved November 25, 2019, from https://www.arup.com/Publications/Smart_Cities.aspx

Asare, E. O., Tompkins, A. M., Amekudzi, L. K., Ermert, V., & Redl, R. (2016). *Mosquito breeding site water temperature observations and simulations towards improved vector-borne disease models for Africa*. Academic Press.

Asís, R., Aiello, A.L, Bariffi F., Campoy, I., & Palacios, A. (2006). La accesibilidad Universal en el marco constitucional español. *Derechos y Libertades, 2*(16), 57-82.

Awerbuch, B., Curtmola, R., Holmer, D., Nita-Rotaru, C., & Rubens, H. (2004). Mitigating byzantine attacks in ad hoc wireless networks. Department of Computer Science, Johns Hopkins University. *Tech. Rep. Version*, *1*, 16.

Baddeley, M., Nejabaty, R., Oikonomou, G., Sooriyabandara, M., & Simeonidou, D. (2018). Evolving SDN for Low-Power IoT Networks. In *Proceedings of the 4th IEEE Conference on Network Softwarization and Workshops (NetSoft)* (pp. 71-79). Montreal, Canada: IEEE. 10.1109/NETSOFT.2018.8460125

Bagheri, M., & Movahed, S. H. (2016). *The effect of the internet of things (IoT) on education business model.* Paper presented at 12th International Conference on Signal-Image Technology and Internet-Based Systems (SITIS), Naples, Italy. 10.1109/SITIS.2016.74

Bajwa, W. I., Coop, L., & Kogan, M. (2003). Integrated pest management (IPM) and Internet-based information delivery systems. *Neotropical Entomology*, *32*(3), 373–383. doi:10.1590/S1519-566X2003000300001

Barth, A., Mitchell, J. C., & Rosenstein, J. (2004).Conflict and combination in privacy policy languages. In *Proceeding of the workshop on Privacy in the electronic society (WPES)* (pp. 45-46). ACM. 10.1145/1029179.1029195

Basu, S., & Munns, C. (2016). *Privacy and Healthcare Data "Choice of Control" to "Choice" and "Control".* Routledge. doi:10.4324/9781315602202

Batista, E., Casino, F., & Solanas, A. (2015). Wandering Detection Methods in Smart Cities: Current and New Approaches. *IEEE First International Smart Cities Conference (ISC2)*, 1-2. 10.1109/ISC2.2015.7366175

Batista, G. E., Keogh, E. J., Mafra-Neto, A., & Rowton, E. (2011). SIGKDD demo: Sensors and software to allow computational entomology, an emerging application of data mining. *Proceedings of the 17th ACM SIGKDD International Conference on Knowledge Discovery and Data Mining*, 761–764. 10.1145/2020408.2020530

Batista, G., Hao, Y., Keogh, E., & Mafra-Neto, A. (2011). Towards automatic classification on flying insects using inexpensive sensors. *2011 10th International Conference on Machine Learning and Applications and Workshops*, *1*, 364–369.

Baumer, D., Earp, J., & Poindexter, J. C. (2004). Internet privacy law: A comparison between the United States and the European Union. *Journal of Computer Security*, *23*(5), 400–412. doi:10.1016/j.cose.2003.11.001

Beard, R., Wentz, E., & Scotch, M. (2018). A systematic review of spatial decision support systems in public health informatics supporting the identification of high risk areas for zoonotic disease outbreaks. *International Journal of Health Geographics*, *17*(1), 38. doi:10.118612942-018-0157-5 PMID:30376842

Belton, P., & Costello, R. A. (1979). Flight sounds of the females of some mosquitoes of Western Canada. *Entomologia Experimentalis et Applicata*, *26*(1), 105–114. doi:10.1111/j.1570-7458.1979.tb02904.x

Benévolo, L. (1974). *Historia de la Arquitectura moderna.* Barcelona, Spain: Gustavo Gili.

Benjamin, L. (2017, Summer). ASPECT: A Survey to Assess Student Perspective of Engagement in an Active-Learning Classroom. *CBE Life Sciences Education*, *16*(2), ar32. doi:10.1187/cbe.16-08-0244 PMID:28495936

Ben-Ner, A., & Putterman, L. (2003). *New economy handbook: Trust in the new economy.* New York, NY: Academic Press.

Bhuiyan, M. Z. A., Zaman, A., Wang, T., Wang, G., Tao, H., & Hassan, M. M. (2018). Blockchain and Big Data to Transform the Healthcare. *Proceedings of the International Conference on Data Processing and Applications*, 62–68. 10.1145/3224207.3224220

Birje, M. N., Challagidad, P. S., Goudar, R. H., & Tapale, M. T. (2017). Cloud computing review: Concepts, technology, challenges and security. *International Journal of Cloud Computing*, *6*(1), 32–57. doi:10.1504/IJCC.2017.083905

Biswas, S., Mazuz, K., & Mendes, R. A. (2014). E-Healthcare Disparities Across Cultures. *International Journal of User-Driven Healthcare*, *4*(4), 1–16. doi:10.4018/IJUDH.2014100101

Blikstein, P. (2013). Digital Fabrication and Making in Education: The Democratization of Invention. In J. Walter-Hermann & C. Büching (Eds.), *Fab Labs: Of Machine, Makers and Inventors* (pp. 203–222). Bielefeld, Germany: Transcript Publishers. doi:10.14361/transcript.9783839423820.203

Boletín Oficial del Estado núm. 162. BOE (2007) REAL DECRETO 907/2007. Ministerio de Medio Ambiente. Gobierno de España., de 7 de julio de 2007.

Boletín Oficial del Estado núm. 294. BOE (2007) REAL DECRETO 1620/2007. Ministerio de la Presidencia. Gobierno de España., de 8 de diciembre de 2007.

Bonet, A. (1978). *Plan Castro*. Madrid, Spain: Ed. COAM.

Borking, J., & Raab, C. (2001). Laws, PETs and Other Technologies for Privacy Protection. *Journal of Information, Law and Technology*. Available at SSRN: https://ssrn.com/abstract=3034261

Boudeguer, A., & Sepúlveda, F. (2004). Accesibilidad en la edificación. In Manual de Accesibilidad Universal. Cap. III. Santiago de Chile, Chile: Servicio Nacional de Turismo de Chile (SERNATUR).

Boulding, W., & Amna, K. (1993). A consumer-side experimental examination of signaling theory: Do consumers perceive warranties as signals of quality? *The Journal of Consumer Research*, *20*(1), 111–123. doi:10.1086/209337

Breaux, T. D., & Rao, A. (2013). Formal analysis of privacy requirements specifications for multi-tier applications. In *Proceeding of the 21st IEEE International Requirements Engineering Conference (RE)*. (pp. 14-23). Rio de Janeiro: IEEE. 10.1109/RE.2013.6636701

Brito Marquina, A., Cantarero García, G., Piñar Mañas, J., Suárez Ojeda, M., Cantarero García, G., Piñar Mañas, J., & Suárez Ojeda, M. (2017). Smart cities: Derecho y técnica para una ciudad mas habitable. Madrid: Reus.

Buhalis, D. (2000). Marketing the competitive destination of the future. *Tourism Management*, *21*(1), 97–116. doi:10.1016/S0261-5177(99)00095-3

Buhalis, D. (2003). *Tourism: Information Technology for Strategic Tourism Management*. Gosport, UK: Prentice Hall.

Buhalis, D., & Amaranggana, A. (2014). Smart Tourism Destinations. In Z. Xiang & I. Tussyadiah (Eds.), *Information and Communication Technologies in Tourism* (pp. 553–564). Heidelberg, Germany: Springer. (Original work published 2014)

Buhalis, D., & Licata, M. (2002). The Future eTourism Intermediaries. *Tourism Management*, *23*(3), 207–220. doi:10.1016/S0261-5177(01)00085-1

Bullón de Mendoza, A. (2009). Los primeros corresponsales de guerra: España 1833-1840. *Cuadernos de Investigacion Historica*, *26*, 345–349.

Burd, B., Barker, L., & Divitini, M. (2017). Courses, content, and tools for internet of things in computer science education. *Proceedings of the ITiCSE Conference on Working Group Reports*. 10.1145/3174781.3174788

Burmester, M., Desmedt, Y., Wright, R., & Yasinsac, A. (2002). Security or Privacy, Must We Choose? In *Proceeding of the Symposium on Critical Infrastructure Protection and the Law* (pp. 1-8). Academic Press.

Burns, B., & Oppenheimer, D. (2016). *Design Patterns for Container-based Distributed Systems*. Paper presented at the 8th USENIX Workshop on Hot Topics in Cloud Computing (HotCloud 16), Denver, CO.

Burns, B. (2018). *Distributed Systems, Patterns and Paradigms for Scalable Microservices*. Sebastopol, CA: O'Reilly Media.

Buyya, R., & Dastjerdi, A. V. (2016). *Internet of Things. Principles and paradigms*. Cambridge, MA: Elsevier.

Buyya, R., & Yeoa, C. S. (2008). *Cloud Computing, and emerging IT platforms: Vision, hype, and reality for delivering computing as the 5th utility*. Elsevier B.V. doi:10.1016/j.future.2008.12.001

Cailly, P., Tran, A., Balenghien, T., L'Ambert, G., Toty, C., & Ezanno, P. (2012). A climate-driven abundance model to assess mosquito control strategies. *Ecological Modelling, 227*, 7–17. doi:10.1016/j.ecolmodel.2011.10.027

Calderoni, L., Maio, D., & Palmieri, P. (2012). Location-aware Mobile Services for a Smart City: Design, Implementation and Deployment. *Journal of Theoretical and Applied Electronic Commerce Research, 7*(3), 74–87. doi:10.4067/S0718-18762012000300008

Calheiros, R. N., Ranjan, R., Beloglazov, A., De Rose, C. A. F., & Buyya, R. (2010). CloudSim: A toolkit for modeling and simulation of cloud computing environments and evaluation of resource provisioning algorithms. *Software, Practice & Experience, 41*(1), 23–50. doi:10.1002pe.995

California PestCast: Disease Model Database—UC IPM. (n.d.). Retrieved January 31, 2020, from http://ipm.ucanr.edu/DISEASE/DATABASE/diseasemodeldatabase.html

Campbell, J., Goldfarb, A., & Tucker, C. (2015). Privacy regulation and market structure. *Journal of Economics & Management Strategy, 24*(1), 47–73. doi:10.1111/jems.12079

Campbell-Lendrum, D., Manga, L., Bagayoko, M., & Sommerfeld, J. (2015). Climate change and vector-borne diseases: What are the implications for public health research and policy? *Philosophical Transactions of the Royal Society B: Biological Sciences, 370*(1665). doi:10.1098/rstb.2013.0552

Canadian Nurses Association. (2003). Privacy and Health Information: Challenges for Nurses and for The Nursing Profession. *Ethics in Practice for Registered Nurses.*

Canbay, Y., Vural, Y., & Sagiroglu, S. (2018). Privacy Preserving Big Data Publishing. In *International Congress on Big Data, Deep Learning and Fighting Cyber Terrorism (IBIGDELFT)* (pp. 24-29). Ankara, Turkey: IEEE. 10.1109/IBIGDELFT.2018.8625358

Cantarero-García, G. (2018). Reflexiones urbanísticas. Referencias del pasado y situación actual de Madrid como ciudad inteligente potencial. In Gestión inteligente y sostenible de las ciudades. Gobernanza, smart cities y turismo. Valencia, Spain: Tirant lo Blanch.

Cardoso, A., & Simões, P. (2011, July). Cloud computing: Concepts, technologies and challenges. In *International Conference on Virtual and Networked Organizations, Emergent Technologies, and Tools* (pp. 127-136). Springer.

Castellani, A. P., Bui, N., Casari, P., Rossi, M., Shelby, Z., & Zorzi, M. (2010). *Architecture and protocols for the internet of things: A case study*. Paper presented at 8th IEEE International Conference on Pervasive Computing and Communications Workshops (PERCOM Workshops), Mannheim, Germany. 10.1109/PERCOMW.2010.5470520

Cator, L. J., Thomas, S., Paaijmans, K. P., Ravishankaran, S., Justin, J. A., Mathai, M. T., ... Eapen, A. (2013). Characterizing microclimate in urban malaria transmission settings: A case study from Chennai, India. *Malaria Journal, 12*(1), 84. doi:10.1186/1475-2875-12-84 PMID:23452620

Cavoukian, A., & Tapscott, D. (1997). *Who Knows: Safeguarding Your Privacy in a Networked World*. McGraw-Hill Professional Publisher.

Chadee, D. D., & Martinez, R. (2000). Landing periodicity of Aedes aegypti with implications for dengue transmission in Trinidad, West Indies. *Journal of Vector Ecology, 25*, 158–163. PMID:11217215

Chan, H., Perrig, A., & Song, D. (2003). Random key predistribution schemes for sensor networks. *2003 Symposium on Security and Privacy*, 197–213. 10.1109/SECPRI.2003.1199337

Chediak, M., Eckhouse, B., & Buhayar, N. (2019). California goes solar. *Bloomberg Business Week*. Retrieved October 26, 2019 from https://www.bloomberg.com/news/articles/2019-10-22/california-prepares-for-a-huge-solar-boom

Chen, Y., & Dong, X. (2013). *The development and prospect of new technology in modern distance education*. Paper presented at International Conference on Information Science and Computer Applications (ISCA 2013), Tel Aviv, Israel. 10.2991/isca-13.2013.7

Chen, C., Xiang, B., Liu, Y., & Wang, K. (2019). A Secure Authentication Protocol for Internet of Vehicles. *IEEE Access : Practical Innovations, Open Solutions, 7*, 12047–12057. doi:10.1109/ACCESS.2019.2891105

Cheng, H.-C., & Liao, W.-W. (2012). *Establishing a lifelong learning environment using IOT and learning analytics*. Paper presented at 14th International Conference on Advanced Communication Technology (ICACT), PyeongChang, South Korea.

Chen, H., & Liu, X. (2006). Adoption of low mobility services: 'Little-Smart' in China as a case. *Info, 8*(6), 69–78. doi:10.1108/14636690610707491

Chen, Y., Why, A., Batista, G., Mafra-Neto, A., & Keogh, E. (2014). Flying insect classification with inexpensive sensors. *Journal of Insect Behavior, 27*(5), 657–677. doi:10.100710905-014-9454-4 PMID:25350921

Christophers, S. R. (1960). *Aedes aegypti: The yellow fever mosquito*. CUP Archive.

Cisco Systems. (2013). *Software-Defined Networking: Why we like it and how we are building on it*. Cisco White Paper. Retrieved from https://www.cisco.com/c/dam/en_us/solutions/industries/docs/gov/cis13090_sdn_sled_white_paper.pdf

Clark, D. D., & Wilson, D. R. (1987). A comparison of commercial and military computer security policies. *Security and Privacy, IEEE Symposium on*, 184–194. 10.1109/SP.1987.10001

Cobb, A., Roberts, S., & Zilli, D. (2016). Active sampling to increase the battery life of mosquito-detecting sensor networks. *AIMS CDT Mini Project, 10*.

Colwill, C. (2009). Human Factors in information security: The insider threat–Who can you trust these days? *Information Security Technical Report, 14*(4), 186–196. doi:10.1016/j.istr.2010.04.004

Continental. (2017). *Press Release: Continental is investing in EasyMile and pushing ahead with the development of driverless mobility*. Retrieved November 20, 2019, from https://www.continental.com/en/press/press-releases/continental-is-investing-in-easymile-70642

Convert, B. (2005). Europe and the Crisis in Scientific Vocations. *European Journal of Education, 40*(4), 361–366. doi:10.1111/j.1465-3435.2005.00233.x

Cornetta, G., Touhafi, A., Mateos, F. J., & Muntean, G.-M. (2018, November). *A Cloud-based Architecture for Remote Access to Digital fabrication Services for Education*. Paper presented at the 4th IEEE International Conference on Cloud Computing Technologies and Applications (Cloudtech), Brussels, Belgium. 10.1109/CloudTech.2018.8713358

Cornetta, G., Mateos, F. J., Touhafi, A., & Muntean, G.-M. (2019). Design, simulation and testing of a cloud platform for sharing digital fabrication resources for education. *Journal of Cloud Computing, 8*(12). doi:10.118613677-019-0135-x

Cornetta, G., Mateos, F. J., Touhafi, A., & Muntean, G.-M. (2019a). Modelling and Simulation of a Cloud Platform for Sharing Distributed Digital Fabrication Resources. *Computers, 8*(2), 47. doi:10.3390/computers8020047

Costello, L. R., & Jones, K. S. (2014). *WUCOLS IV: Water Use Classification of Landscape Species.* Davis, CA: California Center for Urban Horticulture, University of California. Retrieved from https://ucanr.edu/sites/WUCOLS/

Cranmer, E., & Jung, T. (2014) *Augmented Reality (AR): Business Models in Urban Cultural Heritage Tourist Destinations.* Paper presented at the 12th APacCHRIE Conference 2014, Kuala Lumpur, Malaysia.

Cribellier, A., van Erp, J. A., Hiscox, A., Lankheet, M. J., van Leeuwen, J. L., Spitzen, J., & Muijres, F. T. (2018, August). Flight behaviour of malaria mosquitoes around odour-baited traps: Capture and escape dynamics. *Royal Society Open Science, 5*(8), 180246. doi:10.1098/rsos.180246 PMID:30225014

CULTURAbase. (2017). *Turismo cultural.* Ministerio de Cultura y Deporte. Retrieved December 12 from http://estadisticas.mecd.gob.es/CulturaDynPx/culturabase/index.htm?type=pcaxis&path=/t7/p7b/a2016/&file=pcaxis

Dahlqvist, F., Patel, M., Rajko, A., & Shulman, J. (2019). *Growing Opportunities in the Internet of Things.* McKinsey & Company. Retrieved from https://www.mckinsey.com/industries/private-equity-and-principal-investors/our-insights/growing-opportunities-in-the-internet-of-things# in January 2020.

Damar, T., Fleming, G. A., Gandahusada, S., & Bang, Y. H. (1981). Nocturnal indoor resting heights of the malaria vector Anopheles aconitus and other anophelines (Diptera: Culicidae) in Central Java, Indonesia. *Journal of Medical Entomology, 18*(5), 362–365. doi:10.1093/jmedent/18.5.362 PMID:7299790

Damos, P. (2015). Modular structure of web-based decision support systems for integrated pest management. A review. *Agronomy for Sustainable Development, 35*(4), 1347–1372. doi:10.100713593-015-0319-9

Data Protection Laws of the World. (2019). *Technical report. DLAPIPER.* https://www.dlapiperdataprotection.com

De Groot, J. (2019). *What is the general data protection regulation? Understanding and complying with GDPR requirements in 2019.* Retrieved from https://digitalguardian.com/blog/what-gdpr-general-data-protection-regulation-understanding-and-complying-gdpr-data-protection

De Maerschalck, B., Maiheu, B., Janssen, S., & Vankerkom, J. (2010). CFD-modelling of complex plant-atmosphere interactions: Direct and indirect effects on local turbulence. *Proceedings of the CLIMAQS Workshop 'Local Air Quality and Its Interactions with Vegetation', 21–22.*

Delaney, K. J., & Macedo, T. B. (2000). The impact of herbivory on plants: Yield, fitness, and population dynamics. In *Biotic stress and yield loss* (pp. 149–174). CRC Press. doi:10.1201/9781420040753.ch9

Delatte, H., Desvars, A., Bouétard, A., Bord, S., Gimonneau, G., Vourc'h, G., & Fontenille, D. (2010). Blood-feeding behavior of Aedes albopictus, a vector of Chikungunya on La Réunion. *Vector Borne and Zoonotic Diseases (Larchmont, N.Y.), 10*(3), 249–258. doi:10.1089/vbz.2009.0026 PMID:19589060

Delgado, M. (2016). La ciudad ideal como derrota finl de lo urbano. In XIV Coloquio Internacional de Geocrítica. Las utopias y la construcción de la Sociedad del futuro, 215-234.

Department of Biomedical Informatics at Harvard Medical School. (2018). *n2c2 builds on the legacy of i2b2.* Available from https://dbmi.hms.harvard.edu/programs/healthcare-data-science-program/clinical-nlp-research-data-sets

Diario Oficial de la Unión Europea núm. 327. Directiva Marco del Agua (DMA). 2000/60/CE del Parlamento Europeo y del Consejo 22 de diciembre de 2000.

DLA Piper. (2020). *EU general data privacy regulation*. Retrieved from https://www.dlapiper.com/en/us/focus/eu-data-protection-regulation/home

Dong, L., Xianmang, H., LongBin, C., & Huahui, C. (2016). Permutation anonymization. *Journal of Intelligent Information Systems Archive, 47*(3), 427-445.

Eastlick, M. A., Lotz, S. L., & Warrington, P. (2006). Understanding online b-to-c relationships: An integrated model of privacy concerns, trust, and commitment. *Journal of Business Research, 59*(8), 877–886. doi:10.1016/j.jbusres.2006.02.006

Ejaz, W., Imran, M., Jo, M., Muhammad, N., Qaisar, S., & Wang, W. (2016). Internet of Things (IoT) in 5G Wireless Communications. *IEEE Access: Practical Innovations, Open Solutions, 4*, 10310–10314. doi:10.1109/ACCESS.2016.2646120

El Ouazzani, Z., & El Bakkali, H. (2017). New Technique Ensuring Privacy in Big Data: Variable t-Closeness for Sensitive Numerical Attributes. In *The 3rd International Conference on Cloud Computing and Technology Application (CloudTech'17)*, (pp. 1-6). IEEE.

El Ouazzani, Z., & El Bakkali, H. (2019b). Variable Distinct L-diversity Algorithm Applied on Highly Sensitive Correlated Attributes. In *The Fifteenth International Conference on Wireless and Mobile Communications (ICWMC)*, (pp. 47-52). Rome, Italy: ThinkMind.

El Ouazzani, Z., & El Bakkali, H. (2018a). A new technique ensuring privacy in big data: K-anonymity withoutprior value of the threshold k. In *Proceeding of The First International Conference On Intelligent Computing in Data Sciences*. (pp. 52 - 59). Elsevier. 10.1016/j.procs.2018.01.097

El Ouazzani, Z., & El Bakkali, H. (2018b). Proximity Test for Sensitive Categorical Attributes in Big Data. In *Proceeding of the 4th International Conference on Cloud Computing Technologies and Applications (Cloudtech)*. IEEE, 10.1109/CloudTech.2018.8713359

El Ouazzani, Z., & El Bakkali, H. (2019a). Privacy in Big Data Through Variable t-Closeness for MSN Attributes. In M. Zbakh, M. Essaaidi, P. Manneback, & C. Rong (Eds.), *Cloud Computing and Big Data: Technologies, Applications and Security (CloudTech 2017). Lecture Notes in Networks and Systems. 49* (pp. 52–59). Elsevier.

Elyamany, H. F., & AlKhairi, A. H. (2015). *IoT-academia architecture: A profound approach*. Paper presented at 2015 16th IEEE/ACIS International Conference on software Engineering, Artificial Intelligence, Networking and Parallel/Distributed Computing (SNPD), Takamatsu, Japan. 10.1109/SNPD.2015.7176275

Erickson, R. A., Presley, S. M., Allen, L. J. S., Long, K. R., & Cox, S. B. (2010). A stage-structured, Aedes albopictus population model. *Ecological Modelling, 221*(9), 1273–1282. doi:10.1016/j.ecolmodel.2010.01.018

Essays. (2013). *The History Of Smart Cities Concept Information Technology Essay*. Retrieved from https://www.uniassignment.com/essay-samples/information-technology/the-history-of-smart-cities-concept-information-technology-essay.php?vref=1

EU approves GDPR. (2016). *Information Management, 50*(4), 7. Retrieved from https://search-proquest-com.du.idm.oclc.org/docview/1805460371?accountid=14608

EU project. (n.d.a). *FABLAB SCHOOLS EU: Towards Digital Smart, Entrepreneurial and Innovative Pupils*. https://fablabproject.eu/the-project/

EU project. (n.d.b). *NEWTON: Networked Labs for Training in Science and Technology*. http://newtonproject.eu

European Commission. (2017). The Ageing Report 2018 – Underlying Assumptions & Projection Methodologies. *Institutional Papers, 65*. doi:10.2765/286359

European Commission. (2018). *The Silver Economy – Final report*. Luxembourg: Publications Office of the European Union. doi:10.2759/640936

European Commission. (2019). *The Future of Cities – Opportunities, Challenges and The Way Forward*. Joint Research Centre (JRC). doi:10.2760/375209

European Data Protection Board. (2019). *First overview of the implementation of GDPR and the roles and means of the national supervisory authorities*. Retrieved from https://www.europarl.europa.eu/meetdocs/2014_2019/plmrep/COMMITTEES/LIBE/DV/2019/02-25/9_EDPB_report_EN.pdf

European Network for Rural Development. (2018). Smart Villages Revitalising Rural Services. *Eu Rural Review, 26*. Retrieved December 12, 2019, from https://enrd.ec.europa.eu/sites/enrd/files/enrd_publications/publi-enrd-rr-26-2018-en.pdf

European Parliament (2014). *Mapping Smart Cities in the EU*. Directorate general for internal policies. Publications Office. doi:. doi:10.2861/3408

European Union. (2015). *Automated transportation in the (driverless) seat*. Research and Innovation. Retrieved November 15, 2019, from https://ec.europa.eu/research/infocentre/converting.cfm

European Union. (2018). *Legislation environment and climate change*. Retrieved March 27th 2020, from https://eur-lex.europa.eu/summary/chapter/environment.html?root_default=SUM_1_CODED=20&locale=en

Europeana Foundation. (2015). *Transforming the World with Culture: Next Steps on Increasing the Use of Digital Cultural Heritage in Research*. Education, Tourism and the Creative Industries.

Eurostat. (2017). *Household expenditure by purpose in the EU, 2017*. Retrieved November 15, 2019, from https://ec.europa.eu/eurostat/news/themes-in-the-spotlight/household-expenditure-2017

Evangelista, I. R. S. (2018). Bayesian Wingbeat Frequency Classification and Monitoring of Flying Insects Using Wireless Sensor Networks. *TENCON 2018-2018 IEEE Region 10 Conference*, 2403–2407.

Evans, D., Conrad, C. L., & Paul, F. M. (2003). Handbook of automated data quality control checks and procedures of the National Data Buoy Center. NOAA National Data Buoy Center Tech. Document, 03–02.

Evans, D. (2012). *The Internet of Everything. How More Relevant and Valuable Connections Will Change the World*. Cisco Internet Business Solutions Group.

Evans, M. V., Hintz, C. W., Jones, L., Shiau, J., Solano, N., Drake, J. M., & Murdock, C. C. (2019). Microclimate and larval habitat density predict adult Aedes albopictus abundance in urban areas. *The American Journal of Tropical Medicine and Hygiene, 101*(2), tpmd190220. doi:10.4269/ajtmh.19-0220 PMID:31190685

EZ10. (2019). Retrieved November 14, 2019, from https://easymile.com/solutions-easymile/ez10-autonomous-shuttle-easymile/

Farahani, B., Firouzi, F., Chang, V., Badaroglu, M., Constant, N., & Mankodiya, K. (2018). Towards fog-driven IoT eHealth: Promises and challenges of IoT in medicine and healthcare. *Future Generation Computer Systems, 78*, 659–676. doi:10.1016/j.future.2017.04.036

Feng, Q., He, D., Zeadally, S., Khan, K., & Kumar, N. (2019). A survey on privacy protection in blockchain system. *Journal of Network and Computer Applications, 126*, 45–58. doi:10.1016/j.jnca.2018.10.020

Feruza, Y., & Kim, T.-H. (2007). IT Security Review: Privacy, Protection, Access Control. *Assurance and System Security., 2*(2), 17–32.

FitzPatrick, S. M. (2017). *Data privacy and sovereignty changing legal landscape.* Retrieved from https://fr.slideshare.net/tealium/digital-velocity-london-2017-data-privacy-and-sovereignty-sheila-fitz-patrick/6

Flores, O., & Rayle, L. (2016). *How cities use regulation for innovation: the case of Uber, Lyft and Sidecar in San Francisco.* World Conference on Transport Research - WCTR (2016), Shanghai. Retrieved December 12, 2019 from https://reader.elsevier.com/reader/sd/pii/S2352146517305379?token=BD6FAD1CBDA7F54FEE76091A1897E6AFDA7A9457073DA04C9F9F5F5F7FCEF25199A8DB07F00A42D332570A3D95B95008

Fogel, R. (2010). *White Paper, The Education Cloud: Delivering Education as a Service.* Intel World Ahead.

Förster, W. (2006). Housing in the 20th and 21st Centuries: Vienna. Social housing, innovative architecture. Munich: Prestel.

Förster, W. (2018). *The Vienna Model of Social Housing.* Partnerships for Affordable Rental Housing, University of Calgary. Retrieved October 8, 2019 from https://ucalgary.ca/cities/files/cities/forster_the-vienna-model-of-social-housing.pdf

Förster, D., Löhr, H., & Kargl, F. (2015). Decentralized enforcement of k-anonymity for location privacy using secret sharing. In *Vehicular Networking Conference (VNC)* (pp. 279 - 286). Kyoto, Japan: IEEE. 10.1109/VNC.2015.7385589

Franchini, T. (Dir.) & Raventós, T. (Coord.). (2018). Temas de planeamiento urbano. Madrid, Spain: CEU Ediciones.

Freilich, R., & Popowitz, N. (2010). The Umbrella of Sustainability: Smart Growth, New Urbanism, Renewable Energy and Green Development in the 21st Century. *The Urban Lawyer, 42*(1), 1–39.

Frizzo-Barker, J., Chow-White, P. A., Mozafari, M., & Ha, D. (2016). An empirical study of the rise of big data in business scholarship. *International Journal of Information Management, 36*(3), 403–413. doi:10.1016/j.ijinfomgt.2016.01.006

Fuller, C. S. (2018). Privacy law as price control. *European Journal of Law and Economics, 45*(2), 225–250. doi:10.100710657-017-9563-6

Fundación Telefónica. (2011). *Smart Cities: un primer paso hacia el internet de las cosas.* Madrid, Spain: Author.

Ganapati, S., & Schoepp, C. (2008). The wireless city. *International Journal of Electronic Government Research, 4*(4), 54–68. doi:10.4018/jegr.2008100104

Gandomi, A., & Haider, M. (2015). Beyond the hype: Big data concepts, methods and analytics. *International Journal of Information Management, 35*(2), 137–144. doi:10.1016/j.ijinfomgt.2014.10.007

Garau, C., Masala, F., & Pinna, F. (2015). Bechmarking smart urban mobility: A study on Italian cities. *Computational science and its applications—ICCSA, 2015, lecture notes in computer science (LNCS)*, 612–623. . doi:10.1007/978-3-319-21470-2

Gardner, H. (1983). *Multiple intelligences: New horizons.* New York, NY: Basic Books.

Garfinkel, S. (2011, Oct. 3). The Cloud Imperative. *MIT Technology Review.* https://www.technologyreview.com/s/425623/the-cloud-imperative/

Gartner. (2018). *Gartner Forecasts India Public Cloud Revenue to Grow 37.5 Percent in 2018.* https://www.gartner.com/newsroom/id/3874299

Gawanmeh, A., & Alomari, A. (2015). Challenges in Formal Methods for Testing and Verification of Cloud Computing Systems. *Journal of Scalable Computing: Practice and Experience, 16*(3), 321–332. doi:10.12694cpe.v16i3.1104

GDPR. (2019). *GDPR fines after one year: key takeaways for businesses.* Retrieved from: https://gdpr.eu/gdpr-fines-so-far/

Gershenfeld, N. (2012). How to Make Almost Anything: The Digital Fabrication Revolution. *Foreign Affairs, 91*(6), 43–57.

Getting to Smart Growth II. (2003). *100 more policies for implementation/ Smart Network.* Washington, DC: International City/County Management Association.

Gilchrist, A. (2016). *Industry 4.0: The industrial Internet of Things.* Bangken, Thailand: Apress. doi:10.1007/978-1-4842-2047-4

Gilson, L. (2012). *Health Policy and Systems Research: A Methodology Reader.* Alliance for Health Policy and Systems Research and World Health Organization. Retrieved from https://www.who.int/alliance-hpsr/alliancehpsr_reader.pdf

Goel, S., Williams, K., & Dincelli, E. (2017). Got phished? Internet security and human vulnerability. *Journal of the Association for Information Systems*, *18*(1), 22–44. doi:10.17705/1jais.00447

Goldfarb, A., & Tucker, C. (2012). Privacy and innovation. *Innovation Policy and the Economy*, *12*(1), 65–90. doi:10.1086/663156

Goleman. (1995) *Emotional Intelligence.* New York, NY: Bantam Books.

Gori, P., Parcu, P. L., & Stasi, M. (2015). *Smart Cities and Sharing Economy.* Robert Schuman Centre for Advanced Studies. Research Paper No. RSCAS 2015/96. doi:10.2139srn.2706603

Goyal, K. K., Garg, A., Rastogi, A., & Singhal, S. (2018). A Literature Survey on Internet of Things (IOT). *International Journal of Advanced Networking and Applications*, *9*(6), 3663–3668.

Greenfield, A. (2013). Against the Smart City: A Pamphlet. The city is here for you to use, 1. New York, NY: Academic Press.

Greenleaf, G. (2017). Global tables of data privacy laws and bills. *Privacy Laws & Business International Report*, *5*, 14–26.

Gretzel, U., Sigala, M., Xiang, Z., & Koo, C. (2015). *Smart Tourism: Foundations and Developments.* Working Paper, Smart Tourism Research Center, Kyung Hee University.

Gretzel, U. (2018). *Tourism and Social Media. In The Sage Handbook of Tourism Management* (pp. 415–432). Sage. doi:10.4135/9781526461490.n28

Griggs, K. N., Ossipova, O., Kohlios, C. P., Baccarini, A. N., Howson, E. A., & Hayajneh, T. (2018). Healthcare Block-chain System Using Smart Contracts for Secure Automated Remote Patient Monitoring. *Journal of Medical Systems*, *42*(7), 130. doi:10.100710916-018-0982-x PMID:29876661

Grubb, B. (2017). Elon Musk promises 'anywhere in the world in one hour'. *The Sidney Morning Herald.* Retrieved September 28, 2019 from https://www.smh.com.au/technology/elon-musk-promises-anywhere-in-the-world-in-one-hour-20170929-gyrpan.html

Gubler, D. J. (1998). Resurgent vector-borne diseases as a global health problem. *Emerging Infectious Diseases*, *4*(3), 442–450. doi:10.3201/eid0403.980326 PMID:9716967

Gul, L. F., & Simisic, L. (2014, June). *Integration of Digital Fabrication in Architectural Curricula.* Paper presented at the Annual FabLearn Conference Europe, Aarhus, Denmark.

Gul, S., Asif, M., Ahmad, S., Yasir, M., Majid, M., & Arshad, M. (2017). A survey on role of internet of things in education. *IJCSNS*, *17*(5), 159–165.

Hadlington, L. (2018). The "Human Factor" in cybersecurity: Exploring the accidental insider. In Psychological and Behavioral Examinations in Cyber Security (pp. 46-63). IGI Global.

Hajibaba, M., & Gorgin, S. (2014). A review on modern distributed computing paradigms: Cloud computing, jungle computing and fog computing. *CIT. Journal of Computing and Information Technology*, 22(2), 69–84. doi:10.2498/cit.1002381

Hankinson, A. (1982). *Man of war: William Howard Russell of the Times*. Londres, UK: Heinemann.

Hann, I., Hui, K., Lee, T., & Png, I. (2002). *Online information privacy: Measuring the cost-benefit trade-off*. Paper presented at the International Conference on Information Systems, Barcelona, Spain.

Harding, A., Blokland-Potters, T., & Blokland, T. (2014). *Urban theory: A critical introduction to power, cities and urbanism in the 21st century*. Los Angeles: SAGE.

Hassan, F., Domingo-Ferrer, J., & Soria-Comas, J. (2018). Anonymization of Unstructured Data via Named-Entity Recognition. In V. Torra, Y. Narukawa, I. Aguiló, & M. González-Hidalgo (Eds.), *Modeling Decisions for Artificial Intelligence. MDAI 2018* (pp. 296–305). Springer International Publishing. doi:10.1007/978-3-030-00202-2_24

Hawkins, C. (2011). Smart Growth Policy Choice: A Resource Dependency and Local Governance Explanation. *Policy Studies Journal: the Journal of the Policy Studies Organization*, 39(4), 679–707. doi:10.1111/j.1541-0072.2011.00427.x

Hays, S., Page, S. J., & Buhalis, D. (2013). Social Media as a Destination Marketing Tool: Its Use by National Tourism Organisations. *Current Issues in Tourism*, 16(3), 211–239. doi:10.1080/13683500.2012.662215

Healthcare Data Breach Report. (2019). *HIPAA Journal*. Retrieved from https://www.hipaajournal.com/august-2019-healthcare-data-breach-report/

Hernández Muñoz, A. (2015). *Abastecimiento y Distribución de Agua. 6ª edición*. Madrid: Garceta Grupo Editorial.

Hernández Muñoz, A. (2015). *Depuración y Desinfección de Aguas Residuales. 6ª edición*. Madrid: Garceta Grupo Editorial.

Hernández Muñoz, A. (2017). *Saneamiento y Alcantarillado. 8ª edición*. Madrid: Garceta Grupo Editorial.

Herrando Mill, E. (2012). *Auditorías energéticas en el ciclo integral del agua*. Barcelona: Presented at Jornada Técnica SMAGUA.

Higher education in India. (n.d.). https://en.wikipedia.org/wiki/Higher_education_in_India

Hirtan, L., Krawiec, P., Dobre, C:, & Batalla, J. (2019). Blockchain-Based Approach for e-Health Data Access Management with Privacy Protection. In *Proceeding of the 24th International Workshop on Computer Aided Modeling and Design of Communication Links and Networks (CAMAD)*. (pp. 1-7). IEEE. 10.1109/CAMAD.2019.8858469

Hu, R., Stalla-Bourdillon, S., Yang, Mu., Schiavo, V., & Sassone, V. (2017). Regulation, and Practice? A Techno-Legal Analysis of Three Types of Data in the GDPR. In Data Protection and Privacy: The Age of Intelligent Machines. Academic Press.

Huijboom. (2011). The Openness of Government. *European Journal of epractice.eu*. https://joinup.ec.europa.eu/sites/default/files/document/2014-06/ePractice%20Journal-%20Vol.%2012-March_April%202011.pdf

Hui, K., & Png, I. P. L. (2006). The economics of privacy. *Economics and Information Systems*, 1, 271–293.

Hu, L., Qiu, M., Song, J., Hossain, M. S., & Ghoneim, A. (2015). Software defined healthcare networks. *IEEE Wireless Communications*, 22(6), 67–75. doi:10.1109/MWC.2015.7368826

Hur, B., & Eisenstadt, W. R. (2015). Low-power wireless climate monitoring system with rfid security access feature for mosquito and pathogen research. *2015 First Conference on Mobile and Secure Services (MOBISECSERV)*, 1–5. 10.1109/MOBISECSERV.2015.7072871

Hu, Y.-C., Perrig, A., & Johnson, D. B. (2003). Rushing attacks and defense in wireless ad hoc network routing protocols. *Proceedings of the 2nd ACM Workshop on Wireless Security*, 30–40. 10.1145/941311.941317

IBM. (2011) *Ciudades más inteligentes para un desarrollo sostenible. Cómo optimizar los sistemas de la ciudad en una economía basada en el talento.* Institute for Business Value. Retrieved November 9, 2019, from https://www.ibm.com/smarterplanet/global/files/es__es_es__cities__ciudades_inteligentes_para_desarrollo_sostenible_0622.pdf

ICMA. (2003). Getting to Smart Growth II: 100 more policies for implementation. Smart Network International City/County Management Association.

IDAE (2010). *Estudio de Prospectiva. Consumo energético en el sector del agua.* Madrid: Instituto para la Diversificación y Ahorro de la Energía (IDEA). Fundación Observatorio de Prospectiva Tecnológica Industrial (OPTI).

India Age structure. (2018). In *CIA World Factbook.* https://www.indexmundi.com/india/age_structure.html

India, T. W. D. (2018). *Budget 2018: Education sector analysis.* https://www.indiatoday.in/education-today/news/story/budget-2018-education-sector-analysis-1172823-2018-02-19

IPM Cost Calculator. (n.d.). Retrieved January 31, 2020, from http://www.ipmcalculator.com/

Islam, S., Baig, Z., & Zeadally, S. (2019). Physical Layer Security for the Smart Grid: Vulnerabilities, Threats and Countermeasures. *IEEE Transactions on Industrial Informatics*, *15*(12), 6522–6530. doi:10.1109/TII.2019.2931436

Izquierdo, S., & Bartolomé, A. (2019). *Pilares de la divulgación en Humanidades: Geografía, tecnologías digitales y comunicación Historia, pensamiento y humanismo actual. Libro homenaje al profesor Federico Martínez Roda.* Valencia: Universidad de Valencia.

Jadeja, Y., & Modi, K. (2012, March). Cloud computing-concepts, architecture and challenges. In *2012 International Conference on Computing, Electronics and Electrical Technologies (ICCEET)* (pp. 877-880). IEEE. 10.1109/ICCEET.2012.6203873

Jaffe, A. B., Newell, R. G., & Stavins, R. N. (2002). Environmental policy and technological change. *Environmental and Resource Economics*, *22*(1-2), 41–49. doi:10.1023/A:1015519401088

Jaffe, A. B., & Palmer, K. (1997). Environmental regulation and innovation: A panel data study. *The Review of Economics and Statistics*, *79*(4), 610–619. doi:10.1162/003465397557196

Jain, P., Gyanchandani, M., & Khare, N. (2019). Improved k-Anonymity Privacy-Preserving Algorithm Using Madhya Pradesh State Election Commission Big Data. In A. Krishna, K. Srikantaiah, & C. Naveena (Eds.), *Integrated Intelligent Computing, Communication and Security. Studies in Computational Intelligence, 771* (pp. 1–10). Singapore: Springer. doi:10.1007/978-981-10-8797-4_1

Jankauski, M. (2019). Flapping at Resonance: Measuring the Frequency Response of the Hymenoptera Thorax. *bioRxiv*.

Jascow, P. L., & Rose, N. L. (1989). The effects of economic regulation. Handbook of Industrial Organization, 2, 1450–1498.

Joh, E. E. (2019). Policing the smart city. *International Journal of Law in Context*, *15*(2), 177–182. doi:10.1017/S1744552319000107

Juniper Networks. (2016). *SDN and NFV: Transforming the service provider organization.* Juniper White Paper. Retrieved from https://www.juniper.net/assets/us/en/local/pdf/whitepapers/2000579-en.pdf

Kahn, M. C., Celestin, W., & Offenhauser, W. (1945). Recording of Sounds produced by certain Disease-carrying Mosquitoes. *Science*, *101*(2622), 335–336. doi:10.1126cience.101.2622.335 PMID:17789049

Kamatchi, Ambekar, & Parikh. (n.d.). Security mapping of a usage based cloud system. *Network Protocols and Algorithms*.

Kaplan, B. (2014). *Patient health data privacy*. Available at: https://papers.ssrn.com/sol3/papers.cfm?abstract_id=2510429

Kar, J., & Mishra, M. R. (2016). Mitigate threats and security metrics in cloud computing. *J Inf Process Syst*, *12*(2), 226–233.

Karlof, C., & Wagner, D. (2003). Secure routing in wireless sensor networks: Attacks and countermeasures. *Ad Hoc Networks*, *1*(2–3), 293–315. doi:10.1016/S1570-8705(03)00008-8

Khalil, I., Khreishah, A., & Azeem, M. (2014). Cloud computing security: A survey. *Computers*, *3*(1), 1–35. doi:10.3390/computers3010001

Kheng, T. Y. (2010). *Analysis, Design and implementation of Energy Harvesting Systems for Wireless Sensor Nodes* (PhD Thesis).

Khurat, A., Boontawee, S., & Dieter, G. (2017). Privacy policies verification in composite services using OWL. *Journal of Computer Security*, *67*, 122–141. doi:10.1016/j.cose.2017.02.015

Kim, D. J. (2008). Self-perception-based versus transference-based trust determinants in computer-mediated transactions: A cross-cultural comparison study. *Journal of Management Information Systems*, *24*(4), 13–45. doi:10.2753/MIS0742-1222240401

Kitanov, S., & Janevski, T. (2019). Introduction to fog computing. In *The Rise of Fog Computing in the Digital Era* (pp. 1–35). IGI Global. doi:10.4018/978-1-5225-6070-8.ch001

Knightley, P. (1976). *Corresponsales de Guerra*. Barcelona, Spain: Euros.

Kogan, M. (1988). Integrated pest management theory and practice. *Entomologia Experimentalis et Applicata*, *49*(1–2), 59–70. doi:10.1111/j.1570-7458.1988.tb02477.x

Kogan, M. (1998). Integrated pest management: Historical perspectives and contemporary developments. *Annual Review of Entomology*, *43*(1), 243–270. doi:10.1146/annurev.ento.43.1.243 PMID:9444752

Kothari Commission. (n.d.).https://en.wikipedia.org/wiki/Kothari_Commission

Križan, T., Brakus, M., & Vukelić, D. (2015). In-Situ Anonymization of Big Data. In *Proceeding of the 38th International Convention on Information and Communication Technology, Electronics and Microelectronics (MIPRO)* (pp. 292-298). Opatija, Croatia: IEEE.

La DGT y Telefónica prueban un sistema de IoT que anticipa a los conductores sobre peligros en la carretera. (2019). Retrieved October 20, 2019, from https://www.esmartcity.es/2019/09/13/dgt-telefonica-prueban-sistema-iot-anticipa-conductores-peligros-carretera

Lalic, B., Eitzinger, J., Dalla Marta, A., Orlandini, S., Sremac, A. F., & Pacher, B. (2018). *Agricultural Meteorology and Climatology* (Vol. 8). Firenze University Press. doi:10.36253/978-88-6453-795-5

Lande, N. (1995). *Dispatches from the Front. In News Accounts for the American Wars* (pp. 1776–1991). Nueva York, NY: Henry Holt and Company.

Lanjouw, J. O., & Mody, A. (1996). Stimulating innovation and the international diffusion of environmentally responsive technology: The role of expenditures and institutions. *Research Policy*, *25*(4), 549–571. doi:10.1016/0048-7333(95)00853-5

Ledo Iglesias, A. T. (2019). Analysis of Social and Legal Issues on Critical Infrastructures in Spain. *Sixth International Conference on eDemocracy & eGovernment (ICEDEG)*, 375-377. 10.1109/ICEDEG.2019.8734451

Lee, B., Ang, L., & Dubelaar, C. (2015). Lemons on the web: A signaling approach to the problem of trust in Internet commerce. *Journal of Economic Psychology*, 26(5), 607–623. doi:10.1016/j.joep.2005.01.001

Leguineche, M., & Sánchez, G. (2001). *Los ojos de la guerra*. Barcelona, Spain: Mondadori.

Li, T., Liao, C., Cho, H., Chien, W., Lai, C. F., & Chao, H. (2017). An e-healthcare sensor network load-balancing scheme using SDN-SFC. *Proceedings of the IEEE 19th International Conference on e-Health Networking, Applications and Services (Healthcom)*, 1-4. 10.1109/HealthCom.2017.8210833

Liu, D., Ning, P., & Li, R. (2005). Establishing pairwise keys in distributed sensor networks. *ACM Transactions on Information and System Security*, 8(1), 41–77. doi:10.1145/1053283.1053287

Locating outside sensors for optimum accuracy. (n.d.). *Prodata Weather Systems*. Retrieved January 30, 2020, from https://www.weatherstations.co.uk/gooddata.htm

Lom, O., Pribyl, O., & Svitek, M. (2016). Industry 4.0 as a part of smart cities. *2016 Smart Cities Symposium Prague (SCSP)*, 1-6. 10.1109/SCSP.2016.7501015

Lompar, M., Lalić, B., Dekić, L., & Petrić, M. (2019). Filling gaps in hourly air temperature data using debiased ERA5 data. *Atmosphere*, 10(1), 13. doi:10.3390/atmos10010013

Lopez de Avila, A. (2015). *Smart Destinations: XXI Century Tourism*. Presented at the *ENTER2015 Conference on Information and Communication Technologies in Tourism*, Lugano, Switzerland.

Lorenzo, C., Lorenzo, E., Cornetta, G., Muntean, G.-M., & Togou, M. A. (2018, November) *Designing, testing and adapting to create a distributed learning program in open design and digital fabrication*. Paper presented at the International Conference of Education, Research and Innovation (ICERI), Seville, Spain. 10.21125/iceri.2018.0046

Lytras, M. D., & Visvizi, A. (2018). Who uses Smart City Services and What to Make of IT: Toward Interdisciplinary Smart Cities Research. *Sustainability*, 10(6), 1998. doi:10.3390u10061998

Magrabi, S. A. R., Pasha, M. I., & Pasha, M. Y. (2018). Classroom teaching to enhance critical thinking and problem-solving skills for developing IOTApplications. *J Eng Educ Transform*, 31(3), 152–157.

Malhotra, N. K., Kim, S. S., & Agarwal, J. (2004). Internet users' internet privacy concerns (IUIPC): The construct, the scale, and a causal model. *Information Systems*, 15(4), 311–416.

Malone, T. W. (2018). *Superminds*. New York: Hachette.

Mankin, R. W., Machan, R., & Jones, R. (2006). Field testing of a prototype acoustic device for detection of Mediterranean fruit flies flying into a trap. *Proc. 7th Int. Symp. Fruit Flies of Economic Importance*, 10–15.

Manyika, J., Chui, M., Brown, B., Bughin, J., Dobbs, R., Roxburgh, C., & Byers, A. (2011). *Big data: The next frontier for innovation, competition, and productivity*. Retrieved from https://www.mckinsey.com/business-functions/mckinsey-digital/our-insights/big-data-the-next-frontier-for-innovation

Marquez, J., Villanueva, J., Solarte, Z., & Garcia, A. (2016). IoT in Education: Integration of Objects with Virtual Academic Communities. In New Advances in Information Systems and Technologies. Advances in Intelligent Systems and Computing, no. 115 (pp. 201-212). Springer International Publishing.

Martin, R. (n.d.). *Japan is Best Prepared to Capitalize on Cloud Computing*. https://www.techinasia.com/japan-cloud-cloud-computing#fnref:1

Martin, T., Brasiel, S., Graham, D., Smith, S., Gurko, K., & Fields, D. A. (2014, October). *FabLab Professional Development: Changes in Teacher and Student STEM Content Knowledge*. Paper presented at the Annual FabLearn Conference, Stanford, CA.

Martucci, L. A., Zuccatoy, A., & Ben Smeetsk, S. M. (2012). Privacy, Security and Trust in Cloud Computing The Perspective of the Telecommunication Industry. *9th International Conference on Ubiquitous Intelligence and Computing and 9th International Conference on Autonomic and Trusted Computing*. DOI 10.1109/UIC-ATC.2012.166

Matesanz, A., & Hernández, A. (2014). *On the improvement of urban regeneration processes from more than thirty years of rehabilitation experiences*. Retrieved from: http://oa.upm.es/33391/1/papernumber577.pdf

Mayer, C. P. (2009). Security and privacy challenges in the internet of things. *Electronic Communications of the EASST*, 17.

McCann, E., & Paddison, R. (2014). Cities & social change: Encounters with contemporary urbanism. Los Angeles: SAGE.

McGhin, T., Choo, K.-K. R., Liu, C., & He, D. (2019). Blockchain in healthcare applications: Research challenges and opportunities. *Journal of Network and Computer Applications*, *135*, 135. doi:10.1016/j.jnca.2019.02.027

McKeachie, W. J., & Svinicki, M. (2006). *Teaching Tips: Strategies, Research, and Theory for College and University Teachers*. Belmont, CA: Wadsworth.

Mees, A. (1975, December). The revival of cities in medieval Europe: An application of catastrophe theory. *Regional Science and Urban Economics*, *5*(4), 403–425. doi:10.1016/0166-0462(75)90018-6

Mekki, K., Bajic, E., Chaxel, F., & Meyer, F. (2019). A comparative study of LPWAN technologies for large-scale IoT deployment. *ICT Express*, *5*(1), 1–7. doi:10.1016/j.icte.2017.12.005

Mell, P., & Grance, T. (2011). *The NIST Definition of Cloud Computing: Recommendations of the National Institute of Standards and Technology*. https://csrc.nist.gov/publications/nistpubs/800-145/SP800-145.pdf

Meredith, S. (2018). *Facebook-Cambridge Analytica: A Timeline of the Data Hijacking Scandal*. Retrieved from https://www.cnbc.com/2018/04/10/facebook-cambridge-analytica-a-timeline-of-the-data-hijacking-scandal.html

Mershad, K., & Wakim, P. (2018). A learning management system enhanced with internet of things applications. *J Educ Learn*, *7*(3), 23. doi:10.5539/jel.v7n3p23

Metcalf & Eddy. (2013). *Wastewater engineering: treatment and reuse* (4th ed.). New York: McGraw-Hill.

Meyer, R. P., Hardy, J. L., & Reisen, W. K. (1990). Diel changes in adult mosquito microhabitat temperatures and their relationship to the extrinsic incubation of arboviruses in mosquitoes in Kern County, California. *Journal of Medical Entomology*, *27*(4), 607–614. doi:10.1093/jmedent/27.4.607 PMID:2167374

Milberg, S., Smith, J., & Burke, S. (2000). Information privacy: Corporate management and national regulation. *Organization Science*, *11*(1), 35–37. doi:10.1287/orsc.11.1.35.12567

Miorandi, D., Sicari, S., De Pellegrini, F., & Chlamtac, I. (2012). Internet of things: Vision, applications and research challenges. *Ad Hoc Networks*, *10*(7), 1497–1516. doi:10.1016/j.adhoc.2012.02.016

Mohamed, A-B., Gunasekaran, M., Mai, M., & Ehab, R. (2018). *Internet of things in smart education environment: Supportive framework in the decision-making process*. Academic Press.

Mohanta, B., Jena, D., Panda, S. & Sobhanayak, S. (2019). Blockchain Technology: A Survey on Applications and Security Privacy Challenges. *Journal of Internet of Things*, 100-107.

Moorcraft, P. L., & Taylor, P. M. (2008). *Shooting the Messenger. The Political Impact of War Reporting*. Washington, DC: Potomac Books.

More, P. (2015). Review of implementing fog computing. *International Journal of Research in Engineering and Technology*, *4*(06), 335–338. doi:10.15623/ijret.2015.0406057

Moss, T. W., Neubaum, D. O., & Meyskens, M. (2015). The effect of virtuous and entrepreneurial orientations on microfinance lending and repayment: A signaling theory perspective. *Entrepreneurship Theory and Practice*, *39*(1), 27–52. doi:10.1111/etap.12110

Mourtzis, D., Vlachou, E., & Milas, N. (2016). Industrial Big Data as a Result of IoT Adoption in Manufacturing. *Procedia CIRP*, *55*, 290–295. doi:10.1016/j.procir.2016.07.038

Murdock, C. (n.d.). *Variation in mosquito microclimate and implications for vector-borne disease transmission*. Academic Press.

Murray, R. (2016, November). *Unlocking Europe's potential via STEM education*. https://blogs.microsoft.com/eupolicy/2016/11/24/

MyPest Page—IPM Pest and Plant Disease Models and Forecasting. (n.d.). Retrieved January 31, 2020, from http://pnwpest.org/wea/

Naish, M. (2014). *Implementing Public Key Infrastructure (PKI) Using Microsoft Windows Server 2012 Certificate Services*. Digital Certificates.

Namal, S., Ahmad, I., Saud, S., Jokinen, M., & Gurtov, A. (2015). Implementation of OpenFlow based cognitive radio network architecture: SDN&R. *Wireless Networks*, *22*(2), 663–677. doi:10.100711276-015-0973-5

Nargundi, S., & Phalnikar, R. (2013). Data De-Identification Tool for Privacy Preserving Data Mining. *International Journal of Computer Science Engineering and Information Technology Research*, *3*(1), 267–276.

National Academies of Sciences and Medicine. (2016). *Global health impacts of vector-borne diseases: Workshop summary*. National Academies Press.

National committee on vital and health statistics. (2006). Functional Requirements Needed for the Initial Definition of a Nationwide Health Information Network (NHIN). *Report to the Secretary of the U.S. Department of Health and Human Services*. Retrieved from https://ncvhs.hhs.gov/wp-content/uploads/2014/05/061030lt.pdf

Nessus. (n.d.). https://www.tenable.com/blog/nessus-50-released

Neuhofer, B., Buhalis, D., & Ladkin, A. (2015). Technology as a Catalyst of Change: Enablers and Barriers of the Tourist Experience and Their Consequences. In Information and Communication Technologies in Tourism 2015. Lugano, Switzerland: Springer Verlag.

Nissenbaum, H. (2011). A contextual approach to privacy online. *Daedalus*, *140*(4), 32–48. doi:10.1162/DAED_a_00113

NIST National Institute of Standards and Technology Us Department of Commerce. (n.d.). *Blockchain*. Retrieved from https://www.nist.gov/topics/blockchain

Nmap scripts. (n.d.). https://nmap.org/nsedoc/scripts/

Nmap. (n.d.). https://nmap.org/

Norma UNE-EN 16247-5. (2015). *Auditorías energéticas*. Competencia de los auditores energéticos.

O'Connell, L. (2009). The Impact of Local Supporters on Smart Growth Policy Adoption. *Journal of the American Planning Association, 75*(3), 281–291. doi:10.1080/01944360902885495

O'Neil, C. (2016). *Weapons of Math Destruction*. Broadway Books.

OECD. (1997). The OECD Report on Regulatory Reform: Volume 1: Sectoral Studies. OECD.

Okay, F. Y., & Ozdemir, S. (2018). Routing in Fog-Enabled IoT Platforms: A Survey and an SDN-Based Solution. *IEEE Internet of Things Journal, 5*(6), 4871–4889. doi:10.1109/JIOT.2018.2882781

Open University. (n.d.).https://en.wikipedia.org/wiki/Open_University

Openstack. (n.d.). https://www.openstack.org/

Orwell, G. (1949). 1984. New York: Plume. Harcourt Brace Jovanovich.

Ouyang, T.-H., Yang, E.-C., Jiang, J.-A., & Lin, T.-T. (2015). Mosquito vector monitoring system based on optical wingbeat classification. *Computers and Electronics in Agriculture, 118*, 47–55. doi:10.1016/j.compag.2015.08.021

Overby, H., & Steen-Thøde, M. (1990). *Calculation of vertical temperature gradients in heated rooms*. Academic Press.

Ovum. (2014). *Data privacy laws: Cutting the red tape*. Retrieved from https://www.intralinks.com/resources/analyst-reports/ovum-report-data-privacy-laws cutting-red-tape#

Paaijmans, K. P., Imbahale, S. S., Thomas, M. B., & Takken, W. (2010). Relevant microclimate for determining the development rate of malaria mosquitoes and possible implications of climate change. *Malaria Journal, 9*(1), 196. doi:10.1186/1475-2875-9-196 PMID:20618930

Paaijmans, K. P., & Thomas, M. B. (2011). The influence of mosquito resting behaviour and associated microclimate for malaria risk. *Malaria Journal, 10*(1), 183. doi:10.1186/1475-2875-10-183 PMID:21736735

Padfield, N., Haldrup, M., & Hobye, M. (2014, June). *Empowering academia through modern fabrication practices*. Paper presented at the Annual FabLearn Conference Europe, Aarhus, Denmark.

Palega, M., & Knapinski, M. (2018). Threats associated with the Human Factor in the aspect of in-formation security. *Scientific Journal of the Military University of Land Forces, 50*(1), 105–118. doi:10.5604/01.3001.0011.7364

Pallot, M., Trousse, B., Senach, B., & Scapin, D. (2010). *Living Lab Research Landscape: From User Centred Design and User Experience Towards User Co-creation*. Position Paper, First Living Labs Summer School Inria, París. Retrieved November 9, 2019, from http://link.springer.com/chapter/10.1007%2F978-3-642-20898-0_31#

Pampana, E. (1966). *Erradicación de la malaria*. Editorial Limusa-Wiley México.

Panagiotopoulus, P., Ziaee Bigdeli, A., & Sams, S. (2012). *"5 days in August" - How London Local Authorities Used Twitter during the 2011 Riots. In IFIP International Federation for Information Processing 2012* (pp. 102–113). Electronic Government.

PanB. (2015). *E-Tourism*. Doi:10.1007/978-3-319-01669-6_77-1

Pannapacker, W. (2009). *The MLA and the Digital Humanities*. Retrieved November 9, 2019, from https://web.archive.org/web/20120514003204/http://chronicle.com/blogPost/The-MLAthe-Digital/19468

Parimala, S. (2017). A Survey on Security and Privacy Issues of BigData in Healthcare Industry and Implication of Predictive analytics. *International Journal of Innovative Research in Computer and Communication Engineering, 5*(4), 8130–8134.

PCORI Patient-Centered Outcomes Research Institute. (2019). *Improving Outcomes Important to Patients.* Retrieved from https://www.pcori.org

Pedigo, L. P., & Rice, M. E. (2014). *Entomology and pest management.* Waveland Press.

Pellicer, S., Santa, G., Bleda, A. L., & Meastre, R. (2013). A Global Perspective of Smart Cities: A Survey. *2013 Seventh International Conference on Innovative Mobile and Internet Services in Ubiquitous Computing*, 439-444. 10.1109/IMIS.2013.79

Perera, C., Ranjan, R., Wang, L., Khan, S. U., & Zomaya, A. Y. (2015). Big data privacy in the internet of things era. *IT Professional*, *17*(3), 32–39. doi:10.1109/MITP.2015.34

Perera, C., Zaslavsky, A., Christen, P., & Georgakopoulos, D. (2013). Context aware computing for the internet of things: A survey. *IEEE Communications Surveys and Tutorials*, *16*(1), 414–454. doi:10.1109/SURV.2013.042313.00197

Peterson, R. K., Higley, L. G., & Pedigo, L. P. (2018). Whatever happened to IPM? *American Entomologist (Lanham, Md.)*, *64*(3), 146–150. doi:10.1093/ae/tmy049

Petric, M. (2020). *Modelling the influence of meteorological conditions on mosquito vector population dynamics (Diptera, Culicidae).* Ghent University.

Petrić, M., Vandendriessche, J., Marsboom, C., Matheussen, T., Ducheyne, E., & Touhafi, A. (2019). Autonomous Wireless Sensor Networks in an IPM Spatial Decision Support System. *Computers*, *8*(2), 43. doi:10.3390/computers8020043

Phung, K.-H., Tran, H., Nguyen, Q., Huong, T. T., & Nguyen, T.-L. (2018). Analysis and assessment of LoRaWAN. *2018 2nd International Conference on Recent Advances in Signal Processing, Telecommunications & Computing (SigTelCom)*, 241–246.

Piñar Mañas, J. L. (Dir.), Suárez, M. (Coord.), Cantarero G., Cantó, T., Martínez, R., & Navarro, N. (2017). Smart Cities derecho y técnica para una ciudad más habitable. Madrid, Spain: Editorial Reus.

Population of India 2019. (2019). *India Population 2019, Most Populated States.* http://www.indiapopulation2019.in/

Porras-Amores, C., Mazarrón, F. R., & Cañas, I. (2014). Study of the vertical distribution of air temperature in warehouses. *Energies*, *7*(3), 1193–1206. doi:10.3390/en7031193

Porter, M. E. (1991). America's Green Strategy. *Scientific American*, *6*(3), 168. doi:10.1038cientificamerican0491-168 PMID:1925488

Porter, M. E., & Van Der Linde, C. (1995). Toward a new conception of the environment -competitiveness relationship. *The Journal of Economic Perspectives*, *9*(4), 97–118. doi:10.1257/jep.9.4.97

Portney, K. (2005). Civic Engagement and Sustainable Cities in the United States. *Public Administration Review*, *65*(5), 579–591. doi:10.1111/j.1540-6210.2005.00485.x

Posner, R. A. (1981). The economics of privacy. *The American Economic Review*, *71*(2), 405–409.

Potamitis, I., & Rigakis, I. (2015). Novel noise-robust optoacoustic sensors to identify insects through wingbeats. *IEEE Sensors Journal*, *15*(8), 4621–4631. doi:10.1109/JSEN.2015.2424924

Poupineau, S. (2016). *Which smart tourism experiences are more likely to enhance the destination attractiveness?* Retrieved November 9, 2019, from https://www.researchgate.net/publication/308918443_Which_smart_tourism_experiences_are_more_likely_to_enhance_the_destination_attractiveness

Prufer, J. (2018). Trusting privacy in the cloud. *Information Economics and Policy*, *45*, 52–67. doi:10.1016/j.infoecopol.2018.10.003

Quadra-Salcedo y Fernández del Castillo, T., Piñar Mañas, J., Barrio Andrés, M., & Torregrosa Vázquez, J. (2018). *Sociedad digital y derecho*. Madrid: Ministerio de Industria, Comercio y Turismo.

Queralta, J. P., Gia, T. N., Zou, Z., Tenhunen, H., & Westerlund, T. (2019). Comparative study of LPWAN technologies on unlicensed bands for M2M communication in the IoT: Beyond LoRa and LoRaWAN. *Procedia Computer Science*, *155*, 343–350. doi:10.1016/j.procs.2019.08.049

Quiñones, M. L., & Suarez, M. F. (1990). Indoor resting heights of some anophelines in Colombia. *Journal of the American Mosquito Control Association*, *6*(4), 602–604. PMID:2098466

Rahman, G., & Chuah, C. W. (2018). Fog computing, applications, security and challenges [review]. *IACSIT International Journal of Engineering and Technology*, *7*(3), 1615–1621. doi:10.14419/ijet.v7i3.12612

Rajarajeswari, S., & Somasundaram, K. (2016). Data confidentiality and privacy in cloud computing. *Indian Journal of Science and Technology*, *9*(4), 1–8. doi:10.17485/ijst/2016/v9i4/87040

Rajendran, K., Jayabalan, M., & Rana, M. E. (2017). A Study on k-anonymity, l-diversity, and t-closeness techniques focusing Medical Data. *International Journal of Computer Science and Network Security*, *17*(12), 172–177.

Raj, P., & Raman, A. C. (2017). *The Internet of Things: Enabling Technologies, Platforms, and Use Cases*. Boca Raton, FL: CRC Press.

Raman, D. R., Gerhardt, R. R., & Wilkerson, J. B. (2007). Detecting insect flight sounds in the field: Implications for acoustical counting of mosquitoes. *Transactions of the ASABE*, *50*(4), 1481–1485. doi:10.13031/2013.23606

Raymond, D. R., Marchany, R. C., Brownfield, M. I., & Midkiff, S. F. (2008). Effects of denial-of-sleep attacks on wireless sensor network MAC protocols. *IEEE Transactions on Vehicular Technology*, *58*(1), 367–380. doi:10.1109/TVT.2008.921621

Raza, U., Kulkarni, P., & Sooriyabandara, M. (2017). Low power wide area networks: An overview. *IEEE Communications Surveys and Tutorials*, *19*(2), 855–873. doi:10.1109/COMST.2017.2652320

Reed, S. C., Williams, C. M., & Chadwick, L. E. (1942). Frequency of wing-beat as a character for separating species races and geographic varieties of Drosophila. *Genetics*, *27*(3), 349. PMID:17247046

Research Models: Insects, Mites, Diseases, Plants, and Beneficials—From UC IPM. (n.d.). Retrieved January 31, 2020, from http://ipm.ucanr.edu/MODELS/index.html

Resnik, D. (2010). Urban Sprawl, Smart Growth, and Deliberative Democracy. *American Journal of Public Health*, *100*(10), 1852–1856. doi:10.2105/AJPH.2009.182501 PMID:20724685

Reynolds, D. R., & Riley, J. R. (2002). Remote-sensing, telemetric and computer-based technologies for investigating insect movement: A survey of existing and potential techniques. *Computers and Electronics in Agriculture*, *35*(2–3), 271–307. doi:10.1016/S0168-1699(02)00023-6

Roberts, M. (2018). *Serverless architectures*. https://martinfowler.com/articles/serverless.html

Robertson, K. (2006). *Increase Student Interaction with "Think-Pair-Shares" and "Circle Chats"*. colorincolorado.org

Rong, A. (2012). *China economic net*. Retrieved November 12, 2019, from http://en.ce.cn/Insight/201204/12/t20120412_23235803.shtml

Rothschild, M., & Stiglitz, J. (1976). Equilibrium in competitive insurance markets: An essay on the economics of imperfect information. *The Quarterly Journal of Economics*, *90*(4), 629–649. doi:10.2307/1885326

Ruz Bentué, E. (2007). *Smart. City. Innovación urbana para la sostenibilidad, Efficient Urban*. Madrid: Arnáiz and Partners.

Sadki, S. & EL Bakkali, H. (2016). Resolving conflicting privacy policies in m-healthbased on prioritization. *Journal of Scalable Computing: Practice & Experience*, *17*.

Saeed, R., & Rauf, A. (2018). Anatomization through generalization (AG): A hybrid privacy-preserving approach to prevent membership, identity and semantic similarity disclosure attacks. In *The International Conference on Computing, Mathematics and Engineering Technologies (iCoMET)* (pp. 1-7). Sukkur, Pakistan: Academic Press.

Saharan, K. P., & Kumar, A. (2015). Fog in comparison to cloud: A survey. *International Journal of Computers and Applications*, *122*(3), 10–12. doi:10.5120/21679-4773

Sala, L. (2007). *Balances energéticos del ciclo del agua y experiencias de reutilización planificada en municipios de la Costa Brava*. Valencia: Presented at Seminario Internacional Agua, Energía y Cambio Climático.

Sánchez-Corcuera, R., Nuñez-Marcos, A., Sesma-Solance, J., Bilbao-Jayo, A., Mulero, R., Zulaika, U., ... Almeida, A. (2019). Smart Cities survey: Technologies, application domains and challenges fo the cities of the future. *International Journal of Distributed Sensor Networks*, *15*(6). doi:10.1177/1550147719853984

Sánchez, M., Barceló, T., & Cabezuelo, F. (2017). The Smart City Apps as the Core of Place Branding Strategy: A Comparative Analysis of Innovation Cases. *Zer: Revista de Estudios de Comunicación*, *22*(42), 119–135.

Sánchez, M., & Ibar, R. (2015). Convergence and Interaction in the New Media: Typologies of Prosumers among University Students. *Communicatio Socialis*, *28*(2), 87–99.

Savary, S., Willocquet, L., Pethybridge, S. J., Esker, P., McRoberts, N., & Nelson, A. (2019). The global burden of pathogens and pests on major food crops. *Nature Ecology & Evolution*, *3*(3), 430–439. doi:10.103841559-018-0793-y PMID:30718852

Savopoulou-Soultani, M., Papadopoulos, N. T., Milonas, P., & Moyal, P. (2012). Abiotic Factors and Insect Abundance [Editorial]. *Psyche*, *2012*, 1–2. doi:10.1155/2012/167420

Schaffers, H., Komninos, N., Pallot, M., Trousse, B., Nilsson, M., & Oliveira, A. (2011). Smart Cities and the Future Internet: Towards Cooperation Frameworks for Open Innovation. In The Future Internet (pp. 66-56). Berlin: Springer.

Schwäbisches Tagblatt. (2019). *Klare Mehrheit für ein neues Hallenbad*. Online Ausgabe März 2019. Retrieved October 10, 2019, from https://www.tagblatt.de/Nachrichten/Buerger-App-Rund-12-000-machten-mit-409066.html

Sclater. (2010). Cloud Computing in Education. UNESCO Institute for Information Technologies in Education.

Seastrom M. (2011). *Data Stewardship: Managing Personally Identifiable Information in Electronic Student Education Records*. Technical/Methodological Report. National Center for Education Statistics (NCES 2011-602).

Šebesta, O., Gelbič, I., & Peško, J. (2011). Daily and seasonal variation in the activity of potential vector mosquitoes. *Open Life Sciences*, *6*(3), 422–430. doi:10.247811535-011-0019-7

Secretaría de Estado de la España Global. (2017). *España, referente internacional en Ciudades Inteligentes*. Retrieved November 12, 2019, https://marcaespana.es/actualidad/innovaci%C3%B3n/espa%C3%B1a-referente-internacional-en-ciudades-inteligentes

SEGITTUR. (2015). *Informe destinos turísticos: construyendo el futuro*. Retrieved November 13, 2019, https://www.segittur.es/opencms/export/sites/segitur/.content/galerias/descargas/proyectos/Libro-Blanco-Destinos-Tursticos-Inteligentes-ok_es.pdf

Sei, Y., Takenouchi, T., & Ohsuga, A. (2015). (l1, ...,lq)-diversity for Anonymizing Sensitive Quasi-Identifiers. *IEEE Journal of Trustcom/BigDataSE/ISPA*, 596-603.

Sensus. (2012). *Water 20/20: Bringing Smart Water Networks into Focus*. Retrieved from https://c.ymcdn.com/sites/www.ncsafewater.org/resource/collection/A0650A28-4C94-471B-B98E-B0DFD4F76C35/Water_T_AM_09.10_Walsby.pdf

Seol, K., Kim, Y., Lee, E., Seo, Y., & Baik, D. (2018). Privacy-Preserving Attribute-Based Access Control Model for XML-Based Electronic Health Record System. *IEEE Access : Practical Innovations, Open Solutions*, 6, 9114–9128. doi:10.1109/ACCESS.2018.2800288

Sethi, P., & Sarangi, S. R. (2017). Internet of things: Architectures, protocols, and applications. *Journal of Electrical and Computer Engineering*, *2017*, 1–25. doi:10.1155/2017/9324035

Shapiro, J. (2005). *Smart cities: Quality of life, productivity, and the growth effects of human capital (Documentos de trabajo, 11615)*. Cambridge, MA: National Bureau of Economic Research.

Shaw, T., Mcgregor, D., Brunner, M., Keep, M., Janssen, A., & Barnet, S. (2017). What is eHealth (6)? Development of a Conceptual Model for eHealth: Qualitative Study with Key Informants. *Journal of Medical Internet Research*, *19*(10), e324. doi:10.2196/jmir.8106 PMID:29066429

Shi, E., & Perrig, A. (2004). Designing secure sensor networks. *IEEE Wireless Communications*, *11*(6), 38–43. doi:10.1109/MWC.2004.1368895

Shi, W., & Schahram, D. (2016). The promise of edge computing. *Computer*, *49*(5), 78–81. doi:10.1109/MC.2016.145

Shouling, J., Prateek, M., & Raheem, B. (2017). Graph Data Anonymization, De-Anonymization Attacks, and De-Anonymizability Quantification: A Survey. *IEEE Communications Surveys and Tutorials*, *19*(2), 1305–1326. doi:10.1109/COMST.2016.2633620

Shouran, Z., Ashari, A., & Priyambodo, T. (2019). Internet of Things (IoT) of Smart Home: Privacy and Security. *International Journal of Computers and Applications*, *182*(39), 3–8. doi:10.5120/ijca2019918450

Shyr, W.-J., Zeng, L.-W., Lin, C.-K., Lin, C.-M., & Hsieh, W.-Y. (2018). Application of an energy management system via the internet of things on a university campus. *Eurasia Journal of Mathematics, Science and Technology Education*, *14*(5), 1759–1766. doi:10.12973/ejmste/80790

Sikula, O. (n.d.). Vertical Distribution of Air Temperatures in Heated Dwelling Rooms. *Proceedings of Clima 2007 WellBeing Indoors: Rehva World Congress*.

Smith, A., & Cannan, E. (2003). *The Wealth of Nations* (6th ed.). New York: N.Y. Bantam Classic.

Smith, M. E., & Lobo, J. (2019). Cities Through the Ages: One Thing or Many? *Front. Digit. Humanit.*, *6*, 12. doi:10.3389/fdigh.2019.00012

Solove, D. J. (2002). Conceptualizing privacy. *California Law Review*, *90*(4), 1087–1155. doi:10.2307/3481326

Soto Álvarez, G., Soto Benavides, M., Sáez Abarzúa, C., & Morales Miranda, M. (2013). Desalación de agua de mar mediante sistema Osmosis Inversa y Energía Fotovoltaica para provisión de agua potable en Isla Damas, Región de Coquimbo. Documentos Técnicos del PHI-LAC, N° 33. Montevideo: UNESCO.

Spence, N., Hill, L., & Morris, J. (2020). How the global threat of pests and diseases impacts plants, people, and the planet. Plants, People. *Planet, 2*(1), 5–13.

Spiegel. (2019a). *Mietroller-Anbieter Coup stellt Betrieb ein.* Retrieved October 14, 2019, from: https://www.spiegel.de/auto/aktuell/coup-mietroller-anbieter-stellt-den-betrieb-ein-a-1298185.html

Spiegel. (2019b). *Flixbus stellt E-Bus-Experiment ein.* Retrieved October 11, 2019 from: https://www.spiegel.de/wirtschaft/unternehmen/flixbus-stellt-e-bus-experiment-ein-a-1299697.html

Staley, S. (2004). Urban Planning, Smart Growth, and Economic Calculation: An Austrian Critique and Extension. *The Review of Austrian Economics, 17*(2), 265–283.

Sternberg, R. J. (1985). *A Triarchic Theory of Intelligence.* Cambridge University Press.

Stern, V., Smith, R., Van den Bosch, R., & Hagen, K. (1959). The integration of chemical and biological control of the spotted alfalfa aphid: The integrated control concept. *Hilgardia, 29*(2), 81–101. doi:10.3733/hilg.v29n02p081

Stewart, L. A. (2010). *The Impact of Regulation on Innovation in the United States: A Cross-Industry Literature Review.* Information Technology & Innovation Foundation.

Stigler, G. J. (1980). An introduction to privacy in Economics and Politics. *The Journal of Legal Studies, 9*(4), 623–644. doi:10.1086/467657

Stiglitz, J. E., & Weiss, A. (1981). Credit rationing in markets with imperfect information. *The American Economic Review, 71*(3), 393–410.

Stoutjesdijk, P. H., & Barkman, J. J. (2014). *Microclimate, vegetation & fauna.* Brill. doi:10.1163/9789004297807

Suduc, A.-M., Bizoi, M., & Gorghiu, G. (2018). A Survey on IoT in Education. *Revista Romaneasca pentru Educatie Multidimensionala, 10*(3), 103-111.

Suna, Changb, & Suna, & Wanga. (2011). Surveying, and Analyzing Security, Privacy and Trust Issues in Cloud Computing Environments. *Procedia Engineering, 15.* doi:10.1016/j.proeng.2011.08.537

Sun, H., Wang, C., & Ahmad, B. I. (2018). *From Internet of Things to Smart Cities. Enabling technologies.* Boca Raton, FL: CRC Press.

Sun, L. (2011). Smart Growth in Dumb Places: Sustainability, Disaster, and the Future of the American City. *Brigham Young University Law Review, 2011*(6), 2157–2201. doi:10.2139srn.1918386

Tankard, C. (2016). What the GDPR means for business. *Network Security, 2016*(6), 5–8. doi:10.1016/S1353-4858(16)30056-3

Tan, P., Wu, H., Li, P., & Xu, H. (2018). Teaching management system with applications of RFID and IoT technology. *Education in Science, 8*(1), 26. doi:10.3390/educsci8010026

Tayyaba, S. K., Shah, M. A., Khan, O. A., & Ahmed, A. W. (2017). Software Defined Network (SDN) Based Internet of Things (IoT): A Road Ahead. In *Proceedings of the International Conference on Future Networks and Distributed Systems* (pp. 15:1-15:8). New York, NY: ACM 10.1145/3102304.3102319

Telefónica, F. (2011). *Smart cities: un primer paso hacia el internet de las cosas.* Barcelona: Ariel.

Tesconi, S., & Arias, L. (2014, June). *MAKING as a Tool to Competence-based School Programming.* Paper presented at the Annual FabLearn Conference Europe, Aarhus, Denmark.

The biggest healthcare data breaches. (2018). *Healthcare IT News magazine*. Retrieved from https://www.healthcareit-news.com/projects/biggest-healthcare-data-breaches-2018-so-far

The Open Networking Foundation. (2013). *Software-Defined Networking: the new norm for networks*. ONF White Paper. Retrieved from https://www.opennetworking.org/images/stories/downloads/sdn-resources/white-papers/wp-sdn-newnorm.pdf

The Open Networking Foundation. (2014). *Introducing ONOS – a SDN network operating system for Service Providers*. ONF White Paper. Retrieved from onosproject.org/wp-content/uploads/2014/11/Whitepaper-ONOS-final.pdf

The Open Networking Foundation. (2015). *OpenFlow Switch specification version 1.5.1*. TS-025. Retrieved from https://www.opennetworking.org/software-defined-standards/specifications/

The Right to Privacy in Singapore. (1999). *Privacy International*. Technical report.

Thorndike, E. (1904). Introduction to the Theory of Mental and Social Measurements. Davenport, 20(519). doi:10.1037/13283-000

Togou, M. A., Lorenzo, C., Cornetta, G., & Muntean, G. M. (2019). NEWTON Fab Lab Initiative: A Small-Scale Pilot for STEM Education. In Proceedings of EdMedia + Innovate Learning 2019, (pp. 8-17). Waynesville, NC: Association for the Advancement of Computing in Education (AACE).

Togou, M. A., Lorenzo, C., Lorenzo, E., Cornetta, G., & Muntean, G.-M. (2018, July). *Raising students' interest in STEM education via remote digital fabrication: an Irish primary school case study*. Paper presented at Edulearn 2018, Palma de Mallorca, Spain. 10.21125/edulearn.2018.0756

Togou, M. A., Lorenzo, C., Lorenzo, E., Cornetta, G., & Muntean, G.-M. (2019, June). *NEWTON Fab Lab initiative: a small-scale pilot for STEM education*. Paper presented at EdMedia and Innovate Learning Conference, Amsterdam, The Netherlands.

Toledo, C. V., & Spruit, M. R. (2016). Adopting Privacy Regulations in a Data Warehouse A Case of the Anonimity versus Utility Dilemma. In *The 8th International Joint Conference on Knowledge Discovery, Knowledge Engineering and Knowledge Management (IC3K 2016)* (pp. 67 - 72). Porto, Portugal: Academic Press.

Tomalty, R., & Curran, D. (2003). Living it up: The wide range of support for smart growth in Canada promises more livable towns and cities. *Alternatives*, 29(3), 10–18.

Touhafi, A., Braeken, A., Tahiri, A., & Zbakh, M. (2018). *CoderLabs: A cloud-based platform for real-time online labs with user collaboration*. Concurrency and Computation Wiley Online Library. doi:10.1002/cpe.4377

U.S. Department of Energy. (2019). *Net Zero Water Buildings Strategies*. Retrieved from https://www.energy.gov/eere/femp/net-zero-water-building-strategies

U.S. Public Interest Research Group. Public comment on barriers to electronic commerce, Response to call by U.S. Department of Commerce (65 Federal Register 15898), April 25, 2000.

UK Department for Education. (2013). *National Curriculum in England: Design and Technology Programmes of Study*. Retrieved from https://www.gov.uk/governemnt/publication/national-curriculum-in-england-design-and-technology-programmes-of-study

Ukil, A., Bandyopadhyay, S., & Pal, A. (2014). IoT-privacy: To be private or not to be private. *2014 IEEE Conference on Computer Communications Workshops (INFOCOM WKSHPS)*, 123–124.

Ukil, A. (2010). *Security and privacy in wireless sensor networks*. INTECH Open Access Publisher. doi:10.5772/14272

Uniaccess. (2006). *Design of Universal Accesibility Systems for Public Transport.* https://trimis.ec.europa.eu/project/design-universal-accessibility-systems-public-transport

United Nations Conference on Trade and Development (UNCTAD). (2016). *Data protection regulations and international data flows: Implications for trade and development.* Retrieved from https://unctad.org/en/PublicationsLibrary/dtlstict2016d1_en.pdf

United Nations Conference on Trade and Development (UNCTAD). (n.d.). *Online consumer protection legislation worldwide.* Retrieved from https://unctad.org/en/Pages/DTL/STI_and_ICTs/ICT4D-Legislation/eCom-Consumer-Protection-Laws.aspx

United Nations Department of Economic and Social Affairs. (2018). *68% of the world population projected to live in urban areas by 2050, says UN.* UN DESA. Retrieved November 12, 2019, from: https://www.un.org/development/desa/en/news/population/2018-revision-of-world-urbanization-prospects.html

University Grants Commission (India). (n.d.). https://en.wikipedia.org/wiki/University_Grants_Commission

Uthayasankar, S., & Muhammad, M. K., Zahir, I., & Vishanth, W. (in press). Critical analysis of big data challenges and analytical methods. *ScienceDirect. Journal of Business Research.*

Van Dyke, T. P., Midha, V., & Nemati, H. (2007). The effect of consumer privacy empowerment on trust and privacy concerns in e-commerce. *Electronic Markets, 17*(1), 68–81. doi:10.1080/10196780601136997

Vasada, M., & Padhiyar, Y. J. (2016). Smart Tourism: Growth for Tomorrow. *Journal for Research, 01*(12), 55–61.

Veeramanickam, M., & Mohanapriya, M. (2016). IOT enabled Futurus smart campus with effective E-learning: I-campus. *GSTF Journal of Engineering Technology, 3*(4), 81.

Velusamy, R., & Heinrichs, E. A. (1986). Tolerance in crop plants to insect pests. *International Journal of Tropical Insect Science, 7*(6), 689–696. doi:10.1017/S1742758400011747

Verbelen, Y. (2018). *Characterization of Self-Powered Autonomous Embedded Systems for Complementary Balanced Energy Harvesting.* doi:10.13140/RG.2.2.29768.42242

Vimarlund, V. (2011). Capturing the Value of IT investments in Health and Social Care. *International conference in e-Health.*

Visvizi, A., & Lytras, M. (2018). Rescaling and Refocusing Smart Cities Research: From Mega Cities to Smart Villages. *Journal of Science and Technology Policy Management, 9*(2), 134–145. doi:10.1108/JSTPM-02-2018-0020

Wachter, S. (2018). Normative challenges of identification in the Internet of Things: Privacy, profiling, discrimination, and the GDPR. *Computer Law & Security Review, 34*(3), 436–449. doi:10.1016/j.clsr.2018.02.002

WAI. (2019). *Web Accessibility Initiative.* https://www.w3.org/WAI/fundamentals/accessibility-intro/

Wallner, W. E. (1987). Factors Affecting Insect Population Dynamics: Differences Between Outbreak and Non-Outbreak Species. *Annual Review of Entomology, 32*(1), 317–340. doi:10.1146/annurev.en.32.010187.001533

Walters, D. (2011). Smart cities, smart places, smart democracy: Form-based codes, electronic governance and the role of place in making smart cities. *Intelligent Buildings International, 3*(3), 198–218. doi:10.1080/17508975.2011.586670

Wang, X., Chellappan, S., Gu, W., Yu, W., & Xuan, D. (2005). Search-based physical attacks in sensor networks. *Proceedings 14th International Conference on Computer Communications and Networks, 2005. ICCCN 2005,* 489–496.

Wang, X., Chou, J., Chen, W., Guan, H., Chen, W., Lao, T., & Ma, K. (2018).A Utility-Aware Visual Approach for Anonymizing Multi-Attribute Tabular Data. *Proceeding of The IEEE Transactions on Visualization and Computer Graphics*, *24*, 351-360. [Doi:10.1109/TBDATA.2018.2829886]. 10.1109/TVCG.2017.2745139

Wang, X., Gu, W., Schosek, K., Chellappan, S., & Xuan, D. (2004). Sensor Network Configuration under Physical Attacks. Department of Computer Science and Engineering, Ohio State University. Technical Report: OSU-CISRC-7/04-TR45.

Wang, Y. (2010). *English interactive teaching model which based upon internet of things.* Paper presented at 2010 International Conference on Computer Application and System Modeling (ICCASM), Taiyuan, China.

Wang, D., Park, S., & Fesenmaier, D. R. (2011). An Examination of Information Services and Smartphone Applications. *Proceedings of 16th Annual Graduate Student Research Conference in Hospitality and Tourism.*

Wang, D., Park, S., & Fesenmaier, D. R. (2011). The Role of Smartphones in Mediating the Touristic Experience. *Journal of Travel Research*, *51*(4), 371–387. doi:10.1177/0047287511426341

Wang, H., Han, J., Wang, J., & Wang, L. (2014). (l, e)-Diversity-A Privacy Preserving Model to Resist Semantic Similarity Attack. *Journal of Computers*, *9*(1), 59–65. doi:10.4304/jcp.9.1.59-64

Wang, M., Jiang, Z., & Yang, H. (2018). T-Closeness Slicing: A New Privacy Preserving Approach for Transactional Data Publishing. *INFORMS Journal on Computing*, *30*(3), 1–34. doi:10.1287/ijoc.2017.0791

Wang, R., Zhu, Y., Chen, T., & Chang, C. (2018). Privacy-Preserving Algorithms for Multiple Sensitive Attributes Satisfying t-Closeness. *Journal of Computer Science and Technology*, *33*(6), 1231–1242. doi:10.100711390-018-1884-6

Wang, Z. H. (2011). *Smart City Road: Science Governance and Urban Personality / China Telecom Smart City Research Group Compiled.* Electronic Industry Press.

Washburn, D., & Sindhu, U. (2010). *Helping CIOs Understand "Smart City" Initiatives – Defining The Smart City, Its Drivers, And The Role Of The CIO.* In *Making Leaders Successful Every Day.* Forrester Research.

Weber, R. H. (2009). Internet of things–Need for a new legal environment? *Computer Law & Security Review*, *25*(6), 522–527. doi:10.1016/j.clsr.2009.09.002

Weimer, M. (2015). 10 benefits of getting students to participate in classroom discussions. *Faculty Focus.* https://www.facultyfocus.com/articles/teaching-and-learning/10-benefits-of-getting-students-to-participate-in-classroom-discussions/

Weins, K., & Trends, C. C. (2017). *State of the Cloud Survey.* https://www.rightscale.com/blog/cloud-industry-insights/cloud-computing-trends-2017-state-cloud-survey

Williamson, B. (2015, July-December). Educating the Smart city: Schooling Smart citizens through computational urbanism. *Big Data & Society*, *2*(2), 1–13. doi:10.1177/2053951715617783

Wirminghaus, N. (2019). Die E-Scooter kommen - und überschwemmen die Städte mit Elektroschrott. *Der Stern.* Retrieved November 29, 2019, from https://www.stern.de/auto/e-scooter--hype-um-elektrotretroller-bringt-jede-menge-elektroschrott-8654792.html

Wood, A. D., & Stankovic, J. A. (2002). Denial of service in sensor networks. *Computer*, *35*(10), 54–62. doi:10.1109/MC.2002.1039518

World Economic Forum. (2019). The cost of housing is tearing our society apart. *Global Shapers Annual Summit.* Retrieved November 2, 2019, from: https://www.weforum.org/agenda/2019/01/why-housing-appreciation-is-killing-housing/

World Health Organization (WHO). (2009). *Urban planning and Human health in the European City, Report to the World Health Organisation.* International Society of City and Regional Planners (ISOCARP).

Wray, S. (2019). Smart Cities get their houses in order. *SmartCitiesWorld*. Retrieved November 11, 2019, from https://www.smartcitiesworld.net/special-reports/special-reports/smart-cities-get-their-houses-in-order-

Wulf, G. (2010). Agua y energía en California. *Ingeniería del Agua, 17*(3), 201–211.

Xiang, Z., & Fesenmaier, D. R. (2017). Big Data Analytics, Tourism Design and Smart Tourism. In Analytics in Smart Tourism Design Concepts and Methods. Springer.

Xuemin, C., Gangbing, S., & Yongpeng, Z. (2010). Virtual and Remote Laboratory Development: A Review. *Earth and Space 2010: Engineering, Science, Construction, and Operations in Challenging Environments*, 3843-3852.

Yang, Y., Zheng, X., Guo, W., Liu, X., & Chang, V. (2018). Privacy-preserving fusion of IoT and big data for e-health. *Journal of Future Generation Computer Systems, 86*, 1437–1455. doi:10.1016/j.future.2018.01.003

Yerraboina, S., Kumar, N. M., Parimala, K. S., & Aruna, N. J. (2018, June). Monitoring The Smart Garbage Bin Filling Status: An Iot Application Towards Waste Management. *International Journal of Civil Engineering and Technology, 9*(6), 373–381.

Zahumenskỳ, I. (2004). *Guidelines on quality control procedures for data from automatic weather stations*. World Meteorological Organization.

Zárate Martín, M. A., & Rubio Benito, M. T. (2006). *Glosario y buenas prácticas de Geografía Humana*. Madrid, Spain: Editorial Universitaria Ramón Areces.

Zaslavsky, A., Perera, C., & Georgakopoulos, D. (2012, July). *Sensing as a Service and Big Data*. Paper presented at the International Conference on Advances in Cloud Computing (ACC), Bangalore, India.

Zavratnik, V., Kos, A., & Stojmenova Duh, E. (2018). Smart Villages: Comprehensive Review of Initiatives and Practices. *Sustainability, 10*(7), 25–59. doi:10.3390u10072559

Zhang, L., & Yang, J. (2016). Smart Tourism. In J. Jafari & H. Xiao (Eds.), *Encyclopedia of Tourism*. Springer International Publishing. doi:10.1007/978-3-319-01384-8_175

Zigbee FAQ - Zigbee Alliance. (n.d.). Retrieved January 30, 2020, from https://zigbeealliance.org/zigbee-faq/

Z-Wave | Z-Wave Smart Home Products FAQ. (n.d.). Retrieved January 30, 2020, from https://www.z-wave.com/faq

About the Contributors

Gianluca Cornetta obtained his MSc Degree from Politecnico di Torino (Italy) in 1995 and his PhD from Universidad Politécnica de Cataluña (Spain) in 2001, both in Electronic Engineering. In 2003 he joined Universidad CEU-San Pablo in Madrid (Spain), where he is presently an Associate Professor. Prior to joining Universidad CEU-San Pablo, he was a Lecturer in the Departement of Electronic Engineering of Universidad Politécnica de Cataluña (Spain), a Digital Designer at Infineon Technologies Gmbh (Germany), and an ICT Consultant at Tecsidel SA (Spain) in the field of real-time embedded systems. In 2004 he founded the Department of Electronic System Engineering and Telecommunications, which he chaired until February 2008. He is also a research fellow at the Vrije Universiteit Brussel and an invited Professor at the Institut Superieur d'Electronique de Paris (ISEP) where he has taught Wireless System Design in the Advances in Communication Environment (ACE) Master until 2018. His current research interests include RF circuit design for wireless sensor networks, digital communication circuits and distributed real-time embedded systems covering the whole IoT stack from sensor to cloud.

Abdellah Touhafi is professor at the Engineering Sciences Faculty of the Vrije Universiteit Brussel. As member of the Engineering technologies department, he is responsible for the major courses related to electronics design, embedded computing and reconfigurable computing. His research interests are smart and industrial electronics, reconfigurable computing systems, multi-sensorial systems and cloud computing. Those topics are deployed within two emerging applications that are advanced environmental monitoring systems and digital education. He is serving as an editor for the Journal of sensors and is chairing several conferences related to smart cities, cloud computing and industrial electronics. His work has been published in more than 130 scientific publications.

Gabriel-Miro Muntean is an Associated Professor with the School of Electronic Engineering, Dublin City University (DCU), Ireland, where he obtained his Ph.D. degree in 2003 for research on quality-oriented adaptive multimedia streaming over wired networks. He was awarded the B.Eng. and M.Sc. degrees in Software Engineering from the Computer Science Department, "Politehnica" University of Timisoara, Romania in 1996 and 1997 respectively. Dr. Muntean is co-director of the DCU Performance Engineering Laboratory and Investigator with Insight and Lero National Research Centres. His research interests include quality-oriented and performance-related issues of adaptive multimedia delivery, performance of wired and wireless communications, energy-aware networking and personalised technology-enhanced learning. Dr. Muntean has published over 350 papers in prestigious international journals and conferences, has authored 4 books and 19 book chapters and has edited 6 other books, which have attracted over 6000 citations (H-index=44). Dr. Muntean has supervised succesfully 22

PhD students and 10 postdoctoral researchers. He is an Associate Editor of the IEEE Transactions on Broadcasting, Multimedia Communications Area Editor fof IEEE Communications Surveys and Tutorials and reviewer for other important international journals, conferences, and funding agencies. He was the coordinator of the EU Horizon 2020 project NEWTON. He is a senior member of IEEE, and IEEE Broadcast Technology Society.

* * *

Monjur Ahmed is a Senior Lecturer and the Research Leader at Centre for Information Technology (CfIT), Waikato Institute of Technology (Wintec), New Zealand. He holds a PhD from Auckland University of Technology, New Zealand. Monjur's research interests are in Cybersecurity and Decentralised Computing focusing on both technological and human aspects in contemporary computing approaches (e.g. Cloud Computing, Edge Computing, Fog Computing, and IoT). Monjur has over 11 years of teaching, research and management experience at tertiary institutions in Bangladesh, China, New Zealand and United Kingdom.

Gloria Aznar is a Professor of Marketing at CEU San Pablo University in Madrid. Gloria's main focus in Marketing and her research interests lie in the areas of Smart Cities, Online Advertising, Consumer and Development in Sierra Leone. She also delivers conferences in different international congresses and every year is a visitor professor in a different country. Gloria is passionate about Smart Cities and Digital Marketing. She volunteers as a Coordinator in ESADE Business School for Pro Bono consultancy for NGO´s. Gloria coordinates the group of "Semilleros", an incubator group designed to help students develop an understanding of other countries and developing and supporting students in Sierra Leone. In that capacity, her team works with local entrepreneurs to develop their businesses.

Gastón Contreras has a PhD in Physical Sciences from San Pablo CEU University since 2009. He studied at the Politechnic University of Madrid where he obtained in 1990 the title of Aeronautical Technical Engineer in the specialty of Aeromotors and the extraordinary prize at the end of his career in his specialty. Graduated in Physical Sciences with the speciality of Automatic and Industrial Physics from the Universidad Nacional de Educación a Distancia (UNED) in 1998. Master's Degree in Occupational Risk Prevention in the specialities of Safety at Work, Ergonomics and Applied Psychology and Industrial Hygiene. His professional career began at the National Institute of Aerospace Technology (INTA) in the Departments of Power and Energy and in the Department of Remote Sensing. He was an Associate Professor at the Carlos III University of Madrid in the Department of Electricity, Electronics and Automation. Since 2002 he has been a professor-researcher at the Universidad San Pablo CEU where he has been Director of the Department of Building Engineering (2010-2012). Professor Sanglier has taught Conditioning Techniques, Physics I and Physics II and is currently a full professor, Head of the Construction Engineering Area and Coordinator of different subjects of the Masters in Occupational Risk Prevention and Renewable Energy.

Martha Davis is a Senior Director of Content with Endeavor Business Media. She provides editorial leadership to the Endeavor Business Media Energy Group, including the publications of T&D World, Utility Analytics Institute, Transmission Hub, Utility Products, and Distributed Energy magazines. Previously, Martha worked as an executive in the energy industry for about 15 years. She has held various regulatory and government affairs positions and had the opportunity to shape energy policy. Martha has a B.A. from Westminster College in Fulton, MO; completed specialized legal and public policy coursework at American University in Washington, D.C.; M.P.A. Public Affairs and M.B.A. Business Administration both from the University of Missouri. She is currently a doctoral candidate at the University of Denver, Daniels School of Business.

Elizabeth Frank has been a Lecturer in the areas of Finance and Marketing at the School of Business and Economics at the University CEU San Pablo in Madrid, Spain since 2007 and since 2011 she has been International Academic Coordinator of her Faculty cooperating with renowned International Institutions. She is deeply involved in the internationalization of the Faculty where she is currently involved in several international projects. She has been a visiting professor at University of Finance and Administration, VSFS (Czech Republic), University of Economics in Katowice (Poland), Hochschule Augsburg (Germany). Before moving to Academics, Elizabeth worked many years in the IT Sector, for companies such as Oracle, BMC Software and Gartner Inc. She did her final degree in Germany, at the Universität Passau (Diplom-Volkswirtin). Her areas of interest are diverse and include amongst others: Smart Cities, Sustainable, Responsible and Impact Investment (SRI) as well as Innovation in Teaching Methodologies.

Roberto A. González-Lezcano has a PhD in Industrial Engineering, Postgraduate Diploma in Plant Engineering, Postgraduate Diploma in University Didactics, Master in Mathematical Engineering Extraordinary Doctorate Award. Tenured Professor of the Department of Architecture and Design, in the area of Facilities at the Higher Polytechnic School of the CEU San Pablo University. He has been teaching at Building Installations, Electromechanics and Materials, Physics, Mathematics, Mechanical Engineering and Mechanics of Continuous Media and Theory of Structures. Professor accredited by ANECA in the figures of University Tenured Professor. A six-year research period recognized by the CNEAI. He has taught in undergraduate and master's degrees at the Carlos III University of Madrid, Camilo José Cela University, European University of Madrid, Antonio de Nebrija University, Technical University of Madrid and Alfonso X El Sabio University. He has published several books and articles concerning the areas of Energy, Installations and Continuous Media Mechanics. Coordinator and co-author of the collections Abecé de las Instalaciones at Editorial Munilla-Leria and Instalaciones en el Diseño de Edificios (bilingual editions) at Ediciones-Asimétricas.

R. Kamatchi is a Professor, Head of PGDM, ISME School of Management and Entreprenuership, Mumbai. She completed her Ph.D., thesis titled "Security issues of Web services in a Service Oriented Architecture" with Mother Teresa Women's University, Kodaikanal under the guidance of Dr. Atanu Rakshit, Director, IIM, Rohtak. She has 19 years of teaching experience with various premier institutes in Mumbai. She has co authored 5 books and presented more than 60 papers in National and International conferences. She has got 80 Journal publications to her credit. She has conducted various sessions on the topics of Service modeling, Customer Relationship Management, Internet Security, Current IT trends in various students and faculty forums. She is the Board of Studies member in many reputed universities like University of Mumbai, Amity University, Somaiya University etc. She is in the ph.d., examiner panel of many reputed universities like Jain University, North Maharashtra University, Bharathiyar University, Manaonmaniam Sundaranar University, Vishwesaraya Technical University(VIT) etc. She is an IRCA certified Lead auditor. She has authored many course material in the subjects of Customer Relationship

Management, Information Security, Project Management for various universities. She is the approved guide for M.Phil. and Ph.D., programmes with Madurai Kamaraj University, Barathiyar University & Amity University. 7 students completed their M.Phil., dissertation under her guidance and Eight students have submitted their doctoral research under her guidance. She is in the editorial board of various peer reviewed journals and books. She is also a invited reviewer for many journals like INDERSCIENCE, EMERALAD, Science Direct etc. She is also an invited member of various Science & Technology forums like CSI, ISTE, IEANG. She has chaired many sessions in reputed International Conferences.

Eduardo J. López-Fernández has been a PhD Civil Engineer since 2010. He studied Civil Engineering at the School of the Technical University of Madrid and obtained the degree of Doctor at the San Pablo University CEU. His professional career began in Engineering and Project Consultancy, an activity that he continues to develop at present, combining it with teaching, which he approaches while still a student, giving classes in Physics and Mechanics to support engineering students at the UPM. Later he has taught Fluid Mechanics, Hydraulics and Hydrology. Currently, in addition to coordinating the subjects of Analytical Techniques and Normative Aspects of Management in the Master's Degree in Integrated Management at the San Pablo CEU University, he teaches at Water Cycle in Building and Waste Management in the Master of Efficiency and Sustainability in Building and of Installations and Technical Services and Project of Installations in the Degree of Architecture at the San Pablo CEU University in Madrid.

Víctor M. López Millán is an Assistant Professor at the Universidad San Pablo-CEU (CEU Universities), and Assistant Director of the Information Technologies Department. His research interests are complex networks and the application of new networking paradigms to global networks. Previously, he worked in the ICT industry for telco, network equipment manufacturing and consultancy companies. His passion for teaching led him to the university where he currently combines classes and research.

Cedric Marsboom, graduated in 2014 as a Master of Science in environmental engineeringat KU Leuven, Belgium. His MSc thesis focussed on Vegetation dynamics in Nech Sar national park in Ethiopia. Through the use of remote sensing and GIS he was able to determine the leading dynamics behind the degradation of the national park. After his graduation he worked for two years on the ECOPLAN project at the University of Antwerp where he worked on hotspot mapping and modelling of ecosystem services in Flanders. In 2017, he joined Avia-GIS as a spatial analyst where he works on several research and technical development projects. Since 2019 he is CTO of Avia-GIS where he leads the R&D department and focusses on mathematical and spatial modelling.

Gabriel-Miro Muntean was awarded the B.Eng and M.Eng degrees by "Politehnica" University of Timisoara, Romania in 1995 and 1996 and the PhD degree by Dublin City University (DCU), Ireland in 2004. He is an Associate Professor with the School of Electronic Engineering, Dublin City University (DCU), Ireland, and co-Director of the DCU Performance Engineering Laboratory. Dr. Muntean has published over 350 papers in top-level international journals and conferences, authored four books and 18 book chapters, and edited seven additional books, which have attracted over 6000 citations. His research interests include quality, performance, and energy issues related to rich media delivery, technology-enhanced learning, and other data communications over heterogeneous networks. In these research areas, Dr. Muntean has supervised to completion 22 PhD students and has advised 12 postdoctoral researchers. He is an Associate Editor of the IEEE Transactions on Broadcasting, the Multimedia Communications Area Editor of the IEEE Communications Surveys and Tutorials, and a reviewer for important international journals, conferences, and funding agencies. He coordinated the EU-funded project NEWTON http://www.newtonproject.eu in which he collaborated closely with Prof. Cornetta.

Mina Petrić is a PhD student at UGent at the Department of Physics and Astronomy with focus on vector population dynamics modelling. She works with the design and implementation of meteorological Wireless Sensor Networks at Avia-GIS, Belgium.

María Sánchez Martínez has a PhD in Communication. B.A. in Advertising and Public Relations. Associate Professor in Technologies and new media and Online Marketing and Advertising in Universidad CEU San Pablo. Director of the Digital Communication Degree in USPCEU. Member of the research group of Media Convergence (INCIRTV) and Principal Researcher in the research project entitled "Smart Cities: digital content accessibility problems in elderly citizens" financed by the CEU San Pablo University and Banco Santander with approval from the Spanish National Agency for Evaluation and Foresight. Researching lines aimed to digital media, online communication and marketing, smart cities contents and media entrepreneurship in the new economy. Author of several publications between articles and book chapters focused in interactivity, consumer typologies and digital communication's uses, multiscreen content and media convergence. Since 2010 participating as researcher in several internal researching projects and external funded by public or private companies. Visiting professor both Regent's University London and Libera Università Maria SS. Assunta, Rome.

Nurul I. Sarkar holds a Ph.D. from the University of Auckland and is currently Associate Professor and leader of the Network and Security Research Group at the Auckland University of Technology, New Zealand. He is a member of many professional organizations and societies. Dr. Sarkar is a regularly invited keynote speaker, chair, and committee member for various national and international fora. He has published over 180 refereed articles and served on the editorial review boards of several journals. "Improving the Performance of Wireless LANs: A Practical Guide," his second book has been published by Taylor & Francis in January 2014. Dr Sarkar is a member of IEEE Communications Society (ComSoc) and Australasian Association for Engineering Education. He served as conference general Co-Chair for ITNAC'19 and CECNet'18; and TPC Co-Chair/Vice-Chair for ICOIN'19, IEEE DASC'16, SmartGridComm-2016, IEEE ICC'14, APCC'12, TENCON'10 and ITNAC'10. Dr Sarkar served as Chairman of the IEEE joint NZ North, South and Central ComSoc Chapter for more than 10 years which won the 'Best Chapter Achievement Award' in 2012. He is a Senior Member of IEEE.

Jurgen Vandendriessche graduated in 2018 at the Vrije Universiteit Brussel, where he obtained a master degree in Industrial Engineering Sciences, option Electronics ICT. He is currently pursuing a PhD related to microphone arrays and acoustics. His research continues on the work of his predecessors. He teaches courses related to both software and hardware, such as informatics and basic electronics.

Index

Purchase Print, E-Book, or Print + E-Book

IGI Global's reference books are available in three unique pricing formats:
Print Only, E-Book Only, or Print + E-Book.
Shipping fees may apply.

www.igi-global.com

Recommended Reference Books

ISBN: 978-1-5225-8876-4
© 2019; 141 pp.
List Price: $135

ISBN: 978-1-5225-8100-0
© 2019; 321 pp.
List Price: $235

ISBN: 978-1-5225-7847-5
© 2019; 306 pp.
List Price: $195

ISBN: 978-1-5225-6313-6
© 2019; 349 pp.
List Price: $215

ISBN: 978-1-5225-7628-0
© 2019; 281 pp.
List Price: $220

ISBN: 978-1-5225-5855-2
© 2019; 337 pp.
List Price: $185

Do you want to stay current on the latest research trends, product announcements, news and special offers?
Join IGI Global's mailing list today and start enjoying exclusive perks sent only to IGI Global members.
Add your name to the list at **www.igi-global.com/newsletters.**

Publisher of Peer-Reviewed, Timely, and Innovative Academic Research

www.igi-global.com   Sign up at www.igi-global.com/newsletters   facebook.com/igiglobal   twitter.com/igiglobal   linkedin.com/igiglobal

Ensure Quality Research is Introduced to the Academic Community

Become an IGI Global Reviewer for Authored Book Projects

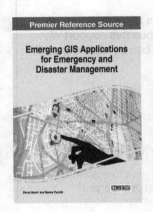

Premier Reference Source

Emerging GIS Applications for Emergency and Disaster Management

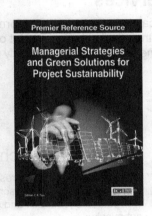

Premier Reference Source

Managerial Strategies and Green Solutions for Project Sustainability

Premier Reference Source

Comparative Approaches to Using R and Python for Statistical Data Analysis

Premier Reference Source

Solutions for High-Touch Communications in a High-Tech World

The overall success of an authored book project is dependent on quality and timely reviews.

In this competitive age of scholarly publishing, constructive and timely feedback significantly expedites the turnaround time of manuscripts from submission to acceptance, allowing the publication and discovery of forward-thinking research at a much more expeditious rate. Several IGI Global authored book projects are currently seeking highly-qualified experts in the field to fill vacancies on their respective editorial review boards:

Applications and Inquiries may be sent to:
development@igi-global.com

Applicants must have a doctorate (or an equivalent degree) as well as publishing and reviewing experience. Reviewers are asked to complete the open-ended evaluation questions with as much detail as possible in a timely, collegial, and constructive manner. All reviewers' tenures run for one-year terms on the editorial review boards and are expected to complete at least three reviews per term. Upon successful completion of this term, reviewers can be considered for an additional term.

If you have a colleague that may be interested in this opportunity,
we encourage you to share this information with them.

IGI Global Proudly Partners With eContent Pro International

Receive a 25% Discount on all Editorial Services

Editorial Services

IGI Global expects all final manuscripts submitted for publication to be in their final form. This means they must be reviewed, revised, and professionally copy edited prior to their final submission. Not only does this support with accelerating the publication process, but it also ensures that the highest quality scholarly work can be disseminated.

English Language Copy Editing

Let eContent Pro International's expert copy editors perform edits on your manuscript to resolve spelling, punctuaion, grammar, syntax, flow, formatting issues and more.

Scientific and Scholarly Editing

Allow colleagues in your research area to examine the content of your manuscript and provide you with valuable feedback and suggestions before submission.

Figure, Table, Chart & Equation Conversions

Do you have poor quality figures? Do you need visual elements in your manuscript created or converted? A design expert can help!

Translation

Need your documjent translated into English? eContent Pro International's expert translators are fluent in English and more than 40 different languages.

Hear What Your Colleagues are Saying About Editorial Services Supported by IGI Global

"The service was very fast, very thorough, and very helpful in ensuring our chapter meets the criteria and requirements of the book's editors. I was quite impressed and happy with your service."

– Prof. Tom Brinthaupt,
Middle Tennessee State University, USA

"I found the work actually spectacular. The editing, formatting, and other checks were very thorough. The turnaround time was great as well. I will definitely use eContent Pro in the future."

– Nickanor Amwata, Lecturer,
University of Kurdistan Hawler, Iraq

"I was impressed that it was done timely, and wherever the content was not clear for the reader, the paper was improved with better readability for the audience."

– Prof. James Chilembwe,
Mzuzu University, Malawi

Email: customerservice@econtentpro.com   **www.igi-global.com/editorial-service-partners**

www.igi-global.com

Celebrating *Over 30 Years* of Scholarly
Knowledge Creation & Dissemination

InfoSci®-Books

A Database of Over 5,300+ Reference Books Containing Over
100,000+ Chapters Focusing on Emerging Research

GAIN ACCESS TO **THOUSANDS** OF
REFERENCE BOOKS AT **A FRACTION**
OF THEIR INDIVIDUAL LIST **PRICE**.

InfoSci®-Books Database

The **InfoSci®-Books** database is a collection of
over 5,300+ IGI Global single and multi-volume
reference books, handbooks of research, and
encyclopedias, encompassing groundbreaking
research from prominent experts worldwide that
span over 350+ topics in 11 core subject areas
including business, computer science, education,
science and engineering, social sciences and more.

Open Access Fee Waiver (Offset Model) Initiative

For any library that invests in IGI Global's InfoSci-Journals and/
or InfoSci-Books databases, IGI Global will match the library's
investment with a fund of equal value to go toward **subsidizing
the OA article processing charges (APCs) for their students,
faculty, and staff** at that institution when their work is submitted
and accepted under OA into an IGI Global journal.*

INFOSCI® PLATFORM FEATURES

- No DRM
- No Set-Up or Maintenance Fees
- A Guarantee of No More Than a
  5% Annual Increase
- Full-Text HTML and PDF
  Viewing Options
- Downloadable MARC Records
- Unlimited Simultaneous Access
- COUNTER 5 Compliant Reports
- Formatted Citations With Ability to
  Export to RefWorks and EasyBib
- No Embargo of Content (Research
  is Available Months in Advance of
  the Print Release)

*The fund will be offered on an annual basis and expire at the end of
the subscription period. The fund would renew as the subscription is
renewed for each year thereafter. The open access fees will be waived
after the student, faculty, or staff's paper has been vetted and accepted
into an IGI Global journal and the fund can only be used toward
publishing OA in an IGI Global journal. Libraries in developing countries
will have the match on their investment doubled.

To Learn More or To Purchase This Database:
www.igi-global.com/infosci-books

eresources@igi-global.com • Toll Free: 1-866-342-6657 ext. 100 • Phone: 717-533-8845 x100

www.igi-global.com

Printed in the United States
by Bookmasters

Printed in the United States
By Bookmasters